AN OUTLINE OF BIBLICAL THEOLOGY

BY *Millar Burrows* WINKLEY PROFESSOR OF
BIBLICAL THEOLOGY YALE UNIVERSITY DIVINITY SCHOOL

Philadelphia

THE WESTMINSTER PRESS

PREFACE

This book falls so far short of what it ought to be that the temptation to make the preface a mere series of apologies is almost irresistible. I shall resist it, however, in the hope that the book's shortcomings will prove so obvious as to be harmless. Much explanation may be saved by calling attention to the first word in the title. Whether what is here presented is theology may be questioned by some readers; there may even be some who will deny that it is biblical; but all must admit that it is only an outline. As such it cannot show how the conclusions stated were reached, or elaborate them. What is certain cannot always be distinguished from what is only more or less probable. Only starting points for further study and discussion can be indicated.

The most regrettable consequence of such a treatment is the loss of the majestic, dramatic sweep of the divine revelation in history as presented in the Bible. There the word becomes flesh, with spirit and life; here it is reduced to dry bones, or at best an X-ray photograph of the living body. But this outline is offered as an aid in the study and use of the Bible itself, not as a digest to make the reading of the Bible unnecessary. Students who have used the mimeographed syllabus in which this text first took shape have told me with engaging frankness that what they valued in it was the collection of Scriptural references. Whatever real life and substance this work may have will be found in the footnotes, and of course they are only partial and typical, not by any means exhaustive. Furthermore, no person should undertake the study of biblical theology without a fairly intimate acquaintance with the Bible and at least an elementary knowledge of biblical history and literature.

Aside from the biblical citations, documentation has been kept to a

*minimum in this volume. Specific references, even to primary sources
outside the Bible (e.g., Philo and the rabbinic literature), are rarely
given. Secondary sources are cited, with few exceptions, only when directly quoted. The bibliography also is very brief, indicating only what
may be especially recommended to students and teachers as good books
to read next.*

*Chapters and verses of the Bible are cited throughout according to
the English text, and no attempt is made to indicate the numbering in
the original when it differs from that in the English. Sometimes, to be
sure, it may be necessary to consult the original to see the point of a reference, but for those who can use the Hebrew and Greek the occasional
difference in the numbering of the verses occasions no serious inconven-
ience. In the transliteration of Hebrew and Greek words the simplest
and most easily printed forms have been adopted, omitting all diacriti-
cal marks. Scholars will know what is meant, and for others the differences are insignificant. Quotations from the Bible follow no one version
consistently. The present text was already in the publisher's hands
when the Revised Standard Version of the New Testament was issued,
and it seemed both inexpedient and unnecessary to undertake all the
changes which would have been involved in making the quotations conform to the new translation.*

*Perverse and foolish though some of the views here expressed may
appear, persistent efforts have been made to secure accuracy of statement, citation, and interpretation. It cannot be hoped, however, that all
errors have been eliminated. The author will be grateful to readers who
inform him of mistakes or serious omissions detected in the book.*

New Haven, Connecticut,   Millar Burrows.
   May 22, 1946.

CONTENTS

I

INTRODUCTION

1. *The Purpose of This Study*

The term " biblical theology " has been used and is used in many different ways. Sometimes it covers the whole field of biblical studies; sometimes it denotes a descriptive history of Hebrew religion and early Christianity, sometimes a delineation of the history of revelation in the Bible as discerned by faith; sometimes it means a theological system grounded in Scripture. In order that it may convey some specific meaning, therefore, we must make clear the sense in which we propose to use it. This requires first some consideration of the need for such a study and the purpose to be accomplished.

In this volume biblical theology is considered primarily as a professional discipline for ministers of the gospel, not in the sense that it is a mystery into which only the clergy should be initiated, but in the sense that as leaders of Christian thought and life ministers particularly need a knowledge of the subject. Religious educators and all who use the Bible in any kind of religious work — indeed, all Christians who are seriously concerned with the significance of the Bible for their own life and faith — will profit also by a study of biblical theology. It is hoped that this book may be of some use to advanced students of the Bible in college courses. But it is the minister who most of all needs a grasp of this subject, and the purpose of the study will therefore be discussed with particular reference to his work.

Jesus, finding his people sick and hungry and lost, like sheep without a shepherd, was moved with compassion, and taught them, and healed them.[1] He chose twelve of his followers that they might be with him and that he might send them out to preach and to heal.[2] As their successor, the Christian minister today must serve people who are lost and sick and hungry, though often unaware of their condition — people

---

[1] Mk. 6:34. [2] Mk. 3:14 f.

grieving, doubting, discouraged, confused as to the ends and the meaning of life; people ruled by their appetites or by their prejudices; people proud, self-satisfied, self-righteous, unsympathetic and uncharitable in their judgments of others, and also people without any self-confidence or self-respect; people with intense but narrow loyalties; people indifferent to religion and people anxiously busy with much serving, devoted in the name of religion to ends of little or no real importance, while ignoring far weightier matters; people earnest and consecrated and eager to be useful; people of many sorts and conditions, all needing spiritual guidance and sustenance. All of them, moreover, are involved in social, economic, and political situations which vitally affect them, and for which as members of a democratic community they have some responsibility. Like a wise physician, the minister must know his people, must be able to diagnose their condition and needs.

He must also have at his command spiritual resources to meet these needs. This calls for something more than the effective presentation of personal opinions. Something more than the professional competence of the expert practitioner is required. The minister differs from the physician, psychiatrist, or social engineer in being not only a specialist equipped with the most up-to-date knowledge and techniques but also the representative of a historic institution and a tradition. He is the bearer of a spiritual heritage which has come down to him from the past with a claim to divine origin and authority. Whatever new applications and developments he may add to the tradition, he cannot simply discard it and put something else in its place without becoming something other than a minister of the gospel. If he regards anything else as more useful or reliable, and feels no inner compulsion to preach the gospel; [3] if he has no sense of being a steward of God's mysteries,[4] of having a sacred trust,[5] he should enter a different profession.

The Christian physician of souls has always in the past found his spiritual *materia medica* in the Bible. The scope and the substance of preaching, with much variety of interpretation and emphasis, have been determined by the Bible. In recent times there has been a marked decline in biblical preaching. The causes of this decline need not be discussed here at length, but some of them are sufficiently obvious. Wider cultural interests have introduced more variety into the materials of which sermons are made. Concern for immediate situations and issues has made the Bible seem remote and alien. New subjects have crowded

---

[3] 1 Cor. 9:16.   [4] 1 Cor. 4:1.   [5] 1 Tim. 6:20.

into the theological curriculum and pushed the Bible into a corner. The absence of any systematic presentation or arrangement in the Bible itself has made its use difficult except for those who know it very well, as few people now do. With all this, modern critical study of the Bible has unquestionably caused confusion and the loss of a sense of divine authority, thus diminishing the confidence with which a preacher could use the Bible. The result, along with much that is clear gain, has been a perceptible thinning out of the content of preaching. Listening for the word of God, the people too often hear only a man's opinions.

What is needed is not merely homiletical ornaments from Scripture. The preacher who knows his Bible finds in it a vast store of texts, illustrations, and effective presentations of spiritual truth and high ideals in attractive literary form. What Christian preaching needs above all, however, is not biblical adornment but the structure and substance of the Scriptures. Our major concern here is with the essential nature and basic features, the real fundamentals, of biblical religion. The Bible is no manual of psychiatry or of social engineering, but it is an incomparable source of the dynamic convictions and motives by which alone life can be made sound and whole.

Meanwhile various marginal ecclesiastical groups, fired by " zeal for God, but not according to knowledge," [6] are making vigorous and aggressive use of the Bible in ways that do more harm than good. The Bible, like medicine, must be rightly used to produce the right results.[7] False ideas and evil institutions all too often and too easily claim the support of the Bible: " The devil himself can quote Scripture." If only to counteract the harmful effects of an ill-informed use of the Bible, the minister must be able to interpret and apply it correctly.

A return to the forms of biblical preaching familiar in former days would not be desirable even if it were feasible. Our new knowledge of the Bible itself makes that impossible. What we need is a better, more informed use of the Bible, growing out of a better understanding of it. The religious resources of the Bible as modern scholarship has enabled us to appreciate them must be made more available for the practical work of the ministry.

This cannot be done by the basic courses in Old and New Testament in the theological seminary. They can only present the general outlines of biblical history and literature, the main points in the progressive unfolding of religious truth, and some more or less detailed exegesis of

---

[6] Rom. 10:2.   [7] 2 P. 3:16.

particular books, with perhaps just a taste of textual and literary criticism. They cannot be expected to put all this into shape for practical use in the work of the church and the nourishment and guidance of the Christian life. There is thus a considerable gap between these courses and the practical courses in homiletics and religious education. To bridge that gap, or at least to throw a preliminary cable across it, is the purpose of the present work.

2. *Scope and Point of View*

The purpose just stated determines the sense in which the term " biblical theology " is here used. It does not imply a complete, logically articulated system of doctrine derived from the Bible. It does not refer to doctrine alone or for its own sake. Theology in the sense of a systematic elaboration of doctrine does not exist in the Bible. The religion of the Bible is an organic whole, including experiences, ideals, practices, and institutions as well as beliefs. It is not something finished and static, but a living historical movement.

Our point of view in interpreting it must therefore be historical. This means not only distinguishing earlier from later stages and tracing developments, but also studying the religion at each stage in its cultural setting and in connection with the whole life of the people. Only such study can avoid misunderstanding and false modernization. The historical point of view emancipates us from the errors of the old proof-text method. It shows the organic growth, structure, and relationships of ideas and practices, and so helps to make clear the proportions and relative importance of the various elements of religion.

But biblical theology is not to be identified with the history of religion in the Bible. History asks what the religion of the ancient Hebrews and early Christians was; biblical theology asks what was God's judgment on that religion, and what significance it has for us. The Bible contains not only a historical record, but also an interpretation and critique of the history from the point of view of the divine will. It judges what religion has been in the light of what it ought to be. In the record, with its interpretation, biblical theology seeks the word of God for the present and for all time. Specific applications to modern thought and life must be left to systematic theology and Christian ethics. Biblical theology can only endeavor to lay a foundation for such applications in a historically sound understanding of the religion of the Bible.

For this purpose a considerable portion of the religious history in the Bible is of little or only secondary importance. Many problems of great interest to the historian of religion have no significance for biblical theology and may here be ignored. Large areas of Hebrew religion, such as animal sacrifice or the veneration of sacred places, require relatively little attention, because they ceased to be important for the religion of the New Testament. At the same time, the historical point of view often makes it possible to find a new practical value even in survivals and echoes of earlier stages and lower levels of religion. They often help us to understand the higher truths which emerged from them or superseded them. They may also help us to understand and evaluate the survival or recrudescence of analogous phenomena in our own day, for every pastor may find primitive religion thriving in his own parish and pews. The most sophisticated among us often become primitive at the very moments when we are likely to be most religious, in times of emotional stress. The religion of the foxhole and the rubber raft is by no means peculiar to wartime experience.

Recognition of all the change and diversity in the Old and New Testaments may make it seem more appropriate to speak of the religions than of the religion of the Bible. There is an underlying unity, however, both historically and theologically. With all its variations, the Hebrew-Christian tradition runs true to type. For Christian faith the focus and principle of unity appear in Christ, who is himself the Word made flesh, the Way, the Truth, and the Life (s. 35). With full recognition of the differences within the Bible, biblical theology may, therefore, judge everything by its relation to the truth as it is in him.

Our attitude, then, is by no means one of disinterested curiosity. We seek the truth for the sake of the most profound issues of our own life, for the sake of salvation. Just because our concern is so deeply practical, however, it is necessary to guard against self-deception. We must make sure that we do not mistake our own preconceptions and prejudices for the truth. Doubtless even historical exposition never quite succeeds in being wholly objective, but that only makes it the more imperative that every effort be made to achieve the greatest possible objectivity. We cannot interpret, reformulate, or apply an idea — we cannot judge its truth or importance for us — until we understand it. Objective exegesis must rigidly exclude subjective eisegesis.

Understanding, of course, requires sympathy and experience. Religious experience and faith cannot be merely observed from the outside: they must be entered into, at least with sympathetic imagination, before they can be understood. Many a learned treatise succeeds only in demonstrating that an irreligious man cannot understand any religion. It does not follow, however, that all religious ideas must be accepted to be understood, or that the teaching of a man or a book must be adopted or rejected as a whole. In that case theology would be either the slave of history or wholly independent of it and hopelessly subjective. Karl Barth is quite wrong when he says that to understand Paul one must commit himself in advance and go all the way with him.[1] The attempt to do that leads only, as in the case of Barth himself, to eisegesis, reading in one's own prepossessions and mistaking them for Paul's thought. We must read Paul as we must read Barth, with discrimination, understanding first and only then accepting or rejecting. To understand we must have some experience and sympathy, but our prejudices, our likes and dislikes, even our needs, must not be allowed to distort our perception of what he actually means through the injection of what we should like to have him say.

3. *Method of Presentation*

The practical purpose of our study demands a topical rather than a chronological order of treatment. This involves several dangers, however, which we must recognize and endeavor to avoid. To prevent a false impression of uniform, unchanging ideas, each topic will here be considered in its chronological development and with reference to the historical background. To prevent distortion of the picture by bringing our own questions to the material and imposing our categories upon it, the outline of topics has been derived, so far as possible, from the Bible itself. To avoid sacrificing proportion by putting all subjects upon the same level of importance, or by stressing those that are most interesting to us, we shall try to observe the scale of proportion and emphasis indicated by the main trend and ultimate outcome of the biblical development. Present usefulness, however, is our chief concern.

Superficially, the topical presentation here offered resembles the old proof-text method, but there is a basic difference. Instead of starting with a doctrinal system and supporting it with texts adduced as having equal authority and relevance regardless of date, authorship, or original historical connection, we seek here to gather up the results of com-

---

[1] *The Epistle to the Romans;* see especially Preface to the Third Edition.

petent, unprejudiced, inductive study, and to find the real meaning of the Bible, whether or not what we find supports our own theological views or can be accepted by us as true.

That the result is actually free from any subjective bias cannot, of course, be claimed. In the discussion of some topics there is doubtless more of the writer's opinions and point of view than there is of disinterested and impersonal exposition, but it is hoped that the reader will not find it hard to detect the places where this is the case and to judge them accordingly.

Needless to say, at many points the interpretations here given are debatable; some of them are highly controversial. Since space does not permit extended discussion of the reasons for adopting the positions taken, conclusions must often be stated with what may seem a dogmatic assurance. The reader is requested to regard such statements merely as propositions for discussion. If this book leads him to search the Scriptures and determine for himself whether these things are so,[1] it will have rendered no mean service.

The Scriptural references cited in the following pages are not exhaustive, but have been selected as typical. The danger of subjectivity in making such a selection cannot be avoided without exceeding the practical limits of this volume. The use of " e.g." or " etc." with the references is avoided because if used at all such an indication would be required with almost every citation.

[1] Acts 17:11.

II

AUTHORITY AND REVELATION

4. *The Problem of Religious Authority*

What has been said in s. 2 about the need of combining a practical interest and an objective approach raises the question of the authority of the Bible, and back of that the whole question of religious authority in general. There is a widespread demand in our day for preaching with authority, only too easily satisfied by dogmatic self-assurance. Over against this the spirit of modern science has made thoughtful people rebel at the very idea of any authority at all in matters of belief or conduct. The question of authority is a timely issue for the cause of Christian unity, for the definition of the terms of church membership, for the nature of evangelistic effort, and for the missionary enterprise. It is involved in the definition of what Christianity is in its ultimate essence, and its differentiation from other ways of life and thought.

It has been indicated in ss. 1, 2, that for biblical theology the Bible is more than a historical source book. We seek in it positive guidance and inspiration for ourselves and for the people to whom we are called to minister, the church, our nation, and the peoples of the world. Christianity, like Judaism before it, has always held that its faith is based on divine revelation, and the authentic record and deposit of that revelation has been seen in the Bible.[1] All branches of historical Christianity have regarded the Scriptures as in some sense and to some degree authoritative for faith and life. Protestantism has held to them as " the only infallible rule of faith and practice " over against the claims made by Roman Catholicism for the authority of the church.

Unfortunately, Protestantism, while agreeing to accept the Bible as its sole authority, has never been able to agree on what the Bible teaches. The result of repudiating the authority of the church has not

---

[1] Jn. 5:39; 2 Tim. 3:15–17.

been unity, but a geometric progression of differences. Yet what seems to the Catholic the logical consequence, that we should submit to the authority of the church, is out of the question. We could not do it honestly, for it would involve not only giving up our freedom of thought and decision in favor of an authority of whose competence we are by no means convinced, but also accepting as true many things which we are bound to say we know to be false. If the authority of the Bible is inadequate, the authority of the church is no more reliable.

The modern mind cannot accept any external compulsion in matters of belief. To believe something because anyone else, or any institution, tells us we must believe it or be damned, seems to us incompatible with the very nature of belief. We cannot believe at will, prone though human nature may be to wishful thinking. The " will to believe " is at least limited by experience and evidence. Something other than mere depravity makes modern man abhor Tertullian's dictum, " I believe because it is absurd." Anything that contradicts what we know or think we know to be true is for us incredible.

That which is divinely inspired must be true, and anything that is not true cannot be divinely inspired. Yet the Bible is full of things that to intelligent, educated persons of today are either quite incredible or at best highly questionable. From the account of creation in the first chapter of Genesis to the description of the heavenly city in the closing chapters of Revelation, statements abound that even the most tortuous interpretation cannot reconcile with modern scientific conceptions of the universe. The historical narratives are full of difficulties and even contradictions.

The Christian minister, of all people, cannot afford to ignore the questions involved in all this for intelligent people today. He must become all things to all men, recognizing their problems and speaking their language, if he would by all means win some of them.[2] Young people in particular, trained in modern ways of thinking, will be lost to the church and alienated from religion altogether if their questions are not frankly and intelligently met. Dogmatic assertion that the Bible is the word of God and must be accepted on faith, without any explanation or reasonable defense of the claim, may win fanatical approval from the narrow-minded, but it can only drive away the people who are most needed in the church, and who need the church and the Bible no less than others do.

2 I Cor. 9:19–22.

Biblical theology must therefore face the question of religious authority in general and the authority of the Bible in particular. First of all, we must find what conception of authority is found in the Bible itself, and what claims the Bible makes for itself. We must then ask whether this conception can be accepted and these claims substantiated. Finally we must determine to what extent and in what sense, if at all, the Bible remains authoritative for us.

All this may seem to make the matter too involved to be worth the trouble. If we cannot accept the authority of the Bible simply and directly, as our fathers did, without elaborate explanations and qualifications, why bother with the Bible at all instead of finding our authority in philosophy and science or in immediate spiritual experience and intuition? The question answers itself, for any other authority would also require explanation and justification. And if the result of the inquiry is in the end a positive gain, if we find that to discard or ignore the religious authority of the Bible would mean a serious loss, perhaps even missing the way to eternal life, the discussion will not have been in vain.

5. The Biblical Conception of Authority and Revelation: the Covenants

In the Bible itself authority is a matter more of what must be done than of what must be believed. Belief is secondary to action, though some belief is required, because without belief man will not act.[1] The New Testament puts much more stress than the Old Testament does on what a man must believe to be saved,[2] yet saving faith in the New Testament is not belief alone; it involves also commitment and action.[3] Biblical religion's first question is always, What must I do?[4]

The Bible throughout assumes and asserts that what man must do has been revealed. Both animal and human life from the very beginning are subjected to God's commandments.[5] From then on man is judged according to his obedience or disobedience to the revealed will of God.[6]

The whole conception of revelation, of course, presupposes the existence of God and the validity, in some sense, of such anthropomorphic ideas as God's showing himself, speaking, commanding, and the like. Regarding the significance and validity of these anthropomorphic expressions in connection with revelation, we shall have more to say in

[1] Jn. 5:40; 20:31; Heb. 11:6.
[2] Acts 16:30 f.; Rom. 10:9.
[3] Jas. 2:19 f.; s. 79.
[4] Mk. 10:17; Acts 2:37; 16:30.
[5] Gen. 1:22, 28–30; 2:16 f.
[6] Gen. 3:11, 17 ff.; 6:22; 7:5.

s. 12. For the present we may confine ourselves to the way in which these matters are represented in the Bible.

The conditions of the divine favor on which all human welfare depends are stated in a series of covenants, beginning with one for all the descendants of Noah,[7] continuing with successive covenants between God and the patriarchs,[8] and culminating in the great covenant with Israel at Mount Sinai.[9] Ratifications and extensions of this covenant as well as other special covenants are mentioned,[10] and especially the covenant with the house of David,[11] but the covenant with the nation at Sinai remains central; it is usually what is meant when the covenant is mentioned.

Israel failed to keep the covenant. The prophets repeatedly denounced the nation's unfaithfulness.[12] Judgment was executed (s. 60), but in the hour of doom Jeremiah promised a new covenant.[13] Postexilic Judaism believed it had received this promise; the Christian church, however, held that Israel was still unfaithful and had now been rejected, the church being put in her place as God's people (s. 51). The old covenant had been abrogated, and the new covenant established.

This is the basis of the terms used for the two major divisions of the Bible, the Old Testament and the New Testament. The Hebrew word for " covenant " was translated in the Septuagint by a Greek word meaning also a will or testament. Hence Paul speaks of the reading of the old testament, and says that Christians are ministers of the new testament.[14] Hence also the blood of Jesus is called the blood of the new testament or covenant,[15] with allusion to Ex. 24:6–8. This idea is developed especially in Heb. 8:1 to 9:20, where the argument depends on the fact that the same Greek word means both " testament " and " covenant."

Since a contract involves the assumption of definite obligations, the covenant between God and Israel necessitated a specific statement of what God promised and also of what he required of Israel. If the initia-

---

[7] Gen. 6:18; 9:1–17.

[8] Chs. 15:18; 17:2, 19; 26:2–5, 24; 28:12–15; Ex. 2:24; 6:4.

[9] Ex. 19:5 f.; 24:3–8; 34:27 f.

[10] Dt., chs. 27; 29:1; Josh. 8:30–35; 24:1–27; 2 K. 11:17; 23:3; 2 Chr. 29:10; Ezra 10:3.

[11] Ps. 89:3 f., 28 f., 34; 132:11 f.; Jer. 33:20 f.; Is. 55:3.

[12] 1 K. 19:10, 14; Ho. 8:1; Jer. 11:9 f.; 22:6–9; Is. 24:5.

[13] Jer. 31:31–34; cp. Ho. 2:14–20; Ezek. 16:59 f., 62 f.; Is. 54:10; 55:3; 59:21; 61:8; note also chs. 42:6 f.; 49:8 f.

[14] 2 Cor. 3:6, 14, A.V.

[15] Mt. 26:28; Mk. 14:24; cp. Lk. 22:20; 1 Cor. 11:25.

tive had been Israel's, a list of promises and expectations might have been formulated and presented to God for his approval, as is done, in effect, when an individual makes a vow.[16] But the initiative was God's; hence his promises and demands had to be revealed. Thus the idea of the covenant carries with it as a corollary the revelation of the law.[17] The long and complicated history of the various law codes incorporated into the Pentateuch is governed by this conception.

Prophetic revelation has the same essential purpose and content as the law: the prophets denounce Israel's failure to obey the revealed will of God.[18] Priests and prophets may differ on the specific content of God's requirements, but for both it is fundamental that he has showed man what is good.[19] Even Jeremiah's new covenant involves a revelation of the law, to be written in the heart.[20] Postbiblical Judaism finds its greatest blessing in the knowledge of God's will: " O Israel, happy are we, for the things that are pleasing to God are made known unto us." [21] The New Testament too is concerned first of all with God's will for man, and hence with the knowledge of what he requires.[22]

Failure to do God's will as he has revealed it incurs judgment; but God does not leave the guilty without hope: he offers the undeserving sinner redemption (s. 61) and reveals the way to obtain it. The promise of the new covenant includes forgiveness.[23] This note sounds strongly in the later prophets, especially Second Isaiah, who again and again proclaims the good news of deliverance.[24] This is the origin of the Christian word " gospel." [25] The law shows what God requires and the penalties of disobedience; the gospel shows the way of deliverance when man has failed to meet the requirements.[26] This is what Paul means by justification, God's free gift to the sinner.[27]

The primary purpose and content of revelation, according to the Bible, are thus practical rather than doctrinal. The object of revelation is not the satisfaction of man's curiosity or even of his mystical aspira-

---

[16] Gen. 28:20–22; Ju. 11:30 f.; 1 S. 1:11.
[17] Ex. 24:3–8.
[18] Jer. 11:1–10.
[19] Jer. 7:21–23; Mi. 6:6–8.
[20] Jer. 31:31–34.
[21] Baruch 4:4.
[22] Mt. 5:17–20; 7:21 ff.; Mk. 10:17 ff.; Lk. 10:25 ff.; Jn. 14:6, 15.
[23] Jer. 31:34.
[24] Is. 40:1 f., 9; 41:27; 52:7; 61:1.
[25] Mk. 1:14 f.; Lk. 4:16–21; 7:22.
[26] Dt. 30:19; Jn. 1:17; 10:10; 20:31.
[27] Rom. 1:16–19; 3:19–26; 6:23; s. 62.

tions, but guidance in the way of life.[28] In revealing his will and the way of salvation God has also made known much of his nature, but even when the knowledge of God is exalted as the very essence of salvation,[29] this does not mean knowledge about God but communion with him (s. 82). The first concern of revelation and authority is what man must do.

6. God's Authority in Matters of Conduct

A true Christian or Jew, whose chief desire is to know and do the divine will,[1] would not think of questioning God's right to command. If it should be asked, however, by what right God demands obedience, the answer of the Old Testament would be, first of all, that Israel in accepting the covenant promised to do God's will.[2] Rabbinic theology makes much of Israel's voluntary commitment as the basis of the authority of the law. Back of that, however, lies God's right as Creator and Ruler of the universe to govern his creatures.[3]

God's authority over man's life may be conceived in either of two ways, both of which are involved in the covenant idea as it is presented in the Bible. Authority may mean power to enforce a demand, rewarding obedience and punishing disobedience, or it may mean superior knowledge concerning the consequences of the acts in question. The former of these two conceptions of authority strongly colors the biblical idea of retribution, with its stress on divine judgments in history and individual life and its promises and warnings for the future (s. 60). The difficulty of maintaining faith in God's justice when the righteous suffer and the wicked prosper (s. 25) may be attributed in part to the conception of God's authority as that of a mighty Ruler who enforces his will by imposing punishments and rewards quite unrelated to the direct, inherent consequences of man's acts. The strong sense of God's sovereignty which permeates the whole Bible (s. 23) doubtless promotes this way of thinking of his authority. However incomprehensible his decrees may seem, man may not question them.[4]

But his commands are not arbitrary; they are true and righteous altogether.[5] God wishes man to do that which is in itself right. His laws

[28] Dt. 29:29; 30:15–20; Jn. 10:10; 20:31; 2 Tim. 3:16.
[29] Jn. 17:3.
[1] Ps. 1:2; 40:8; Mt. 6:33.
[2] Ex. 24:7 f.; Dt. 27:11–26.
[3] Ps. 100:3.
[4] Is. 45:9; 64:8; Jer. 18:1–10; Rom. 9:20 f.
[5] Dt. 32:4; Neh. 9:13; Ps. 19:7–9.

are not those of an arbitrary despot. Even though men may be unable to perceive the reasons for them, they are grounded in wisdom and justice; their purpose is that man may have life, and therefore they embody what God in his wisdom knows to be good for man.[6] Such contrary instances as God's inciting David to take a census and then punishing him for it [7] and Ezekiel's statement that God gave Israel " statutes that were not good, and ordinances wherein they should not live," [8] are only the exceptions that prove the rule. What is right is not so because God commands it; he commands it because it is right, and it is right because it is good for man. This may be true even of what we may call strictly religious rather than moral requirements, such as the observance of the sabbath.[9]

Since what God commands is what is good for man, his authority is not merely that of power to enforce a demand but that of superior knowledge. It is like the authority of a wise physician whose instructions we disregard at our peril, because he knows whereof he speaks. In practical affairs men constantly recognize and seek this kind of authority, the authority of the expert. Confident of God's absolute goodness and perfect wisdom (ss. 24 f.), we are assured that what he wills is what we should choose for ourselves if we could know all the implications and consequences of our acts as he knows them.

Comparing God to a wise physician or an expert, whose authority resides in his superior knowledge of the consequences of different lines of conduct, may suggest that God's demands are governed by conditions which he did not establish but merely recognizes. This would make him subject to something beyond his own will. But God differs from any human expert or specialist in that he is himself the Creator who established the order of things according to which man's salvation and welfare depend upon a particular kind of behavior. He knows what is good for man because he has made the world and all that is in it, including man himself.

7. God's Authority in Matters of Belief

The point of view we have achieved with regard to God's authority over man's conduct resolves our basic difficulty regarding authority in matters of belief (s. 4). Acceptance of the authority of superior knowledge and firsthand experience is universally recognized as thoroughly

---

[6] Dt. 30:19.
[7] 2 S., ch. 24.
[8] Ezek. 20:25.
[9] Mk. 2:27.

compatible with independence and honesty. Refusal to accept it shows only stubborn conceit and prejudice, once the competence of the authority in question has been reasonably established. As a matter of fact, we have all accepted on authority of this kind the very beliefs that lead us to reject certain statements in the Bible as untrue. We have not proved for ourselves by independent investigation that the earth is round or that it was not created in six days, yet we are thoroughly convinced of the truth of these propositions by what we consider competent, irrefutable authority.

Just as God wishes man to do what is inherently right, so he wishes man to believe the truth. The authority of God is, in the last analysis, the authority of ultimate reality, the authority of objective truth. There are, to be sure, a few suggestions in the Bible that God may deliberately mislead the wicked; [1] but to suppose that he really wished or required men to believe what was not true would contradict the basic Scriptural conception of his nature.[2] The only compelling authority for belief is the authority of truth itself, either conclusively demonstrated or so convincingly attested as to be indubitable.

The Bible itself, as a matter of fact, does not demand belief in defiance of reason and experience. It does demand faith, over and over again, where evidence is lacking or incomplete and belief is difficult, as in the case of Ahaz when threatened by the coalition of Israel and Syria.[3] It demands faith, also, in the sense of recognizing and accepting new truth when it is presented.[4] It condemns refusal to believe anything without a conclusive demonstration.[5] It also honors the faith that may accompany honest doubt.[6] It condemns dogmatic assurance at the cost of dishonesty.[7]

Recognition of the authority of superior knowledge makes clear the connection between authority and revelation. If we can be sure that the Bible is the word of God, no greater guarantee of its truth could be asked, for God is the supreme Knower.[8] The authority of what is revealed thus resides in the fact of revelation itself, if only we can recognize it as such and be sure of its authenticity. From this point of view

---

[1] 1 K. 22:10–23; Is. 6:9 f.; Jer. 4:10; Ezek. 14:9; 2 Th. 2:11.
[2] Num. 23:19; 1 S. 15:29; Ps. 19:9; 100:5; Is. 65:16; Jn. 17:17; Heb. 6:18; 1 Jn. 1:5.
[3] Is. 7:1–9.
[4] Mk. 3:22–30; 4:9–12.
[5] Jn. 4:48; 20:29; 1 Cor. 1:21–24.
[6] Mk. 9:23 f.
[7] Job 13:7; 42:7.
[8] Is. 40:13 f.; Rom. 11:33 f.

the question of authority, for belief as for conduct, is a question of recognizing genuine revelation, or of determining the authenticity of what purports to be revelation.

In other words, the authority of the Bible depends upon the reality of its inspiration. The word " inspiration," as commonly used, designates the divine origin of what is revealed and also the process by which it is communicated to man. Since this double usage involves no serious confusion, it will be adopted here.

8. *The Criteria of Revelation: Evidence of Divine Origin*

The authenticity of the revelation given in the Bible has been thought to be established in four ways: by competent and reliable testimony, by evidence of divine origin, by the way in which it was received as distinguishing it from knowledge gained in other ways, and by its own inherent truth and worth. A frank appraisal of each of these in turn will show that the first three are fallacious or at best inconclusive, leaving the fourth as the only tenable ground of assurance.

We have already found (s. 4) that the testimony of the church, which the Roman Catholic accepts as the sufficient and final guarantee of the inspiration of the Bible, is not conclusive for the Protestant, to say nothing of the unconvinced non-Christian. The same must be said of the claims to inspiration in the Bible itself: it is the validity of these claims that has to be established, and a witness cannot by his own testimony establish his competence to testify.

Direct evidence of divine origin would seem to be impossible in the nature of the case, for the ultimate origin of experiences and ideas cannot be determined by any kind of investigation. The whole problem of epistemology is involved here. What may be called indirect evidence, however, is adduced by two classic arguments for the inspiration of the Bible, known respectively as the proof by miracles and the proof by the fulfillment of prophecy.

Both of these arguments are used to some extent in the Bible itself. The proof by miracles corresponds to the biblical conception of " signs and wonders." In the Old Testament these sometimes occur in a series of " judgments " in history (s. 60), such as the plagues in Egypt.[1] They serve to authenticate and enforce revelation.[2] The New Testament similarly appeals to miracles.[3] Jesus and the apostles condemned the de-

[1] Ex. 7:3 f.
[2] Num. 14:11.
[3] Acts 2:22; 14:3; 2 Cor. 12:12; Heb. 2:3 f.

mand for signs to support the gospel,[4] yet Jesus himself saw in his miracles evidence of the nearness of the kingdom of God.[5] The fourth evangelist explicitly treats the miracles as " signs," [6] and this conception
was evidently strong in the early church.[7] Interest in the miraculous
was characteristic of the times, both among the Jews and in the Hellenistic world. What is remarkable in the New Testament is the resistance
to the general demand.

For the purpose of authenticating revelation the argument from miracles is of no use to us. To the modern mind the miraculous element in
the Bible constitutes a difficulty rather than evidence of inspiration.
The credibility of the biblical miracles will be discussed later (s. 43),
but even if it is granted, we cannot use the miracles to prove the divine
origin of the Bible, because we are dependent on the Bible itself for
the record of their occurrence. The argument from miracles is thus like
trying to prove the credibility of a witness by facts for which we have
only his own testimony. It is as inconclusive as his direct assertion of
his own competence.

The argument from the fulfillment of prophecy shares the same weakness. It too has Scriptural precedents. The fact that a prediction is not
fulfilled shows that it was not divinely inspired,[8] and, conversely, the
fulfillment of a prediction shows that it was spoken by a true prophet.[9]
The uniqueness and supremacy of Yahweh over against the false gods
of the nations are maintained by Second Isaiah on the ground that only
Yahweh can give knowledge of the future.[10] But again the argument
cannot be used to establish the authenticity of revelation in the Bible.
For many events, to be sure, we have abundant evidence of their occurrence in addition to the biblical record, but unless the statement that
they had been predicted is accepted on the authority of the Bible itself,
there is nothing to prove that the supposed prediction was not written
after the event took place. In other cases, where the prophecy was de-
monstrably written before the event that is traditionally regarded as its
fulfillment, the interpretation is open to question, if not obviously false.
This is true of the prophecies supposed to be predictions of the birth,
life, death, and resurrection of Jesus, and used as such in the New

4 Mk. 8:11 f.; 1 Cor. 1:22; Jn. 4:48; 6:30–37.
5 Mk. 3:27; Mt. 12:28; s. 64.
6 Jn. 2:11, 18–22; 20:30.
7 Acts 2:43; 4:30; 5:12; 8:13; Rom. 15:18 f.
8 Dt. 18:21 f.
9 Ezek. 33:33; cp. Am. 3:3–8.
10 Is. 41:21–24, 26; 43:9 f.

Testament itself, from Mt. 1:22 f. on. The argument from prophecy will not convince any intelligent and informed person who does not already believe that the Bible is inspired.

The attempt to demonstrate the inspiration of the Bible by any such evidence is as futile as the reliance upon the testimony of the church or on the claims to inspiration in the Bible itself.

9. *The Canon*

The third ground on which the authenticity of the revelation given in the Bible is defended is the way in which its contents were communicated to man. This, it has often been claimed, distinguishes revealed truth from knowledge received or achieved in other ways. We must, therefore, examine the process of inspiration, both as represented in the Bible and as claimed for it.

Before this can be intelligently considered, however, we must decide what we mean by the Bible. The decision as to which books were to be accepted as constituting an authoritative canon or rule of faith and practice was not definitively made at one time and unanimously accepted by the whole church. The canon has been variously defined at different times and by different portions of the church, and there has never been universal agreement on it even temporarily.

The first part of the Bible to be regarded as an authoritative body of sacred literature was the Pentateuch. The book of the law referred to in Deuteronomy [1] and Joshua [2] was probably the book of Deuteronomy itself,[3] which may therefore have been the first Hebrew book claiming anything like canonical authority. The Chronicler often mentions the book of the law of Moses,[4] probably meaning the whole Pentateuch.[5] The canonization of the Pentateuch was certainly complete by the time of the Samaritan schism, i.e., not later than the fourth century B.C. The religion of Israel was now distinctly the religion of the written law, founded on the word of God in a very different sense from what the prophets meant by the word of Yahweh.

The prophetic books seem to have been regarded as a sacred collection by the end of the third century B.C., for Ben Sira, after speaking of

[1] Dt. 17:18; 28:58, 61; 29:20 f.; 31:9, 24–26.
[2] Josh. 1:8; 8:31, 34; 24:26.
[3] Cp. Dt. 17:18–20; 1 K. 2:3; 2 K. 14:6; 22:8–20.
[4] 2 Chr. 17:9; 23:18; 25:4; 31:3; cp. Ezra 3:2; Neh. 8:1–8, 13–15; 9:1–3; 10:34, 36; 13:1–3.
[5] Cp. Dan. 9:11, 13.

Isaiah, Jeremiah, and Ezekiel, mentions " the twelve prophets." [6] The twelve minor prophets are named together in 2 Esdr. (4 Ezra) 1:39 f. In addition to our major and minor prophets (except Daniel and Lamentations), the second division of the Hebrew Bible, known as " the prophets," contains also the historical books (except Ruth, 1 and 2 Chronicles, Ezra, Nehemiah, and Esther), which are called " the former prophets." Just when and how this whole prophetic collection was made and added to the law as sacred Scripture is not known.

The remaining books of the Old Testament are grouped as a third part of the Hebrew canon under the general name of " the writings " (or Scriptures). The translator of Sirach speaks already in his preface of " the law and the prophets and the other books of our fathers." The New Testament refers to the law and the prophets,[7] Moses and the prophets,[8] and once " the law of Moses and the prophets and the psalms." [9] There were many disputes among the rabbis of New Testament times regarding the sacredness of various books, and the Hebrew canon was not definitively determined until early in the second century A.D. The threefold division of the canon is still retained in the Hebrew Old Testament.

Meanwhile the Septuagint, made for Greek-speaking Jews in Egypt, had included many books and portions of books that were not in the Hebrew canon. Some of them had never existed in Hebrew. The Greek-speaking church, followed to this day by the Roman Catholic church and the Oriental churches, accepted as its Bible the whole Septuagint, but the Protestant Reformation rejected everything not found in the Hebrew canon, setting apart as " Apocrypha " the fourteen additional books and parts of books, and denying them Scriptural authority. Some of them are actually as valuable and as truly inspired as some of the books that were retained, or more so. It is unfortunate that the decisions of the second-century rabbis were given such weight by the Reformers. The order of the books in our English Bibles, with the exception of the Jewish version, still follows in general the order of the Septuagint rather than that of the Hebrew Old Testament.

The definition of the New Testament canon was a matter of difference of opinion in the church for several centuries. The great uncial Codex Sinaiticus of the fourth century A.D. still includes the Epistle of

[6] Ecclus. 48:20, 22; 49:6–8, 10.
[7] Mt. 5:17; 7:12; 11:13; 22:40; Lk. 16:16; Jn. 1:45; Acts 13:15; 24:14; Rom. 3:21.
[8] Lk. 16:29–31; 24:27.
[9] Lk. 24:44.

Barnabas and the Shepherd of Hermas in the New Testament. Even in the sixteenth century Luther felt free to condemn the epistle of James as " an epistle of straw."

All these facts make it impossible to maintain a hard-and-fast conception of inspired Scripture as comprising the sixty-six books of the Protestant Bible, no more and no less. In Rev. 22:18 f. a curse is pronounced on any man who adds to the book or subtracts from it; to suppose that this applies to the canon, however, is to assume naïvely that the writer intended his book to stand at the end of the Bible. Even though we accept the canon of the Protestant churches by general consent as our standard of Christian faith and practice, we cannot ascribe equal authority to everything in it or exclude entirely from the category of inspired Scripture such books as Ecclesiasticus and the Wisdom of Solomon. Our conception of revelation and authority must be one that will allow some elasticity in the definition of Scripture.

10. *Tradition and the Written Word*

A defensible view of the inspiration of the Bible must also contemplate something quite different from verbal dictation and inerrancy. In the first place, most Christians must read the Bible in translation, and no translation can be infallible. Strict literalism in the use of the Greek and Hebrew texts also is excluded by the differences of interpretation among equally competent commentators. In fact, the text itself has suffered extensive corruption, so that the original wording can no longer be determined in detail.

Before the books of the Bible were written at all, the materials they contain had passed through many vicissitudes. Much of the narrative material in both Old and New Testaments rests on oral tradition, handed down in some cases for many generations before being reduced to writing at all. Some written records may have been kept even as early as the time of Moses, but the development, change, and combination of traditions are clear from the internal evidence of the Bible itself.

Many of the laws also were doubtless at first transmitted orally.[1] Moses may have put some of the laws into writing, but certainly no large collection of documents was carried about in the wilderness. The teaching of the law was committed to the priests and Levites.[2] In Canaan, after the conquest, the priests of various shrines decided cases

---

[1] Ex. 18:16, 20.   [2] Lev. 10:11; Dt. 33:10; 2 Chr. 15:3; 17:9.

brought to them, using both divination and legal tradition.[3] The various codes that can be distinguished in the Old Testament may have grown up in part by the formulation, accumulation, and codification of precedents at such places as Dan, Bethel, and Jerusalem.

The prophets, especially the earlier ones, were preachers rather than authors, and their words were for the most part preserved only in the memories of their disciples, who repeated them among themselves and reported them to others, thus establishing a tradition.[4] The wisdom literature also was based on wise sayings handed down from one generation to another.[5]

After the composition and canonization of the Pentateuch were completed (s. 9), new situations continued to arise, necessitating new interpretations and applications of the law. The same process of tradition that had produced the legal literature now produced a great body of new traditions, long transmitted orally out of reverence for the written law, and only much later written down and codified in the great collection known as the Talmud. These are the traditions of the elders and scribes referred to in the gospels; they were of the greatest importance to the Pharisees (s. 52) and have continued to be so for orthodox Judaism, but Jesus rejected them.[6]

Christianity, thus delivered from Jewish tradition, was not long in developing its own. The gospel was spread largely by preaching and testimony.[7] Jesus' own deeds and sayings were at first preserved mainly, if not entirely, by oral tradition. Lk. 1:1–4 and Jn. 21:24 show the dependence of the evangelists on such traditions. Since the sayings of Jesus were found helpful for moral guidance, a tendency arose to regard the gospel as a new law, and Jesus himself as another Moses (note the division of the gospel of Matthew into five " books " and the sharp contrast drawn in Mt., ch. 5, between the Mosaic law and the teaching of Jesus; also the portions, especially ch. 18, showing the compilation of sayings into a manual of church discipline).

Recognition of the period of oral tradition back of the written gospels and their literary sources, however short that period may have been as compared with the generations of oral tradition back of some of the ma-

---

[3] Dt. 17:8–11.
[4] Is. 8:16.
[5] Job 8:8; 15:17 f.; Prov. 1:2–6; 4:10–12; 13:14; 22:17; 24:23; Eccl. 12:11; Jer. 18:18; Ezek. 7:26.
[6] Mk. 7:1–23.
[7] Mk. 16:20; Lk. 1:1 f.; 24:47, 48; Acts 1:8; Heb. 2:3 f.; 1 P. 1:12.

terial of the Old Testament, has made the question of the authenticity of Jesus' sayings more acute than it was from the point of view of literary criticism. While few New Testament scholars accept without reservations the method and results of " form criticism," it is now clear that we cannot make a list of sayings that are certainly authentic and from them reconstruct Jesus' teaching in detail. Many points are uncertain and will probably always remain so. The main outlines, to be sure, have not been affected. Whatever critical investigation may do with this or that element, the main structure, with all its most characteristic features, stands out as clearly as ever. The net result of recent investigation, however, is that every saying must be considered on its own merits when we undertake to determine what Jesus taught on any subject. Sometimes we must depend upon cumulative evidence when it is impossible to establish with certainty the genuineness of particular sayings. In any case, allowance must always be made for the influence the interests of the church may have had on the selection, transmission, and modification of the material.

For the standardization of doctrine also tradition became important to the church. The prominence of the twelve as authoritative witnesses in Acts, ch. 1, suggests that a tendency in this direction was at work very early. Paul indignantly repudiates reliance on apostolic tradition for his gospel.[8] As variant interpretations of the gospel and what seemed to the leaders of the church to be dangerous heresies arose, conformity to tradition became more and more the standard of orthodoxy.[9] In so far as this tended to literalism and undue stress on orthodox belief, it was unfortunate; yet it preserved some historical continuity, preventing such a complete break with the historic origins of the faith as preoccupation with Greek philosophy might otherwise have brought about.

The desire for fixation and standardization, and so assurance of accuracy, led — how early we cannot tell — to reduction of the oral traditions to writing. We have already observed the possibility that some of the laws of the Pentateuch were actually written by Moses himself, if not literally by the finger of God.[10] The Bible explicitly states that this was done.[11] Writing was already well known in Palestine, and long before the time of Moses other nations had written law codes. But the

---

8 Gal., chs. 1 f.; but cp. 1 Cor. 11:23; 15:3.
9 1 Tim. 1:10 f.; 4:6; 6:3; 2 Tim. 1:13 f.; 4:3; Jude 3, 17; 2 P. 3:2; 1 Jn. 4:2; Rev., chs. 2 f.
10 Ex. 31:18; 32:16.
11 Ex. 34:1, 4, 27 f.; Dt. 31:9, 24–26; Josh. 1:8; cp. Dt. 27:1–3; Josh. 8:30–35.

tradition, oral or written, remained fluid for many centuries, with much revision and expansion. New laws were repeatedly evoked by the transition to agricultural and commercial life and the continued development of social and political institutions.

The prophetic books, like the books of the law and the histories, were products of compilation, selection, arrangement, and revision. Jeremiah dictated a record of his own preaching,[12] but the present book of Jeremiah includes much more than his own words. Whether or to what extent the later prophets were authors is uncertain. The apocalyptic writings were definitely literary compositions, not compilations of matter originally delivered orally; combination of different documents, however, is still evident. Compilation and editorial combination are equally apparent in the books of poetry and the wisdom literature, including Ecclesiastes and Job, though the last is mainly the individual product of a great literary genius. Aside from the brief books of Ruth, Esther, and Jonah, the narrative literature of both Old and New Testaments in its present form is the work of compilers and editors, and even these books are not free from the effects of such activity. In addition to all this it should be noted that even in those books and portions of books which most distinctly bear the stamp of great individual minds, most of the Bible is anonymous. The original parts of the prophetic books in the Old Testament and the epistles of Paul in the New Testament are the chief exceptions.

All these facts must be taken into account in our view of the inspiration of the Bible. To be sure, if the real author of the Scriptures is God, it makes no difference when or by whom any particular book or passage was written. Inspiration may have been granted to compilers and editors as well as prophets and apostles. But a naïve conception of inspiration as verbal dictation or even automatic writing is incompatible with the facts that we have reviewed. The very differences of style among the various writers would be enough to exclude such an idea: one does not alter his style to suit the personality of each stenographer to whom he gives dictation. The writer of Revelation claims prophetic inspiration and calls his book a book of prophecy,[13] indicating even that the writing was done by direct revelation.[14] Such a claim for a whole book, however, is unique.

[12] Jer., ch. 36.
[13] Rev. 1:1-3, 10 f.; 22:7-10, 16, 18 f.
[14] Rev. 1:11, 19; 2:1, 8, 12, 18; 3:1, 7, 14; 10:4; 14:13; 19:9; 21:5.

Comparison of parallel passages should be enough of itself to show the impossibility of maintaining a theory of verbal dictation. The differences between the accounts of the same events in Kings and Chronicles, for example, cannot all be ascribed to the errors of copyists. Did God incite David to take a census,[15] or was it Satan?[16] Both cannot be true, and two contradictory statements cannot have been dictated by one and the same Spirit. Similar discrepancies abound in the gospels. Did Jesus say " kingdom of God " or " kingdom of heaven " in the parables reported in Mk., ch. 4, and Mt., ch. 13? Here the meaning is the same, but the words are different, and Jesus did not say both at the same time. Did he say " the poor in spirit "[17] or " ye poor " and " you that are rich "?[18] It is extraordinary how such differences can be noted and calmly discussed by the same interpreters who none the less insist on verbal inspiration and inerrancy. Insignificant as these discrepancies are for Christian faith, they are entirely incompatible with any conception of inspiration as including the very words used by the writers of the Bible.

If our only authority resided in the exact contents of the original revelations received by the prophets, lawgivers, and the rest, we should now have no authoritative Scripture at all, for we can never know just what those contents were. Even if we had the original manuscript of each book, we should not know what previous changes had been made by copyists and editors in the sources used by the writer, or what alterations had occurred still earlier in the course of oral tradition; we should therefore have to suppose, as many in fact do, that it was the final compiler or editor who was divinely guided in his work and so enabled to correct errors in his sources. But we do not have the original manuscripts, and those we have are manifestly full of mistakes.

To be of any real significance and practical value for us, the Bible which is our authority must be the Bible we now have, with all the imperfections and uncertainties involved in it. Unless the inspiration of the Bible is to be treated as a purely academic question, of no practical religious significance for us today, it must mean something that can be predicated of the imperfect Bible which we can use for our inspiration and guidance. It must apply to a revelation still to be found there in spite of all the alterations made by editors and scribes, not one that has been effaced by them, as exact verbal infallibility would have been.

[15] 2 S. 24:1.   [17] Mt. 5:3.
[16] 1 Chr. 21:1.   [18] Lk. 6:20, 24.

By and large it is not the wording of the final record but the original vision of the prophets, the wisdom of the sages and lawgivers and apostles, the insight of the historians and evangelists, and the clear insight of Jesus into the mind of God that should be attributed to inspiration. Not the books, not the words, but the men were inspired.[19] It is in this sense that the Scriptures were inspired of God.[20]

11. *The Spoken Word*

The foregoing section has made clear how much of the written word, including such vitally important elements as the pronouncements of the prophets and the teachings of Jesus, goes back to communications originally made by the living voice. If anything in the Bible can be said to have been directly inspired from above, it must have been the spoken word of God's living representatives. Back of the spoken word itself, of course, lies the inner experience of the speaker. It is this which in the strictest sense is inspired. But if inspiration may be claimed in any sense for the words of Scripture, it must surely be claimed for the words of those who had such experiences.

The words reported in the Bible are often attributed to specific directions given by God himself. When a revelation is received in the form of an audition (s. 12), it may simply be verbally repeated: so Moses [1] (cp. the frequent expression, " Speak unto the children of Israel that they . . . ," or, " Speak unto the children of Israel and say unto them . . ."); so also Balaam,[2] Michaiah,[3] and the prophets in general.[4] Only in the case of Balaam, however, is automatic trance utterance unmistakably indicated.[5] Aside from verbal auditions, it is the idea, the word rather than the words, that the prophet delivers; in fact even the report of an audition is often accompanied by considerable narrative, explanation, or elaboration. The general relation between the revelation received and the message delivered is suggested by Ps. 39:3, " As I mused, the fire burned; then I spoke out with my tongue." [6]

The spoken word of the prophet is often accompanied and enforced

---

19 2 P. 1:21.
20 2 Tim. 3:16.
1 Ex. 4:11–16.
2 Num. 22:18–20; 23:12–26.
3 1 K. 22:14, 19–23.
4 Jer. 1:7–9; 25:1–9; 37:2; Is. 51:16; Mt. 1:22; 2:15; Lk. 1:70.
5 Num. 24:3 f., 15 f.
6 Cp. Job 32:18–20; Am. 3:7 f.; Jer. 20:9; Acts 18:5; 1 Cor. 9:16; 2 P. 1:21.

by object lessons and dramatic actions.[7] Jesus' actions at his last supper with his disciples followed this prophetic tradition of dramatized symbolism (s. 98).

In so far as the spoken words were a part of the speaker's inner experience they may be called inspired in the same sense and to the same degree as the experience itself. In so far as they are merely his own expression of what he has experienced, we must reserve the concept of inspiration for the experience. But how can we determine whether or not such an experience was truly God-given? We must consider more closely the forms of experience out of which came the words recorded in the Bible.

12. The Experience of Inspiration

The Old Testament records " divers portions " and " divers manners " of revelation.[1] From the very beginning God appears directly to individuals. Sometimes these theophanies are narrated with naïve anthropomorphism.[2] Sometimes it is said only that God appeared and spoke.[3] Sometimes he appears and speaks to a man in a dream; [4] so also in the New Testament.[5] Sometimes it is God's angel that appears,[6] though in several of these instances there is a curious confusion or lack of sharp distinction between Yahweh and his angel, which cannot be wholly explained by the combination of sources (s. 40). In the New Testament also an angel brings guidance, often in dreams, to chosen individuals.[7] A special type of revelation by angels is the characteristic explanation of apocalyptic visions by angelic interpreters.[8]

Outstanding among Old Testament theophanies is the one at Sinai, when the law was given and the covenant established.[9] Connected with this are other appearances to Moses and to the elders of Israel.[10] The historical basis of the tradition that the law was revealed to Moses at Sinai cannot now be determined, much less the psychological form of

---

[7] I K. 11:29–36; Is. 7:3; 8:1–4, 18; 20:1–4; Jer. 13:1–11; 18:1–10; 19:1 f., 10; 27:2; 28:10–14; 32:6–15; Ezek., chs. 4; 5:1–5, 11 f.

[1] Heb. 1:1.

[2] Gen. 3:8–21; 18:1–33; 32:24–32; Ex. 4:24–26; 33:12–23.

[3] Gen. 12:7; 17:1; 26:2; Ex. 6:3.

[4] Gen. 15:1, 12 f.; 20:3, 6; 26:24; 28:11–17; Job 4:12–17; 33:14–16.

[5] Mt. 2:22; Acts 16:9; 18:9.

[6] Gen. 16:7–14; 21:17; 22:11, 15; Ex., ch. 3; Num. 22:9–35; Ju. 6:11 ff.; 13; 2 S. 24:15–17.

[7] Mt. 1:20; 2:12 f., 19; Lk. 1:11, 26; Acts 5:19 f.; 8:26; 27:23 f.

[8] Zc. 1:9, 18; Ezek. 40:3 f.; Dan. 8:15 f.; 10:4–12, 18–21; Rev. 17:1, 7.

[9] Ex., chs. 19; 20:18–22; Dt. 4:11 f.; 5:4.

[10] Ex. 24:1 f., 9–18.

his experience. In spite of later additions, it need not be doubted that some of the laws were promulgated by Moses himself. Whether he received them in visions and auditions is another question. The accounts of his experiences, especially the revelation at the burning bush,[11] give that impression. It would not necessarily follow that all his laws came to him in that fashion. Some may have been decisions rendered in particular cases,[12] and taken thereafter as precedents. In general it is probable that Moses' laws were at least formulated in times of prayer and meditation, and were issued in the assurance that they expressed the will of God. Such an origin is possible also, though less likely, for the laws added later to the Mosaic corpus. On the whole, whatever divine influence may have governed their formulation and adoption would seem rather to have been a general endowment of practical wisdom (s. 13).

Further theophanies in the wilderness are recorded.[13] Later appearances of God to individuals include those to Samuel[14] and Solomon.[15] Theophanies are referred to in rather general terms in the Psalms;[16] cp. also the great theophany of Job, chs. 38 to 42.

Along with all this the Bible, especially the New Testament, teaches that God is invisible;[17] in fact it is flatly stated that no man has ever seen him.[18] Early portions of the Old Testament reflect the idea that to see God or his angel is dangerous, if not fatal.[19] The prohibition of images[20] indicates a similar feeling, and even such passages as Ex. 24:10 and Ezek., chs. 1 and 10, notably avoid any description of God. Efforts to avoid anthropomorphism are evident also in the representations of God as appearing in dreams or being represented by his angel. Other expressions of the same reverential attitude are the reference to clouds, smoke, and flame in connection with theophanies, and the later conception of the Glory of Yahweh (s. 28). In Psalms the experience of communion with God is sometimes called seeing God;[21] cp. Jesus' promise to the pure in heart,[22] though this may refer to the future life.

[11] Ex., ch. 3.
[12] Ex. 18:13 ff.
[13] Ex. 16:10; Lev. 9:23; Num. 14:10; Dt. 31:15.
[14] 1 S., ch. 3.
[15] 1 K. 3:5; 9:2; 11:9.
[16] Ps. 18:6–16; 97:2–6; 144:5–7.
[17] Col. 1:15; Heb. 11:27; 1 Tim. 1:17.
[18] Jn. 1:18; 1 Jn. 4:12.
[19] Gen. 32:30; Ex. 19:21; 24:11; Ju. 6:22 f.; 13:22; cp. Is. 6:5.
[20] Ex. 20:4; Dt. 5:8.
[21] Ps. 17:15; 27:4, 8 f.; 63:2; 69:17; 105:4.
[22] Mt. 5:8.

Most of the theophanies include a verbal revelation: God appears in order to speak. Sometimes also he speaks without appearing.[23] The expression " God said " is used first of the words of command by which the creation is brought about in Gen., ch. 1, leading to the first commandment given to man.[24] In Gen., ch. 2, another primeval commandment is given.[25] God also speaks to himself.[26] Gen., chs. 3 and 18, records protracted conversations between God and men. From Gen. 8:15 on we find often the expression, " And God spake unto . . . , saying." The verb " commanded " also is used frequently.[27]

Revelations in dreams have been mentioned; these, too, usually include a verbal communication. God also speaks often in waking visions, which cannot always be distinguished from dreams. One of the Hebrew nouns meaning " vision " is used in the titles of the books of Isaiah,[28] Obadiah, and Nahum.[29] Num. 12:6-8 contrasts God's speaking to prophets in visions and dreams and his speaking to Moses directly. Some prophetic visions involve appearances of God himself;[30] note also the later apocalyptic visions of God.[31] Joel 2:28 f. promises prophetic visions to " all flesh " in the future,[32] though it is not said that God himself will be seen. False prophets too have visions.[33] Jer. 23:23-32 condemns false prophets who prophesy dreams.[34] In the New Testament, God, an angel, the Spirit, and the exalted Christ speak in visions.[35]

For the verbal content of these experiences, various expressions are used. Several Hebrew nouns are translated " word " in our English versions, the most common one (*dabar*) being derived from the same root as the verb meaning " speak." The plural of this noun is used sometimes of the laws, especially those of a particular type;[36] it is occasionally used also of prophetic utterances.[37] More commonly the term

23 Gen. 4:6, 9, 13; 6:13; 7:1; 9:1, 8.
24 Gen. 1:28.
25 Gen. 2:16 f.
26 Gen. 1:26; 2:18; 3:22; 6:3, 7; 11:6.
27 Gen. 2:16; 6:22; 7:5.
28 Cp. 2 Chr. 32:32.
29 Cp. Ezek. 1:1; 8:3; 40:2; Hab. 2:2 f.
30 Am. 7:7; Is., ch. 6; Ezek., chs. 1; 10.
31 Dan. 7:9 ff.; cp. Rev. 1:12-18; 20:11.
32 Cp. Acts 2:16 ff.
33 Is. 28:7; 29:11 f.; Jer. 14:14; Ezek. 12:22 f.; Zc. 13:4.
34 Cp. Dt. 13:1-5; 1 S. 28:6, 15.
35 Acts 9:1-16; 10:3, 17; 11:5; 2 Cor. 12:1; Rev. 1:10-20.
36 Ex. 20:1; 34:27 — the same noun is translated " commandments " in ch. 34:28, though it is not the noun usually so rendered.
37 Jer. 30:1 f.

is used in the singular, " the word of Yahweh," for both commands and promises and also for revelation in general.[38] Jer. 18:18 makes the " word " the special property of the prophets as the law is that of the priests. Prophetic inspiration is commonly indicated by the expression, " The word of Yahweh came [literally, " was "] to . . ." — so from Abraham [39] and Samuel [40] to Jeremiah.[41] The same expression appears in the editorial titles of Hosea, Micah, and Zephaniah. The word is also sent [42] or even seen,[43] or, in the legal literature, commanded.[44]

Within the sayings of the prophets themselves two other expressions are more common: " Thus Yahweh has said " and " oracle of Yahweh " (so modern translations; the standard English versions render " saith "). Still another expression is the " burden " of Yahweh,[45] used chiefly in late or disputed passages and in editorial titles. The psalms refer often, using various Hebrew terms, to the word or words of God, including both commands and promises.[46]

The nature of the actual experiences indicated by all these expressions is extremely difficult to determine. Many of the accounts doubtless record actual visions and undoubtedly also auditions with specific verbal content (cp. Augustine's " Take, read," and Joan of Arc's angelic voices). In other cases the vision seems to be merely a form of literary expression, and the statement that God spoke, or that his word came to the prophet, may often mean simply that the idea came into the prophet's mind with a burning conviction of its divine origin.

Some passages in the wisdom literature suggest an experience essentially the same as that of the prophets,[47] but on the whole the inspiration of the sages seems to have been of a different kind (s. 13). The great theophany of Job, chs. 38 to 42, is poetry rather than history, yet it may reflect the poet's own experience.

Postbiblical Judaism in general held that direct inspiration belonged to the past. While prophetic experience was not entirely extinct, the nearest approach to it ordinarily was the occasional voice from

[38] 1 S. 3:1, 7, 21.
[39] Gen. 15:1.
[40] 1 S. 15:10.
[41] More than 20 times.
[42] Is. 9:8.
[43] Is. 2:1; Jer. 2:31; 38:21.
[44] Ex. 19:7; 35:1; Dt. 4:2.
[45] 2 K. 9:25; Jer. 23:33-40.
[46] Ps. 33:4, 6; 103:20; 119:9, 11, 103, 105, 130; 130:5.
[47] Job 4:12-17; 33:14-16.

heaven (*bath qol*), which was not acknowledged as authoritative in controversies regarding the law (i.e., the written law and even its traditional interpretation could not be affected even by a direct word from heaven). Such a *bath qol* was heard at Jesus' baptism and again at his transfiguration. Whether it was heard in the former instance by Jesus alone or by others also is not clear,[48] but all accounts agree that at the transfiguration the voice addressed the disciples.[49] Another instance is given in Jn. 12:28–30.

Otherwise there is little, if any, evidence that Jesus had such experiences as those of the prophets. His inspiration was of another kind (s. 13). He seems not to have expected that his disciples would speak by direct revelation, yet cp. Mk. 13:11 and Mt. 11:25. Instances of direct verbal guidance in dreams and visions have been cited above from the book of Acts; there are also cases of such guidance without any indication of a dream or vision.[50] The prophetic experience was certainly common in the early church (s. 87). Paul not only insists that his gospel was given to him in the first place by revelation; [51] he also claims both mystical experiences and direct divine guidance.[52]

Regarding all these experiences we must conclude that the divine origin of the message is quite independent of the psychological form of its reception. Inspiration, like conversion (s. 77), is not a matter of a particular type of experience. To say that " men spake from God being moved by the Holy Spirit " [53] does not necessarily imply either the presence or absence of such phenomena as visions and auditions. Nor does the occurrence of such phenomena guarantee the presence of divine inspiration. False as well as true revelations exist, false prophecy as well as true prophecy, false spirits as well as true spirits; and while some individuals may have a special gift for the discerning of spirits,[54] the final decision is left to each individual, with no external criterion beyond consistency with what is already accepted as authoritative.[55] Theophanies, visions, and auditions cannot prove the fact of revelation; for that matter, we are again dependent upon the testimony of the Bible itself for their occurrence.

48 Mt. 3:16 f.; Mk. 1:10 f.; Lk. 3:21 f.; cp. Jn. 1:32–34.
49 Mk. 9:7, and parallels; cp. 2 P. 1:17 f.
50 Lk. 1:11 f., 26 ff.; Acts 5:19 f.; 8:26, 29; 10:19; 12:7–9.
51 Gal. 1:12, 16; cp. 2 Cor., chs. 10 to 13.
52 1 Cor. 14:6, 18 f.; 2 Cor. 12:1–10; Gal. 2:2.
53 2 P. 1:21.
54 1 Cor. 12:10.
55 Dt. 13:1–5; 1 Jn. 4:1–3.

If we could make a psychological analysis of the prophets' experience, we should probably find that the experience of the false prophets was psychologically indistinguishable from that of the true prophets. It must be recognized also that the specific content of such experiences is at least conditioned and may be wholly given by previous experience, native endowment, and the cultural background. On the other hand, to recognize that the visual and auditory factors in the experience come under the head of hallucination does not necessarily exclude an authentic revelation. It remains possible, until the contrary is proved, that these factors are merely incidental, like the sparks from an anvil.

13. *The Gift of Spiritual Insight*

Not only knowledge or guidance given directly in particular experiences, but also that achieved through special insight and wisdom is recognized by the Bible as God-given and treated as revelation.[1] Even technical knowledge and skills come under this head.[2] Wisdom in government also is a divine gift.[3]

As already observed, the Old Testament laws should probably be regarded as inspired largely in this sense. Whether given by Moses himself or by later legislators, they were doubtless derived largely from the tribal traditions of the Hebrews and the common legal concepts of the times. Similarly the Babylonian Code of Hammurabi claims that its laws were given by the god Shamash, though, as Chiera says, everybody knew they were the same old laws.[4]

A special problem is posed in this connection by the incorporation of foreign laws in the Hebrew codes. The relation between the Hebrew Book of the Covenant[5] and the Code of Hammurabi is still disputed, but recent study shows that along with distinctive Israelite laws the Old Testament contains many others of foreign origin, probably taken over from the Canaanites. For biblical theology the important point in this connection is not the origin of any particular law or group of laws but the fact that for Israel they are all given the sanction of the divine will and subsumed under the basic idea of the covenant. Whether the form or content of such laws was derived from ancient Hebrew custom, from the earlier codes of Babylonians, Canaanites, or other peoples, or

---

[1] Job, ch. 28; Ps. 94:10; Prov. 2:6; Dan. 1:17.
[2] Ex. 28:3; 31:1-6.
[3] 1 K. 3:4-15; 4:29-34; cp. Is. 11:2.
[4] E. Chiera, *They Wrote on Clay*, p. 77.
[5] Ex. 20:23 to 23:19.

from the immediate inspiration of a particular individual, the essential revelation in the matter was that this was what God required.

The same problem arises also in the wisdom literature, for Prov. 22:17 to 24:22 evinces dependence upon the Egyptian "Wisdom of Amenemope." Canaanite elements in the Psalms and the prophetic books have been detected recently. All this, however, is quite compatible with inspiration. It does not even disprove inspiration by visions and auditions, for, as noted in s. 12, the ideational content of mystical experience, like that of normal learning, is always limited and conditioned by the individual's previous experience. Still less does it exclude divine influence in endowing men with the wisdom by which existing material might be selected and incorporated into Israel's religious tradition. God's will for Israel may very well have been expressed in such material: whether this was so or not in any particular instance cannot be determined by objective evidence. Even the inspiration of the prophets may have belonged in part to this category. The strong convictions expressed as the word of Yahweh may often have come through observation of current tendencies and profound reflection on their implications. They would be none the less inspired if they came in this way.

Certainly permanent mental and spiritual endowment rather than particular, immediate inspiration is responsible for most of the material preserved in the wisdom literature, whether original or derived from earlier sources. Wisdom is regarded in the wisdom literature as communicable by teaching, but only to those with an inborn capacity for it; [6] cp. W.S. 7:27, "And from generation to generation, passing into holy souls, she maketh men friends of God and prophets." Its content is not information or metaphysical knowledge, but prudence and intelligence in practical and spiritual matters, its basis being simple piety.[7] This conception of wisdom underwent various developments. On the one hand wisdom came to be identified with the law and legal learning; [8] on the other hand it was connected with the Greek idea of the Logos.[9]

Jesus' message seems to be the expression of clear, steady insight rather than the result of separate, particular revelations. He could speak with assurance because he knew the Father.[10] Kinship with the wisdom of the sages is suggested by Lk. 7:35; 11:49. The rest of the

---

[6] Prov. 4:1; 14:18; 17:16; 18:15; 24:7.
[7] Job 28:28; Ps. 111:10; Prov. 1:7; 9:10; 15:33.
[8] Ecclus. 24:1–23, and the rabbinic literature.
[9] W.S. 9:1 f. and Philo; see s. 35.
[10] Mt. 11:27.

New Testament preserves little of this conception, except as it is implied by the Johannine idea of the Logos.

Several of the references already given connect wisdom with the Spirit of God (s. 27), showing that not only the immediate and particular revelations of the prophets and others but also permanent gifts of insight and understanding are to be attributed to the Spirit.[11] Hellenistic Judaism identified wisdom with the Spirit as well as the Logos.[12] Paul names wisdom and knowledge among the gifts of the Spirit.[13] Wisdom as a divine gift in answer to prayer appears also in James.[14]

The biblical conception of revelation, however, cannot be wholly reduced to the existence of truth and the endowment of men with the intellectual and spiritual capacities by which it can be apprehended. Revelation, as represented in the Bible, has specific content. The current tendency to define revelation in terms of something other than the communication of definite ideas, whatever partial justification it may have, is not true to the biblical conception of revelation. In the Bible revelation does not mean the disclosure of metaphysical truth, but it does mean definite guidance for life and for the faith that leads to life.

It must be remembered also that not wisdom in general but particular individual gifts of spiritual insight, given only to faithful and approved servants of God, are regarded as the vehicle of revelation. The native wisdom of the natural man, however highly cultivated, is helpless to attain any knowledge of " the deep things of God "; [15] they are known only by the more profound wisdom which the Spirit gives to the spiritual man.[16]

14. *The Relation Between Revelation and Discovery*

The emphasis on the divine initiative implied by the concepts of revelation and inspiration, together with the disparagement of human wisdom mentioned at the close of the preceding section, may seem to imply a condemnation of all human efforts to achieve knowledge by way of discovery. It is true that the Hebrews had little of the intellectual curiosity that animated Greek philosophy and has produced modern science. The writer of Ecclesiastes decries the pursuit of knowledge as worse than

---

[11] Cp. also Num. 27:18; Dt. 34:9.
[12] W.S. 1:6 f.; 7:22 ff.; 9:17.
[13] 1 Cor. 12:8.
[14] Jas. 1:5; 3:13–17.
[15] Job 11:7; 28; Jer. 9:23 f.; 1 Cor. 1:17 to 2:5.
[16] 1 Cor. 2:6–16; Jas. 1:5–8; cp. Mt. 11:25–27.

futile.[1] Something of the same feeling seems to be involved in the story of the tree of the knowledge of good and evil in Gen., ch. 3. Yet we have seen that even practical knowledge and wisdom, within due limits, are not only praised but regarded as a divine gift.

What may be called an intermediate idea between revelation and discovery is implied by the ancient practice of divination and the consulting of oracles. Here the conception that all reliable knowledge must come from God is combined with the assumption that man can induce God to grant special revelations for immediate needs. This is of course very different from discovery by systematic observation and experiment. It is when men have no hope of learning by natural means what they wish to know that they resort to such practices, which of course are usually based on nothing better than superstition and have often been kept alive by priestly fraud.

The Hebrews, like other peoples of all times, were not always content to wait for God's initiative in granting revelation, or to depend upon what had already been revealed. Faced with specific questions, they sought immediate, specific answers. Pagan forms of divination are frequently mentioned and strongly condemned in the Bible under such terms as witchcraft and sorcery.[2] The basis of condemnation is in general reliance on other means of guidance than the revealed will of God. The same is true of necromancy, which was officially condemned by Yahwism but was evidently practiced by many Israelites.[3] The periodic recrudescence of such superstitions in the modern world gives these passages a timeliness not often recognized by Christian preachers. Deuteronomy condemns all efforts to secure knowledge of what is hidden as both presumptuous and unnecessary, because God has revealed all that man needs to know for salvation, leaving him without excuse if he fails to find the way of life.[4]

Certain forms of divination, however, are at least tacitly approved in the Old Testament. Signs were a characteristic Hebrew way of getting answers to life's riddles.[5] In Is. 7:10 ff. (s. 31) God himself offers a sign; this comes therefore under the head of revelation rather than divination. The interpretation of dreams [6] may be regarded as a kind of

[1] Eccl. 1:18.
[2] Dt. 18:10–14; Lev. 19:26, 31; 20:6, 27; 1 S. 15:23; 2 K. 1:1–4; 17:17; 21:6; Mi. 5:12; Is. 19:3; 47:9, 12 f.; Gen. 41:8, 24; Dan. 1:20; 2:2, 27; 4:7, 9; 5:7, 11, 15; Acts 16:16–24.
[3] 1 S., ch. 28; Is. 8:19; Dt. 18:11; Lev. 19:31.
[4] Dt. 29:29; Rom. 1:18–20.
[5] Ju. 6:17 ff., 36–40; 1 S. 14: 8–10; 2 S. 5:23 f.; 2 K. 20:8–11.
[6] Gen., chs. 40 f.; Dan., chs. 2; 4.

divination, out when the dream is given for the express purpose of conveying a divine message, it too belongs rather to the category of revelation (s. 12).

Divination by second sight or trance vision, induced at will, is exemplified by Balaam [7] and Elisha.[8] Here we touch again the borderline between divination and revelation. Old Testament prophecy is an important form of revelation, but if we draw the distinction on the basis of the divine or human initiative, some of the earliest prophets were diviners rather than recipients of revelation — so perhaps the ecstatic prophets of 1 S., ch. 10, and the " sons of the prophets "; [9] so clearly the court prophets of 1 K., ch. 22, who are asked the same kind of question to which Saul and David sought answers by the ephod and ark.[10]

The condemnation of divination did not, of course, apply to seeking oracles by means that had been divinely ordained and entrusted to the legitimate priesthood. The Old Testament refers sometimes to inquiring of God without indicating the means employed.[11] Sometimes the sacred lot was used.[12] The root from which the Hebrew word for law, *torah,* is derived means both " teach " and " cast " and the noun may have meant originally the casting of the lot. The ark [13] and the ephod [14] were used as means of securing oracles. The Urim and Thummim had some connection with this practice.[15] Clearly the Old Testament does not indicate that man's attitude with regard to revelation must be a wholly passive waiting for God to speak, or a dependence on revelation granted in the past.

The New Testament neither sanctions nor explicitly condemns any of these means of seeking answers to immediate questions,[16] but its constant emphasis on an immediate personal relation to God and its frequent instances of direct divine guidance of individuals leave no room for anything in the nature of divination or oracles. At the same time, the recognition of such personal guidance allows some human initia-

[7] Num., chs. 22 to 24.
[8] 2 K. 3:11–15.
[9] Cp. 2 K., ch. 2.
[10] Cp. 2 Chr., ch. 20.
[11] Gen. 25:22 f.; 1 S. 14:36 f.; 23:2, 4; 2 S. 5:19, 23–25.
[12] 1 S. 10:17–24; Acts 1:15–26.
[13] 1 S. 14:18 f.
[14] 1 S. 23:9–12; 30:7.
[15] Ex. 28:30; Lev. 8:8; Num. 27:21; Dt. 33:8; 1 S. 14:41, LXX: " If there is unrighteousness in me or my son Jonathan, Lord God of Israel, give Urim; and if thou sayest this, In thy people Israel, give Thummim "; ch. 28:6.
[16] Cp., however, Acts 1:15–26.

tive in seeking knowledge from God, at least to the extent of praying for it.[17]

All this is still quite different from an independent investigation and search for truth by reason and experiment. The apparent antithesis between revelation and discovery, however, is practically resolved by the biblical conception of all knowledge as ultimately dependent on revelation. From this point of view, discovery is only the recognition of something that has been revealed. For Amos the fact of prophecy implies a divine revelation in the same way that any observed event may imply an unseen cause.[18] So any discovery is dependent, first, upon the existence of what is discovered, a reality capable of being apprehended by the human mind, and, secondly, upon the endowment of man with the capacity to discover and recognize it (s. 13).

All knowledge, however received or achieved, comes through the experience of realities outside ourselves, interpreted by means of the data of previous experience and in turn enabling us to reinterpret our previous experience. This is as true of spiritual experience as it is of physical and social experience. Revelation itself can be received only in and through experience, and not only such special experiences as visions and auditions but any experience may be a vehicle of revelation if perceived with a new sense of significance. The sight of a basket of summer fruit [19] or an almond branch [20] or an opportunity to buy a piece of real estate [21] is such a means of revelation when he who experiences it also hears God speak to him.

There is thus no inherent or inevitable conflict between revelation and discovery. What God reveals, man must discover or at least recognize, and man can discover only what has been revealed. This does not mean that there is no revelation except what man finds by investigation on his own initiative. If there can be no discovery without revelation, it does not follow that there can be no revelation without discovery, if by discovery is meant the result of a deliberate effort to find truth. What the Bible means by revelation depends wholly on the divine initiative. More often than not it comes, or seems to come, without any searching on man's part, often indeed taking him by surprise. Even such unsought revelation, however, presupposes some fitness in the recipient. If the instrument is not attuned to the right wave length, the broadcast will not be received. No man is wholly worthy, but not everyone is capable of being an instrument of revelation at all.

17 Cp. Jas. 1:5.
18 Am. 3:1–8.
19 Am. 8:1.
20 Jer. 1:11.
21 Jer. 32:6 ff.

But if revelation, as conceived in the Bible, is not always or even often preceded by a search on man's part, it may and sometimes does come after and perhaps through such a search. Who knows what hard thinking had preceded Paul's sudden vision on the road to Damascus? Revelation and discovery are not necessarily identical or coextensive, like the obverse and reverse of a coin, but they certainly are not mutually exclusive.

Investigation and discovery, when pursued and used for worthy ends, help to realize God's purpose in the creation of man (s. 48), as expressed in the commandment, " Replenish the earth and subdue it." [22] The disparagement of human wisdom in the Bible does not apply to a humble effort to " think God's thoughts after him," but to that narrow, self-satisfied knowledge that fails to recognize its own limits and despises everything outside of its own ken. This is the knowledge that puffs up,[23] scorning the faith and insight of those not in its own circle, and refusing even to acknowledge the existence of anything that cannot be measured by its own instruments. Such arrogant knowledge keeps itself hopelessly ignorant of all that is most important for man. It is only " knowledge falsely so-called," [24] the wisdom of fools.[25] It is especially the self-interested, insincere, and therefore corrupt learning of those whose desires dull their insight and warp their judgment,[26] so that they are " led away with divers lusts, ever learning, and never able to come to the knowledge of the truth." [27] Unfortunately even religious interests and motives, such as dogmatic assurance or fear of change, may exclude the light of revelation.[28]

The relation between revelation and discovery is further clarified by the distinctions between general and special revelation and between natural and revealed theology, to which we now turn.

15. *General and Special Revelation; Natural and Revealed Theology*

The distinction between general and special revelation has not always been made in the same way or at the same point. It is not made at all in the Bible, yet it is implied by the different types of revelation recognized by the Bible. As the terms are used here, general revelation means a divine communication or demonstration of truth given or at least made accessible to all men and peoples, while special revelation

22 Gen. 1:28.
23 1 Cor. 8:1.
24 1 Tim. 6:20.
25 Rom. 1:22.

26 1 Tim. 6:5.
27 2 Tim. 3:6 f.
28 Mk. 3:29 f.; 7:13; Mt. 23:23 f.; Acts 6:14.

means any particular communication to an individual or a limited group.

According to the Bible, some knowledge of God and his will is open to all men. *Nature* as his work reveals his power and majesty, the excellence of his " name " (s. 54), and the littleness of man.[1] It is a God-given witness also to his impartial goodness and care for his creatures.[2]

In *history* also his mighty acts and judgments demonstrate that he alone is God, and while much of the revelation of God in history comes under the head of special revelation in the sense that it was given for Israel's special benefit (*v. i.*), stress is often laid also on the fact that the nations see God's works and are convinced of his power.[3] In fact, God's dealing with Israel itself, both in punishment and in blessing, serves to reveal his greatness to other peoples also.[4]

The human *conscience and reason* also convey to mankind in general a partial knowledge of God and his will. In keeping with Greek ideas of natural law, Paul uses the words " nature " and " natural " in this connection: the Gentiles " show the work of the law written in their hearts " when they " do by nature " the things that the law requires.[5] As opposed to the " natural " relation of the sexes, pagan vice is " contrary to nature." [6] So Paul appeals to the Corinthians to judge in themselves and recognize what nature itself teaches,[7] though to be sure in this instance he applies the concept to the rather trivial question of wearing the hair long or short, actually a matter of social convention. Even an apostle is not exempt from the common human tendency to mistake convention and prejudice for the law of nature. (Paul uses the adjective " natural " elsewhere as the opposite of " spiritual," especially with reference to the limitations of the natural man's knowledge; cp. s. 45. Man's life rather than the universe at large is probably meant in Jas. 3:6 by " the course of nature " which may be set on fire by the tongue. Jude 10 refers contemptuously to what men " know naturally, as brute beasts.")

A general revelation in conscience and reason may be referred to in Jn. 1:9 f., for while the phrase " coming into the world " probably modifies " true light," the position of the verse as well as the expression

---

[1] Job 12:7–9; Ps. 8; 19:1–6; Is. 40:26; Jer. 5:22; Rom. 1:20.
[2] Mt. 5:44 f.; 6:26–30; Acts 14:15–17.
[3] Ex. 7:5; Is. 26:9.
[4] Dt. 4:5 f.; 29:24–28; Is. 52:10; Jer. 33:9; Ezek. 37:27 f.; 38:16, 23; Zc. 8:23.
[5] Rom. 2:14 f.
[6] Rom. 1:26 f.
[7] 1 Cor. 11:13 f.

" every man " indicates a reference to a general revelation to all mankind, though unrecognized by most men, preceding the special revelation to Israel (vv. 11–13) and the incarnation (vv. 14 ff.). This corresponds to the conception of Wisdom as coming into the world and seeking a dwelling among all peoples.[8]

The open book of nature, history, and the reason and conscience of mankind is the concern of science, philosophy, and natural theology. General revelation is thus another expression for the existing nature of things that lies back of all discovery (s. 14). General revelation is " given " only in the sense that it is there to be found; it is " received " only by those who have eyes to see and ears to hear and the experience and understanding to interpret correctly. Natural theology deals with what can be known by observation and reason, in other words with the data of general revelation. What is called " revealed theology " deals, strictly speaking, with the subject matter of special revelation.

All general revelation is only partial and preliminary. God has given a much fuller revelation to his chosen people. In part this was conveyed by his dealings with them; there is thus, as noted above, a special as well as a general revelation in history. God's inexorable justice and his gracious help are revealed by the whole series of judgments and marvelous deliverances throughout Israel's history.[9] His judgments on Israel's foes meant salvation for Israel,[10] yet Israel also had to suffer judgments for disobedience (s. 60).

The conviction that God is revealed in history, and especially in the history of his chosen people, explains why there is so much history in the Bible. It is told, not for the sake of the record itself, but for the revelation of God's judgments in the events narrated. Sometimes God's righteous acts are celebrated as ground for praise and rejoicing, especially when they are executed upon hostile peoples; [11] sometimes they are used to give assurance for the future; [12] often they are used to bring conviction of sin.[13]

The special revelation of God given in the history of Israel reaches its culmination in the incarnation of God in Christ. As a topic sentence sums up a paragraph or one chapter gives the gist of a whole book, or

[8] Ecclus. 1:9 f.; 24:6 f.; cp. Prov. 8:31; s. 28.
[9] Ex. 6:6 f.; Dt. 4:34 f.; 11:2–7; Ps. 103:6 f.
[10] Num. 33:4; Ps. 105:5–7.
[11] Ju. 5:11.
[12] Is. 43:16–19.
[13] Ju. 2:1 ff.; 1 S. 12:6 ff.; Acts 7:2–53; 13:16 ff.

as a man's character is revealed by one act, so all the saving truth of Scripture is summed up in the person of Jesus. His life and death express God's character and reveal his will. This conception is not found everywhere in the New Testament. It is nowhere elaborated or explained, but it is most clearly stated in Jn. 1:14, 18; 14:9 f.; and Heb. 1:1-4 (see further ss. 28, 35).

Special revelation includes not only God's acts in history, culminating in the incarnation, but also his direct communications to chosen individuals, interpreting his acts. The giving of the law, the experiences and messages of the prophets, and the teachings of Jesus and the apostles constitute such special revelations. So far as our present purpose is concerned these have already been sufficiently discussed in ss. 12 f.

16. *Truth and Revelation*

The foregoing sections have been concerned with the third of the criteria of authentic revelation mentioned at the beginning of s. 8, namely, the way in which it is received. Our examination has shown that there are indeed " divers portions " and " divers manners " of revelation, and that the same mode of reception may be found with false as with true ideas. The conclusion must therefore be that the reality of revelation can no more be determined from the type of experience by which it comes than it can by any external attestation or evidence. We are thus thrown back on the final criterion, the inherent truth and value of what is revealed. This is, of course, obvious with respect to general revelation. The whole question, as related to the authority and inspiration of the Bible, has meaning only with reference to special revelation. In what follows, when we use the term " revelation " we shall have in mind special revelation. Our point here is that the authenticity of anything that purports to be a special revelation can be determined only by its inherent worth.

If truth is the only criterion of authentic revelation, does it follow from the truth of any idea, however arrived at, that it must have been revealed? The answer to this question is implied in what has already been said. For general revelation it must be in the affirmative. To say this is not to make " revealed " a mere synonym for " true," or to express a mere value-judgment without metaphysical implications. It is rather to express our faith that God exists, that what is true is his thought, and what is right is his will, that man is his creature, and therefore that all valid knowledge of truth and right must come from him. All knowledge is revealed in the sense that it is ultimately dependent upon God.

The recognition that there is such a thing as general revelation, however, implies that not all knowledge is given by immediate inspiration, even when it appears to come in that way. A man may conceive an idea that is true, but may be mistaken in supposing that it was directly revealed to him. It may have come actually by tradition; it may have arisen from a subconscious memory of something previously learned; it may be a true intuition without being necessarily a direct revelation. There is reason to suspect that the apostle Paul himself unconsciously attributed to immediate revelation some elements of his gospel which he had actually received from Christian tradition. In such a case our question is whether the knowledge has come from God immediately or ultimately.

This question is a matter of only secondary importance. What we are most concerned to know about a proposition is whether or not it is true. If it is, we do not need to know how or by what process it came from God. Since we cannot determine by other criteria that it is revealed, and from this conclude that it is true, we must determine its truth as best we can, and it is then not essential that it should have come by immediate inspiration.

Indeed, comforting as it is to feel that direct inspiration may be and is given to individuals in times of need, it would not be fatal to Christian faith if proof were forthcoming that all revelation actually came through the same means and processes as other knowledge, so that there was no such thing as direct inspiration. As a matter of fact, this cannot be proved. If psychologists cannot conclusively prove or disprove the reality of telepathy or scientifically establish the real source of alleged communications from the dead, they are equally unable to determine the origin of every impression that enters men's minds in the guise of revelation. But in comparison with the necessity of knowing God's truth, it is unnecessary and relatively unimportant to know how that truth has come to us.

How, then, can we know what is true? Without digressing into a discussion of epistemology and metaphysics, in which there will always be abundant room for differences of opinion, we can only say that in the quest of certainty in religious belief we are dependent upon the same means and methods by which we must determine the truth or falsehood of any idea on any subject or for any purpose. The only final proof is the test of experience, and even here a question of the interpretation of experience may be involved.

Must we, then, await a conclusive demonstration of truth before we can accept anything as revealed? We cannot *know* it is revealed until we know it to be true, and even then we cannot know that it came by special rather than general revelation; but we must often, perhaps more often than not, commit ourselves by an act of faith without such knowledge. What we believe to be good and true, and therefore take as a working principle of our living, we may accept, at least tentatively and practically, as revealed. The basis of such a commitment may be an inner conviction so intuitive and unreasoned, so far beyond our own experience, and yet so compelling that we can only regard it as a witness of God's Spirit in our hearts (s. 27). We must act on such convictions, as we must always act on the best knowledge and judgment we have. " I was not disobedient to the heavenly vision," says Paul to Festus in Acts 26:19, and what a loss to the world it would have been if he had disobeyed it! Any man disregards his own visions at the peril of shutting out from himself any further light.[1] To follow blindly every strong impulse or inhibition on the assumption that it is the voice of God is decidedly dangerous, of course. That is the way fanatics and bigots are made. The danger in movements that emphasize direct divine guidance is that people of sensitive conscience may be led into unwise acts by the assumption that any suggestion that seems hard and unpleasant must come from above. Attention has already been called to the Bible's warnings against false spirits and false revelations (s. 12). But we cannot defer action until all the evidence is in and the proof is complete. We must proceed on the basis of what appears to be true by the best light we have, walking often by faith and not by sight.[2] This applies to what is offered as revelation in the Bible as much as to what comes by any other route. It applies to the experiences of the men who made the Bible.

17. *The Subject Matter of Revelation*

The distinction between natural and revealed theology, as we have seen in s. 15, involves not only a difference of process but also a difference of content; not only a difference in the way knowledge comes but also a difference in its subject matter. The definition of natural theology as dealing with what can be known by reason and observation, and

---

[1] Is. 63:10; Eph. 4:30; Rom. 1:28; Mk. 3:28–30.   [2] 2 Cor. 5:7.

of revealed theology as dealing with what can be known only by revelation, presupposes a division between certain truths or realms of truth that are accessible to human observation and logical thought and others that are beyond the reach of man's experience and reason.

Traditionally this has meant that natural theology can demonstrate such truths as God's existence, man's freedom, and the immortality of the soul, while the doctrines of the Trinity, the incarnation, and the atonement could never have been discovered without revelation and cannot be rationally demonstrated. The present widespread agreement that the demonstrations formerly offered were not so conclusive as was supposed would seem, on this basis, to reduce the realm of natural theology to the vanishing point, forcing its doctrines back into the realm of revealed theology. This leads easily to the common conclusion that what is asserted in the Bible but cannot be proved must be accepted on faith as revealed, which carries with it the obligation to believe everything in the Bible, even though it be not only undemonstrable but even contrary to reason and experience. The only logical alternative, from this point of view, is to deny the inspiration of the Bible altogether, since blind faith has no means of distinguishing true and false within the Bible. The tragic controversy between religion and science in modern times is a consequence of this conception of revelation.

A more fruitful distinction of subject matter is that between the spheres of religious and secular knowledge, the matters that properly concern religion and those that are of no religious importance. The age of the earth, the antiquity of human life, and the process by which human life emerged in the world may be taken as examples of purely secular concerns. They seem important for religious faith only when one's view of inspiration compels him to defend anything stated in the Bible on any subject. The origin of man and the universe in the will of a wise and loving God is a matter of vital religious concern, but it is quite independent of questions of time or process (see further s. 39). There is, of course, no a priori reason for assuming that revelation could not or would not take place concerning matters belonging to the sphere of secular interests; neither is there any reason to shut off any area as sacred and therefore not subject to investigation. Scientific study of religious as well as any other phenomena is not only legitimate but helpful. If science could prove or disprove even the existence of God, it would thereby render a great service. Actually the limits imposed on science by the necessary definition of the various fields of scientific research and the choice of method preclude such an achievement. The real concern of the Bible, moreover, is not with the subject matter of the sciences.

The significance of this distinction for biblical theology is that it enables us to recognize either truth or falsehood in the Bible and discriminate between different areas of truth without forcing upon us premature and unwarranted generalizations. If the right of the Bible to be considered inspired must be determined by the truth and value of what it tells us, it does not follow that every statement on any subject must be true. Not truth in general, or in all fields, is required. For religion the question of truth in the Bible is a question of reliable guidance in faith and conduct.

18. *The Truth of the Bible*

Coming now to the Bible, not with the assumption that it is inspired and therefore everything in it must be true, but with the realization that we cannot know whether it is inspired or not until we find whether or not what it tells us is true, what do we actually find?

In the field of the physical sciences we find at once that many mistaken and outmoded conceptions appear in the Bible. That the earth is flat, the center of the universe, created in a week — these and other equally indefensible ideas are either explicitly stated or taken for granted. The protracted struggle of theology to defend the inerrancy of the Bible against the findings of astronomy, geology, and biology has been a series of retreats, ending in a definite defeat which has led all wise theologians to move to a better position. There are many insights that strike us as remarkable in such an ancient book, but they are as irrelevant for Christian faith as the mythological presuppositions of the times, which the writers of the Bible on the whole accepted without question (s. 38). Having distinguished the areas of truth with which religion is vitally concerned from those that have no immediate relevance for religious faith, we are not disturbed by the unscientific notions in the Bible. We recognize that for ancient Hebrew or early Christian writers to express themselves in terms of modern science would have been as impossible, and also as unhelpful, as it would have been for them to write in English.

Much ink has been wasted also, and is still wasted, in the effort to prove the detailed historical accuracy of the biblical narratives. Actually they abound in errors, including many contradictory statements. Archaeological research has not, as is often boldly asserted, resolved the difficulties or confirmed the narrative step by step. It has solved some problems and afforded confirmation at some points; it has also raised many new problems and confirmed some of the adverse conclusions of historical criticism. The stress on revelation in history throughout the Bible makes the question of historical truth somewhat more important for faith than that of scientific fact. Historical information is not, of course, the essential content of revelation. Even fiction may be true to life and convey religious truth. For such books as Ruth, Jonah, Esther, and the narrative portions of Daniel and Job the question of historical fact is as irrelevant as it is for the parables of Jesus. Conversely, the most exact account of events would convey no revelation without a sound religious interpretation. On the other hand, if the Bible purports to record revelations of God in historical events, the reality of the revelation presupposes the actual occurrence of the events. Accuracy of detail is not essential, provided the spiritual interpretation has a valid basis in what actually occurred.

Both scientific and historical issues are raised by the supernatural element in the Bible. The general conception of the miraculous as a part of the world-view will be discussed in s. 43; here we are concerned with the historical reality of the particular supernatural events narrated in the Bible. It is important in this connection to realize that the question whether a given miracle really occurred is one which rarely if ever can be answered on the basis of objective evidence. One's decision will inevitably be affected by prior judgments regarding the possibility of the supernatural in general and the kind and amount of evidence consequently necessary to establish the reality of what is represented as miraculous. In general it may be said that many of the events recounted as miracles in the Bible are explicable from a naturalistic point of view, though explanations of this sort are in the nature of the case merely conjectural, and their possibility does not prove them to be correct. Other miracles are recognized by modern scholarship as purely legendary, like many events of a nonmiraculous character.

Assuming that an event took place, what is important for us is its religious significance. At this point the natural and the supernatural are on the same plane. The Bible treats purely natural events as divine acts along with what we call the supernatural; in fact, ancient thought does not draw the distinction as we do (s. 43). The attestation of revelation by miracles has already been discussed in s. 8. The Bible itself, as a matter of fact, teaches that what is miraculous is not necessarily of divine origin and spiritual significance, for there are also " lying wonders." [1]

Much more crucial is the question of the validity of the biblical interpretation of history. The inclusion of the early historical books in the prophetic division of the Hebrew canon is true to the intention of their authors and editors, which was to exemplify and demonstrate the prophetic interpretation of history and so induce faith and repentance. Therefore, to deny that God acts in the history of nations, rewarding righteousness and punishing evil, and that in so doing he reveals himself and his will, is far more serious than to deny the accuracy of the narrative at one point or another. To modern thought it is clear that Israel's prophets and historians attributed to divine judgment much that was actually due to causes entirely independent of moral, social, or spiritual considerations. They made the same error with regard to history in the large that Job's friends made with regard to individual retribution. Whether, apart from such exaggeration or artificial simplification, they were right in their basic interpretation of history is a matter not subject to historical verification or refutation; it remains a question which only revelation and faith can answer. At any rate, true or false, the conviction that God acts in human history is basic for the religion of the Bible.

At one point the question of historical accuracy is of decisive concern for Christian faith. The centrality of Jesus for the whole religion of the New Testament as the culmination of the whole revelation of God in history makes vitally important the question of the historicity of Jesus. Even here the record need not be complete and accurate in every detail, for then the differences in the gospel accounts would destroy their validity, but if God really revealed himself to man in the person of Jesus Christ (s. 15), it is essential not only that Jesus actually lived, but that he was the person portrayed in the gospels, and that he preached the gospel attributed to him. As to his existence modern historical scholarship leaves no room for reasonable doubt. The reliability of the records of his life and teaching, however, has become a serious problem as the result of modern criticism.

It is now clear that we cannot reconstruct the order of events in Jesus' life, nor be sure of the settings and contexts of his sayings or their exact wording. We cannot even make a list of sayings that are certainly authentic. The church preserved what it found helpful in winning new

---

[1] 2 Th. 2:9; cp. Ex., chs. 7 to 9; Dt. 13:1–3; Mk. 13:22; Rev. 13:14; 16:14; 19:20.

converts, guiding the life and faith of believers, and meeting the attacks of its enemies. This had three results: (1) an inevitable change in the proportions and relative emphases of the original gospel through the selection of material, (2) the unconscious coloring and alteration of some sayings, and (3) even the creation of some entirely new sayings (probably through accepting as sayings of Jesus words spoken by prophets in his name). All this might have been disastrous if the religion of Jesus had been one of legalism and literalism, but in that case he would have taken more pains to ensure the accurate transmission of his teaching. Even sayings not actually spoken by Jesus may have been truly inspired by his spirit.

Like the oral tradition, the composition of our written gospels also was animated by practical motives. The individual evangelists, as well as the preachers and teachers who preceded them, had special interests which affected their choice, arrangement, and presentation of material. Along with such special aims, all four shared the primary motive explicitly stated in Jn. 20:30 f. The fourth gospel stands by itself as a spiritual interpretation of the significance of Christ in the believer's experience. The evangelist's own spiritual experience and insight enabled him to supplement the revelation given by Jesus. The difference between the fourth gospel and the synoptics at this point, however, is only relative. Theological interpretation plays a large part along with history in all the gospels as a result of their practical, evangelistic purpose. At the same time, for all this, the gospels preserve a clear and undoubtedly authentic picture of a distinct personality and a definite message.

The distinction between religious and nonreligious areas of truth does not dispose of all the errors in the Bible. Even in matters of religious concern the Bible is by no means of uniform value throughout. Not only are false ideas expressed; wrong practices are sanctioned or allowed to pass without protest, such as slavery, polygamy, and wars of conquest and extermination. The Bible can be a reliable guide only when it is rightly used and interpreted in the light of the central revelation in Christ (s. 15).

The will of God is the immediate concern of the Old Testament laws. These include much that is universally and permanently valid. The constant insistence on justice between a man and his neighbor, on respect for life, and on the rights of the poor and the oppressed will never be outgrown. Jesus quoted Lev. 19:18 as his second great commandment.[2]

---

[2] Mk. 12:31.

Whether what the law commanded was actually in every detail God's will even for ancient Israel we cannot tell; in any case the social order for which the laws were intended has passed away. None of us would now attempt, as our Puritan forefathers did, to formulate a constitution for a modern state on the pattern of the laws of Moses. Fundamental social principles and perhaps even sound practical suggestions for applying them may still be found even in Leviticus and Numbers. The Christian pulpit has by no means exhausted the resources of the Pentateuch in this direction. But the laws have no binding force on the Christian; he is not under the law but under grace (s. 53).

The truth of the prophetic utterances recorded in the Bible involves the characteristic prophetic interpretation of history, which we have already considered, and also the basic conceptions of God and his will and the warnings and promises for the future enunciated by the prophets. The truth of the prophetic conception of God cannot be demonstrated; it must be left to faith (ss. 8, 79). The predictive element in prophecy calls for some further consideration here. Prophecy, of course, is not essentially or primarily prediction, but *speaking for* another person, namely, God (s. 87). The prophet's preaching of righteousness and judgment included, as motivation to right action, warnings and promises for the future. Not all the predictions thus made came true. They were not divinely given previews of history, but rather the expression of convictions as to the inevitable outcome of what had already been done and was being done, based on the prophetic theology and philosophy of history. They were also usually and characteristically conditional. The prophet hoped that his warnings might induce repentance and so avert judgment.[3] Here again the main question is the truth of the underlying interpretation of history.

The apocalyptic literature is essentially predictive. Its purpose is comfort and assurance rather than warning, and its promises are not conditional like the predictions of the prophets. The visions in Daniel and Revelation, like those in the extracanonical apocalypses, cannot be accepted as inspired pictures of future events, even when we can be sure what their symbolism is intended to represent. Their chief value is the confidence they express in the invincible justice of God, regardless of present appearances, and their testimony to the fact that theistic faith demands an eschatology (cp. s. 74).

This question arises in its most crucial form in connection with the

[3] Am. 5:14 f.; Jer. 26:3, 13; contrast Jonah, ch. 4.

predictive element in the teaching of Jesus. His gospel was above all the good news of the coming of the kingdom of God, which he said would occur very soon, within the lifetime of some of his hearers.[4] The eschatological discourse couples the assurance of the coming of the Son of Man within that generation with the most solemn affirmation of the unchangeable truth of Jesus' words.[5] This problem is a very serious one for Christian faith, but discussion of it must be postponed until we have examined the content of Jesus' eschatological teaching (s. 74).

As regards relevance to the moral and social needs of the modern world, the prophetic literature is on the whole more valuable than the law. Not only what literary criticism may select, with more or less accuracy, as the original pronouncements of the prophets whose names the books bear, but also the later material interpolated or added by scribes and editors is often of great moral and spiritual value, the supreme example being the work of the anonymous " Second Isaiah."

The truth of the wisdom literature lies in its keen observation of life and human nature and the general soundness of its ideals. On the whole it is less profound and inspiring than some other parts of the Bible, but no little moral and spiritual profit may still be derived from it. The timeless truth of the book of Job is widely though still insufficiently recognized. The spiritual values in the Psalms are shown by their constant devotional use by Christians, though the fact that an unchristian spirit of hatred and vengeance appears in some of them must be recognized also.

The epistles of the New Testament constitute a distinct category, resembling in some respects the wisdom literature of the Old Testament. They were obviously written in response to the needs of particular groups, with no idea that they would ever be regarded as sacred literature, though 2 P. 3:16 already cites Paul's letters along with " the other scriptures." They contain a great deal of profound spiritual insight and sound guidance for Christian conduct, along with some things of dubious value. For the inspiration and truth of Paul's epistles, and by implication other parts of the Bible, 1 Cor., ch. 7, is especially enlightening (note especially vv. 10, 12, 25, 40).

There is thus no escaping the necessity of " picking and choosing " in our use of the Bible. What, then, is left of the authority of the Bible? Has it still any real significance for us, or any vital importance?

---

[4] Mk. 1:14 f.; 9:1.   [5] Mk. 13:30 f.; cp. Mt. 10:23.

19. *The Authority of the Bible*

Since the only sound criterion for determining whether anything is an authentic revelation is its intrinsic value, and since the contents of the Bible vary greatly in their value even in matters of religious importance, we cannot take the Bible as a whole and in every part as stating with divine authority what we must believe and do. This conclusion involves no difficulty for faith when we have abandoned the idea of mechanical inspiration and verbal infallibility, and have accepted the principle that what is ultimately authoritative for us is that which commands the assent of our own best judgment, accepted as the witness of the Spirit within us. The only ultimate basis of assurance is the witness of the Spirit with the believer's own spirit.[1] And only the individual can decide whether or not the assurance he feels is the witness of the divine Spirit of truth. The Bible itself gives no warrant for any delegation of responsibility to an external, intermediate authority, whether an institution or a book. It condemns one who allows an alleged revelation to another person to supersede the word that he has himself received.[2] Any insight into truth and right that has the inner attestation of the Spirit is an authoritative revelation for us, regardless of how it comes to us. It is so in spite of the fact that we know how subject to error our own judgment is, for we have nothing that can take its place. If God does not speak to us in our own minds and consciences, he does not speak to us at all.

This does not mean, be it noted, that the individual may interpret the Bible as he pleases and claim divine authority for his interpretation.[3] The meaning of the Bible is what its writers meant by it, and that is a question for objective exegesis. The correct interpretation is not always ascertainable, but whether or not we have the means to determine what it is, only one interpretation can be correct (s. 20). The only admissible authority at this point is the same as that of science and scholarship in all fields, the authority of demonstrated fact. Whatever negative effects historical criticism has had, it has rendered a positive service in emancipating exegesis from individual caprice and unfettered imagination and restoring the authority of the original intention.

When we have determined the meaning, we still have to decide whether it is true. Neither the Bible nor any other statement of what

[1] Rom. 8:16; Jn. 14:26; 15:26; 16:13 f.; 1 Jn. 5:6-10.
[2] 1 K. 13:11-22.
[3] 2 P. 1:20.

is to be believed and done can be accepted wholesale in advance. But if, having tried various sources and means of knowledge and insight, we find that one of them actually contains all that is best and most important for us, then we can say that here we have found our authority. That is what we do find in the Bible. On the most basic questions of faith and life we get from it more light than we get anywhere else. This is a statement of experience. It may not be true for all people individually; but historically, for our culture, it is a fact that our best spiritual insights and highest ideals have come to us through the experiences recorded in the Bible. The present generation has received most of this indirectly, as a part of its cultural tradition. It could receive much more from the Bible directly if it knew the Bible.

Thus the question of authority cannot be settled by a simple appeal to the letter of the Bible. Truth from God may be found outside the Bible, and the fact that an idea or ideal is stated in the Bible does not guarantee its truth or divine origin. The Bible is the word of God in the sense that it contains the record of a long series of authentic and supremely important revelations, each to be understood, evaluated, and applied on its own merits, and also in the sense that as a whole, rightly understood and properly used, it expresses the highest ideals and most profound truths given to man, including all that he needs for salvation here and hereafter. It is the permanent, universal standard of Christian faith and practice, because in it are preserved the historic origins of Christianity, by comparison with which all later variations and developments must be understood, evaluated, and, if need be, corrected.

The practical implication of this point of view is that the minister need not be concerned to give his people a clear grasp of the nature of authority and inspiration before presenting to them the specific teachings of the Bible. He should know where he stands and be able to answer questions, and for that reason these subjects have been discussed here at the outset of our study, but in practical use the Bible may be allowed to make its own impression, care being taken only that it be directly known and rightly understood.

20. *Use and Interpretation of the Bible*

Correct interpretation has been shown to be necessary to make the Bible a true guide for faith and practice. Wrong methods of interpretation and use have prevented Christians hitherto from arriving at any unity in their understanding of the Scriptures.

The proof-text method of citing Scripture to establish points of doctrine is unsound and inconclusive. Experience has shown that it is futile and divisive. While the citation of verses and parts of verses apart from their contexts and with meanings not intended by the writers may claim precedents within the Bible itself, such as Paul's use of Gen. 15:6 [1] and Hab. 2:4,[2] it is invalidated by the fact that selection and combination can produce any desired result. The exegetical principle of interpreting Scripture by Scripture must therefore be used with caution.

Prophecy has been especially abused in this way. The early church, eager to prove the Messiahship of Jesus, mustered everything in the Scriptures that seemed to its uncritical understanding relevant.[3] This use of prophecy had a sound basis in the fact that Jesus was in truth the real answer to his people's deepest hopes, and regarded his own mission as fulfilling Scripture (ss. 29 ff.). It led, however, both to misinterpretation of the Scriptures (e.g., the use of Ps. 16:8 ff. in Acts 2:25–31) and to misunderstanding of the nature and work of Jesus (s. 36). Present-day efforts to derive blueprints of the future from indiscriminate combinations of texts are self-refuting by virtue of the fact that they do not agree among themselves.

Allegorical interpretations of Scripture were used from early days to make the Bible agree with itself and with the preconceived ideas brought to it by its interpreters. This method of interpretation had been applied by the Stoics to Homer and pagan mythology, and Philo and his predecessors had adapted it to the Old Testament, finding Greek philosophy anticipated by Moses just as modern scientific ideas are now found in the Bible. Palestinian rabbis also used allegorical exegesis on occasion, and from either Hellenistic or rabbinical models, or both, it was learned by Paul.[4] Its greatest development in the New Testament is found in Heb., chs. 7 to 10. It must be abandoned by the modern interpreter unless the passage interpreted was clearly intended as allegory.

Logical deduction was a favorite method of exegesis with the rabbis. Jesus' use of Ex. 3:6 and Ps. 110:1 [5] resembles such rabbinical exegesis, as does Paul's use of Gen. 13:15 and ch. 17:8,[6] but it is noteworthy that Jesus used this method only in debate, not in applying the law to

---

[1] Rom. 4:3; Gal. 3:6.
[2] Rom. 1:17; Gal. 3:11.
[3] See especially Mt., chs. 1; 2; Acts, chs. 1 to 12.
[4] 1 Cor. 10:4; Gal. 4:21–31.
[5] Mk. 12:26 f., 35–37.
[6] Gal. 3:16.

life. Only when checked by sound historical criticism is this method of exegesis valid.

In the use of Scripture as a guide for conduct Jesus rejected every form of legalism (s. 53). In the matter of washing before eating he condemned making the word of God of no effect by tradition; [7] in the matter of divorce he put torah against torah; [8] in the matter of sabbath observance he subordinated the law to a new principle, simply stated as axiomatic.[9] He subsumed the whole law under love for God and love for one's neighbor,[10] summarizing the latter in the Golden Rule.[11] So also Paul [12] and James.[13] That Christians nevertheless persist in literalism and legalism is deplorable.

A sound interpretation of any part of the Bible must be, first of all, objective and disinterested. Wishful thinking, reading one's own opinions and desires into the Bible and then claiming its authority for them, has been responsible not only for false exegesis but for division and unchristian attitudes throughout the history of the church, and not least in Protestantism. Our only hope of assurance and agreement is in the growing consensus of competent scholarship.

Correct interpretation requires recognition of the fact that the knowledge of truth and right revealed in the Bible is not stated in abstract, universal propositions, but in specific, concrete applications to particular situations, and in literary, not scientific or philosophical, language. It is also presented in terms of ancient thought and life, the only terms available to the writers or meaningful for their first readers. Consequently it needs constant reformulation in terms of new knowledge and experience, and constant reapplication to new situations.

With all this it is equally important to recognize the facts of diversity and development within the Bible. The Bible presents not a uniform but a progressive revelation. Its true unity and final significance are to be found in the general direction and the outcome of the process, culminating in the supreme and central revelation of God in Christ (s. 15).

[7] Mk. 7:13.
[8] Mk. 10:2–12.
[9] Mk. 2:27; cp. ch. 3:4.
[10] Mk. 12:29–31.
[11] Mt. 7:12.
[12] Rom. 13:9 f.; Gal. 5:14.
[13] Jas. 2:8.

III

GOD

21. *Monotheism*

The existence of God, a pressing problem for modern thought, is no problem at all for the writers of the Bible. Even Ecclesiastes does not doubt that God exists, and Job's question is not whether God is but what he is, in particular whether or not he is just (s. 25). From Gen. 1:1 on, God's existence is taken for granted. Only the wicked and fools deny it,[1] and even their denial is a practical rather than a theoretical atheism: they leave God out of their plans, thinking he will not observe them or hold them responsible.[2]

Jesus and the writers of the New Testament also assume the reality of God. Paul at Athens begins with the God already worshiped by his hearers.[3] The only suggestion in the New Testament of any question as to the existence of God is the statement of Heb. 11:6 that he who comes to God must believe that he exists.

For biblical theology, therefore, there is no problem of the existence of God. It is natural theology rather than revealed theology which concerns itself with that subject. For the ancient Hebrews the pressing danger and temptation was not atheism but polytheism. The question was not whether there was any God but whether there was one God or many.

Hebrew religion grew out of primitive Semitic religion, and the ancestors of the Hebrews were doubtless polytheists.[4] From the time of Moses on, Israel worshiped Yahweh, the jealous God who would not tolerate the worship of any other god with him.[5] The later Old Testament writers were convinced that no other god had any real existence, but it had not always been so. Just when and how the Hebrews had be-

---

[1] Ps. 14:1.
[2] Job 22:13 f., 17; Ps. 10:4, 11, 13; 36:1 f.; cp. Jas. 4:13-15.
[3] Acts 17:23.
[4] Josh. 24:2.
[5] Ex. 20:3.

come monotheists is still a moot question. The Old Testament contains no explicit denial of the existence of other gods that can be definitely dated earlier than the sixth century B.C. Lacking such specific and datable statements, we cannot say when monotheism first emerged in Hebrew religion.

It is clear that the Old Testament combines into one several gods originally worshiped as separate deities. The different tribal groups composing the Israelite nation undoubtedly had their own distinct gods before they formed a federation as worshipers of Yahweh. Gods of other peoples also were from time to time identified with Yahweh, who appropriated their names as his own. For example, El Elyon, to whose priest Abraham gave a tenth of his spoils after the defeat of the five kings,[6] was not Abraham's own God, but was later identified with him. It has recently been shown, indeed, that El Elyon, who is called " Possessor [or Creator] of heaven and earth," [7] was himself a combination of the god of earth, El, and the god of heaven, Elyon.[8]

Abraham and the other patriarchs may have worshiped only one God, with such exceptions as the one just noted, but there is no reason to suppose that they ever questioned the real existence of the gods worshiped by other peoples. At most they were henotheists, not monotheists.

Along with the successive identification of other gods with the Hebrews' God, the process by which henotheism developed into monotheism included a gradual delocalization of the idea of God's presence. The fact that the Hebrews came to Canaan in the first place from another land, bringing their religion with them, involved a break with any local associations their worship may have had previously.[9] The name by which Abraham and the other patriarchs knew God, El Shaddai (E.VV., God Almighty),[10] means " God of the mountain " and thus suggests an original localization. In Abraham's time, however, El Shaddai was widely worshiped as a great heavenly deity.

Israel's worship of Yahweh, identified now with El Shaddai, begins with Moses.[11] The origins of Yahwism are still obscure, and scholars are not agreed on the question. A tradition that the worship of Yahweh was

---

[6] Gen. 14:17–24.
[7] Gen. 14:19.
[8] G. Levi Della Vida, *Journal of Biblical Literature.* LXIII (1944), pp. 1–9.
[9] Gen. 12:1 ff.
[10] Ex. 6:3.
[11] Ex. 3:13 ff.; 6:3.

very ancient is preserved in Gen. 4:26; this is, in fact, the view of the J source throughout, and may have been true for some of the tribes, particularly Judah. The tribes that left Egypt under the leadership of Moses, however, became worshipers of Yahweh at that time. Many scholars favor the Kenite hypothesis, according to which Moses learned the worship of Yahweh from his Kenite father-in-law, Jethro, " the priest of Midian," [12] whose sheep he was tending on Horeb, " the mountain of God," when Yahweh first spoke to him.[13] In that case Ex. 18:12 records the formal inauguration of Israelite worship of Yahweh under the tutelage of Jethro, though the traditional interpretation sees Jethro here as the first proselyte to Judaism. This hypothesis, while uncertain and questioned by many, seems very probable.

The great theophany at Sinai, when the law was given,[14] established or confirmed a connection between Yahweh and Mt. Sinai which persisted long after the conquest of Canaan.[15] The connection was not so binding, however, as to prevent Yahweh from working wonders in Egypt and overthrowing Pharaoh's army at the Red Sea, as later he came from Sinai to destroy the army of Sisera at the river Kishon.[16] The narratives imply, indeed, that while Yahweh " came down " to Sinai to reveal himself to Israel, his dwelling was in heaven.[17] His presence with his people as they moved through the wilderness was objectified by the pillars of cloud and fire, and also, after the departure from Sinai, by the ark and tabernacle.

The conquest demonstrated his control of the land of Canaan. His triumph over the Canaanite baals made him Lord of Canaan, and a new tendency toward localization in that land set in, becoming even stronger after the ark was brought to Jersualem and the temple was built. For David, being exiled from Yahweh's territory involved the worship of other gods.[18] His desire to build a house for Yahweh brought the reply that Yahweh had always lived in a tent and desired no house,[19] but Solomon was allowed to build the temple, and called it a house for Yahweh to dwell in forever.[20]

[12] Ex. 2:16; 3:1; 18:1.
[13] Ex. 3:1.
[14] Ex., ch. 19.
[15] Ju. 5:4 f.; Ps. 68:7 f.; also, if Sinai and Horeb are the same, 1 K. 19:8 ff.
[16] Ju., ch. 5.
[17] Ex. 19:11, 18, 20; 24:9 f.
[18] 1 S. 26:19.
[19] 2 S. 7:5-7.
[20] 1 K. 8:13-27 is a Deuteronomic addition, though the idea that Yahweh really lived in heaven had doubtless persisted from the time of Moses.

Most modern scholars agree that Yahwism as established by Moses was still henotheistic or monolatrous rather than monotheistic. In spite of recent efforts to prove that Moses was a monotheist (so especially W. F. Albright),[21] that contention remains improbable. The records of the time of Moses, though edited by later men who were monotheists, still include statements that imply the existence of other gods than Yahweh.[22] For the time of the conquest and settlement Ju. 11:24 has the same implication, though it may be a mere *argumentum ad hominem*. The long and bitter struggle between Yahwism and Canaanite baalism, dramatically pictured centuries later in Ho., ch. 2, shows how easily the Israelites were tempted to worship other deities. The later history of the united kingdom and the two kingdoms of Israel and Judah involves similar conflicts between Yahweh and the gods of other nations. Political relationships were important here, for in the ancient world the recognition of a conquering nation commonly entailed the worship of its deities.

The greatest crisis of all for Yahwism was caused by the effort of Jezebel in the ninth century to make the baal of Tyre the national god of Israel. Elijah's prayer on Mt. Carmel [23] and the cry of the people when the fire fell from heaven [24] seem to mean that Yahweh alone exists, unless the meaning is simply, " Yahweh is the god for us." It is possible, though not certain, that Elijah's faith was in reality monotheistic. If 2 K. 19:15–19 is an authentic prayer of Hezekiah, monotheism existed in Judah in the eighth century, but this prayer is probably of Deuteronomic origin and uncertain date. Dt. 4:35 is definitely monotheistic, but again its date is uncertain. Not until we come to Second Isaiah (6th, if not 5th, century) do we find monotheism clearly stated and vigorously defended, with biting satire on idolatry.[25]

The prophets before Second Isaiah may have had an implicit monotheism, either in the sense that they believed there was only one God but did not find occasion to say so, or in the sense that they held a conception of God that logically implied monotheism though they were not

[21] *From the Stone Age to Christianity*, pp. 196–207, 227 f., 331 (note 29) ; *Archaeology and the Religion of Israel*, pp. 116–119; cp. T. J. Meek, *Journal of Biblical Literature* LXI (1942), pp. 21–43, and my discussion in *Jewish Quarterly Review*, XXXIII (1943), pp. 476–478.

[22] Ex. 18:11; Num. 33:4.

[23] 1 K. 18:36 f.

[24] 1 K. 18:39.

[25] Is. 40:18–26; 41:1–10, 21–29; 42:8 f.; 43:9–13; 44:6–20; 45:5, 7, 11 f., 14, 16, 18; 46:1–11.

themselves fully aware of that implication. In the latter sense at least the faith of the eighth-century prophets was implicitly monotheistic. It was a practical, if not a theoretical, monotheism, for their conviction that Yahweh controlled all nations and used them for his purposes,[26] if carried to its logical conclusion, would — and later certainly did — lead to monotheism. Whether Amos and Isaiah and the rest saw this or not we cannot tell from what they say; at least they say nothing to the contrary.

Recognition of God's power in nature also promoted progress toward monotheism. A good example of practical monotheism, applied to nature rather than the history of nations, is Jer. 14:22, where the creation of the world is stressed.[27] Creation does not necessarily imply monotheism, since many polytheistic religions have creator gods, but the fact that one God has created the whole universe makes monotheism a natural inference.

The centralization of the cult under Josiah [28] would naturally tend toward monotheism, if Yahwism was not already monotheistic by that time (621 B.C.). The local shrines might be thought to have different Yahwehs, but the one temple could have one Yahweh alone. This may have been the original meaning of Dt. 6:4. At the same time, the centralization of worship at Jerusalem also strengthened the connection between Yahwism and Zion.

The final emergence of monotheism in the religious consciousness of the Hebrews is probably to be explained as the result of the prophetic interpretation of history, confirmed by national disaster. The warnings of the prophets came true. Yahweh's power over other nations and his superiority to their gods had been shown by the destruction of many kingdoms by Assyria and then the destruction of the Assyrian empire itself; the fall of the northern kingdom proved to Judah that Yahweh would punish unfaithfulness to him. It was not so easy to recognize the destruction of Judah itself as his work. Ordinarily it would have seemed to mean that Marduk, the god of Babylon, had overthrown Yahweh. But the prophets, from Amos on, had said that Yahweh would not spare even his chosen people; Micah had said that even Jerusalem would be destroyed,[29] and Jeremiah had given stern warning that the presence of the temple was no guarantee of inviolability.[30] Therefore, when the na-

---

[26] Is. 10:5–19.
[27] Cp. Ps. 96:5; 2 K. 19:15 and Second Isaiah.
[28] 2 K., ch. 23.

[29] Mi. 3:12.
[30] Jer. 7:8–15; 26.

tion fell in 586 B.C., it was clear that Yahweh himself had punished his people's persistent disobedience.[31] The false prophets of security and complacency, who had hitherto been much more popular than the true prophets of judgment, were therefore repudiated.

Thus Hebrew monotheism was reached in a way unparalleled in other faiths, not by logical inference from the unity of the world (as in some forms of Greek and Hindu philosophy), not through military conquest and political unification (as Re was exalted in Egypt and Marduk in Babylonia, though without the achievement of monotheism in either case), but actually through national disaster. Only the moral interpretation of history made this possible. Hence Hebrew monotheism is distinctly ethical monotheism.

For the postexilic religion and for later Judaism monotheism was assured and assumed. Thus Job presupposes it, for the problem with which the book deals exists only for ethical monotheism (s. 25). To be sure, Yahwism remained strongly bound to Jerusalem and the temple as its center. Pride in the holy mountain of God is frequently expressed in the Psalms. Through the postexilic period and into New Testament times, until the destruction of the second temple in A.D. 70, Jerusalem was the holy city. Orthodox Jews to this day bewail the temple at the Wailing Wall and hope for its restoration in the days of the Messiah. The transcendence of God was not forgotten, however, but rather was stressed increasingly.[32] The conceptions of the Glory of Yahweh and the Shekinah (s. 28) reconciled the transcendence of God with his local manifestations.

The Samaritans claimed that not Zion but Mt. Gerizim was meant by Deuteronomy as Yahweh's chosen shrine, as may indeed have been the case originally. The controversy survives to this day. It is the basis of the conversation between Jesus and the woman of Samaria in Jn., ch. 4, which provides the occasion for the definite and final denial of any localization of God's presence for Christianity. This is true to the spirit of Jesus, though he honored the temple and drove out its desecrators.[33] The impossibility of limiting God to any earthly dwelling is expressed also in Acts 17:24.

The New Testament throughout takes monotheism for granted. Many even of the pagans who were converted when the gospel spread beyond

[31] Lam. 1:18; 2:17; 3:40 f.; cp. Jer., ch. 44.
[32] Is. 66:1 f.
[33] Mt. 5:34 f.; Mk. 11:15–18, and parallels.

Palestine were already more or less consistent monotheists. There were others, however, whose conversion from polytheism to Christianity gave new importance to the belief in one God alone. The question of eating meat dedicated to pagan deities was evidently one of considerable importance at Corinth, as Paul's careful and elaborate discussion of it shows.[34] It continued to be so for the church in the Roman empire for some time after the New Testament period.

For Christianity today the issue between monotheism and polytheism may seem to be of no vital interest. The missionary enterprise, however, still has to deal with it in some parts of the earth. For modern thought, moreover, it is not unrelated to the apparently more vital issue between theism and atheism. It is at bottom the question whether there is any unified and reliable control of the universe, or whether we are at the mercy of an unpredictable interplay of forces in a welter of worlds that is not a cosmos, a system, a universe at all. The polytheistic Babylonians and other Gentile peoples were in constant fear and uncertainty; Israel worshiped the one God whose ways had been made known, and whose faithfulness reached to the clouds.[35]

22. *Personality; Anthropomorphism; Transcendence and Immanence*

The biblical conception of God is always strongly personal. Any idea of God that makes him anything other than a Person is a radical departure from biblical thought, whatever else may be said about it. There are in the Old Testament, to be sure, some echoes of the widespread primitive conception of an impersonal force or quality possessed by superior persons, animals, and objects, like the *mana* of Melanesian religion and the "medicine" of the American Indians. The basic Semitic word for God, *'ēl*, apparently meant originally "power." It retained that meaning in such idiomatic expressions as "mountains of God" for "mighty mountains,"[1] "cedars of God" for "mighty cedars,"[2] or "to the god of my hand" for "in the power of my hand."[3] The earliest conception of God's Spirit in the Old Testament is that of a mysterious force like wind (s. 27), but this is not identified with God himself. Whatever part such impersonal conceptions played in Hebrew

---

34 1 Cor. 8:1–13; 10:1 to 11:1.
35 Ps. 36:5.
1 Ps. 36:6 — A.V., "great mountains"; A.S.V., "mountains of God."
2 Ps. 80:10 — A.V., "goodly cedars"; A.S.V., "cedars of God."
3 Gen. 31:29; Prov. 3:27; Mi. 2:1.

religion, they were manifestly, from the earliest times of which we have any knowledge, overshadowed by the personal way of thinking about God.

The oldest ideas of God reflected in the Old Testament, in fact, are quite naïvely anthropomorphic. In considering the theophanies of the Old Testament (s. 12) we have observed the intimacy and informality of God's dealings with men as represented in the J narratives of the Pentateuch. Yahweh lives in the sky and must come down to see what men are doing.[4] In extraordinary cases men may ascend to his heavenly abode.[5] Some effort to avoid crude anthropomorphism is evident in later sources, however, and in the poetic and prophetic literature anthropomorphic expressions are for the most part obviously figurative, as they are in later Jewish sources and the New Testament.[6]

Anthropopsychic and anthropopathic ideas of God are characteristic of biblical thought from beginning to end. Feelings like those of men are often attributed to God. Even the notion that God is jealous of man and afraid of human progress (the Prometheus motif) appears in Gen. 3:22; 11:6 (s. 38). Yahweh's jealousy with regard to the worship of other gods, originally connected with the " demonic " side of his nature,[7] remains characteristic of both Mosaic and prophetic religion.[8] Other emotions attributed to God will appear in the discussion of his moral attributes (ss. 24–26). At the same time the contrast between man and God is strongly emphasized.[9] In view of this contrast and the obviously figurative nature of many anthropomorphic expressions, it is only reasonable to suppose that the statements attributing to him human thoughts and emotions partake of the same character.

At the same time, however much he may differ from man, God is a distinct and real Person. Certainly the biblical conception of God is not humanistic: God is not only far above man but quite independent of man's existence.[10] The biblical conception is not pantheistic or in any sense monistic: God is not the universe but its Maker.[11] Neither is the biblical conception deistic: God is not separated from the world; it is

---

[4] Gen. 11:5, 7; 18:21.

[5] Ex. 24:9–11, where the language suggests that the holy mountain pierces the sky.

[6] Mt. 5:34 f.

[7] Ex. 4:24–26; 19:21–25; s. 23.

[8] Ex. 20:5; 34:14; Dt. 4:24; 5:9; 6:15; Josh. 24:19; Ezek. 39:25; Joel 2:18; Na. 1:2; Zc. 1:14; 8:2.

[9] Job 9:32; Is. 40:18, 22; 42:5; 55:8; Eccl. 5:2; Lk. 12:4 f.

[10] Job 38:26; Ps. 50:12; Acts 17:25.

[11] Ps. 19:1; cp. Job 26:14.

his work, and good; [12] he is still at work in it; [13] he is its Ruler, constantly present in his world and controlling it; indeed it is impossible to get away from his presence.[14] In other words, God's relation to the world involves both transcendence and immanence. A theology that denies or unduly emphasizes either of these aspects cannot justly claim to be Scriptural. Sometimes in the postexilic period of Old Testament religion the majesty and transcendence of God were so stressed that a gap seemed to be left between him and the world (s. 28), but his presence and activity in the world were never wholly ignored. In short, the biblical conception of God is theistic. It is throughout strongly personal, though increasingly spiritual.[15]

The mechanical procedures of modern life, our expanding knowledge of the universe, and the abstract ideas of modern science and philosophy have made belief in a personal God more difficult for us than it was for earlier generations. One aspect of the problem will be considered later in connection with Providence and miracles. The exposition and defense of theism in terms of modern thought must, of course, be left to systematic theology and the philosophy of religion. A few general remarks by way of interpreting biblical theism, however, are in order here.

In the first place, the historical derivation of the Hebrew-Christian conception of God has nothing to do with its validity. Monotheism may be traced back to polytheism, polytheism to animism, and animism to animatism, which may then be explained as merely a spontaneous, unreflecting, and erroneous reaction of the primitive mind to its environment, a naïve assumption that objects which affect our welfare are persons like ourselves and can be dealt with as persons. Historically the theistic interpretation of the universe is a direct descendant of that primitive and mistaken assumption. So is modern science a direct descendant of primitive magic (s. 93). Ideas, like men, must be judged on their own merits, not by their pedigrees. Sometimes their worth is in proportion to the distance they have traveled from their origins. The process of development from primitive misconceptions to profound spiritual apprehensions of truth may reasonably be adjudged a work of divine revelation (s. 13).

Another point to be kept in mind is that the language of the Bible is not the language of philosophy or science; it is the language of worship. It must be understood as poetry, not as factual description or analysis.

[12] Gen. 1:10-31.
[13] Jn. 5:17.
[14] Ps. 139:7-13; Acts 17:28.
[15] Jn. 4:24.

Strictly speaking, the Bible does not present a doctrine of God but a way of thinking about God. This does not mean, however, that the writers of the Bible had a conception of the divine nature to which their language did not correspond. Unlike some of the ancient Stoics and many modern thinkers, they did not indulge in an accommodation of language for the expression of emotional attitudes while holding an abstract, impersonal view of the real nature of God. There is not the slightest reason to suppose that any of their thoughts of God ever verged on the impersonal or the abstract.

As a matter of fact, they were not interested in exploring the nature of God. The very thought of attempting to describe what God is in himself would have seemed to them impious.[16] What concerned them was always God's relation with man and the world. All that their statements imply as to the essential nature of God — and, to be sure, it is a great deal — is that the capacity for personal relations with man is included in the nature of Deity.

Any belittling limitation of God by the thought of him as a Person is prevented by the " how much more " of Jesus,[17] a form of thinking and speaking found also in Jewish literature. Jesus does not limit God by speaking of him and to him as Father; he says that if even human fathers, evil as they are, respond with kindness to their children's requests, much more will God give his children what is good. The clue to what may be expected of God is found in what is best in man. It is from this point of view that biblical theism must be understood and judged and accepted.

As to the difficulty of adjusting faith in a personal God to a modern conception of the universe, it may still be true that the divine foolishness of the gospel is superior to the greatest wisdom of men.[18] The insight of simple faith may pierce closer to the heart of reality than reason and learning can ever penetrate without it.[19] Only he who becomes like a little child can enter the kingdom of heaven; [20] only he who is born again can see it; [21] only the pure in heart can see God.[22]

23. *Power, Majesty, Sovereignty; the Kingdom of God*

The growth of the Hebrew conception of God until Yahweh came to be thought of as the supreme and only Sovereign of the universe has

[16] Dt. 29:29.
[17] Mt. 7:11; cp. Lk. 18:6 f.
[18] I Cor. 1:18 ff.
[19] Mt. 11:25.

[20] Mt. 18:3.
[21] Jn. 3:3.
[22] Mt. 5:8.

been traced in s. 21. The concept of royalty afforded the most natural means of expressing this idea.

The most primitive root of the idea of God's majesty is the idea of his fearful, demonic aspect. This is closely related to the idea of the holy as the " numinous " (s. 25).[1] Such adjectives as " terrible," [2] " dreadful," [3] " fearful," [4] and the expression " to be had in reverence " [5] all translate a form of the Hebrew word meaning " fear." The standard expression for piety or religion in the Old Testament is " the fear of Yahweh " (s. 81). In Jer. 20:11 a stronger Hebrew word is translated " terrible." [6]

While the emphasis on the awe-inspiring and the dangerous aspect of Yahweh's nature seems to have been especially characteristic of the Mosaic period, it persisted later. The conquest of Canaan enhanced the sense of Yahweh's power as Israel's war god, " Yahweh of armies " (Yahweh Sabaoth). The result of the conflict with baalism, together with the prophetic teaching of Yahweh's control of world history (s. 21), exalted him further in the eyes of his people; and his power over nature was shown in creation and providence, and in such miracles as the drying up of the Red Sea and the Jordan and the storm by which Sisera's host was overthrown.[7] The writer of Job regards God as the power behind all nature and life, whose ways cannot be questioned. Second Isaiah uses God's power over nature and history as the ground for assurance of the restoration and redemption of his people. Many expressions are used to convey the idea of God's power and majesty, including terms translated " strength," " might," " power," " dominion," and the like, and also such titles or epithets as " Rock," " Fortress," " strong Tower."

The sense of God's transcendent majesty found expression in the postexilic period through the use of various circumlocutions for the divine name (s. 28). Among such indirect designations of God in postexilic sources are " the Power," [8] " the Height," and " the Majesty."

1 Note the connection between holiness and fear in Is. 8:12 f., reading with the University of Chicago translation, " Nought that this people call holy shall you call holy; and what they fear you shall not fear "; also Is. 6:1-5; Ps. 99:1 f., 5.

2 Dt. 7:21; 10:17; Neh. 9:32; Job 37:22; Ps. 47:2; 66:3, 5; 68:35; 76:12.

3 Dan. 9:4; Mal. 1:14, A.V.

4 Ex. 15:11; Dt. 28:58.

5 Ps. 89:7, A.V.

6 The word used in Gen. 31:42, 53, and rendered " fear," may mean " kinsman " (so Albright).

7 Ju., chs. 4 f.

8 Cp. Mk. 14:62.

The Apocrypha evince a fondness for the divine epithets " Most High " and " Almighty." We have seen (s. 21) that the ancient name El Shaddai, commonly translated " God Almighty," did not mean this originally, but it was already so interpreted when the Septuagint of Job was made. The name El Elyon, on the other hand, does mean " High God " and may have been understood in the sense " Most High " even before the god so named was identified with Yahweh.

The rabbinic literature especially stresses the creation as showing God's majesty and power. Naïve and even grotesque ways of expressing God's omnipotence are sometimes used by the rabbis; at the same time the earlier dread of God gives way to reverence, and the sense of God's majesty is combined with an equally strong sense of his nearness and goodness. In the prayer book this finds expression in the frequent combination of two ancient ways of addressing God: " Our Father, our King."

The idea of God as King is the basis and essence of the conception of the kingdom of God. The Greek, Aramaic, and Hebrew nouns ordinarily translated " kingdom " all mean primarily " kingship " or " sovereignty," though they are used also in the derived senses of " reign " and " realm." The Old Testament speaks of God's kingdom in the sense of his sovereign rule of the universe.[9] In Judaism this idea of the kingdom of God (or kingdom of heaven) is very prominent. The prayer book, referring to the crossing of the Red Sea, says, " Then they saw thy kingdom " (i.e., royal power). The rabbinic literature speaks of making God King (literally, causing him to reign) in the sense of accepting him as King. The same idea is expressed also as taking upon one the kingdom of God or receiving his kingdom. A similar expression is " taking the yoke of the kingdom of heaven." The rabbis speak also of " taking the yoke of the commandments," [10] the distinction being that taking the yoke of the commandments means obeying for the sake of rewards, whereas taking the yoke of the kingdom of heaven means devotion to God in love, apart from self-interest, i.e., full acceptance of God's sovereign rule.

This basic meaning of the concept lies at the root of Jesus' use of the term " kingdom of God " (or " kingdom of heaven " as Matthew usually expresses it). Most of Jesus' sayings about the kingdom involve

---

[9] 1 Chr. 29:11 f.; Ps. 22:28; 47:2, 7 f.; 93:1; 96:10; 97:1; 99:1; 103:19; 145:10–13; Is. 52:7; Dan. 4:3, 17, 34; 5:21; 6:26.

[10] Cp. Mt. 11:29.

also the further meanings to be discussed in ss. 64 ff., referring to new or future manifestations of God's royal power, but in one or two cases the meaning seems to be the eternal, timeless fact of God's kingship and rule. In Mk. 10:15 and parallels the idea of entering the kingdom of God may have an eschatological significance (s. 73), but receiving God's kingdom must mean, as in Jewish sources, accepting him as King. So too the idea of seeking the kingdom in Mt. 6:33 (Lk. 12:31) probably means, not merely accepting the divine sovereignty, but actively endeavoring to make it real and effective in one's own life and in the lives of others. A rabbinic text says that before Abraham's time God was King in heaven, but Abraham made him also King on earth. The prayer that God's kingdom may come on earth as in heaven is thus a prayer that his sovereign rule, which has always existed, may prevail on earth and overcome all opposition (s. 64).

In the rest of the New Testament the kingdom of God is not clearly spoken of in this sense; in fact, it is relatively rarely mentioned at all. Paul's description of the kingdom, however, as " righteousness, peace, and joy in the Holy Spirit " [11] has essentially the same meaning; it may be paraphrased as " the life which is governed by God's will." In 1 Cor. 4:20 Paul seems to mean by the kingdom of God something like the divine government of the world. Elsewhere his use of the term is eschatological. In Acts, chs. 1 to 12, there are only two references to the kingdom, both quite general.[12] Jn. 3:3 uses the expression " see the kingdom of God," which in Jewish usage means to see God's royal power in such works as the deliverance of Israel at the Red Sea, but the expression " enter into the kingdom of God " in v. 5 may imply a different meaning (s. 73). The concept of God's kingdom is most important in the teaching of Jesus himself, and there we may say that the meaning is based on the Old Testament conception of the eternal sovereignty of God, though it involves also special manifestations and realizations of God's rule, with an ultimate eschatological significance (ss. 64, 73).

Aside from the idea of the kingdom of God, Jesus does not especially stress God's power and majesty.[13] The preaching of the early church in Acts, chs. 1 to 12, assumes but does not emphasize this aspect of the divine nature, and with Paul the idea of God's greatness is usually implicit rather than explicit, except in such doxologies as Rom. 11:33–36. For Paul God's power is especially manifested in the resurrection of

[11] Rom. 14:17.
[12] Acts 1:3; 8:12.

[13] But cp. Mt. 5:34 f.; 10:28; 11:25.

Jesus, which gives assurance that the same power will redeem us.[14] The Cross is the power as well as the wisdom of God,[15] and Paul's own ministry demonstrates God's power.[16] Paul also stresses the sovereignty of God in connection with human freedom and responsibility (s. 76).

Other parts of the New Testament also speak of the divine power and majesty.[17] The greatest emphasis is in Revelation, where such titles as " He who was and who is and who is to come," " the First and the Last, the Beginning and the Ending, the Alpha and the Omega," " the Living One," " the Eternal One," and " the King of the ages " occur frequently. Nine times in Revelation God is called " the Almighty." [18] Other divine titles expressing majesty and power are used in Heb. 8:1 and 2 P. 1:17, and in a number of liturgical formula in the pastoral epistles; [19] also in Jude 24 f. and the doxology added to the Lord's Prayer in Mt. 6:13.[20] In short, while the New Testament has no theoretical discussions of God's omnipotence like those in rabbinical literature, this attribute is basic throughout.

24. *Wisdom and Knowledge*

God's incomparable superiority to man consists not only in his power but also in his knowledge of all things and his infinite wisdom in governing the universe. The same terms used to designate human knowledge, wisdom, and the like, are applied also to God. Thus Prov. 3:19 f. speaks of Yahweh's wisdom, understanding, and knowledge as shown in creation. God's knowledge, however, far surpasses that possessed by man.[1] Second Isaiah especially exalts God's plans and thoughts, with particular emphasis on his knowledge of future events.[2] The book of Job stresses God's wisdom over against man's ignorance.[3] This attribute of God, however, is less emphasized in the Old Testament than his majesty, holiness, and righteousness. Later Jewish sources laid great weight on God's foreknowledge in connection with the problem of predestination and freedom (s. 76).

---

[14] Rom. 6:4; 2 Cor. 13:4; worked out especially in Ephesians.
[15] 1 Cor. 1:18, 24.
[16] 1 Cor. 2:4; 4:20; 2 Cor. 4:7; 6:7.
[17] Cf. Jn. 10:29; 19:11.
[18] Elsewhere in the New Testament only 2 Cor. 6:18, an Old Testament quotation.
[19] 1 Tim. 1:17; 6:15 f.
[20] Not in the best MSS. A.S.V. and R.S.V. omit; cp. Lk. 11:4.
[1] Josh. 22:22; 1 S. 16:7; Job 23:10; chs. 38 to 41; Ps. 1:6; 37:18; 44:21; 94:11; 103:14; 138:6.
[2] Is. 44:25; 46:10; 48:3, 5.
[3] Job 5:13; 9:4; 12:13, 16; 36:5; 38:36 f.

Jesus says that only God knows the time of the end, or perhaps of the destruction of the temple.[4] God knows what his children need.[5] Only the Father knows the Son.[6] Jesus tells the scoffing Pharisees that God knows their hearts; [7] and this characteristic Old Testament idea is repeated in Acts.[8] Paul refers in a general way to God's knowledge [9] and praises his wisdom.[10] His conception of the Cross as the power and wisdom of God and of the simple gospel as the divine mystery and wisdom [11] have been noted in s. 23. Rev. 7:12 ascribes wisdom to God along with power and might. In fact, even where it is not stated, we may safely assume that God's omniscience is presupposed throughout the New Testament. It is a self-evident corollary of God's being the Creator and Ruler of the universe.

25. Holiness, Righteousness, Justice

The idea of holiness, which ultimately came to mean complete purity and righteousness, had originally no such moral significance; it meant, rather, the " numinous " quality of Deity, the *mysterium tremendum*, or, more particularly, the " otherness " of God, his separation from everything ordinary, earthly, or human. This idea has already been encountered in connection with God's dread majesty (s. 23). The Hebrew word translated " holy " is used also in a general way for the sacred as against the profane. It is applied to places, times, objects, and persons set apart for religious uses and purposes, and the cognate verb means " consecrate." The lack of any intrinsic ethical meaning is shown by the fact that the Hebrew terms for the male and female sacred prostitutes of Canaanite religion mean literally " holy men " and " holy women," indicating merely that they are set apart for a cultic function.

The word " holy " may even be applied to something that is taboo, such as the use of a mixture of two kinds of seed.[1] In this sense the quality of holiness is communicable by contact.[2] Later reinterpretation explains this by the idea of the inviolability of God's private property.

---

[4] Mk. 13:32 — this verse is probably authentic even if all the rest of the eschatological discourse is not.

[5] Mt. 6:8, 32; Lk. 12:30.

[6] Mt. 11:27; Lk. 10:22; cp. Jn. 10:14 f.

[7] Lk. 16:15.

[8] Acts 1:24; 15:8; cp. 1 Jn. 3:20.

[9] 1 Cor. 3:20; 2 Cor. 12:2 f.

[10] Rom. 11:33; 16:27; 1 Cor. 1:18 ff.

[11] 1 Cor., chs. 1 to 3.

[1] Dt. 22:9; cp. s. 57.

[2] Ex. 29:37; Lev. 6:18; Hg. 2:12.

What the holiness of the ark meant is shown by the story of Uzzah,[3] though the word " holy " is not used here. The idea that God was angry and punished Uzzah is a consequence of reinterpretation, through the specific association of holiness with Yahweh, but the original absence of ethical implications is evident in the unfairness of such a punishment for such an act.

The basic idea of separation in the concept of holiness included separation from the " unclean " (s. 57), and finally from everything evil and sinful. The old associations lingered, especially in connection with ritual and priestly interests. In the Holiness Code ritual and ethical implications are inextricably combined.[4] The ethical meaning of holiness is already strong in Am. 4:2; yet in Is. 6:3 it is still combined with the sense of the numinous.

Apart from the concept of holiness, however, the idea of Yahweh's righteousness is much older than the time of Amos. The covenant idea already involves confidence in the reliability of Yahweh, his fidelity to his obligations and promises. This is the meaning of the word commonly translated " truth " in the English versions. It is the opposite of capriciousness and arbitrariness (the unpredictable demonic quality attributed to Yahweh in Ex. 4:24–26). The word ordinarily translated " mercy " or " loving-kindness " also means " loyalty." Mi. 7:20 uses both of these words.

Being righteous and faithful himself, Yahweh requires the same virtues in man. The earliest Mosaic legislation doubtless included ethical requirements. The conquest of Canaan and the syncretism and baalization of Yahwism which followed, as well as the later development of the official cultus, promoted ritualism, but the Mosaic tradition was preserved by the prophets, the early historians, and the Deuteronomic school. For J, Yahweh is the Judge of all the earth who does right.[5] The laws and histories from the beginning represent him as champion of the oppressed and afflicted. His judgments on the nations in general and on Israel in particular are based largely on moral and social grounds, the exploitation and oppression of weaker nations and of the poor and helpless.[6] This idea is repeatedly stressed in the Psalms.[7]

Habakkuk is troubled by Yahweh's punishment of his people through the agency of the wicked Babylonians, but receives assurance of God's justice and its ultimate vindication.[8] Jeremiah goes beyond previous

[3] 2 S. 6:6–10.   [5] Gen. 18:25.   [7] Ps. 9:7 f.; 99:4.
[4] Cp. Lev. 19:2 ff.   [6] Am., chs. 1 f.   [8] Hab. 1:5 f., 12 f.; 2:2–4.

prophets in applying the idea of divine retribution to individuals as well as nations, but this raises the problem of God's justice, for which Jeremiah has no solution.[9] A hard-and-fast doctrine of exact individual retribution is enunciated by Ezekiel.[10] Whether this is the first definite statement of the doctrine, coming from the time of the exile, or whether it is a much later summing up of the results of a development beginning with Jeremiah, depends upon the unsettled question of the date of Ezekiel. In any case the assertion of exact rewards and punishments in this life, being belied by experience, made the problem of theodicy acute.

The psalms often express disillusionment and doubt,[11] generally with the answer characterized by Fosdick as the " Wait and see " solution of the problem of evil.[12] The most radical attack upon the doctrine of retribution is in the book of Job, which emphatically asserts but does not explain the existence of undeserved suffering. While Job expects some kind of vindication even after death,[13] he does not find the answer to his questions in a future life (cp. s. 69). He receives no proof of the goodness and justice of God, but instead a conviction of his own inability to criticize or judge God, with such an overwhelming experience of God's reality and power that he is content to trust without understanding.[14]

Various partial solutions of the problem are offered elsewhere in the Old Testament. In addition to the " Wait and see " answer of the Psalms there is the conception of suffering as disciplinary and redemptive in purpose. As applied to the nation this means restoration after punishment has evoked repentance (s. 60). The wisdom literature applies the idea to the suffering of the righteous, which is to be received as chastening by a loving Father.[15] The most profound idea in the Old Testament on this subject is Second Isaiah's conception of Israel as the Servant of Yahweh who gladly suffers to make God known to the nations (s. 30). The centrality of the Cross in the New Testament carries with it the idea of vicarious suffering, but for the believer the main emphasis is on the patient endurance of undeserved suffering in devotion to God's will.[16]

---

[9] Jer. 12:1–3; 31:29 f.
[10] Ezek., chs. 18; 33.
[11] Ps. 73:3–14.
[12] *A Guide to the Understanding of the Bible*, p. 167.
[13] Job 19:25–27.
[14] Job 42:1–6.
[15] Job 5:17–19; Prov. 3:11 f.; cp. Heb. 5:8; 12:4–11.
[16] 1 P. 2:19–24; 4:1, 12–19.

All this obviously leaves a wide margin of mystery. The Bible gives no complete answer to man's questions. There is still need for Job's submission and trust, and only a future life can bring justice to the millions who suffer wrongly on earth.

The idea of judgment and retribution after death appears in the apocalyptic literature, its first clear expression being Dan. 12:2 (ss. 69 ff.). The wisdom literature on the whole, with the conspicuous exception of Job, retains the idea of retribution in this life. Throughout the Old Testament God's justice is maintained.

Postbiblical Judaism strongly emphasizes the holiness of God, both in the old sense of separateness and otherness and in the sense of separation from sin. The rabbis say that sin puts the Shekinah to flight. Naturally the idea is closely connected with the law, the teachers of which are called holy. God's justice in the sense of fairness in judging is much emphasized in connection with the future judgment (s. 70). His decisions cannot be questioned. The problem of theodicy is felt, but the solution is consistently sought under the principle of retribution, carried over to the future life and the eschatological order.

Jesus takes God's righteousness for granted and gives warnings of judgment as well as promises of rewards (s. 55). The problem of evil does not trouble him; in fact, he sees evidence of God's impartial goodness in the very facts of nature which seem to others evidence of indifference.[17] He recognizes and faces evil but does not feel it as throwing doubt on God's power or justice. Satan is still active, but his kingdom is doomed and God's kingdom is near (s. 64).

The vivid expectation of imminent judgment (s. 70) prevented the early church from feeling any need of theodicy. Paul says much of the wrath and judgment of God but also thinks of his justice as the ground of his gift of salvation.[18] The problem of theodicy comes up for Paul in connection with the hardness of Israel in rejecting the gospel. He finds the solution in the idea of the fulness of the Gentiles as well as God's unquestionable power over his creatures.[19]

The later writers of the New Testament refer more or less incidentally to God's holiness and justice. Retributive justice in judgment is stressed in Revelation and Hebrews. 1 P. 4:13 comforts Christians in persecution with the thought that they are partakers of Christ's sufferings.[20] In general the stress on divine righteousness and judgment is

---

[17] Mt. 5:45.
[18] Rom. 3:19–26

[19] Rom. 9:19–24; 11:25.
[20] Cp. Phil. 3:10; Col. 1:24.

great in the later books because God's justice could not be so taken for granted in the Gentile world as in a Jewish environment.

26. *Mercy and Love; Fatherhood*

The conception of God as loving comes to expression in the Old Testament somewhat later than the idea of his justice, though the idea of the covenant implied from the beginning the gracious choice of Israel and at least a kind of favoritism. Hosea is the first of the prophets to stress the love of God for Israel even to the extent of forgiving and restoring the unfaithful nation.[1] God's mercy is here connected with his holiness. In fact, the Old Testament often connects justice and mercy quite closely. The word " justice " appears sometimes where we might expect such a word as " mercy " or " grace," especially in the deliverance of the wronged and oppressed. This conception, which is as old as Ju. 5:11, makes the words for justice and mercy almost interchangeable, and " justice " and " salvation " become practically synonyms.

The importance of the idea of God's mercy is shown by the number of words used for it (grace, mercy, compassion, goodness, long-suffering). The fact that the word usually translated " mercy " or " loving-kindness " involves the idea of loyalty has been noted previously. It implies fidelity to God's own nature and to his covenant.[2] The idea of the chosen people caused difficulties with regard to God's mercy as well as his justice (s. 102).

Postbiblical Judaism puts great stress on the love and mercy of God. Rabbinic literature says he is full of love for his creatures; he was moved by love in the creation of the world. He loves all men, even the wicked, but especially his chosen people. The problem of reconciling mercy and judgment is met in various ways, the tendency being to make mercy predominate over justice.

The idea of the Fatherhood of God is very ancient, older even than the idea of God as King. Early Semitic personal names often combine a divine name or designation with the word meaning " father " or " my father " (so Abraham, Abimelech, Abishua, Absalom, Abijah, Eliab, and many others). The primary conception involved includes both authority and protection, the latter becoming more prominent as the idea of kingship comes into use for the former. What is indicated is not a matter of man's nature (s. 48) but of God's character and attitude.

---

[1] Ho. 2:19; 11:8 f.   [2] Cp. especially Ex. 34:6 f.

The Old Testament frequently refers to God as Father of the king (s. 33), of the people, and even of individuals. In view of the importance of the Fatherhood of God for the religion of Jesus, it is desirable to recognize the roots of that idea in the Old Testament and Judaism. In the Old Testament, Ps. 103:13; Jer. 3:19; Mal. 2:10 (though Abraham as father of the nation may be meant here); and Is. 63:16 f. are especially noteworthy. In the Apocrypha, we note Sir. 23:1, 4, and W.S. 2:16; in the Pseudepigrapha, Jubilees 1:24 f.; Test. of Levi 17:2. Two especially striking passages in the rabbinic literature are Aboth 3:15 (quoting Dt. 14:1), " Beloved are Israel, for they were called children of God," and, even more remarkable, ch. 5:20, " Be strong as the leopard and swift as the eagle, fleet as the gazelle and brave as the lion to do the will of thy Father which is in heaven "; also Sotah 9:15, " On whom can we stay ourselves? — on our Father in heaven." [2a]

These passages show plainly that the difference between the teaching of Jesus and Judaism at this point has been greatly exaggerated. This has been a result both of ignorance of Jewish literature on the part of Christian scholars and of a false feeling that at all costs Jesus' teaching must be shown to be new and original. It seems not to have been commonly recognized that what is important for us is not that Jesus' teaching be new but that it be true. What is significant is that he selected just this aspect of Jewish faith for his major emphasis. The meaning of the idea for him appears in many sayings.[3] The major stress both in the Old Testament and Judaism and in Jesus' use of the term " Father " is on kindness and care. In fact the relationship is one of grace rather than nature (s. 48): men are God's sons by adoption (s. 62).

Paul shows by his use of the Aramaic word for Father [4] that even the Greek-speaking church treasured the word most characteristic of Jesus' teaching. The Lord's Prayer was doubtless used in the earliest forms of Christian worship. The addition of the doxology in some manuscripts of Matthew reflects such use. God is called Father in Acts 1:4, 7; 2:33 also. Paul frequently speaks of God as the Father of Christ, but also as the Father of believers.[5] Elsewhere in the New Testament God is often called the Father of Christ (cp. s. 28 on the meaning of God's Fatherhood in the doctrine of the Trinity), and sometimes the Father of be-

[2a] H. Danby, *The Mishnah*, pp. 452, 458, 306.
[3] Mt. 5:43-48; 6:1-18, 25-34; 7:7-12; 11:25-27; 18:14, 19; 25:34; 26:39, 42; Mk. 14:36; Lk. 12:32; 23:34, 46.
[4] Rom. 8:15; Gal. 4:6; cp. Mk. 14:36.
[5] Rom. 1:7; 1 Cor. 1:3; 8:6; Phil. 4:20; Col. 1:12.

lievers,[6] though the expression " the Father " is frequently used without any specified application (so especially 1 and 2 John).

In other ways also, of course, the conception of God's love is expressed in the New Testament. Such parables as the lost sheep, lost coin, prodigal son, importunate widow, grudging neighbor, and unrighteous steward all emphasize the perfect love of God. The sermons in Acts, chs. 1 to 12, stress God's readiness to forgive along with judgment. Paul speaks constantly of the grace and love of God, with other words also to the same effect. The free gift of salvation shows not only God's justice but also his love.[7] The gospel and epistles of John emphasize especially God's love.[8] Other New Testament books also repeatedly speak of grace and mercy, though the eschatological emphasis on judgment in Revelation somewhat obscures this major emphasis of New Testament religion.

27. *The Holy Spirit*

From Gen. 1:2 to Rev. 22:17 the Spirit of God or Holy Spirit is frequently mentioned in the Bible. The conception thus indicated seems rather surprising in a monotheistic religion and calls for some explanation.

Since the King James Version is still widely used, it may still be necessary sometimes to point out that in 1611 " Holy Ghost " meant exactly what " Holy Spirit " means now, just as a priest might then be called a " ghostly comforter." The older expression is now misleading and should be abandoned entirely.

We have already seen (s. 22) that the earliest Hebrew conception of the Spirit of Yahweh was related to the impersonal conceptions of primitive dynamism, not as a general power or quality like mana which certain persons or objects possess naturally and permanently, or which can be communicated, but as a force that comes suddenly and inexplicably upon particular individuals at particular times. The Hebrew word for spirit (*ruah*) means primarily " wind " (so also Greek *pneuma;* note the untranslatable play on the word in Jn. 3:8). The stories of the judges and Saul exemplify the early idea. Here the Spirit is clearly an activity or power of Yahweh, but in earlier times it was probably an impersonal force like the wind, invisible but producing effects that

---

[6] 1 P. 1:17; Rev. 21:7.   [8] Jn. 3:16; 1 Jn. 4:8–10.
[7] Rom. 5:8; 2 Cor. 5:14, 18 f.

could be seen. When associated with Yahweh, as with a human person (s. 47), the *ruah* is an emanating force, an active extension of his personality. In this sense it is associated with the idea of breath, as in Job 4:9 (A.V., " by the breath of his nostrils "; A.S.V., " by the blast of his anger ").

Sometimes it is said that the Spirit simply " was " (or " came to be ") upon a man;[1] sometimes that it " came mightily " (literally, " rushed ") upon him.[2] Again it is said that the Spirit " clothed " (or perhaps " clothed itself with ") a person.[3] Deeds of physical or military prowess are the results of this sudden endowment, which equips the recipient for leadership in Israel, especially in battle. Saul was thus endowed, exactly like one of the judges.[4] After his disobedience, the Spirit of Yahweh left him and an evil spirit from Yahweh troubled him[5] — here the word seems to indicate a personal being like a demon. The preceding verse says that the Spirit of Yahweh " came mightily upon David from that day forward," suggesting either a repeated, habitual coming or a permanent possession.[6] In Num. 27:18 f.; Dt. 34:9 we meet the presumably later idea of an official endowment preceding or accompanying the imposition of hands.[7] Nothing is said of the Spirit's coming to Solomon or later kings.

The Spirit produces also prophetic frenzy.[8] Elisha asks and receives a double portion of Elijah's spirit;[9] later it is suggested to him that Yahweh's Spirit may have taken up Elijah and dropped him somewhere in the mountains.[10] These statements are puzzling: does " Spirit " here mean the whirlwind of v. 11? — and what is the spirit of which Elisha received a double portion? In 1 K. 22:21–23 a lying spirit (evidently personal) is put in the mouths of the false prophets;[11] v. 24 speaks of the Spirit of Yahweh as going from one prophet to another. In these passages the idea of a personal being and the idea of an impersonal divine inbreathing seem to be interchangeable. Joel 2:28 f. promises the

[1] Ju. 3:10.
[2] Ju. 14:6.
[3] Ju. 6:34; 1 Chr. 12:18; 2 Chr. 24:20 (cp. mg.).
[4] 1 S. 11:6.
[5] 1 S. 16:14–23.
[6] Cp. Ju. 13:25.
[7] Cp. Acts 6:5 f.; 8:14–17; 13:2 f.
[8] 1 S. 10:10; 19:23; Num. 11:24–29; cp. s. 12.
[9] 2 K. 2:9, 15.
[10] 2 K. 2:16.
[11] Cp. 2 K. 19:7.

outpouring of the Spirit on all flesh, with universal prophesying, dreams, and visions.[12]

In Is. 11:2 the conception of a divine power and influence almost passes over into the use of " spirit " for disposition or character. Here a permanent possession is clearly indicated.[13]

In Gen. 1:2 the Spirit of God is connected with the creation, unless we should here translate *ruah* " wind." [14] In Gen. 2:7 the word for breath is a different one, but chs. 6:17 and 7:15 have " spirit of life." [15] The Spirit also produces fertility, prosperity, and blessings in general.[16] The expression " Holy Spirit " occurs in Ps. 51:11 and Is. 63:10, 11; " thy good Spirit " in Neh. 9:20; cp. Ps. 143:10, where the Spirit teaches or leads. God's Spirit is inescapable.[17] In Is. 40:13 Yahweh's Spirit means apparently his mind (cp. s. 47 on man's spirit). In general the Spirit of God in the Old Testament means his power and active influence in the world. The literal meaning " wind " or " breath " seems always present in the background.

Later Jewish sources frequently use the expression " Holy Spirit " (literally, " Spirit of holiness "), not in connection with creation but chiefly in connection with prophecy or the composition of the Scriptures. Joel's promise of the outpouring of the Spirit in the Messianic age is used, and there are some references to an inner working of the Spirit in the present. The Greek (Stoic) idea of spirit as a fine substance pervading the universe appears in the Wisdom of Solomon.[18]

The Spirit is especially important in the New Testament. In Mk. 12:36 (Mt. 22:43) Jesus uses a rabbinic expression connecting the Spirit with the composition of the Scriptures.[19] More characteristic is Mk. 3:29, which implies that Jesus' work is the work of the Spirit, and that to attribute it to Beelzebul is blasphemy; so also Mt. 12:28.[20] In Lk. 4:18 (the authenticity of which is very doubtful) Jesus applies Is. 61:1 to his own mission (s. 30). The eschatological discourse promises the Spirit to the disciples in persecution.[21] The association of the Spirit

---

[12] Cp. Acts, ch. 2.
[13] Cp. Gen. 41:38; Dan. 4:8 f., 18; 5:11–14; also Ex. 28:3; 31:3; 35:31 and s. 12.
[14] Cp. Ps. 33:6, " breath."
[15] Both words occur in Ps. 18:15; cp. also Gen. 6:3 f. (translate, " My spirit shall not abide in man forever ") and s. 48.
[16] Is. 32:15; 34:16; 44:3 f.
[17] Ps. 139:7.
[18] W.S. 1:7; cp. 7:22–24 and s. 47.
[19] But cp. Lk. 20:42.
[20] Cp. Lk. 11:20.
[21] Mk. 13:11, and parallels; cp. Mt. 10:20; Lk. 12:12.

with the inspiration of the Scriptures and with the Messianic age agrees with Judaism; the connection with Jesus' own work is new, except as it implies that he is the Messiah (s. 31).

The prominence of the Spirit in the gospels reflects the interest of the early church. For the evangelists it is clear that Jesus' work is done in the power of the Spirit.[22] Luke especially stresses the Spirit, particularly in Acts, chs. 1 f. The work of the Spirit in the church begins at Pentecost.[23] Later the Spirit falls upon the converts at Samaria[24] and at Caesarea.[25] The early Hebrew idea of the Spirit is reflected in ch. 8:39 (cp. the " wind " of ch. 2:2). The Spirit is also the agency of guidance, revelation, and prophecy.[26] In addition to these cases of special endowment there are also suggestions of a permanent possession of the Spirit.[27]

Paul develops the idea of the Spirit further. The conception of special manifestations and gifts of the Spirit is carried over from the early church.[28] In 1 Cor. 12:11 the Spirit is personified. Paul's special contribution, however, is his idea of the Spirit as the characteristic, sustaining, permanent power of the Christian life. Paul speaks interchangeably of the Spirit, the Spirit of Christ, the Spirit of the Lord, the Spirit of Jesus, and the Spirit of him who raised Jesus; also of being in Christ, being in the Spirit, having Christ in you, and having the Spirit.[29] While this recalls the Stoic conception of spirit as rarefied substance, Paul's idea is closer to the Hebrew and early Christian conception of the active power of God, now identified with the influence and activity of Jesus.[30] He even explicitly identifies Lord and Spirit.[31] For Paul the possession of the Spirit is both the means of overcoming the power of sin in the flesh (s. 63) and an " earnest " of complete redemption hereafter.[32]

The gospel and epistles of John have not only the traditional associations[33] but also distinctive ideas. The statement that God is spirit and must be worshiped in spirit[34] combines the metaphysical idea of spirit as against matter[35] with the idea of inner meaning as against outer form.[36] Most characteristic is the connection of the coming of the Spirit to the disciples with the return of Jesus, and the idea of the Spirit as

22 Mk. 1:10, 12, and parallels.
23 Acts, ch. 2.
24 Acts 8:14–17.
25 Acts 10:44.
26 Acts 10:19; 11:27 f.
27 Acts 6:3, 5; 11:24.
28 1 Cor., chs. 12 to 14.
29 Rom. 8:9–11.

30 Cp. Acts 2:33.
31 2 Cor. 3:17.
32 2 Cor. 1:22; 5:5; cp. Eph. 1:14.
33 Jn. 1:32 f.; 3:34; 1 Jn. 4:1.
34 Jn. 4:24.
35 Cp. Is. 31:3.
36 Cp. Jn. 6:63.

the Paraclete.[37] Salvation means a new birth in the Spirit.[38] 1 John also refers to the present possession of the Spirit.[39]

The emphasis on possession of the Spirit as the distinctive mark of the Christian life and of the new Messianic age continues in the sources for the later Hellenistic church.[40] The Spirit as the agent of revelation is prominent in Revelation; [41] the agency of the Spirit in the composition of the Scriptures appears also elsewhere.[42]

28. *Hypostases; the Trinity*

In addition to the idea of the Spirit, the Old Testament and Jewish sources use also other concepts to express the presence and operation of God in the world. For the New Testament and later Christianity these are important chiefly because they afforded means for expressing Christological ideas and finally the doctrine of the Trinity. They are technically designated by the term " hypostases," the word adopted by the church for the " persons " of the Trinity. The Greek word *hypostasis* means " substance "; [1] so Heb. 1:3 calls Christ the imprint of God's *hypostasis* (A.V., person; A.S.V., substance; R.S.V., nature). The later technical use of the term, however, implies a power emanating from God, constituting a more or less distinct entity, and usually more or less strongly personified. So the Old Testament, especially in Ezekiel and P, uses the expression " the Glory of Yahweh " to express God's manifest presence in the world, particularly in the tabernacle and temple (s. 22). Later Judaism, especially rabbinic theology, made much use of the similar idea of the Shekinah (dwelling). Other terms also (Name, Place, Power [2]) were similarly used to express the immanent activity of God without sacrificing his transcendence, but only two of these were important for Christian thought, the Wisdom and the Word of God.

Wisdom in connection with revelation has been discussed in s. 13. In Prov., chs. 1 to 9, the divine Wisdom is personified, though only as a poetic figure. Especially important historically is ch. 8:22–31, where Wisdom has a part in the creation as God's " master-workman " (or perhaps " favorite "). Ecclus., ch. 24, carries the picture farther and

---

[37] Jn. 7:39; 14:16–18, 26; 15:26; 16:7; 20:22; cp. 1 Jn. 2:1.
[38] Jn. 3:5–8.
[39] 1 Jn. 4:13; 5:6–8.
[40] Acts 19:2 ff.; Heb. 2:4; 10:29; 1 P. 1:2; 4:14; Jude 19.
[41] Rev. 1:10 and often, especially in chs. 2 f.
[42] Heb. 3:7; 9:8; 10:15; 1 P. 1:11 f.; 2 P. 1:21.
[1] Cp. Heb. 11:1.
[2] Cp. Mk. 14:62.

identifies Wisdom with the law of Moses. In the Wisdom of Solomon it is even more highly personified than in Proverbs and at the same time is identified with God's Word and Spirit,[3] while chs. 7:22 to 8:2 develop the idea in terms of the Stoic conception of spirit (s. 27). Philo carries much farther this line of thought. God has become for him the Absolute, pure Being, and the connection between the Absolute and the world is made by an elaborate scheme of " powers " in which Wisdom plays an important part along with the Logos (v. i.). Palestinian Judaism did not follow this development, but rather continued Sirach's identification of Wisdom and the law.[4]

In connection with revelation we have discussed the Old Testament idea of the word of Yahweh (s. 12). Nowhere in the Old Testament is there any hypostatization of the word; i.e., the word is not regarded as an independent, active being; but primitive Semitic psychology regarded a person's words as an active extension of his personal presence, and Yahweh's word is so conceived in the Old Testament.[5] The translation of Hebrew *dabar* by the Greek word *logos* in the Septuagint made it easy to read into many Old Testament passages the conception of the Logos found in Philo and in Jn. 1:1-18. In John this idea resembles closely the conception of Wisdom in Prov., ch. 8, and the Wisdom of Solomon, and we have seen that the Wisdom of Solomon identifies Wisdom and Logos. In Philo the relation between Wisdom and Logos is rather fluid, following the exigencies of allegorical interpretation of the Pentateuch. Basic for Philo are the Stoic use of *logos* for the immanent Reason of the universe and the dualistic type of thought (later developed in Neoplatonism) by which the same term was used to designate the divine emanation connecting God and the world.

Such ideas are quite foreign to the personal, concrete way of thinking characteristic of the Old Testament and the teaching of Jesus. The early church in Palestine appears to have been equally innocent of such conceptions, though Acts 8:10 attests the existence of similar notions in Samaria. Paul speaks of the wisdom of God, but never as personified or hypostatized: the only divine Wisdom he knows is Christ crucified.[6] The idea of the Logos would seem well suited as a vehicle for Paul's Christology, but he does not use it. The one great instance of its use in the New Testament is the prologue of the fourth gospel; strangely enough the word " wisdom " does not appear in the gospel or epistles of

[3] W.S. 9:1 f., 4, 9, 17.
[4] But cp. Enoch 42:1-3.
[5] Is. 55:10 f.
[6] 1 Cor. 1:24.

John, and after the prologue *logos* is used only of the spoken word, except perhaps in 1 Jn. 1:1 f. The idea of the Logos does not recur elsewhere in the New Testament. The warrior Logos of Rev. 19:11–16 [7] is
hardly a hypostasis. In Heb. 4:12 f. the *logos* of God probably means
the Scriptures or the gospel.[8] Even in Jn. 1:1–18 the use of the Logos
idea seems to have been merely a point of contact which meant less to
the evangelist than to his later readers.

What may be called the classical doctrine of the Trinity arose after
the apostolic age as an answer to the theological problem of reconciling
the Deity of Christ with monotheism. (The relation of the Holy Spirit
to the Father and the Son was only a secondary problem at first.) The
Old Testament provides no preparation for this doctrine except the idea
of the Spirit. The New Testament has all the elements of the doctrine
but no statement of it, because the problems that led to its formulation
were not yet felt.

Jesus expresses the consciousness of his Sonship and of working by
the power of the Spirit (s. 27), but suggests nothing like the triune nature of Deity; indeed it is hard to imagine him speaking in such terms.
The " Trinitarian formula " of Mt. 28:19 f. is not authentic (*v.i.*).
Acts 2:33 brings together the exalted Christ, the Father, and the gift of
the Holy Spirit, but without indicating their relationship.[9] Paul's benediction in 2 Cor. 13:14 involves the elements of the doctrine but again
indicates no attempt at an analysis of the nature of God.[10] So also 1 P.
1:2. In Jn. 14:16 f., 26; 15:26 the Father, the Spirit, and Christ are
brought together similarly with little indication of their metaphysical
relationships, though ch. 15:26 became important in the later filioque
controversy. Mt. 28:19 f., while not a saying of the historical Jesus, expresses the faith of the later church; it still gives no explicit statement
of the triune nature of God, though this may be implied. The one verse
in the New Testament which clearly states the doctrine of the Trinity,
1 Jn. 5:7, A.V., is not in the best Greek manuscripts and is omitted by
A.S.V. and R.S.V.

The fact that the Bible nowhere clearly stated the doctrine of the
Trinity made possible and perhaps inevitable the Trinitarian controversy of the third century. The religious and irreligious motives ani-
mating all parties in that heated series of disputes are clear enough. As
finally formulated, the doctrine was an attempt to affirm the Deity of

---

[7] Cp. W.S. 18:14–16.   [9] Cp. Acts 10:38.
[8] Cp. 1 P. 1:23–25.   [10] Cp. Gal. 4:6.

Christ, and thus guard the reality of redemption in him, without sacrificing monotheism. For this purpose concepts derived from the Bible were used, but recourse was had also to Greek metaphysical ideas which Jesus would undoubtedly have regarded as rank paganism. The distinction between the one *ousia* (essence) and the three *hypostaseis* (substances) represents nothing in either the Old Testament or the New. When the western church used *substantia* instead of *essentia* for *ousia*, and *persona* instead of *substantia* for *hypostasis*, and when the *personae* even came to be thought of as three distinct Persons in something like our common sense of the word, theology went even farther afield from the straight path of biblical monotheism. Indeed, a radical departure from the fundamental attitude of the religion of the Bible was made when theology first began to attempt any metaphysical analysis of the nature of God.

But if the doctrine of the Trinity as a statement of what God is in himself cannot be justified on the basis of Scripture, the fact that it employs biblical concepts enables us to use it in a different sense as a summary of that revelation itself. When we turn our attention from the analysis of God's nature to a statement of what has been revealed, we recall that God is made known to man in three ways. He reveals himself in nature, in history, and in the spiritual experience of individuals (s. 15). In other words, we know him as the God of natural theology, as the God of historic revelation, and as the God of personal experience; and we believe that these three are one God. The God revealed in nature is " the Father Almighty, Maker of heaven and earth." The God revealed in history is God, the Son, the eternal Logos, speaking by the prophets and incarnate in Christ. The God known in personal experience is the Holy Spirit, by whose witness with and in our own spirits we know that we are sons of God, and by whose power we are enabled to live as such.

Our senses acquaint us with different aspects of an object in the material world, and our minds identify the object thus variously experienced as one and the same. We recognize also that it must have other qualities which we cannot experience merely because we have no organs to report them to us. In its real essence, moreover, it may be quite different from the idea of it which we infer from the data of our senses. So by the three channels of nature, history, and inner experience we learn of God, and by faith we combine what is revealed to us in these three ways as all coming from and pertaining to the one God. At the same time

we do not suppose that what is revealed exhausts the richness of his nature, nor need we assume that the threefold form of the revelation corresponds to any trichotomy or inherent distinction in the divine Being.
It is one and the same God whose glory the heavens declare, whose
righteousness and love are disclosed in the historic revelation recorded
in Scripture, and whose living, saving presence is not far from any one
of us.

If this interpretation of the Trinity is accepted as in closer accord
with the language and meaning of the Bible than the orthodox doctrine,
a few further distinctions are necessary. The word " Father " as used in
this connection does not signify the loving care that Jesus expressed by
his use of the term; it refers to the creative and ruling power of God
seen in nature. This is equally true of the First Person of the Trinity in
the creeds. It is in the Second Person, God as revealed through history
and particularly in Christ, that we know him as loving and good. Again,
what for us is the Second Person, God as known in historical revelation,
was of course for the prophets and for Jesus himself the Third Person,
the Spirit, the God of immediate personal experience. This also applies
to the orthodox doctrine as well as to our reinterpretation of the Trinity.
It is merely a further reminder that the distinction of Persons is true
only for our knowledge of God, not for his inner Being, which we cannot know.

It was no accident that the Trinitarian controversy of the fourth century led on to the Christological controversy of the fifth century. The
doctrine of the Trinity and the Person of Christ are inseparably connected. From the biblical revelation of God we therefore pass to the
consideration of him in whom the eternal Word became flesh and dwelt
among us.

IV

CHRIST

29. *Christ as Prophet and Lawgiver*

Christian theology has often represented the redeeming work of Christ as threefold, the work of Prophet, Priest, and King. This conception of the Messiah's work appears already in the pseudepigraphic Testaments of the Twelve Patriarchs.[1]

In the Messianic hope of the Old Testament and of later Judaism in general the Messiah (s. 31) was not commonly thought of as a prophet, though the idea of an anointed prophet appears once in the Old Testament.[2] The Servant of Yahweh in Second Isaiah (s. 30) does the work of a prophet,[3] and in Is. 61:1 [4] either the Servant or the prophet himself says that Yahweh has anointed him to preach good tidings.

Many of Jesus' contemporaries believed that he was a prophet.[5] Jesus himself, whatever else he thought of himself and his mission, clearly regarded himself as a prophet.[6] As a teacher of the nature of God and his will, Jesus sometimes reminds us of the wisdom teachers of the Old Testament and sometimes of the rabbis of his own time, but as a proclaimer of judgment and the imminent kingdom of God he resembles most closely the prophets, and in his emphasis on right relations with man instead of ritualism as God's chief demand he stands in the line of the prophetic tradition. The conception of his work as that of a prophet seems to apply particularly to his ministry on earth, yet he is also a prophet for believers of all ages in the sense that he reveals God's will to man. As the incarnate Word (s. 35) he brings to its ultimate completion the prophetic method of conveying the word of God by symbolic action and dramatization, both teaching God's will and living it.

The Old Testament calls Moses a prophet and predicts, according to the traditional interpretation of the ambiguous Hebrew, that God will

---

[1] Test. of Levi 8:1–15.
[2] 1 K. 19:16.
[3] Is. 40:9; 42:6 f.; 49:6, 9; 52:7.

[4] Cp. Lk. 4:16–21.
[5] Mk. 6:15; 8:28; Mt. 21:11, 46.
[6] Mk. 6:4; Lk. 13:33.

raise up another prophet like him.[7] Popular Judaism in the time of Jesus connected this prediction with the Messianic hope,[8] and in Acts it is applied to Jesus.[9] But Moses was, above all, the great lawgiver. The gospel of Matthew presents Jesus as the second Moses, whose " I say to you " supersedes and at the same time fulfills the Mosaic law.[10] In Matthew alone Jesus says that the whole law and the prophets hang on the first great commandment and the second one which is like it; [11] the " Golden Rule " *is* the law and the prophets.[12] The " Great Commission " given by the risen Jesus to his followers is that they shall " make disciples of all the nations, . . . teaching them to observe all things whatsoever I commanded you." [13] So also Acts 1:2 says that Jesus " was received up after that he had given commandment through the Holy Spirit unto the apostles." The idea of Jesus' commandments appears also in the Johannine literature.[14] The exclamation of Jesus' hearers in the synagogue at Capernaum [15] may be translated, " A new torah! " The idea that love fulfills the law is expressed also by Paul; [16] cp. also Jas. 2:8. The conception of Jesus as lawgiver, however, is characteristic of Matthew and goes with his understanding of the Christian life (s. 10).

The same conception is evident in our day in the tendency to use particular sayings of Jesus as legal maxims, to be obeyed literally by all who claim to be his followers. The error and danger of this legalistic view of the gospel will occupy us later (s. 56). The idea of Jesus as prophet is much less dangerous, much more true to his own purpose, and much more fruitful for the Christian life than the conception of him as lawgiver. The truth in the latter idea, however, must not be forgotten. Following Jesus in love for God and man does fulfill all that was good in the laws of Moses.

30. *Christ as Priest and Suffering Servant*

So far as our evidence goes, Jesus never spoke of himself as a priest; indeed, it is hard to imagine him doing so. The whole priestly side of

---

7 Dt. 18:15-19.
8 Jn. 1:21, 25.
9 Acts 3:22 f.; 7:37.
10 Mt. 5:21 ff.; cp. s. 56.
11 Mt. 22:40; cp. Mk. 12:31; Lk. 10:28.
12 Mt. 7:12.
13 Mt. 28:19 f.
14 Jn. 13:34; 15:10, 12, 14, 17; 1 Jn. 2:7 f.; 2 Jn. 5.
15 Mk. 1:27.
16 Rom. 13:8-10; Gal. 5:14.

religion seems to have had little interest for him (s. 86). If he gave a new *torah* (s. 29), it was conspicuously lacking in anything like the ritual legislation of the Pentateuch.

The essence of the conception of Christ as Priest, however, is the conception of a vicarious atonement by suffering; this is found also in the prophecy of the Suffering Servant of Yahweh in Second Isaiah, and there is at least a debatable possibility that Jesus thought of himself as fulfilling that prophecy.

No Christian can read Is., ch. 53, without being reminded of Jesus. From the earliest days the church has seen in this chapter a prophecy of the Cross. The chapter is a part of the series of Servant Songs in Second Isaiah.[1] The relation of these poems to their context and the meaning of the concept of the Servant are still much disputed.

The word commonly translated " servant " means primarily a slave, but is used also of the subjects of a king or the worshipers of a god, and also in the special sense of a high royal official. In other parts of the Old Testament the designation " servant of Yahweh " or " my servant " is applied often to Moses; it is applied also to David, the Davidic king, and the promised future king.[2] Even Nebuchadrezzar is called " my servant " in Jer. 27:6. Thus the term might designate any chosen agent of God, including the Messiah.

One of the passages just cited, Ezek. 37:25, speaks also of " Jacob my servant," evidently meaning the people of Israel; so also ch. 28:25 and Jer. 30:10 f.; 46:27 f. These are all clearly dependent upon Second Isaiah, and the designation of Israel as Yahweh's servant occurs in Second Isaiah, both outside of the four Servant Songs [3] and once in the midst of one of them.[4] The burden of proof is therefore on those who maintain that the Servant of the songs, including ch. 53, means anything else than Israel.

Many scholars, nevertheless, think the Servant is an individual. This requires a difference of authorship between the songs and the rest of Is., chs. 40 to 55, and also the deletion of ch. 49:3. Those who take this position, moreover, do not agree as to the individual designated. Their strongest argument is the fact that in ch. 49:5 f. the Servant seems to be distinguished from Israel. It is possible, however, to take Jacob and

---

[1] Is. 42:1–4; 49:1–6; 50:4–11; 52:13 to 53:12, with some variation of opinion as to the number and extent of the songs.
[2] Jer. 33:26; Ezek. 34:23 f.; 37:24 f.; Zc. 3:8; cp. Ps. 89:20, 39.
[3] Is. 41:8 f.; 43:10; 44:1 f., 21; 45:4.
[4] Is. 49:3.

Israel in these verses as in apposition with the Servant. It is also possible in such instances of personification, in line with the ancient concept of corporate personality (s. 49), to treat the personified group and its constituent parts as distinct.[5] In any case, more important than the identification of the Servant as intended by the prophet is his idea that the salvation of the world must be accomplished by vicarious suffering (ss. 25, 75).

The interpretation of Is., ch. 53, as referring to the Messiah is not attested for Judaism earlier than the second century A.D., but it is suggested by the fact that Enoch uses the language of Second Isaiah in connection with the Son of Man, who is identified with the Messiah (s. 31), e.g., " the elect " [6] and " the light of the Gentiles." [7] The Enochic Son of Man, however, does not suffer and die. It may be significant in this connection that Ps. 89 calls the ruling Davidic king Yahweh's elect, servant, anointed, and first-born. The idea of a suffering messiah does not appear in Jewish sources before the second century, when it is applied, not to the Davidic Messiah, but to another messiah from the house of Joseph.[8] The later Targum, in identifying the Servant of Is., ch. 53, with the Messiah, eliminates the idea of suffering.

The gospels indicate that Jesus saw in the figure of the Servant a picture of himself and his mission. Many scholars believe that this application of the prophecy was first made by the church after the crucifixion, but evidence for its origin in Jesus' own teaching is to be found not merely in the very doubtful use of Is. 61:1 in Lk. 4:18 but also in the important Q saying, Mt. 11:5 (Lk. 7:22), the reply of Jesus to the disciples of John. While Is., ch. 61, is not commonly regarded by critics as one of the Servant Songs, Jesus certainly did not draw the distinctions made (perhaps erroneously) by modern criticism. The fact, already noted, that the heavenly voice at the baptism and transfiguration combines Ps. 2:7 and Is. 42:1 indicates an identification of Messiah and Servant, though it does not clearly show who made the identification. Jesus' predictions of his own suffering in Mk. 9:12; 14:21 refer to prophecy, and Is., ch. 53, is the only passage that could be meant; in fact in some of the predictions of Jesus' rejection and suffering there

---

[5] Cp. Is. 49:14–21; Jer. 31:15.

[6] Enoch 39:6; 40:5; 51:3, 5; 52:6; cp. Is. 42:1.

[7] Enoch 48:4; cp. Is. 42:6; 49:6.

[8] Torrey has recently argued that this idea is already found in Zc. 4:14; 12:10 ff.; and Dan. 9:25 f. (*Journal of Biblical Literature*, LXI, Part I, March, 1942, p. ii); also in 1 Enoch 90:38 (*Journal of the American Oriental Society*, LII, 1, March, 1942, p. 57). Another paper, not yet published, gives additional material.

are echoes of the language of Is., ch. 53. (The essential authenticity of these predictions is thoroughly probable, in spite of the obviously later addition of circumstantial details regarding the crucifixion and resurrection.) Further echoes of Is., ch. 53, occur in the sayings at the Last Supper. Foreseeing his rejection by his people, and regarding his mission as fulfilling the purpose of God revealed in Scripture, Jesus could hardly have failed to see the connection, so clear to his followers, between his experience and the picture of the Servant in Is., ch. 53. Why he did not call himself the Servant we cannot tell, unless it was because the word did not do justice to his consciousness of a filial relation to the Father.

The main reason given for believing that it was the church that first applied the Servant prophecies to Jesus is the fact that the disciples were unprepared for the crucifixion and found its explanation in Is., ch. 53. According to Lk. 24:13 ff. it was the risen Christ that opened the Scripture to them, showing them that the Messiah had to suffer. But the gospels sometimes say that during Jesus' ministry the disciples failed to understand what he was trying to tell them, and in particular that they resisted the idea of his suffering.[9] This is true to human nature, which often refuses to listen to what is unpleasant. In any case, whether or not Jesus himself so taught, the church certainly met the problem of the Messiah's death by using, along with the category of Messiahship, the category of the Servant. In Acts 8:26–39 Philip preaches Christ from Is. 53:7 f. The Greek word used by the Septuagint for the Servant in Is., ch. 53, is applied to Jesus in Acts.[10] The fact that this word means both " child " and " servant," while the Hebrew word used in Second Isaiah does not have this ambiguity, leads some to believe that the connection between Jesus and the Servant was made first in the Hellenistic church.

Paul does not call Jesus the Servant of the Lord, but in 1 Cor. 15:3 he says that Christ died according to the Scriptures, which can only mean Is., ch. 53. John also does not use the term Servant, but in ch. 1:29, 36, Jesus is called " the Lamb of God who bears the sin of the world." [11] The synoptic evangelists leave no doubt that for them Jesus is the fulfillment of the Servant prophecies. Is. 42:1 ff. is quoted in Mt. 12:18; Is. 53:12 in Lk. 22:37 (the quotation in Mk. 15:28 is not in the best mss.); there are also many echoes elsewhere, as already noted.

The favorite title for Jesus in Revelation is " the Lamb." The Greek word used here is not the one used in John or in the Septuagint of Is. 53:7, but is peculiar to Revelation in the New Testament; a reference

---

[9] Mk. 8:32.   [10] Acts 3:13, 26; 4:27, 30.   [11] Cp. Is. 53:4 f., 7, 11.

to Is., ch. 53, however, is indicated by the designation " the Lamb that was slain." [12] Heb. 9:28 echoes Is., ch. 53; in 1 P. 1:19; 2:22–25 the chapter is definitely quoted and applied to Christ, and the designation " the righteous one " in ch. 3:18 may reflect Is. 53:11.

It is thus fair to say that from Acts on the identification of Jesus with the Suffering Servant of the Lord is constant in the New Testament, and there is no compelling reason to doubt that Jesus himself originated the idea. He did fulfill the ideal of the prophecy, even though what the prophet had in mind was a quite different fulfillment.

The conception of the Servant as achieving salvation for others by his own suffering finds its fulfillment in the New Testament in the conception of the Cross as Christ's atoning sacrifice of himself for man's salvation, the effective offering which he has made once for all as our High Priest. The idea of a Messianic priest is not found in the Old Testament, in spite of the emphasis on the anointed priest in P. Zc., chs. 3 f., almost makes the high priest Joshua a second Messiah along with Zerubbabel. The Messiah of the Testament of Levi (s. 29) is a member of the tribe of Levi instead of Judah.. The only basis in the Old Testament for the conception of Christ as priest is the fact that in Is., ch. 53, the idea of vicarious suffering is associated with the ritual term " guilt offering." [13]

The origin of the idea of Jesus as the priest whose offering is his own life is not clear. Philo connects the priestly legislation of the Pentateuch with the Logos, and it is probable that the idea of vicarious suffering came first and the idea of priesthood later, perhaps through an allegorical interpretation of the Old Testament. Certainly this is the way the conception appears in the New Testament. The writer of the epistle to the Hebrews, where the idea is expressed and developed, may have been its originator, though more or less dependent upon an earlier allegorical tradition. For him Christ is not merely the successor of the Levitical priesthood; his priestly office is anterior and superior to that of Levi, being eternal " after the order of Melchizedek." [14] As our High Priest Christ has not only offered an effective and final sacrifice; [15] he has also established the new covenant [16] and entered the true holy of holies, the heavenly tabernacle, where he makes intercession for us.[17] His work as priest thus includes both sacrifice and intercession.[18]

The conception of the atoning efficacy of the Cross is, of course, not

---

[12] Rev. 5:6, 9, 12.
[13] Is. 53:10.
[14] Heb. 4:14–16; chs. 5; 7; cp. Ps. 110:4.
[15] Heb. 9:11–14, 25 f.
[16] Heb. 9:16–22.
[17] Heb. 4:16; 9:24.
[18] For the latter cp. Rom. 8:34; 1 Jn. 2:1.

confined to these chapters in Hebrews. It pervades every part of the New Testament quite apart from the idea of Christ as priest. Its significance will be clearer when we examine the biblical idea of atonement (s. 75).

31. Christ as King: Messiah; Son of David

That Jesus ever spoke of himself as the promised King, or thought of his work as that of a monarch, is at best doubtful, though, as we shall see presently, it is by no means impossible. It is certain, however, that his followers began very early to think of him as the royal Son of David whose coming the prophets had foretold.

Royalty is the original implication of the word " Christ," which is the Greek *christos,* meaning " anointed." In the Septuagint this word is used to translate the Hebrew word *mashiah,* from which comes our Anglicized term " Messiah." The ceremony of consecration by anointing with oil was used in Israel for prophets (s. 29), for priests (often in P), and especially for kings. Samuel anointed Saul [1] and David; [2] Zadok anointed Solomon.[3] David referred to Saul as " Yahweh's Anointed "; [4] in the Septuagint this is translated by the same Greek expression used in Lk. 2:26 for the expected Messiah.

While the king was honored as Yahweh's anointed, the monarchy was not an unqualified success from the religious point of view. There were those who had doubts as to its being really an expression of God's will. Such later questioning is reflected in the warning attributed to Samuel in 1 S. 8:11–18 and in the admonition of Dt. 17:14–17, which is attributed to Moses but obviously reflects the experience of Solomon's reign.[5] Something of the same attitude is shown also by the Deuteronomic historians' designation of every king as either good or bad, and more often bad than good.

During the reigns of the " bad " kings the prophets, from Isaiah on, promise the coming of a good king who will reign with justice.[6] Jeremiah looks for a long, unbroken succession of Davidic kings, but his conception of the righteous Branch [7] was later applied to the expected Messiah, as were all these prophecies. Some of the terms applied to the coming

[1] 1 S. 10:1.
[2] Ch. 16.
[3] 1 K. 1:39.
[4] 1 S. 24:6, 10.
[5] Cp. 1 K. 10:26–29; 11:1–8.
[6] Is. 9:2–7; 11:1–9; 32:1–8; Jer. 23:1–6; 33:15–17.
[7] Cp. the similar idea, expressed in different Hebrew words, in Is. 11:1.

ideal ruler suggest divine qualities, though no more so than the terms applied to the reigning monarch in the royal psalms (s. 33). In some of these prophecies it is impossible to tell whether the reference is to a future king, near or remote, or to one already reigning or at least born. The language sometimes suggests an ode in honor of a newly born crown prince; so especially Is. 9:6, perhaps celebrating the birth of Hezekiah.

The prototype for the prophecies of an ideal ruler seems to have been a group of poems in honor of David, written in the form of predictions uttered long before his time, the " blessing poems." [8] The content of the later prophecies was doubtless suggested by the idealized memory of David's glorious reign. Possibly the widespread hope of a returning king played some part also (cp. Alexander, Nero, Friedrich Barbarossa, Arthur).

One of the most famous passages commonly taken as a Messianic prophecy was not so intended, even in the sense of a prediction of a good king. The meaning of Is. 7:10-16, though still much debated, must be something corresponding to the situation depicted in vv. 1-3 and serving as a sign to Ahaz to confirm Isaiah's promise in vv. 4-9. What is probably meant is that by the time a child already conceived is born, good times will have returned to Judah, so that the child will be named " God is with us." Who the " young woman " [9] was cannot be determined. Mi. 5:2-7, another important text for Christianity, combines references to Assyria with apparent reflections of the later Dispersion; it is therefore either composite or all late. In any case it expresses the hope of a coming deliverer who will be of David's line. [10]

The promise of divine favor and support to the Davidic dynasty is sometimes expressed as a covenant. [11] The destruction of the kingdom of Judah and the exile seemed to belie all this, [12] but hope was not relinquished. Now, instead of an uninterrupted continuance of David's line, its restoration is promised: so Am. 9:11 (an exilic addition to the book); Jer. 30:8 f.; Ezek., ch. 34. [13] Haggai, after the exile, hailed Zerubbabel as the signet of Yahweh. [14] Zc. 3:8 salutes " my servant the

---

[8] Gen., ch. 49, in which vv. 10-12 may well refer to David himself, and Num. 24:17-19; cp. s. 49.

[9] So the Hebrew; the Septuagint reads " virgin."

[10] Implied by the reference to Bethlehem.

[11] Ps. 89:3 f., 19-37; cp. Is. 55:3.

[12] Ps. 89:38-45, 49-51; Lam. 4:20.

[13] Based on Jer. 23:1-4.

[14] Hg. 2:21-23.

branch." [15] The emphasis on the anointed priest in P may indicate a deliberate suppression of the idea of political restoration.

The royal title " anointed " is not applied to the promised ruler in any of the Old Testament prophecies; [16] this fact, however, is probably not significant. Since " Messiah " means simply " king," any promise of a king may be called Messianic in a general sense. The only possible reference to the coming deliverer and ruler as Yahweh's Anointed is Is. 45:1. The present text calls the Persian conqueror Cyrus the *Mashiah Yahweh*,[17] but the name of Cyrus may be a gloss. The application of the distinctive designation of the Hebrew kings to a foreign ruler is unique, whether due to the prophet himself or a later scribe.

Not much is made in the later Old Testament books of the promise of a son of David, though the Chronicler magnifies David and stresses the promise to him and his descendants, perhaps thus reflecting a revival of the hope of national independence. While the term " Messiah " is still not used of an expected king, some of the pre-exilic royal psalms, in which the reigning king is called Yahweh's Anointed, may already have been given a Messianic interpretation in the Greek or Roman period.

The first use of the term in what we call a Messianic sense is in the pseudepigraphic Psalms of Solomon (ca. 50 B.C.), where the Greek text has " Lord Christ," [18] " his Christ," and " the Lord's Christ," [19] all as equivalent to " the king, the son of David." Enoch and 4 Ezra also have " his Anointed "; 2 Baruch, " the Anointed." Rabbinic sources constantly use *mashiah*, both with and without the definite article; also " King Messiah " and " Messiah, Son of David."

Christian theology from the beginning has identified Jesus with the Messiah. This indeed was the main burden of apostolic preaching.[20] In its Greek form the title came to be used as a proper name, and the very word " Christian " is derived from it. In view of this unanimity and emphasis it is a strange fact that we cannot be sure whether or not Jesus himself claimed or accepted this identification. Certainly he rejected for himself the primary content of the traditional hope, literal kingship. For this reason, probably, he discouraged the application of the title " Messiah " to him during his ministry: it suggested the wrong idea of what he

15 Cp. ch. 6:12, which originally must have referred to Zerubbabel.
16 " Messiah," Dan. 9:25 f., A.V., is a misleading translation.
17 Cp. " my shepherd," ch. 44:28.
18 Cp. Lk. 2:11.
19 As in Lk. 2:26.
20 Acts 17:3.

wished to accomplish, and it aroused unnecessary suspicion and opposition on the part of both Jewish and Roman authorities. According to Mark, he silenced the demons who recognized him as Messiah; [21] he repeatedly charged those whom he healed not to tell anybody; [22] after his transfiguration he told the disciples not to tell what they had seen.[23] Peter's confession at Caesarea Philippi receives enthusiastic approval in Mt. 16:17, but in Mk. 8:30 Jesus charges the disciples to tell no man of him, and proceeds to talk about the Son of Man (s. 32).

The rest of the evidence is equally inconclusive. The triumphal entry into Jerusalem and the cleansing of the temple were not necessarily intended as Messianic demonstrations. In Mk. 12:35–37 Jesus argues against the belief that the Messiah was David's son: if authentic, this means at least that Jesus rejected the Davidic ideal of Messiahship, but how much more it means or how it applies to himself, if at all, we cannot tell. At his trial Jesus answers in the affirmative the high priest's question, " Art thou the Christ, the Son of the Blessed? " [24] At least he does not repudiate the title, yet he goes on as in Mk., ch. 8, to speak in terms of the Son of Man.

Mark evidently believed that Jesus was the Messiah, but that he forbade the public use of the title until the end of his ministry. Many modern scholars suppose that Mark inferred this idea of the Messianic secret from the fact that he could find no evidence of Jesus' having publicly claimed to be the Messiah, and that actually Jesus did not consider himself the Messiah at all. But in that case the fact that he was so different from what the Messiah was expected to be makes it all the more strange that his followers should ever have thought of regarding him as Messiah. We can only conclude that his use of the title is uncertain, and that in any case he rejected the traditional content of the concept.

For the church there was no question from the very beginning that Jesus was the promised Messiah. The emphasis on his Davidic descent in the New Testament indicates the importance attached to his being the Messiah. He was not merely a descendant of David; he was the particular Son of David promised by the prophets. This is implied by the

[21] Mk. 1:24 f., 34; 3:11 f.
[22] Mk. 1:43 f.; 5:43; 7:36.
[23] Mk. 9:9.
[24] Mk. 14:61 f. — Matthew's " Thou sayest " probably means the same thing, cp. Mk. 15:2, and parallels; in Luke, Jesus gives an evasive reply.

annunciations to Joseph and the wise men [25] and to Mary and the shepherds.[26] Jesus himself never claims Davidic ancestry as a basis of Messianic authority, but on the contrary even questions the Davidic descent
of the Messiah.[27] The idea is not referred to in Acts, chs. 1 to 12 (though
mentioned in ch. 13:23), but the genealogies of Matthew and Luke are
probably Palestinian and show two different attempts to prove that Jesus was the Son of David. The rest of the New Testament, while occasionally recalling his descent from David, puts the main stress on other
ideas of the origin of his Messianic or divine nature. In general the main
importance of this idea for the New Testament is merely the fulfillment
of prophecy; it is even possible that the very idea of Jesus' being a descendant of David arose by inference from prophecy.

This was the one point on which his followers definitely and sharply
differed from other Jews. Their emphasis on this claim, and the necessity of defending it, led them to ask questions about Jesus, and Christian theology ever since has been largely concerned with Christology.
Since Jesus had not done what was expected of the Messiah,[28] and had
even been crucified, it was necessary to reinterpret the concept of Messiahship, which was accomplished largely by resorting to other categories (ss. 30, 32–35). The resurrection of Jesus was much stressed as
evidence that he was the Messiah in spite of the crucifixion.[29]

Some scholars believe, indeed, that the disciples first thought of Jesus as a divinely chosen and approved man who became Messiah by being raised from the dead. It is true that in Acts 2:36 Peter says God exalted Jesus and " made him both Lord and Christ." During his lifetime,
Jesus was anointed with the Holy Spirit and with power, and God was
with him.[30] The resurrection showed that he was the one ordained to be
the Judge.[31] The prominence of the resurrection in the preaching of the
early church was doubtless due to its importance in the disciples' own
experience: it restored and confirmed their faith, sorely tried by the
crucifixion, that Jesus was the Messiah. The supposition that their belief in his Messiahship came only after the resurrection, however, involves the assumption that the baptism and temptation, the transfiguration, and even Peter's confession are wholly legendary. Nowhere else in
the New Testament is there any trace of the idea that Jesus did not be-

25 Mt. 1:21–23; 2:2.   29 Acts 2:22–36; 17:31.
26 Lk. 1:31–33; 2:10 f.   30 Acts 10:36, 38.
27 Mk. 12:35–37.   31 Acts 10:42; 17:31.
28 Lk. 24:21; Acts 1:6.

come Messiah until his resurrection; [32] if the idea ever actually existed in the early church, it was certainly soon abandoned.

For the Gentile churches the concept of Messiahship was much less significant than it was for the Jewish church. The proof from prophecy was still used, as shown by the synoptic gospels, but other categories were more meaningful for converts from paganism, and the title Christ became for them simply a surname. It is already so even for Paul, who uses it both alone and in various combinations (Jesus Christ, Christ Jesus, the Lord Jesus Christ, Jesus Christ our Lord). The Davidic descent of Jesus is mentioned in Rom. 1:3, but the idea of Jesus as King is unimportant for Paul except in a spiritual sense.[33]

More attention is paid to the traditional Messianic hope in John, doubtless because of the anti-Jewish polemic which is one of the aims of the fourth gospel. The Hebrew title is both transliterated and explained.[34] In the dialogues the term Christ is often used by the Jewish antagonists of Jesus with reference to the popular hope. The Samaritans call Jesus " the Christ, the Saviour of the world." [35] In ch. 7:42 the Jews refer to the Davidic descent of the Messiah. The titles " King " and " King of the Jews " are used also, with emphasis on the spiritual character of Jesus' kingship; [36] cp. the attempt to make Jesus king by force, ch. 6:15.

The synoptic evangelists use the title " Christ " much as Paul does. Matthew is fond of the title " Son of David," inserting it several times where Mark and Luke do not have it. That the danger of political complications from the claim to Messiahship persisted even outside of Palestine is shown by Acts 17:7. Revelation uses various Messianic and royal titles for Jesus, but not with the idea of a literal Davidic kingship.[37] The word " Christ " is still used with the definite article, i.e., as a title rather than a surname,[38] but the familiar combination " Jesus Christ " occurs also several times. The remaining books of the New Testament usually omit the article and make the title practically a surname, used in various combinations. The Davidic descent of Jesus is recalled incidentally in 2 Tim. 2:8.

In the early prophetic hope the primary idea of the Messiah's work was to restore Israel's independence and glory and to give justice to the oppressed. In orthodox Judaism the association of the Messiah with na-

---

[32] On Rom. 1:4 cp. s. 33.
[33] 1 Cor. 15:24 f.; v.i.
[34] Jn. 1:41; 4:25.
[35] Ch. 4:42.

[36] Chs. 18:33–39; 19:13–22.
[37] Rev. 3:7; 5:5; 22:16; also chs. 17:14; 19:16.
[38] Chs. 11:15; 12:10; 20:4, 6, Greek.

tional independence has remained prominent, but in the New Testament it disappears. Christ's work as king becomes either spiritual or eschatological. The stress on the spiritual kingdom in the fourth gospel has just been noted. Paul thinks of the kingdom of Christ as present, but his language if not his thought is more concrete and " mythological " (s. 38) than that of John. Connecting the idea of Christ as king with the traditional conception of him as seated at the right hand of God in heaven,[39] Paul thinks of him as reigning and overthrowing his enemies during the present age, at the end of which he will deliver the kingdom to the Father.[40] Closely related to this is the conception of the warrior Logos in Rev. 19:11–16, which seems to refer to the present age.[41]

Elsewhere the kingdom of Christ is thought of chiefly as eschatological, in connection with the parousia (s. 67). So Mt. 25:31–46 (s. 70). In Acts 17:7 the Christians at Thessalonica are accused of subversive activity because they claim that in addition to the emperor " there is another king, one Jesus." [42] The millennial reign of Christ and the martyrs appears only in Rev., ch. 20 (s. 68). The glad cry of Rev. 11:15 seems to refer to the eschatological consummation.[43]

For the Christian of today the basic significance of this whole conception is twofold: (1) it emphasizes the continuity of the Old and New Testaments, and (2) it gives definite content to the concept of the rule of God by making it also the rule of Christ. Paul's conception of a present, heavenly rule of Christ implies that Jesus not only reconciles us to God and gives us new spiritual power, but also fights for us and with us against all the forces of evil outside of ourselves. Such a conception of his continuing work has an obvious relevancy for any hope of turning the kingdoms of this world into the kingdom of our Lord and of his Christ. It has a tremendous dynamic potentiality for triumphant Christian living and social action. It is open, however, only to those who can take with sobering seriousness the enduring personal existence of Jesus and his real activity in the present world.

The eschatological aspect of Christ's kingship will be considered further in s. 73. Its implications with regard to the Person of Christ cannot

---

[39] Acts 2:34, quoting Ps. 110:1; Acts 7:55 f.; Rom. 8:34; Eph. 1:20; Col. 3:1; Heb. 1:3, 13; 8:1; 10:12; 12:2; 1 P. 3:22.
[40] 1 Cor. 15:24–28.
[41] Cp. Rev. 3:21; 7:17.
[42] Contrast Jn. 19:12, 15.
[43] Cp. Rev. 22:1, 3.

be understood apart from the other titles applied to him in the New Testament.

32. *Son of Man*

Jesus' favorite designation of himself was " Son of Man." This has traditionally been taken as expressing his human nature, as " Son of God " expresses his divine nature, and it is true that in common Semitic idiom " son of man " means " human being " and " son of God " means " divine being." In Ps. 8:4 and in Ezekiel's characteristic designation as son of man [1] the expression means practically " mere mortal." As used in the gospels, however, it has a quite different connotation, arising out of particular historical associations. The references to the coming of the Son of Man on the clouds of heaven, as in Mk. 14:62, show that Jesus' use of this title is based on Dan. 7:13 f., where " one like a son of man " means a being in human form. In vv. 18, 27, this mysterious figure is apparently explained as a personification of " the people of the saints of the Most High," i.e., the Jewish nation, as a corporate personality (s. 49), to whom will be given " the kingdom and the dominion and the greatness of the kingdoms under the whole heaven." Possibly, however, the " one like a son of man " is not the nation itself but its angelic patron or representative.[2]

In the pseudepigraphic Similitudes of Enoch [3] the Son of Man becomes a definite individual, " that (this) Son of Man," also called the Anointed, the Elect, and the Righteous One. In other words, the expression is here definitely a Messianic title, but the Messiah of Enoch is not the Davidic king but a being from heaven, who will come with the angels, sit on " the throne of his glory " and judge the nations.[4] In 4 Ezra (2 Esdras), ch. 13, " the likeness of a man," called also " that man " and " my Son " (s. 33), comes up out of the sea, flies with the clouds of heaven, and executes judgment. In apocalyptic thought there was thus the hope of a coming judge and deliverer who was called Son of Man and sometimes Messiah, but who was a very different figure from the Davidic Messiah of the prophetic hope. The fact that the gospels clearly echo the terminology of both Daniel (clouds of heaven) and Enoch (angels, throne of his glory, *et al.*) shows that the background of

---

[1] Ezek. 2:1, and often.
[2] See ch. 10:16, 18, for the expression, and ch. 10:12 f. for the idea of angelic princes of the nations; cp. s. 40.
[3] 1 Enoch, chs. 37–71, early first century B.C.
[4] See especially chs. 46:1–4 ; 48:2 f.; 62.

the term " Son of Man " as used in the sayings of Jesus is the apocalyptic tradition. The fact that Enoch frequently uses language evidently derived from Second Isaiah (s. 30) is significant in view of the way Jesus alludes to Is., ch. 53, while speaking of the Son of Man (s. 30), though Enoch does not apply to his heavenly Son of Man the ideas of rejection and vicarious suffering.

Jesus' use of the term, however, is not entirely explained by this apocalyptic association. The pertinent sayings fall into two distinct groups: in some Jesus clearly refers to himself, speaking of his earthly ministry and without any apocalyptic language or associations; [5] in others the apocalyptic reference is prominent, but nothing in the sayings indicates clearly that Jesus is speaking of himself (though the parallels show that the evangelists so understand him).[6] There is no sufficient reason to question the authenticity of either group of sayings; hence it seems clear (1) that Jesus called himself the Son of Man, (2) that he also spoke of the coming apocalyptic Son of Man, and therefore (3) that he identified himself with the apocalyptic Son of Man, since he would hardly use the same designation for himself and also for a quite different being.

As we found in connection with the Messiah and the Servant, this identification is certainly made by the evangelists and undoubtedly goes back at least to the early Palestinian church. Here again some scholars hold that the church made the connection in the light of the resurrection experience, believing that Jesus was now at God's right hand in heaven,[7] awaiting the time when he would come back on the clouds to complete his work.[8]

Paul, in spite of his apocalyptic interest, never uses the title Son of Man, though it may underlie his idea of the Man from heaven.[9] The background of this idea is apparently Iranian, as may be true also of Enoch's conception of the Son of Man, and indeed of the whole apocalyptic hope (s. 69). John speaks of Jesus as the Son of Man with imagery recalling Daniel, yet different.[10] What is sometimes called the Son of Man Christology is especially characteristic, however, of the synoptic gospels, though they use the title only in sayings of Jesus, or what the

---

[5] Mt. 8:20; 11:19.
[6] Cp. Mk. 8:38; Mt. 10:32 f.; Lk. 12:8.
[7] Mk. 16:19; Acts 7:56.
[8] Acts 1:11; 3:21; cp. s. 67.
[9] Rom. 5:15, 19; 1 Cor. 15:21, 45–47.
[10] Jn. 1:51; 3:13 f.; 5:27; 6:27; 8:28; 12:23, 34; 13:31.

evangelists apparently suppose to be his sayings.[11] Revelation goes back directly to Daniel and reproduces the expression " one like unto a son of man." [12] The title does not appear in the rest of the New Testament, though Ps. 8:4 ff. is applied to Christ in Heb. 2:6–8. Evidently the conception of Jesus as the apocalyptic Son of Man was most popular in the primitive Palestinian (Galilean?) church, which was closest to Jesus himself. It had less significance for the later Hellenistic church.

The work of the Son of Man is primarily judgment, which is closely connected with the biblical idea of kingship; in fact the Hebrew verb translated " judge " means also more generally " rule " (s. 60). Thus in Mt. 25:31–46 the Son of Man is called also the King. In the sayings of Jesus and the thought of the synoptic evangelists the relation between the kingdom of God and the kingdom of the Son of Man is not entirely clear, but there is no evidence of any sharp distinction.[13]

Since the Son of Man of the apocalyptic literature is a divine, or at least superhuman, being existing in heaven before he comes to earth on the clouds of heaven, Jesus' use of this term as a self-designation affords an indication that he may have thought of himself as more than human and as having a personal pre-existence in heaven. There is no further suggestion of this in any of his sayings as reported in the synoptic gospels, to say nothing of any direct assertion.

33. *The Son of God*

No designation of Jesus comes nearer to including the whole meaning of New Testament Christology than the term " Son of God." In this case the historical background of the expression does not help us greatly in understanding its significance as used in the New Testament, though it may help us to understand how the term came to be used as a Messianic title.

The king of an ancient Oriental monarchy was often deified, and he was commonly the head of the state cult. Saul does not seem to have had such a position, but David at least took steps in that direction, bringing the ark to Jerusalem and dancing before it,[1] officiating at the altar on the threshing floor of Araunah as royal priest,[2] and assuming

---

[11] Cp. Mk. 2:28.
[12] Rev. 1:13; 14:14.
[13] Cp. Mk. 9:1 and Mt. 16:28, also Mt. 19:28; 25:34; Lk. 12:31 f.; 22:29; see further s. 73.
[1] 2 S., ch. 6.
[2] Ch. 24:25.

the right to appoint priests even from his own sons.[3] Solomon built the temple as an annex to his palace. There is no clear evidence that the Hebrew kings were ever actually deified, though commentators have difficulty in explaining away the fact that the king is hailed as God in Ps. 45:6.

On the whole the king was rather the appointed representative and agent of Yahweh. As such he was called Yahweh's son.[4] In Ps. 2 (probably the coronation ode of a king of Judah) the ruler is hailed as having just become God's son: unless some notion of an actual transformation of nature is involved, which is hardly likely, the " begetting " must mean adoption. Ps. 89:26 f. similarly says that the king shall call God his Father, being made God's first-born. (This interpretation, of course, presupposes that these psalms were not originally meant to refer to the future Messiah.)

The prophecies of a coming ideal king, as noted in s. 31, sometimes use terms suggesting a divine nature;[5] they do not, however, speak of him as God's son. The meaning of the statement in Is. 9:6, " Unto us a child is born, unto us a son is given," is probably that a prince of the house of David has just been born (cp. v. 7, " upon the throne of David and upon his kingdom "). In the postbiblical apocalyptic literature the promised king is sometimes called the Son of God,[6] though all such references may be later Christian interpolations. The origin of the Messianic use of the term Son of God in either Judaism or Christianity cannot now be determined with certainty. The most probable explanation is that it arose out of the Messianic interpretation of Ps. 2:7.

Jesus sometimes spoke of himself as the Son, but in a way quite different from the Old Testament idea of the king as God's son. The heavenly voice at the baptism and transfiguration of Jesus echoes Ps. 2:7 in combination with Is. 42:1, and Jesus' temptation is put in terms of doubt as to his Sonship in a special, Messianic sense. The " beloved son " in the parable of the wicked husbandmen[7] refers by implication to Jesus as contrasted with the prophets who were merely messengers, but the story in its present form is suspiciously allegorical, and such a sharp differentiation between Jesus and the prophets is foreign to his other sayings. In Mk. 13:32 (Mt. 24:36) " the Son " is mentioned with the angels over against the Father; this is the conclusion of the eschato-

---

[3] Ch. 8:18; cp. s. 86.
[4] 2 S. 7:14.
[5] So especially Is. 9:6.

[6] 1 Enoch 105:2 and often in 4 Ezra.
[7] Mk. 12:6, and parallels.

logical discourse and may be the only genuine part of it after the prediction of the destruction of the temple (s. 66). In Matthew many manuscripts and versions omit " neither the Son "; the original text probably included this, however, for it is not likely that any Christian
copyist would insert a statement limiting the knowledge of Christ. Luke
has no parallel here, and in Acts 1:7 there is no reference to the angels
or the Son. In Mt. 11:27 (Lk. 10:22) the Son is said to have unique
knowledge of the Father. Such a claim to unique revelation seems
strange immediately after the thanksgiving for revelation to babes, yet
the connection may be merely editorial. If the saying is authentic, the
idea of Sonship has no Davidic connotation for Jesus; the implication
is rather a uniquely close and confidential relationship, though not necessarily implying anything as to origin or metaphysical nature.

However Jesus himself may have understood his Sonship, the conception of him as the Son of God in the early church was probably a
corollary of his Messiahship. In Mk. 3:11 f.; 5:7 (the confessions of
the demons) Sonship and Messiahship seem to be equivalent. The
high priest's question in Mk. 14:61 makes them equivalent also, though
Jewish scholars claim that a high priest in the first century would not
have spoken of the Messiah as " the Son of the Blessed." The Messianic
hope of the Old Testament did not involve more than a human king,
with no more deification than was attributed to the historic kings of Israel and Judah. This remains true of the Davidic Messiah in Judaism.

There is little evidence, as a matter of fact, for the use of the term
Son of God in the early Palestinian church. Jesus was still regarded as
a real, distinct person, the chosen and approved Servant (s. 30), who
had been raised from the dead and exalted to heaven, whence he would
come as Judge (s. 70).[8] The confession of faith in Acts 8:37, A.V., is
omitted by the best manuscripts (A.S.V. relegates it to the margin);
it is probably an interpolation reflecting later liturgical use of such a
confession at baptism. In ch. 9:20, however, Paul at Damascus proclaims that Jesus is the Son of God. Since chs. 1 f. of Lk. are probably of
Palestinian origin, vv. 32 and 35 are significant in this connection also.

The belief that Jesus became the Son of God at his baptism (Adoptionism) appears later among the Ebionites, who are often considered
the survivors and successors of the primitive Palestinian church. Some
interpreters see in the accounts of Jesus' baptism evidence that the
early disciples held this view. Just what the experience at his baptism

[8] On the term " child " in Acts 4:27, 30, A.V., cp. s. 30.

meant to Jesus himself we do not and cannot know. If the *bath qol* (s. 12) originally quoted all of Ps. 2:7 (as it actually does in the " Western " text of Lk. 3:22), Jesus may have felt that he was then and there adopted as God's Son, but the omission of the last line and the combination with Is. 42:1 in the present text indicate rather the confirmation of a previous sense of Sonship and the approval of his life up to that time. Since there is no trace of Adoptionism elsewhere in the New Testament, we must conclude that if the idea existed at all in the early church it was soon abandoned by the main body of the disciples. In Jn. 1:29–37 nothing is said of Jesus' being baptized at all; the descent of the Spirit is a sign to John the Baptist that Jesus is the Son of God. Whether this is a bit of anti-Adoptionist polemic or whether the baptism is merely presupposed is not certain. The Ebionite doctrine may have been simply a later inference from the baptism narratives.

The birth-stories of Matthew and Luke attest the idea of a divine nature by miraculous conception and birth. There is no hint of this in any saying of Jesus or anywhere else in the New Testament. The idea is more Hellenistic than Jewish, but related ideas are not unknown in Judaism. Since Sarah, Rebekah, and Rachel were all barren, a series of miraculous conceptions (though not without human paternity) was necessary to fulfill the promise to Abraham. The reading of the Sinaitic Syriac in Mt. 1:16, " Joseph . . . begat Jesus," may reflect such a view of Jesus' birth. Hellenistic Judaism goes farther: Philo " frequently is near to denying Abraham's paternity and representing Isaac as the direct child of God through Sarah, to whom virginity has been miraculously restored." [9] Such a confusion of paternity as between a god and a human father is " one of the commonest elements in the Hellenistic religions." [10] The translation of " young woman " in Is. 7:14 as " virgin " in the Septuagint may reflect an idea of the virgin birth of the Messiah in Hellenistic Judaism. In the Hellenistic church this translation at least supported the belief in the virgin birth of Jesus, if it did not give rise to it. The relatively early origin of the belief is shown by the fact that it is a different idea from pre-existence and logically hard to combine with it, since it implies the creation of a new person. Matthew and Luke have the virgin birth without pre-existence; John has pre-existence without the virgin birth; Mark has neither. The very absence of references to the virgin birth in the rest of the New Testament favors the early origin of the belief. It may even have been Palestinian,

[9] E. R. Goodenough, *By Light, Light*, p. 154.   [10] *Ibid.*

though later than the genealogies, which it makes irrelevant except as fulfilling prophecy.

For Paul the thought of Jesus as Son of God is basic, but what it means to him is entirely different from the Old Testament conception of the king as God's son. In Rom. 1:4, Paul seems to imply that the resurrection made Christ the Son of God in a greater sense than he had been before, but other statements show abundantly that Paul thought of Jesus as having been already the Son of God before his incarnation. Paul's conception of Jesus' eternal Sonship implies a unique nature and relationship to God, but not identification with God, for confession of Jesus as Lord (s. 34) is " to the glory of God the Father," [11] and in the end Christ will deliver the kingdom to the Father, becoming himself subjected to him, " that God may be all in all." [12]

When and how Jesus first came to be thought of as having been pre-existent eternally cannot be determined. There is no indication that he ever thought of himself in that way, unless (as noted in s. 32) it is implied by the fact that he identified himself with the apocalyptic Son of Man. For the early Palestinian church further evidence is lacking. Paul, however, uses many expressions that point to the pre-existence of Christ as a heavenly being. Such general statements as that God sent his Son [13] do not necessarily imply personal pre-existence, nor does the allegorical interpretation of the rock in the wilderness as being Christ.[14] But 2 Cor. 8:9, " though he was rich, yet for your sakes he became poor," can hardly mean anything other than a voluntary descent from heaven to earth.

The clearest expressions of the belief are Phil. 2:6–11 and Col. 1:15–17. Porter considers the former a hymn merely quoted by Paul to illustrate the mind of Christ,[15] but such a quotation would have had no point if Paul had not believed that Christ had actually so humbled and emptied himself. Porter deletes Col. 1:15–17 as a later interpolation,[16] but similar terms are used in 1 Cor. 8:6, where Porter thinks Paul is quoting from the letter of the Corinthians.[17] It is true that Paul's experience and doctrine of salvation did not require a pre-existent Christ; in seeking to describe and interpret his experience, however, Paul used inherited cat-

---

[11] Phil. 2:11.
[12] 1 Cor. 15:24, 28.
[13] Rom. 8:3; Gal. 4:4.
[14] 1 Cor. 10:4.
[15] F. C. Porter, *The Mind of Christ in Paul*, pp. 204 ff.
[16] *Op. cit.*, pp. 179 ff.
[17] *Op. cit.*, pp. 117–121.

egories which involved pre-existence. His Christ is not a deified man; he is the eternal Son of God who existed in heaven, came to earth, died and rose, and now reigns in heaven.[18]

The fourth gospel repeatedly designates Jesus as the " unique " Son of God.[19] The characteristic adjective commonly translated " only be-gotten " in these passages actually means " unique in kind." It is used of Isaac in Heb. 11:17 and by Josephus, and of the divine Wisdom in W.S. 7:22. Philo speaks of the Logos as God's first-born Son.[20] As the Son, Christ is constantly distinguished from the Father throughout the fourth gospel: the Father is greater than Christ,[21] and Jesus says re-peatedly that the Father has sent him, that he speaks not his own words but the Father's, and that he does not his own will but the Father's.[22] He is in the Father and the Father in him; [23] indeed he and the Father are one,[24] and he who has seen him has seen the Father.[25] Evidently this means moral unity, not personal identity, for he prays that the disciples also may be one with him and with one another even as he and the Fa-ther are one.[26]

Hebrews frequently calls Jesus the Son of God, drawing a strong con-trast between the revelation given by the prophets and that given by the Son.[27] The superiority of the Son to the angels [28] and to Moses [29] is em-phasized. Ps. 45:6 is quoted as though spoken to the Son,[30] and Ps. 102:25 ff. is applied to Christ.[31] Here and in the remaining books of the New Testament, which frequently call Jesus the Son of God, any per-ceptible association with the Davidic king has disappeared, and the title has become purely an expression of Jesus' divine origin and nature.

34. Lord

Another appellation that came to be felt, especially by Paul, as ex-pressing the very essence of faith in Christ is the term Lord. Unfortu-

[18] Cp. 1 Cor. 15:47.
[19] Jn. 1:14, cp. v. 18; 3:16, 18; 1 Jn. 4:9.
[20] Cp. Ps. 89:27.
[21] Jn. 14:28.
[22] Jn. 5:19, 30, 36 f.; 6:44, 57; 8:16, 18, 28; 10:37; 12:49; 14:23 f.; 15:10, 15; 16:28, 32.
[23] Chs. 10:38; 14:11.
[24] Ch. 10:30.
[25] Ch. 14:9.
[26] Ch. 17:21 f.
[27] Heb. 1:1–3.
[28] Ch. 1:4–14.
[29] Ch. 3:5 f.
[30] Ch. 1:8.
[31] Ch. 1:10–12.

nately its significance is somewhat obscured by the fact that the Greek word so translated, *kyrios,* has an even wider application than the English word, being used with much the same range of meaning as the German *Herr.* Its primary meaning is the master of a slave, but it is also an imperial title and a term of polite address. In addition to these uses, it is the principal designation of the gods of the mysteries and similar cults.[1] Even more important for New Testament usage is the fact that the Septuagint uses this word not only for two Hebrew nouns of similar meaning (*'adon, ba'al*) but also for the ancient proper name of the Hebrew God, Yahweh. This corresponds to the practice of substituting the Hebrew word *Adonai* for the divine name in the public reading of the Old Testament in the synagogue. In keeping with this practice the Authorized Version and the Revised Standard Version represent the name Yahweh by LORD, where the American Standard Version inadvisedly uses the erroneous form Jehovah. The Old Testament does not apply the title Lord to the Messiah, unless *'adon* in Mal. 3:1 is so intended.

In the gospels the Greek noun is used in all the ways noted above. It is frequently used of a slave owner.[2] It is translated " Sir " in a number of places, and perhaps should be in others. In Jn. 20:15 Mary uses it in this way, thinking that she is addressing the gardener. Mk. 11:3 indicates that it was commonly used of Jesus during his ministry, and that he sanctioned the practice, but just what it implied is not clear. The corresponding Aramaic word *mar* was used in the same connections as the Hebrew and Greek words, and in particular was used by the disciples of the rabbis as a title of respect for their teachers. It is still used in the Syriac-speaking churches for the bishops. The double address, " Lord, Lord," in Mt. 7:21–23 (Lk. 6:46) seems to imply something more than this, yet in Mt. 25:11 the bridesmaids address the bridegroom in exactly the same way. In Mk. 12:36 f. (quoting Ps. 110:1) Jesus says that David calls the Messiah his lord, implying that the Messiah was his superior and therefore not his son. From all this it appears probable that the use of the term by the disciples was in the first place simply the common usage of a rabbi's students.

After the resurrection, however, the situation is quite different. In Acts 2:36 Lord and Christ are put side by side as Messianic titles.[3] Old Testament usage had given the words meaning Lord strong associations of deity, in spite of their common use in lesser meanings. In Acts, chs. 1 to 12, *kyrios* is used both of God and of Jesus, and in almost a third

---

[1] 1 Cor. 8:5.   [2] Cp. Mt. 10:24 f.   [3] Cp. ch. 10:36.

of the places where it occurs one cannot be sure which is meant. Possibly Messiah was the most popular title for Jesus in the Judean church, Son of Man in the Galilean church, and Lord in the Hellenistic church; in any case, judging by Acts 2:36 and 10:36, we may say that in the early Palestinian church the title " Lord " was already on the way to becoming a divine title for Jesus.

" The Lord " is Paul's favorite designation of Christ, " the name that is above every name." [4] The fundamental Christian confession of faith is, " Jesus is Lord." [5] In 2 Cor. 3:17 f., as noted in s. 27, Paul seems to equate Lord and Spirit, though the reference here may very well be to God rather than Christ. In John, while the word *kyrios* appears frequently in common polite address, meaning " Sir," it is used also in confessions of faith.[6] Jesus is regularly designated " the Lord." [7] In the remaining New Testament books we find frequently the combinations mentioned in s. 31, and also " the Lord " alone for both God and Christ. As in Acts, it is sometimes impossible to tell which is meant. In the general epistles, as in Paul's, the word is clearly used as a divine title, meaning more nearly " God " than " Messiah."

35. *The Logos*

The Johannine identification of Christ with the eternal Logos has been considered in s. 28. It has a distinctly philosophical sound as well as a philosophical background, but we cannot tell how far the evangelist would have gone with regard to its metaphysical associations and implications. It clearly implies eternal, though not necessarily personal, pre-existence. Christ is here the incarnation of a divine hypostasis. Personal pre-existence seems implied in ch. 8:58, as also in ch. 17:5 and the references to Christ's coming down, being sent, and being from the Father.[1] In ch. 1:3, 10, it is said that the work of creation was done " through him." [2] The Logos not only was with God in the beginning but was God (or God was the Logos), though the omission of the definite article with the Greek word for God may be significant in view of the fact that Philo uses this word without the article for the Logos, but never with the article.

---

[4] Phil. 2:9, 11.
[5] Rom. 10:9.
[6] Jn. 20:13, 28.
[7] So also Luke, but in general the synoptic gospels do not use the term as a divine title.
[1] Jn. 6:46; 7:29; 8:42, 47; 16:28.
[2] Cp. 1 Cor. 8:6; Col. 1:16; Heb. 1:2.

The idea of the Logos is metaphysical rather than mythological, in the sense that it is a substantial rather than a personal concept. At the same time the fourth evangelist by his use of the idea of eternal Sonship (s. 33) combines a " mythological " concept with the " metaphysical " idea of the Logos. Paul also uses substantial as well as personal terms, together with some which can hardly be classified as either. Christ is God's image; [3] the fullness of Deity dwells in him.[4] The special meaning attached to the latter term in Gnosticism may be a development from this verse itself rather than an indication of a pre-Christian Gnostic background for Paul's language. In any case, the resemblance of the ideas expressed by these terms to the Logos conception is obvious. Much in Paul's language may be part of his effort to become all things to all men,[5] utilizing expressions and ideas more or less extraneous to his own main interests and natural ways of thinking. His identification of Lord and Spirit (s. 34) is clearly not mechanical or mathematical; the point is that the power that works in the Christian is the same as that which worked in Christ himself. While substantial, metaphysical conceptions are sometimes suggested by Paul's language, he evidently thought chiefly in personal terms, and his idea of the relation between God and Christ was one of a relation between two real and distinct persons.

For both Paul and John, in fact, the personal point of view is clearly primary, doubtless in part because of their common Jewish background and also because of their knowledge of the real person, Jesus. The use of substantial concepts is hardly more than a pedagogical point of contact in presenting the gospel to people of Greek background and ways of thinking. Both writers combine Jewish monotheism, Hellenistic philosophy, and the tradition of the historic Jesus without full realization of the logical problems involved in such a combination. In both cases the philosophical element is the least influential of the three, indicating no special training or interest in Greek metaphysics. In both cases also the basic interest is religious rather than theological, redemptive rather than intellectual.

Ideas akin to those of Jn., ch. 1, and Col. 1:15–17 appear again in Heb. 1:1–4, one of the most important Christological passages in the New Testament. Terms characteristic of Hellenistic thought are here used of Christ: the " effulgence " (radiation, emanation, light stream) of God's " glory " (splendor), and the " imprint " (translated " im-

---

[3] 2 Cor. 4:4; Col. 1:15.   [4] Col. 1:19; 2:9.   [5] 1 Cor. 9:22.

age " but not the word used by Paul) of his " substance " (*hypostasis*, cp. s. 28), " upholding all things by the word of his power." [6]

36. *Other Christological Terms*

Many other terms are used to express the significance of Jesus. The word " Savior " is used often, though perhaps not so commonly as we might suppose. In Hebrew the word meaning " savior " has the same varied applications as the verb meaning " save " (s. 61), of which it is a participle. Neh. 9:27 calls the judges saviors. 2 K. 13:5 says that when Israel was oppressed by the Syrians in the time of John, Yahweh gave them a savior who delivered them. Obad. 21 speaks of saviors who will appear on Mt. Zion to judge Edom. In Is. 19:20 a savior is promised to the Egyptians. Elsewhere (with special frequency in Second Isaiah) Yahweh himself is called Israel's Savior.

The Greek word meaning " savior " was used in the Hellenistic world for the lords of the cults and also for the rulers. It was used as a divine epithet by the Ptolemies and Seleucids. A famous inscription hails the emperor Augustus as " savior of the world."

This term " savior " does not occur in any saying of Jesus. For the early Palestinian church we have only Acts 5:31 and Lk. 2:11. The only occurrence in a certainly authentic letter of Paul is Phil. 3:20.[1] The Johannine literature uses it only in Jn. 4:42 and 1 Jn. 4:14. It does not appear in Matthew (but note ch. 1:21 and the meaning of the name Jesus), or in Mark; Luke has it only in chs. 1:47 (of God) and 2:11, and in Acts 5:31 and 13:23. It is not used in Revelation, Hebrews, 1 Peter, or James. Its chief use is in the pastoral epistles and in 2 Peter and Jude, referring sometimes to God and sometimes to Jesus (especially in combination with Lord).

The term Redeemer, commonly applied to Jesus in present usage, is often used with reference to Yahweh in the Old Testament,[2] and later Jewish sources apply it to the Messiah. It is nowhere in the Old Testament applied to the promised king, and the New Testament never uses it of Jesus.

In Rev. 3:14, Jesus is called " the beginning of God's creation." [3] The important passage at the beginning of Hebrews, already considered in s. 35, states explicitly Christ's agency in the creation of the world and thus implies his pre-existence; cp. the idea of Christ's eternal priest-

---

[6] Cp. Col. 1:17.
[1] Cp. Eph. 5:23.

[2] So especially Second Isaiah.
[3] Cp. Prov. 8:22; Col. 1:15, 18.

hood " after the order of Melchizedek " in ch. 7:1–3 (s. 30). 1 P. 1:20 says that Christ was foreknown before the foundation of the world; v. 11 says that the spirit of Christ was in the prophets.

In most of the rest of the New Testament there is a rather conventional use of traditional terminology, expressing deep conviction and devotion but not distinctive or even very clear ideas. The book of Revelation is an exception. The mythological point of view dominates the Christology of Revelation; in fact, the historical Jesus is hardly recognizable in the descriptions of chs. 1:12–16; 19:11–16; and elsewhere. Ch. 12 is an extraordinary example of the application of mythological conceptions to Christ. The power and majesty of Christ are stressed,[4] and he shares with God many divine attributes and titles, such as " the Alpha and the Omega, the first and the last," [5] and " the Living One." [6] He sits on the throne with the Father; [7] prayer is addressed to him as to God; [8] in the new Jerusalem God and the Lamb will be the temple.[9] Honor and glory are ascribed to the Lamb.[10] In chs. 2:23; 5:6 expressions used elsewhere in the Bible of God are used of Christ.[11] The description of Christ in ch. 1:12–16 is based on that of the Ancient of Days rather than that of the " one like a son of man " in Dan., ch. 7. Yet Jesus calls God his God and his Father and says he has received dominion from him.[12] In ch. 3:5 God is the Judge and Christ gives the decisive testimony before him, as in Mt. 10:32 f.

With regard to the use of all these titles and categories we may observe that they represent the endeavor of the church to interpret Christ in terms that had meaning and associations for themselves and their contemporaries. This was necessary in order to convey at all their sense of his significance. The danger in thus interpreting Jesus in traditional terms was that the old associations and content of the familiar concepts would unduly color and even distort the impression of Jesus, instead of being modified and enlarged in accordance with what Jesus really was and taught. As Porter puts it, the tendency was to say, " Jesus is the Messiah," instead of, " The Messiah is Jesus." [13] In the New Testament

[4] Rev. 1:5; 2:26; 6:14 ff.
[5] Chs. 1:17; 2:8; 22:13; cp. 1:8; 21:6.
[6] Ch. 1:18; cp. chs. 4:9 f.; 10:6.
[7] Chs. 3:21; 7:17; 22:1, 3.
[8] Ch. 7:10.
[9] Ch. 21:22.
[10] Ch. 5:12 f.
[11] Cp. 1 Chr. 28:9; Rom. 8:27; Zc. 3:9; 4:10.
[12] Rev. 2:27; 3:2, 5, 12, 21.
[13] *The Mind of Christ in Paul*, p. 144.

the memory of Jesus is still sufficiently strong to counteract this tendency, though it is already in evidence. Another danger not entirely avoided even in the New Testament was that of letting the traditional terms become so stereotyped as to lose all vital meaning.

Not the terminology but the total conception that it was intended to express is most important. Perhaps the heaping up of different titles is more significant than the use of any one of them, for it shows that no one title was felt to be adequate. No Jewish or Hellenistic category exactly fits Jesus, and all together fail to exhaust the sense of his significance. That must always be true of any modern attempt to describe him or account for him in our own terms, yet we must keep trying in order to make him real to men.

37. Christ's Relation to Man and to God

The extent to which Jesus is regarded in the New Testament as having a different nature from that of man is hard to determine. Apparently it varies. How far his own conception of himself as Son of Man and Son of God put him above and apart from his followers we cannot say; certainly he regarded himself as a real man, and certainly not as part man and part God, or as a being of two natures. He came eating and drinking, the friend of publicans and sinners.[1] He objected to being called good [2] and to being appealed to as a judge or divider over men.[3] His use of the expressions " my Father " and " your Father " for God both unites him with his followers and separates him from them: in no recorded saying does he join himself with the disciples in saying " our Father," though it is quite possible that he actually did so in practice. He makes no statements on the subject of his relation to man. That was not what he was concerned to teach; indeed the question whether he was really and fully a man probably never occurred to him even in thinking of himself as the apocalyptic Son of Man or as the Son who alone knew the Father.

The conception of the early Palestinian church, as shown in Acts 10:38, has already been considered (s. 31). Here we may note also ch. 2:22: "A man approved of God . . . by miracles and signs which God did by him." Jesus is the man ordained of God to judge the world.[4] While emphasizing faith in him as Messiah and Son of Man, the early church clearly thought of Jesus as genuinely and fully human.

[1] Mt. 11:19.
[2] Mk. 10:18.
[3] Lk. 12:14.
[4] Acts 10:42; 17:31.

Paul's idea of the heavenly, pre-existent Christ makes him distinctly different from men. To become man, he " emptied himself, taking the form of a servant," being " made in the likeness of men " and " found in fashion as a man." [5] The constant emphasis on the exalted, spiritual Christ somewhat obscures the human Jesus in Paul's letters, though Paul recalls that God sent his Son " in the likeness of sinful flesh," [6] " born of a woman, born under the law," [7] " of the seed of David according to the flesh." [8] Whatever may have been true of Paul's preaching, his letters show a notable lack of interest in the earthly ministry of Jesus, though his dependence on the teaching of Jesus, especially in matters of conduct, is closer than may be supposed.

John, together with the Logos Christology, stresses the reality of the incarnation.[9] Even the reality of the resurrection body of Jesus is emphasized.[10] Probably a polemic against incipient Docetism is one of the purposes of the gospel, as it is clearly of the epistles.[11] There is even some stress on such human qualities as weariness,[12] sympathy,[13] and distress over his own suffering,[14] though John has no account of the temptation or the anguish in Gethsemane. With all this, John makes much also of qualities that distinguish Jesus from other men, especially his refusal to be guided by the advice of others.[15] Certainly, while the picture of Jesus in John has great devotional value, the picture given by the synoptic evangelists is much more human and real.

In Revelation the human existence of Jesus is assumed but not mentioned aside from the fact of his death.[16] The writer is mainly interested in the conquering heavenly Christ. Hebrews, however, like John, in spite of its high Christology, stresses the human qualities of Jesus (often designated simply by that name). He was tempted, learned obedience by suffering, and achieved sinlessness through decision and struggle — an idea unique in the New Testament.[17] 1 P. 2:19–24, with the

---

5 Phil. 2:7 f.
6 Rom. 8:3.
7 Gal. 4:4.
8 Rom. 1:3.
9 Jn. 1:14; 19:34.
10 Ch. 20:27; cp. ch. 21:13; Lk. 24:39, 43.
11 1 Jn. 4:2; 2 Jn. 7.
12 Jn. 4:6.
13 Ch. 11:33–38.
14 Chs. 12:27; 13:21.
15 Chs. 2:4; 7:2–10.
16 Rev. 11:8.
17 Heb. 2:9 f., 14, 18; 4:15; 5:7–9; 12:2 f.; 13:12.

practical interest of encouragement under persecution, emphasizes the example of Jesus, but Jas. 5:10 f. cites instead the examples of the prophets and Job. 1 Tim. 2:5 speaks of " the man Christ Jesus " as the " one mediator between God and men." The incarnation is referred to in something of the Johannine manner in 1 Tim. 3:16; 2 Tim. 1:10.

Here again the problem has not yet been felt: Jesus was a real human being for the New Testament writers, but also the eternal Son of God. While the recollection of Jesus was still strong in the apostolic age, with increasing time and distance the Christ of worship and inner experience became more real to the average Christian than the historical Jesus. The preservation of the traditions of Jesus' life and so of his distinct character and personality in spite of this tendency is to be explained by the apologetic use of the fulfillment of prophecy, the soteriological importance of the Cross, and above all the ethical use of the example of Jesus. Even Paul does not quite substitute Christology for Christ: his heavenly Christ has the character of the historical Jesus. John makes more use than Paul of historical tradition, presenting his Christology in the form of a biography, yet he obviously and perhaps deliberately reads back into the earthly life of Jesus his own inward experience of the abiding Christ. The synoptic gospels remain our only means of determining what Jesus really was, and even they are not written as history but as testimony.

In four New Testament passages the word God is actually applied to Jesus, though either the text or the meaning is uncertain in all but one of them, namely, the confession of Thomas in Jn. 20:28, " My Lord and my God." [18] In Jn. 1:18 some manuscripts read " son " instead of " God," and while the textual evidence favors the latter reading, the context distinctly favors the former. Just how much is meant by the evangelist in ch. 20:28 is uncertain, but only a Hellenistic background can explain the use of the word in such a connection at all. In the other two instances translators and commentators differ (cp. A.V. and A.S.V.), but the Greek of Titus 2:13 is most naturally translated, " The glorious appearing of our great God and Saviour Jesus Christ," and the language of 2 P. 1:1 is most naturally taken to mean, " The righteousness of our God and Saviour Jesus Christ." The writers of these passages were probably influenced by the use of the word " God " in emperor worship. A fifth passage, in which the Greek is ambiguous, should be mentioned here: Rom. 9:5 reads, in the American Standard Version, " Of

[18] For Jn. 1:1, " the Word was God," cp. s. 35.

whom is Christ as concerning the flesh, who is over all, God blessed forever." The margin reads, " Of whom is Christ as concerning the flesh; he who is over all, God, be blessed forever." The new Revised Standard Version makes a full stop after " flesh."

However these debatable passages may be interpreted, it is clear that by the end of the New Testament period the process of deification had gone far. Christians converted from paganism may often have thought of Jesus as the real God of the cult, replacing their former deities. The difficulty of reconciling such an idea of him with monotheism would not have bothered such Gentile believers as it would those who came from Judaism. The New Testament, however, never quite puts Christ in the place of God. Jesus is moved by the Spirit of God, he is the Son of God, God is in him and he is in God; he is the incarnation of the eternal, divine Logos, the radiation of God's glory and the imprint of his very substance, the image of the invisible God, the first-born of all creation, sharing titles and attributes with God, reigning with him, being addressed in prayer with him, being even called " my Lord and my God " and perhaps " our God and Saviour, Jesus Christ." Yet he is never identified with God, but always remains a distinct person. The relationship is never philosophically worked out.

Underlying all forms of expression was the basic experience that in and through Jesus the disciples were somehow dealing with God himself. It was the same experience and the same faith that we have found expressed in the doctrine of the Trinity (s. 28), the faith that God the Father and God the Son are one God.

V

THE UNIVERSE

38. *Mythology, Philosophy, and Science*

The ancient Hebrews and the early Christians had no philosophy or science, but current conceptions were presupposed in their religious thinking and acting. Consequently, in order to perceive the essential religious message in which alone revelation is to be found in the Bible, we must be able to disentangle it from the world-view in terms of which it is expressed.

The ancient Hebrew and early Christian world-views were never systematically presented or even definitely formulated. Hebrew mentality lacked the type of intellectual curiosity that produced Greek philosophy. Even primitive man, however, has some curiosity regarding the origins and reasons of things. Spontaneously attributing feelings and conscious purposes like his own to everything about him that attracts his attention by helping or hindering his pursuits (animatism and animism, s. 22), he naïvely answers his questions of how and why by stories of the acts of personal beings. Mythology is thus primitive man's philosophy. Another and perhaps more important source of mythology is ritual (s. 93), but many myths are clearly etiological.

Several types of etiological myth which are found the world over are exemplified in the Old Testament. Nature myths, explaining natural phenomena, are seen in the stories of creation (s. 39) and also in the simpler, more primitive instance of Gen. 3:14. Gen. 3:22–24 is a typical mortality myth, including a motive rare in Hebrew myths, though common elsewhere — the divine jealousy of man (cp. ch. 11:6). In fact, Gen., ch. 3, combines several mythological motives that were doubtless originally treated in separate stories. The keen psychological and spiritual insight of the story in its present form (s. 58) shows it to be a relatively late and sophisticated adaptation of the primitive myths on which it was based. Why clothing is worn, why man must work for a living, and why woman must suffer in childbirth, are some of the questions answered. Cult myths, explaining ritual practices, appear in the accounts of the origins of the Sabbath,[1] circumcision,[2] and the use of particular holy places and objects.[3] The story of the first Passover [4] may be largely a cult legend. Culture myths and legends, explaining phenomena of civilization, social institutions, and ethnic or national conditions and relations, are preserved or reflected in Genesis.[5] The development and combination of all these elements with other legendary and historical material was due in part to delight in the story for its own sake.

Before the end of the Old Testament period, Greek thought was known to some extent in Palestine, but its influence is not yet apparent in any of the canonical writings (including Ecclesiastes). Greek influence is clearly evident in some of the Apocrypha, especially the Wisdom of Solomon. Philo not only interprets Genesis allegorically, but even denies the literal truth of some of the stories. On the whole, however, Jewish thought was still mythological rather than philosophical. The cosmological speculations in Enoch show keen curiosity, but the ideas are naïve and distinctly mythological in character.

Later Judaism and early Christianity on the whole took the mythological elements of the Old Testament quite literally. The extension of the conception of revelation from the laws and the words of the prophets to the narrative literature carried with it the belief that all these stories were inspired. Some of the rabbis apparently knew something of philosophy, but their literal acceptance of the Old Testament prevented them from discarding the ancient stories. There is no reason to doubt that Jesus accepted the Old Testament narratives without question, as did Paul and the whole early church.

Echoes of Platonic and Stoic thought may be heard in Paul's letters, but he could not have sympathized with Stoic pantheism and materialism. The Johannine idea of the Logos (ss. 28, 35) is likewise little more than an unphilosophical use of a current term as a point of contact. In Hebrews we find something resembling the Platonic conception of the world of ideas, though not quite the same.[6]

---

[1] Gen. 2:3.
[2] Ch. 17:10 ff.
[3] Chs. 12:8; 28:10–22.
[4] Ex., ch. 12.
[5] Gen. 4:20–22; 9:20–27; 11:1–9; 25:22 f., 25, 27, 27–34.
[6] Heb. 8:1–5; 9:23 f.

The book of Revelation has a syncretistic background including mythological ideas, not all of which have been traced to their sources or perhaps even recognized yet. The thought of western Asia was still expressed in mythological rather than philosophical forms (cp. Gnosticism). Apocalyptic Judaism had affinities with this wider world of thought, and, in spite of the pervasive influence of the Old Testament, many items in Revelation were probably derived from the Gentile environment. Indeed, there may be more of such influence in the Old Testament itself than has been recognized, and orthodox editing may have eliminated still more of it.

In short, the revelation preserved in the Old Testament and the New Testament alike is presented throughout in terms of a prescientific, mythological world-view. This must be recognized in any attempt to understand and evaluate the religious ideas of the Bible. To prevent misunderstanding, it is also important that the sense in which we use the word " mythological " be clearly defined. In discussing Christological concepts (s. 35) we have used the term in one sense, as the equivalent of " personal " in contradistinction to " substantial " or " metaphysical " ideas. This use of the term has no implication of either primitiveness or falsehood: the " mythological " conception of the pre-existent, incarnate, and exalted Son of God may conceivably be not less but more true than the " metaphysical " idea of an impersonal divine hypostasis.

The sense in which we speak of the Hebrew and early Christian world-view as mythological is related to this but not quite the same. It involves the personal, even anthropomorphic element, treating as the acts of a personal being or beings what a scientific world-view sees as the operations of impersonal forces and laws. But for the modern man who accepts the scientific point of view a mythological conception in this sense is at the same time false, or at best only a poetic, figurative expression of truth. Much of ancient Hebrew and early Christian thought is obviously mythological in this sense. The mythological element must be distinguished and eliminated before we can accept whatever spiritual truth may be hidden behind it.

A third way of using the word " mythological " is now somewhat in vogue among theologians. It regards myth as a symbolic, approximate expression of truth which the human mind cannot perceive sharply and completely but can only glimpse vaguely, and therefore cannot adequately or accurately express. This meaning again overlaps those just stated but is not coextensive with either of them. It implies, not false-hood, but truth; not primitive, naïve misunderstanding, but an insight more profound than scientific description and logical analysis can ever achieve. The language of myth in this sense is consciously inadequate, being simply the nearest we can come to a formulation of what we see very darkly.

What was originally a myth in the sense of a primitive story, naïvely accepted as true though quite incompatible with what we now know, may nevertheless involve a true insight and be later accepted by theo-logians and philosophers as myth in the more sophisticated sense just indicated. Greek philosophy did just that with the ancient Greek myths, and modern theologians do it with the stories of the Bible. The pro-cedure is quite legitimate if both writers and readers understand what is being done. It has perhaps the further justification that we can never be sure just how literally primitive man himself meant his stories to be understood, or at just what point in the history of thought they began to be used as symbolic representations of dimly apprehended realities.

39. Creation, Flood, etc.: Cosmography

The considerations adduced in the foregoing section make it all the more important that we understand the world-view in terms of which the spiritual insights of the Bible are expressed. The distinction between the intellectual and cultural framework and the real content and con-cern of revelation has been brought out in s. 17. By means of this dis-tinction we are able to hold fast the treasure while discarding the earthen vessel in which it is contained. But, to change the figure, we cannot translate the divine message into our own language until we know the vocabulary and syntax of the language in which it has come to us.

The Old Testament preserves two distinct creation myths, with ech-oes of a third. The P account [1] presents a clear cosmogony implying def-inite ideas of the nature of the world and rather advanced theological conceptions. The order of creation (marine life first, then vegetable, an-imal, and, finally, human life) is notably like that conceived by modern biology, but this is not to be taken as showing that the Almighty in dic-tating an account of his own work came remarkably near the truth (Goldwin Smith). There are striking parallels with Babylonian crea-tion myths, and some with Egyptian myths, but the polytheism, anthro-

[1] Gen. 1:1 to 2:4a.

pomorphism, and exuberant mythological features of the Babylonian accounts are conspicuously absent. In the framework of an ancient myth, inherited from the proto-Semitic ancestors of both Hebrews and Babylonians and handed down in somewhat different forms among the two peoples, P expresses a profound conception of God's relation to the world and to man, of the unity of mankind, and of man's responsibility to God. In this religious teaching Christian faith finds a revelation of truth, to be reformulated in terms of modern knowledge but by no means invalidated by it.

The J story of creation [2] is simpler in style, more naïve in conception, more characteristically Israelite, and undoubtedly more primitive than the P account. It shows no such close relation to known myths of other peoples. In the order of creation and the conception of the first state of the world (earth dry, mist necessary to make life possible, man created first, then the garden, then animals, and woman last) it is quite incompatible with the other story. It is equally incompatible with modern science. The essential religious teaching, however, is the same as that of P. The preservation of the two accounts side by side shows that the editors of Genesis were not concerned with the differences in process, but with the religious conceptions of ultimate origin and purpose which were common to both.

The third way in which the creation was thought of by the Hebrews and other peoples was the myth of the primeval conflict between God and the dragon of chaos. While known from Babylonian and Canaanite sources, this myth is only echoed in the Old Testament by occasional literary allusions. The Hebrew word for the abyss, *tehom*,[3] corresponds etymologically to the Babylonian name of the primeval monster, *Tiamat*, but in this case the original idea has entirely disappeared. Not so with Rahab [4] and Leviathan.[5] Apparently the attitude of the later Old Testament writers to this myth was like that of Christian poets to pagan mythology.

Accepting the Old Testament stories without apparent consciousness of their discrepancies, the rabbis of postbiblical times discussed the question whether the creation was *ex nihilo,* and decided in the affirmative. Hellenistic Judaism, under Platonic influence, thought of a spir-

[2] Gen. 2:4b–25.
[3] Gen. 1:2.
[4] Ps. 89:10; Is. 51:9.
[5] Ps. 74:14; Is. 27:1 — the latter has a close parallel in a mythological text from Ras Shamrah.

itual creation preceding the material creation. Jesus and the early
church undoubtedly accepted the creation stories without question.
Passing references to the creation appear in Mk. 13:19; Rom. 1:20;
2 P. 3:4.[5a]

In the account of the flood we have again two distinct stories, but in
this case the editor found it possible to weave them together, although
the result involves strange discrepancies. As in the P account of creation, there is striking similarity in general outline and in many details
between the Hebrew and Babylonian flood stories, together with great
differences in the theological presuppositions and implications. Fundamentalists have recently made much of supposed archaeological demonstrations of the historicity of the flood, but the evidence does not
stand examination. The flood story is not history but myth. For Old
Testament theology the main point in it is the promise that it will not
be repeated. Hellenistic Judaism used the story of the flood as a redemption myth comparable to the myths of the mystery cults. In the New
Testament it is used as a warning of divine judgment.[6] Noah is also one
of the examples of faith cited in Heb., ch. 11. In 1 P. 3:20 f. the flood
is a type of baptism. It has no theological significance for Christian
faith today aside from the fact that the world depends upon God for its
existence and is subject to his judgment.

The story of the sons of God and the daughters of men [7] is a frag-
ment of very primitive mythology, doubtless going back to a polytheistic stage of proto-Hebrew or Canaanite religion. Why it was preserved
by the editors of the Pentateuch is not apparent. Since it stood in the
Torah and met a theological need, it was much used in postbiblical Judaism to explain the origin of the demons and of sin. The New Testament nowhere refers to it.

Gen., ch. 1, pictures the earth as a flat disk, surrounded by a river,
with a " firmament " shutting out the waters above it except when the
windows of heaven are opened, and with waters below the earth which
cause floods when the " fountains of the great deep " are unstopped.[8]
Job 9:6 mentions the pillars of the earth; ch. 26:11, the pillars of
heaven. In Is. 40:22 the earth is a circle, but in ch. 11:12 it has corners
(literally, " wings ") — the same word is translated " uttermost part "
in Is. 24:16 and " end[s] " in Job 37:3; 38:13.

5a On the agency of Christ in creation, cp. s. 35.
6 Mt. 24:37 f.; Lk. 17:26 f.; 2 P. 2:5; 3:5 f.
7 Gen. 6:1-4.
8 Cp. chs. 7:11; 8:2.

The recesses [9] of the north [10] recall the Canaanite conception of the dwelling of the gods in the north. Like the echoes of Canaanite mythology mentioned above, the references to this idea may be mere literary allusions without any theological implications for the Hebrew writers.

A common idea in later Judaism was the series of heavens. Paul speaks of being caught up into the third heaven,[11] which in rabbinic theology was the dwelling of God. Generally, however, the New Testament like the Old has only heaven (literally, " the heavens ") in contrast to the earth. The underworld as the abode of the dead will be considered in s. 65.

In general the cosmography of both Old and New Testaments remained popular rather than philosophical. With some notable exceptions, it was naïvely anthropocentric (s. 48). It was always geocentric. The loss of this geocentric point of view is one important aspect of the problem that modern science has created for religious faith. Since the primary concern of religion, however, is the relation between God and man, faith need not be overconcerned with such other worlds and beings as may exist beyond our ken. If science should ever discover other inhabited worlds than ours, with beings capable of fellowship with us and communion with God, religion will then properly be concerned with them. Meanwhile we have more than enough to do in bringing our own world into obedience to Christ. In any case, relative size and position do not affect the importance of man in God's sight. Value cannot be determined by merely spatial considerations. In short, for most of the practical purposes of religion the geocentric, anthropocentric point of view of the Bible is still adequate. On the other hand, our enlarged ideas of the universe add new force to the wondering awe of Ps. 8.

40. Angels

Belief in angels is a part of the prescientific, mythological world-view of the Bible. The earliest form of the belief found in the Old Testament is evidently a survival of primitive animism and polytheism. The polytheistic background is still apparent in the " sons of God " or " sons of gods " mentioned several times.[1] In the Ras Shamrah texts the gods are called " sons of gods," and Ps. 29 is probably an Israelite adaptation of a Canaanite hymn.

[9] A.S.V., " uttermost parts "; A.V. translates variously.
[10] Ps. 48:2; Is. 14:13; Ezek. 38:6, 15; 39:2.
[11] 2 Cor. 12:2.
[1] Gen. 6:1-4; Ps. 29:1; Job 1:6; 2:1; 38:7; cp. the " host of heaven " in 1 K. 22:19.

Our word " angel " comes from the Greek word for " messenger," which is used in the Septuagint to translate a Hebrew noun meaning both " messenger " and " angel " (it appears in both senses in 2 K. 1:3). In other words, the Bible has no special word to designate angels but uses in both Old and New Testaments the common Hebrew or Greek word for a messenger. To bring this out, we shall here use the word " messenger " throughout the discussion of this topic. Sometimes it is actually impossible to tell whether a human or a superhuman messenger of God is meant.[2] In Hg. 1:13 the prophet is called Yahweh's messenger; cp. Is. 42:19 (of the Servant, s. 30, thought of as a prophet); 44:26. The herald of Yahweh's advent in Mal. 3:1 may be a prophet, since the name Malachi is the Hebrew for " my messenger " as used in this verse.[3]

The most common and characteristic use of the term in the earliest sources is as a designation of the theophanic messenger, who is practically interchangeable with Yahweh himself (s. 12). It is impossible to determine from the Hebrew text whether one special messenger having this function is meant, or whether any messenger may be sent for this purpose. In Gen., chs. 18 f., we find Yahweh himself,[4] three men,[5] the men and Yahweh,[6] two messengers,[7] and again the men;[8] note also Gen. 32:23–32 and Ho. 12:3 f. The common assumption that the messenger of Yahweh is introduced to avoid anthropomorphism (s. 12) hardly fits Gen., chs. 18 f., or the other anthropomorphic passages in J. Either J itself combines earlier and later sources, or the writer was inconsistent, being hardly conscious of any distinction between the appearance of a messenger of Yahweh and an appearance of Yahweh himself in human form. This is in accord with the early Semitic idea that one who sent a messenger was personally present in the messenger and his words. In some places God is so far identified with a human messenger that the reference of the personal pronoun shifts imperceptibly from the speaker to God himself.[9]

The (or a) messenger of Yahweh was thought of as a paragon of wisdom and goodness.[10] Yet even the messengers are not infallible.[11] In 2 S. 24:16 f. (cp. 2 K. 19:35) the (or a) messenger of Yahweh appears as his agent, inflicting disease on men.

While the increasing sense of the transcendence of God after the ex-

---

2 Ju. 2:1; cp. the prophet of ch. 6:8.
3 This word is not used in Ps. 8:5; cp. A.S.V.
4 Gen. 18:1, 13, 33.
5 Ch. 18:2.
6 Ch. 18:16 ff., 22 ff.

7 Ch. 19:1, 15.
8 Ch. 19:10, 12, 16.
9 Dt. 29:2–6; Jer. 9:2 f.
10 1 S. 29:9; 2 S. 14:17; 19:27.
11 Job 4:18.

ile might lead us to expect to find the theophanic messenger prominent in D and P, the idea does not appear in these sources; note, however, the " messenger of his face " in Is. 63:9, and the " messenger of the covenant " in Mal. 3:1. In the heavenly judgment scene of Zc., ch. 3, the (a) messenger of Yahweh appears as the opponent of the *satan* (s. 41). Zc., chs. 1 to 8, also presents for the first time what becomes characteristic of the later apocalyptic literature — the idea of a messenger who explains the visions to the seer (s. 12). In Ezekiel and Daniel this figure is simply called a man. Gen. 48:15 f. suggests the idea of a special guardian messenger.

In addition to such references to a single messenger the word appears sometimes in the plural. Jacob sees messengers of God on the ladder at Bethel [12] and is met by messengers of God at the place he names Mahanaim, saying, " This is God's host." [13] The messengers are charged with the care of the righteous, encamp round about them and chase their enemies.[14] Sometimes [15] the term is applied to divine messengers and agents in general.

The myth of the fallen angels, prominent in later Jewish and Christian theology, does not appear in the Old Testament, though when it arose it could attach itself to Is. 14:12, a reflection of a Canaanite myth that may actually have been the prototype of the Jewish idea. In postbiblical Judaism the fall of Satan and his angels was one of the two favorite explanations of the origin of the demons (the other being Gen. 6:1–4). References to the devil and his angels in the gospels, and to angels as possibly hostile to the Christian in Rom. 8:38, may allude to this idea; cp. also the obscure reference in 1 Cor. 11:10 and the messenger of Satan in 2 Cor. 12:7.

Two new developments in angelology appear in Daniel: individual divine messengers with personal names, in particular Gabriel [16] and Michael,[17] and heavenly " princes " of particular nations.[18] Many commentators hold that the " one like a son of man " in ch. 7:13 ff. (s. 32) was such a heavenly being.

Postbiblical sources show an exuberant growth of angelology. 1 Enoch speaks of spirits, sons of God, watchers, holy ones,[19] and also of the seven archangels.[20] The part of Raphael in the story of Tobit illus-

[12] Gen. 28:12.
[13] Ch. 32:1 f.; cp. Josh. 5:13–15; 1 K. 22:19.
[14] Ps. 34:7; 35:5 f.; 91:11.
[15] Job 33:23; Ps. 78:49; 104:4.
[16] Dan. 8:16; 9:21.

[17] Chs. 10:13, 21; 12:1.
[18] Chs. 10:13, 20 f.; 12:1.
[19] Cp. Dan. 4:13, 23.
[20] 1 Enoch 20; 81:5; 90:21 f.

trates popular views. Angelic beings appear also in Bel and the Dragon, Susanna, and 2 Maccabees. According to Acts 23:8 the Pharisees believed in both angel and spirit (as well as the resurrection), the Sadducees in neither. Josephus says that the Essenes had secret names for the messengers. Philo identifies the Old Testament messengers with the Greek heroes. Enoch and the rabbinic literature say the messengers are made of fire and do not eat, drink, or multiply. Philo says they are incorporeal. Various types and categories, based in part on Old Testament ideas (cp. s. 42), appear in these sources, but the chief occupation of the messengers is praising God. Enoch ascribes the operations of the heavenly bodies and winds to such beings. They are connected also with judgment, with recording men's deeds, with guarding men, and, in short, with all God's activities in the world. Michael is their chief; prominent also are Gabriel, Raphael, and others (a striking number have the old type of Semitic name formed with -el).

Jesus apparently accepted the current beliefs on this subject, but made little use of them. In the resurrection (s. 69) the righteous will be like the messengers in heaven.[21] There is joy in the presence of God's messengers when a sinner repents.[22] Lazarus was carried by the messengers into Abraham's bosom, in accordance with Jewish belief.[23] In his last need Jesus could have prayed, and the Father would have sent legions of messengers.[24] The messengers are mentioned especially in connection with the parousia and judgment (ss. 67, 70).[25]

Numerous references in Acts indicate that Jewish beliefs were carried over by the early church.[26] Acts 12:15 suggests the idea of the spirit double, which may be the meaning of ch. 23:8; cp. the puzzling reference to the heavenly messengers of the little ones in Mt. 18:10. Paul too retains current ideas. In addition to general references,[27] we may note the connection with the parousia, as in the sayings of Jesus,[28] the new idea that believers shall judge the messengers,[29] a curious reference in connection with the veiling of women,[30] and the retention of the Jew-

---

[21] Mk. 12:25.
[22] Lk. 15:10; cp. v. 7.
[23] Lk. 16:22.
[24] Mt. 26:53; cp. Lk. 22:43.
[25] Mk. 8:38, and parallels.
[26] Acts 5:19; 6:15; 7:30, 35, 38, 53; 8:26; 10:3, 22; 11:13; 12:7–11, 23.
[27] 1 Cor. 4:9; 13:1; 2 Cor. 11:14; Gal. 1:8; 4:14.
[28] 1 Th. 4:16; 2 Th. 1:7.
[29] 1 Cor. 6:3.
[30] 1 Cor. 11:10.

ish idea that the law was given by the mediation of messengers.[31] Col.
2:18 attacks angelolatry.[32] There are few references to this subject in
the gospel of John,[33] and none in the Johannine epistles. Abundant references in the synoptic gospels correspond to popular conceptions of
the time, as in the infancy stories of Matthew and Luke, the angelic
ministrations to Jesus at his temptation [34] and in Gethsemane,[35] and the
appearances at the tomb of Jesus.[36] Matthew's explanations of the parables of the tares and the dragnet [37] carry on the tradition of the eschatological function of the messengers, which is highly developed in Revelation.[38] Revelation by a messenger of Jesus is claimed in Rev. 1:1. A
peculiar and obscure idea is that of the messengers of the seven churches
in chs. 1:20 and 2 f.; commentators differ on the meaning, some thinking that the local bishop is referred to, others that each church is
thought to have a personified heavenly double (cp. the " one like a son
of man " and the " princes " of the nations in Daniel).

A distinctive use of angelology appears in Heb. 1:4 to 2:16, as part of
the argument for the superiority of Christ; there are also more general
references in chs. 12:22 and 13:2, the latter perhaps referring to Gen.,
ch. 18. Unimportant references occur in 1 Peter and 1 Timothy. An obscure allusion in 2 P. 2:11 finds its explanation in the parallel passage,
Jude 9, which refers to the pseudepigraphic Assumption of Moses. The
idea of fallen angels (s. 39) appears in Jude 6 (2 P. 2:4); cp. Mt. 25:41.
Nowhere in the New Testament are the current ideas questioned; they
recur most frequently and specifically in the latest books.

Whether the belief in angels is to be regarded merely as an element
in the outmoded world-view of biblical times, or whether it still has
some validity, is a question on which intelligent people may differ. It
cannot be said that we know there are no such superhuman personal beings in the universe, though it must be admitted that we have no evidence of their existence. On the whole it seems best to regard the idea of
such divine messengers as a part of the ancient mythological framework
of biblical religion which we have discarded. A legitimate reinterpreta-

[31] Gal. 3:19; cp. Acts 7:53; Heb. 2:2.
[32] On Rom. 8:38 cp. s. 42.
[33] Jn. 1:51; 5:4; 12:29; 20:12.
[34] Mk. 1:13.
[35] Lk. 22:43.
[36] Mk. 16:4 f.; Mt. 28:2–7; Lk. 24:2–7, 23.
[37] Mt. 13:39, 41, 49.
[38] Rev. 3:5; 12; and throughout in the visions.

tion of the belief is suggested by Ps. 104:4: [39] the forces of nature are God's messengers and servants. As a part of the language of worship the angels may at least symbolize the transcendent majesty of God, and also remind us that there is still much we do not know about the universe. Otherwise the angels no longer serve any vital religious purpose, and Christian faith actually makes little use of them.

41. *Demons; Satan*

What has just been said about angels applies also to their evil counterpart, the demons. Primitive animism left a deposit of ideas regarding malignant spirits. The Old Testament is remarkably free from such ideas, perhaps because the records were edited by advanced theologians who allowed only occasional fragments of early conceptions to slip through their fingers as parts of stories that were preserved for the sake of higher spiritual values. The Hebrew word translated " demons " (A.V., " devils ") occurs only in two passages, both poetic and both referring to pagan deities.[1] Another word rendered " devils " in the Authorized Version is translated " he-goats " (mg., " satyrs ") in the American Standard Version; it too occurs only twice [2] and refers to pagan deities. Several words regarded by some scholars as indicating types of demons more probably refer to the animals and birds that haunt ruins and desolate places (jackals, wolves, owls, etc.). Lilith (A.S.V., " night-monster ") in Is. 34:11–15 was doubtless a female demon, as in Assyrian sources and late Jewish legends. In Lev. 16:8, 10, 26, Azazel (A.V., " scapegoat ") probably was a demon of the wilderness who had to be propitiated; in Enoch the name is used for Satan.

Like angelology, demonology flourished in later Judaism. The demons are called also unclean spirits and evil spirits, as in the gospels. The rabbinic sources call them " workers of evil." Their origin is discussed and explained in two ways: by the story of Gen. 6:1–4 and by the myth of the fall of Satan and his angels (ss. 39 f.). God did not create evil; the demons were free creatures who rebelled against his will. Common belief regarded the demons as very numerous, filling all space, causing disease, teaching evil, and tempting men to sin. The demon Asmodeus in Tobit illustrates the abundant folklore on this subject.

In the synoptic gospels demons play an extremely prominent role, and there is no reason to doubt that Jesus himself believed in their reality

---

[39] Cp. Heb. 1:7.   [1] Dt. 32:17; Ps. 106:37.   [2] Lev. 17:7; 2 Chr. 11:15.

and took them seriously. Like both Jews and Gentiles of his time, he regarded such afflictions as epilepsy and insanity, if not ordinary sickness, as the work of demons; hence, healing meant exorcism. In his work and the work of his disciples, casting out demons was as important as preaching.[3] (For the significance of Jesus' miracles see ss. 43, 64, 103.)

Exorcism undoubtedly continued to be an important part of the work of the early church.[4] Paul mentions demons only in 1 Cor. 10:20 f. in connection with pagan sacrifice, though the gift of healing [5] probably included exorcism. The fourth gospel does not represent Jesus' miracles as acts of exorcism, but mentions demons only in the charge of Jesus' adversaries that he has a demon.[6] The synoptic evangelists, however, reflecting the characteristic craving of the Hellenistic world for the marvelous, glory in the stories of exorcism. Demons are mentioned more or less incidentally in other parts of the New Testament.[7]

The word *satan* is a Hebrew common noun meaning " adversary." It is commonly used in this sense in the Old Testament with reference to both human and superhuman adversaries.[8] The earliest use of the word as the title of a particular supernatural being is in Zc. 3:1 f., not as a proper name, but with the definite article: the high priest Joshua is placed on trial, being prosecuted by " the adversary," but acquitted by Yahweh (or his messenger). Both the noun and its cognate verb are here used: the adversary (*satan*) stands at Joshua's right hand to be his adversary (*le-sitno*). So in Ps. 109:4 the psalmist complains that slanderers are his adversaries (*yistenuni*), and in v. 6 one of them calls for an adversary (*satan*) to stand at his right hand. Apparently in Hebrew legal procedure the plaintiff and defendant stood together before the judge, with the former at the right of the latter. In Zc., ch. 3, the adversary is rebuked for his charge against Joshua, but he is not regarded as hostile to God.

A similar scene is presented in Job 1:6–12 and 2:1–7. Here " the adversary " (still with the definite article) appears at the heavenly court among the " sons of God." This time he is not only a plaintiff or prosecutor but an inspector who makes his rounds on earth and reports in

---

[3] Mk. 1:32–34; 3:14 f.; but cp. ch. 1:38.
[4] Acts 5:16; 8:7; 16:16–18; 19:11–20.
[5] 1 Cor. 12:9, 28, 30.
[6] Jn. 7:20; 8:48 f., 52; 10:20 f.
[7] Rev. 16:13; 18:2; Jas. 2:19; 1 Tim. 4:1.
[8] Num. 22:22; 1 S. 29:4.

heaven the evil deeds of men. Unable to charge Job with sin, he accuses him of selfish motives. He is not simply rebuked but is allowed to put his claim to the test by afflicting Job. From this point he drops out of sight, since the poet has no further use for him, though the original folk story may have had another heavenly scene in which the adversary was condemned for making a charge he could not sustain.

While the *satan* of Job tries to provoke him to blasphemy, the idea of direct instigation to sin appears first in 1 Chr. 21:1. In 2 S., ch. 24, Yahweh himself moves David to take a census, but in this account the temptation comes from another who is called *satan*. Whether the absence of the definite article here means that the word has now become a proper name, or whether we should translate " an adversary " (A.S.V., mg.) cannot be determined. In either case, the change from 2 S., ch. 24, indicates a theological development which made it impossible to suppose that God would tempt David to sin and then punish him for it. The influence of Zoroastrianism, if its dualism of Ahura Mazda and Angra Mainyu had developed by that time, may have been a factor in the development in Judaism.

In postbiblical Judaism Satan plays a very important part as the head of the powers of evil. In Enoch the word *satan* is clearly a proper name, designating the head of a highly developed hierarchy of demons. Other names also are used for him in Enoch and the other pseudepigrapha. He is called Belial (an Old Testament expression meaning " worthlessness "), Beelzebul or Beelzebub (in 2 K. 1:2 the name of the god of Ekron), Azazel (*v.s.*), *et al.* He is represented as an angel, originally good but fallen, the enemy of man, whom he seeks to destroy by attacking the body with disease and the soul with temptation. Identified with the serpent of Gen., ch. 3 (where no such idea is intended), he is held responsible for the sin of Adam and so for the fact of death.[9]

In the New Testament, Satan appears first in the temptation of Jesus.[10] In Mark and Matthew he is called Satan; in Matthew and Luke, " the devil " and " the tempter." Later on, Jesus' opponents charge that he casts out demons by Beelzebul,[11] the prince of the demons.[12] Jesus replies that Satan's kingdom is in that case divided and therefore doomed (cp. s. 64). The coming of the kingdom of God will be the end

9 W.S. 2:24.
10 Mk. 1:12 f.; Mt. 4:1–11; Lk. 4:1–13.
11 So the Greek.
12 Mk. 3:22 ff., and parallels.

of the kingdom of Satan.[13] In Lk. 10:17–20 Jesus sees Satan fallen as lightning from heaven.[14] Confidently expecting the end of Satan's power, Jesus was undismayed in the face of demonic activity.[15]

Other references are of less significance. In Mk. 8:33 Jesus calls Peter " Satan," evidently meaning tempter (unless the Aramaic noun was used in the original sense of " adversary " without reference to Satan). In Lk. 22:31, which may not be authentic, Jesus says that Satan has asked for Peter to sift him like wheat. In Mt. 13:19 (probably secondary) Satan is called " the evil one." [16] In other places it is impossible to tell whether the same Greek words mean " the evil one " or " evil." [17] In Mt. 5:39 the meaning must be either " evil " or " the evil man."

No change of idea in the early church is apparent. Temptation is ascribed to Satan in Acts 5:3; in ch. 10:38 the sick whom Jesus healed are said to have been " oppressed of the devil." [18] Paul frequently speaks of Satan by name and also by other current designations (evil one, tempter, destroyer, snake, Belial, the god of this age), attributing to him temptation [19] and perhaps physical ills.[20] In the gospel of John he is sometimes called the ruler of this world.[21] Revelation speaks of him often under various appellations, including along with those already mentioned the dragon, the old serpent, Abaddon and Apollyon (the Hebrew and Greek for " destruction "), and the angel of the abyss who is king of the locusts. His expulsion from heaven and warfare with God's angelic host are told in ch. 12. Chapter 20 tells of his being bound during the millennium, loosed after it for the warfare of Gog and Magog, and finally cast into the lake of fire and brimstone for eternal torment (ss. 66–70).

Thus, having once emerged, the conception of a personal devil retained its prominence both in Judaism and in the religion of the New Testament. However unacceptable to the modern mind, the idea met a religious need, representing at least a realistic recognition of evil in the

[13] Cp. Mk. 1:15 and the saying at the end of Mark in the Freer ms., " Fulfilled is the limit of the years of the authority of Satan."

[14] Cp. Is. 14:12.

[15] See further s. 64.

[16] So also Eph. 6:16; 1 Jn. 2:13 f.; 3:12; 5:18 f.

[17] Mt. 5:37; 6:13; so also Jn. 17:15; 2 Th. 3:3.

[18] For the designation " the devil," cp. Eph. 4:27; 6:11; Jn. 8:44; 13:2; 1 Jn. 3:8, 10; Heb. 2:14; 1 P. 5:8; Jas. 4:7; Jude 9; and often in Revelation and the pastoral epistles.

[19] 2 Cor. 2:11.

[20] 1 Cor. 5:5; 2 Cor. 12:7.

[21] Jn. 12:31; 14:30; 16:11.

world and in man himself. Used frankly as mythological, the figure of Satan may still serve to symbolize everything in the universe that is contrary to God's will and therefore to be fought by the Christian.

42. *Other Spiritual Beings*

The world-view which embraced angelology and demonology made room also for other beings, some of them doubtless survivals from animism or polytheism and others creatures of the imagination of later times. Their nature and role are sometimes obscure. Devoid of religious significance for modern theology, they are treated here as a part of the world of thought which must be understood if the Bible is to be interpreted rightly.

Gen. 3:24 tells of God's placing the cherubim at the entrance of Eden to guard the tree of life. This recalls the common practice in Egypt and western Asia of placing images of demonic beings as guards before temples and palaces. Ezek. 28:13 f. has an obscure reference to Eden and the cherub. The cherubim flanking the ark in the tabernacle and temple doubtless represented the same kind of creature referred to in these passages.[1] The cherub on which the Glory of Yahweh rested in the temple is mentioned in Ezek. 9:3. Ezekiel's plan for the new temple has no cherubim for the ark, which had been destroyed, but cherubim are to be carved on the walls.[2]

The idea that must lie back of this symbolism is that of other passages that represent Yahweh as sitting or riding on (A.V., dwelling between) the cherubim, or as being borne by them in his chariot.[3] The conception is similar to that of the living creatures of Ezekiel;[4] in fact Ezek. 11:22 suggests a connection with the cherubim of the temple. The original nature of the cherubim, however, is hardly to be deduced from Ezekiel's elaborate but confusing descriptions. Comparative archaeological materials indicate that the cherub was probably a composite being like the sphinx or griffin.

Later Judaism took the cherubim as a special category of angels. The

---

[1] Ex. 25:18–22; 37:7–9; Num. 7:89 describe the cherubim of the tabernacle; cp. the cherubim woven into the curtains and veils, Ex. 26:1, 31; 36:8, 35. The somewhat different cherubim of the temple are described in 1 K. 6:23–28; 8:6 f. (2 Chr. 3:10–13; 5:7 f.); cp. those woven into the veil and carved on the walls and doors and the bronze lavers (1 K. 6:29–35; 7:29–36; 2 Chr. 3:7, 14).

[2] Ezek. 41:18–25.

[3] 1 S. 4:4; 2 S. 6:2; 22:11; 2 K. 19:15; Ps. 18:10; 80:1; 99:1.

[4] Ezek. 1:5–28; 10:1–22; 11:22.

New Testament barely mentions them in Heb. 9:5, though Revelation has four living creatures obviously suggested by those of Ezekiel.[5] Aside from such use in apocalyptic imagery, the cherubim serve only to enhance the impression of awe and majesty in the presence of God. Since scientific description and philosophical analysis can never replace poetry as the language of religion, we can still profitably use in worship the passages referring to the cherubim.

The same may be said of the seraphim, now commonly grouped vaguely with the cherubim (as in the Te Deum) but mentioned in the Bible only in Is. 6:2 f. The Hebrew word is the one translated " fiery " in the story of the serpents in the wilderness.[6] In some obscure and remote way these creatures were probably derived from primitive serpent-worship, but their function in Is., ch. 6, is like that of the living creatures in Ezekiel. Like the cherubim, they are regarded in later Judaism as a particular class of angels.

References to good and evil spirits have been encountered in ss. 40 f. The Old Testament refers often to men and women described in the English versions as having " familiar spirits," the whole expression representing a single Hebrew word which might be translated " necromancer." In Is. 29:4 and perhaps in Lev. 20:27 this word appears to mean, not the necromancer, but his " control." Sometimes our English versions speak of " spirits " where the meaning is probably " winds," the ambiguity of the Greek and Hebrew words (s. 27) making a clear distinction impossible.[7]

In s. 28 the Hellenistic idea of " powers " has been noted. In Jewish sources and the New Testament this term and others are used for beings hardly distinguishable from angels or demons. In the New Testament they usually appear as hostile to the Christian. Rom. 8:38 names principalities and powers together with angels in such a connection; here height, depth, life, and death are probably not thought of as personal beings, though Gnosticism made such a use of the terms. In several New Testament passages it is uncertain whether such words as authority, dominion, principality, and the like are used as abstract nouns or as designations of spiritual beings.[8] The latter meaning is clear in some cases,[9] and therefore probable in others, though sometimes the

---

[5] Rev., chs. 4 to 7; 14:3; 15:7.
[6] Num., ch. 21; cp. 2 K. 18:4.
[7] Ps. 104:4 and Heb. 1:7, 14; Zc. 6:5; Rev. 1:4; 3:1; 4:5; 5:6.
[8] 1 Cor. 15:24; Col. 1:16; 2:10; Eph. 1:21; 1 P. 3:22.
[9] Eph. 3:10; 6:12.

apparent personification may be purely literary.[10] Paul's conception of
sin in Rom., ch. 7, and of vanity in ch. 8:20, should probably be regarded as abstractions rather than personifications.

The " elements " of Gal. 4:3, 9; Col. 2:8, 20, are the spirits believed
to rule and operate the heavenly bodies and other natural phenomena.[11]

43. Providence and Miracles

The historicity of the miracle stories has been discussed in s. 18.
Here we are concerned with the idea of the miraculous as a part of the
conception of the universe, the way in which the miracle stories were
accepted and understood by the Hebrews and early Christians. Just as
the origins of the universe were thought of in mythological terms, so
the operations of nature were conceived as the acts of personal beings
(s. 38). This continued to be true after the emergence of monotheism
and throughout biblical times. Jesus, like his Hebrew ancestors, spoke
and thought in simple, concrete terms (by no means a sign of lack of
intellectual ability). So also did Paul and all the writers of the New
Testament. In spite of contrary ideas among philosophers, popular
thought in the Hellenistic world was still largely mythological and an-
imistic, and the people to whom Paul preached were not philosophers.[1]

For the Old Testament, later Judaism, and the New Testament there
were innumerable good and evil beings in the universe (ss. 40–42), all
subject to the one God. The world was not a *kosmos* or " nature," but
" creation," made and directly ruled by God. There was conflict between the good and evil powers, the kingdom of God and the kingdom
of Satan.[2] In this conception of opposed empires of good and evil, basic
for the apocalyptic literature and shared by Jesus, Iranian influence is
probable. It was no real dualism, for the control was always in God's
hands and the outcome of the conflict certain (ss. 64, 73).

Since the conception of the universe was thus personal rather than
mechanical or abstract, the dominating idea was not natural law or force
but will — the will of God and the obedient or rebellious wills of his
creatures. In spite of increasing emphasis on the transcendence of God
in later Old Testament religion and postbiblical Judaism, his care for
his creatures and his immediate presence and activity in the world were

[10] Cp. Rev. 6:8; 20:13 f.
[11] In 2 P. 3:10 the same Greek word means the natural elements; in Heb. 5:12 it is
used of the rudiments of Christian truth.
[1] 1 Cor. 1:26.
[2] Mt. 12:25–28.

always maintained (s. 22). Jewish sources refer often to God's mercy in giving rain, for example. Of course, God's control of history involves direct action. The rabbis, even in stressing man's freedom (s. 76), insisted on God's sovereign control of the universe.

Jesus does not discuss such questions, but he too, while assuming human freedom, stresses the divine sovereignty (s. 23). He explicitly asserts direct providence.[3] That God answers prayer directly, which is either stated or assumed throughout the Old Testament and Jewish literature, is also confidently and repeatedly stated by Jesus.[4] Since God knows our needs, anxiety and long prayers are unnecessary.[5]

Providence involves miracles, at least in the sense of direct intervention by God in the ordinary course of events. For ancient thought, which has no conception of natural law and does not distinguish between ultimate and contingent causes, or between origin and process, a miracle is simply an unusually striking and significant exercise of the divine will which governs all things. The rabbis glory in the wonders done by God for the fathers. Josephus, telling the stories for sophisticated pagan readers, says apologetically, " I repeat what the Scriptures tell, which each one may think of as he wishes." In the ancient world miracles were expected of any great religious teacher, and legend attributed them to some of the rabbis as to great men of the Hellenistic world.

Jesus regarded his own works of exorcism as the work of the spirit of God.[6] A keen interest in the miraculous is evident in the synoptic gospels and Acts, reflecting the common attitude of the whole ancient world at that time. All this is simply a part of the prescientific world-view. It expresses the implications of theistic faith without critical analysis or any attempt at philosophical interpretation or justification. What we call the supernatural was normal from this point of view. Daily bread and other necessities — in fact, even the continuance of life and the existence of the universe — depended upon the continual exercise of God's will.[7] An ancient Jewish prayer says that God daily renews the work of Genesis.

The sharp contrast between this whole point of view and the world-view now prevalent, which is not so much an expression of scientific and philosophical theory as it is a result of our mechanical way of life, pro-

---

[3] Mt. 10:29 f.; Lk. 12:6 f.
[4] Mt. 7:7–11; Lk. 11:5–13; 18:1–8.
[5] Mt. 6:7 f., 25–32; Lk. 12:22–30.

[6] Mt. 12:28; Lk. 11:20.
[7] Ps. 104:24–30; 145:15 f.

duces a strain on Christian faith. Instead of being a support, miracles are now a major problem for faith in the religion of the Bible (s. 8). In this connection we may remind ourselves that revelation was impossible except in terms which had meaning for the recipients (s. 18). If the faith that is expressed in the Bible in terms of ancient conceptions has permanent validity, it is capable of translation into terms of our modern world-views, and must be so translated for the modern believer. Indeed, it can and must be repeatedly reformulated as our understanding of the universe is superseded by more adequate conceptions.

The basic issue for religious faith in this connection is whether the universe is governed by a personal God (s. 22), however the nature and process of the divine government may be conceived. If it is not, biblical religion is basically false. If it is, the intellectual problems involved in believing it may be a part of the secret things which belong to God.[8] They are subject to investigation, but faith and practice need not wait for a solution. It has been said that whether or not we believe the miracle-stories of the Bible, we constantly want miracles for ourselves. The Christian should not expect God to make exceptions for his benefit. But there are certainly miracles in the sense of especially significant events, and also in the sense of events not predictable by known causes and processes. It is not wise to set limits upon what God can or may do. A Christian's prayer is always, " If it be possible, . . . nevertheless, not as I will but as thou wilt." [9]

[8] Dt. 29:29.   [9] Mt. 26:39.

VI

MAN

44. *Flesh and Body*

The central biblical conceptions of sin and salvation are presented in the framework of an ancient idea of human nature, and in words whose connotations are sometimes quite different from what they suggest to us. The characteristic Hebrew view of human nature regards man as a living body with various qualities, but with no sharp division between body and soul. The later Greek idea of the body as mortal and the soul as immortal is foreign to early Hebrew thought, though a kind of personal survival after the destruction of the body was always taken for granted (s. 65).

The word meaning literally " flesh " is often used for mankind or human nature in general. In Gen. 2:24 " one flesh " means practically " one person." The idea of all mankind is expressed by " all flesh " (cp. our " everybody "); " no flesh " means " nobody." These usages carry over also in later Jewish and Christian writings.[1] Sometimes human as against divine powers or agencies are designated as " flesh and blood." [2] In such connections flesh as human is contrasted with spirit as divine.[3]

The New Testament also uses " flesh " to designate the physical as against the spiritual nature of man, or rather the lower as against the higher nature. So Mk. 14:38, and, especially, Paul. Since this lower nature is to Paul wholly evil and dominated by sin (s. 57), he calls unregenerate men " carnal " and contrasts walking according to the flesh with walking according to the Spirit.[4] Being in the flesh is the opposite of being in the Spirit.[5] Spirit and flesh are at war, and the works of the flesh are the opposite of the fruits of the Spirit.[6] The Christian has crucified the flesh.[7] Paul uses also the term " members " for this lower nature.

---

[1] Cp. Mk. 13:20.
[2] Mt. 16:17; Gal. 1:16; Eph. 6:12.
[3] Is. 31:3.
[4] Rom. 8:4 ff., 12 f.; 2 Cor. 10:2.

[5] Rom. 7:5; 8:9.
[6] Gal. 5:17, 19.
[7] V. 24.

Paul's idea is not that the material body as such is evil. He can also speak of living in the flesh in the common sense of remaining physically alive even when wholly controlled by Christ.[8] Evil thoughts and attitudes are included in what Paul means by the " flesh " in the special, quasi-technical sense; but the flesh is not necessarily defiled, nor the spirit undefiled, for Paul can urge his followers to cleanse themselves from every defilement of flesh and spirit.[9]

John uses the term " flesh " in the Old Testament manner.[10] In Jn. 1:14 " became flesh " means " became man " (i.e., assumed human nature). In ch. 6:51, however, " flesh " means " body." [11] Sometimes the word indicates outer form and appearance as against inner reality and meaning.[12] Elsewhere it means, as with Paul, the earthly, natural side of man, not necessarily but usually with the connotation of sinfulness,[13] though John's usage, more than Paul's, implies something of the Hellenistic dualism of matter and spirit, world and God, and even a rather ascetic attitude (s. 104). The remaining books of the New Testament add nothing distinctive or new in this connection.

Both Hebrew and Greek have words meaning " body," but use them much less frequently than " flesh " and usually with reference to dead bodies.[14] Paul uses " body " in the same way as "flesh," and also in the ordinary sense with no implication of corruption or sinfulness, even telling the Corinthians that their bodies are to be honored as members of Christ and temples of the Holy Spirit.[15] In this literal sense he speaks of the body as the " outer man." [16] How far he is from ascetic dualism in all this is shown by the fact that even in the future life the Christian will have a body, albeit a spiritual one,[17] not subject to the mortality of the flesh (s. 69).

45. Soul

Traditional Christianity has always been concerned with the salvation of the soul, but in the Bible the Hebrew and Greek words translated " soul " have by no means the same associations and implications

[8] Gal. 2:20; cp. Phil. 1:22–24, also 2 Cor. 7:5.
[9] 2 Cor. 7:1.
[10] Jn. 17:2.
[11] Cp. Mk. 14:22; Mt. 26:26; Lk. 22:19; 1 Cor. 11:24.
[12] Jn. 6:63; 8:15.
[13] Jn. 1:13; 3:5 f.; 1 Jn. 2:16 f.
[14] Is. 66:24; Mt. 5:29 f. (cp. 18:8 f.; Mk. 9:43–48); 10:28; Lk. 12:4 f.
[15] 1 Cor. 6:15, 19.
[16] 2 Cor. 4:16.
[17] 1 Cor., ch. 15.

as the English word. To remove current misunderstandings it is necessary to consider in some detail the usage of these terms, and since they are not uniformly translated we must consider the original Greek and Hebrew words. The Hebrew noun is *nephesh;* the corresponding Greek word in the Septuagint and the New Testament is *psyche.*

a. *Nephesh* means primarily " breath." It is so translated in Job 41:21, where it refers to the breath of a crocodile. The cognate verb is used in the sense " take breath, be refreshed." [1]

b. *Nephesh* is often used also with the meaning " living being," human or otherwise. In Gen. 2:7 the first man became a living *nephesh* when Yahweh's breath (a different word) was breathed into his nostrils. V. 19 applies the same expression to the animals.[2] Everywhere but in Gen. 2:7, in fact, the expression refers to the subhuman creatures. Paul, using, of course, the Greek word *psyche,* quotes Gen. 2:7 in 1 Cor. 15:45, contrasting Adam as a " living soul " with Christ as " life-giving spirit." Elsewhere, however, the Greek word is not applied to other than human beings except in Rev. 16:3, where the Hebrew expression of Genesis is translated literally.

c. Both *nephesh* and *psyche* frequently mean simply " life " and are so translated. There are other words for life in the abstract in both Greek and Hebrew, but *nephesh* and *psyche* are used for the life of a particular person or animal.[3] This usage is important as background for interpreting some passages where the meaning is not immediately clear.

d. Frequently the best translation of the Hebrew or Greek word is " person." The Hebrew word is sometimes so translated,[4] and might well be so rendered in other places also.[5] In H and P it is even used for a dead person.[6] The Greek word also often means " person," though it is not actually so translated in the English versions.[7] The Hebrew word is used regularly with this meaning in enumerations; [8] *psyche* also is

---

[1] Ex. 23:12; 31:17; 2 S. 16:14.

[2] Translated " living creatures " here and in chs. 1:20, 21, 24; 9:10, 12, 15 f., but simply " life " in 1:30.

[3] For *nephesh* see Gen. 9:5; 19:17, 19; 32:30; 45:5; Ex. 4:19; 21:23; Num. 35:31; Ju. 12:3; Job 2:4, 6; 6:11; Prov. 12:10; for *psyche* see Mt. 2:20; 6:25; Mk. 3:4; 10:45; Jn. 10:11, 15, 17; 13:37; 15:13; 1 Jn. 3:16; Acts 20:10, 24; 27:22; Rom. 11:3; 16:4; Phil. 2:30; Rev. 8:9.

[4] Gen. 14:21; 36:6, A.V.; Num. 5:6, A.V.; 31:19; 35:15, 30; Dt. 27:25; Jer. 43:6; Ezek. 16:5; 33:6.

[5] Prov. 19:15.

[6] Num. 6:6.

[7] Acts 3:23, quoting Dt. 18:19 (Acts 2:43 is not so clear a case) ; also Rom. 13:1.

[8] Ex. 16:16; 1 Chr. 5:21.

used in enumerations,[9] just as we speak of a ship as having so and so many " souls " on board. Rev. 18:13 refers to slaves as " bodies and souls of men."

e. Closely related to the meanings " life " and " person " is the meaning " self." Thus " my soul " often means I, me, myself, etc.[10] The meaning " self " is not always clearly distinguishable from the meaning " person," especially as the writers were hardly aware of a difference. The meaning " self " appears commonly in the use of " my soul," " your soul," etc., instead of a reflexive pronoun. Sometimes *nephesh*, when used this way, is translated by a reflexive pronoun,[11] and sometimes it should be so translated where it is not.[12] In New Testament Greek there is no clear case of this characteristic Semitic idiom, though it may well be involved in Lk. 12:19.[13] Often in sayings of Jesus the Greek reflexive pronoun doubtless represents this idiomatic use of *nephesh* in the original Aramaic.[14] The meaning " self " should therefore be kept in mind as a possibility wherever the word " soul " is encountered in the English New Testament; in fact " self " comes as near as any English word can to a comprehensive rendering of the Greek and the Hebrew and Aramaic nouns.

f. Sometimes the *nephesh* is the seat of physical appetite and desire. Thus Eccl. 6:2 f. does not refer to the need of spiritual satisfaction; in v. 7 *nephesh* is the word translated " appetite," [15] and in v. 9 it is translated " desire." [16] In the same way *psyche* also is used of the animal nature, desires, and appetites, especially where distinguished from the spirit [17] or the mind.[18] With this use goes Paul's use of the adjective *psychikos* in the sense of physical, animal, natural; [19] cp. Jude 19, where it is translated " sensual " and explained as " not having spirit."

g. The Hebrew and Greek words are used also for the seat of emotion or (less often) thought. Sometimes [20] *nephesh* is translated " heart."

---

[9] Acts 2:41; 7:14; 27:37; 1 P. 3:20 in an Old Testament allusion.

[10] Num. 23:10; Ju. 16:30; Is. 46:2; 51:23; Ps. 124:7; cp. the use of " my soul " and " my spirit " in Lk. 1:46 f.

[11] Job 18:4; 32:2; Is. 47:14; Am. 2:14 f.

[12] 1 S. 18:1, 3; 20:17; Jer. 26:19.

[13] Cp. Gen. 49:6.

[14] The Syriac uses the same idiom in translating Mk. 3:26; 5:5, 30; 8:34, *et al.*

[15] So also Prov. 23:2.

[16] So Jer. 44:14; also A.S.V. in Ex. 15:9; Ps. 78:18, 30; A.V., " lust." Cp. Ps. 107:9; Prov. 16:24; Eccl. 2:24; 4:8; 7:28.

[17] 1 Th. 5:23; Heb. 4:12.

[18] Mk. 12:30; cp. v. 33.

[19] 1 Cor. 2:14; 15:44, 46.

[20] Ex. 23:9; Lev. 26:16, A.V.; Dt. 24:15; Prov. 23:7; Ho. 4:8.

Once [21] *psyche* is so rendered. In other cases [22] *nephesh* is translated "mind"; the reference in many of these passages, however, is to the attitude or disposition rather than the intellect or reason, for which other terms are used (s. 46). Only once in the New Testament is *psyche* rendered "mind," [23] and here too the attitude and will are meant (cp. the similar idea in Acts 4:32, where the same noun is translated "soul").

Clearly the word "soul" in the Bible has a much broader meaning than in current usage now. The fact that translators are often compelled to use other English words to translate the same Hebrew or Greek noun raises the question whether they should not have done so in many more instances.[24] Nowhere in the Old Testament, as a matter of fact, is the meaning exactly what we ordinarily mean by the soul. Sometimes, to be sure, *nephesh* indicates something that departs at death, but in such instances the word probably has merely its original meaning, "breath." [25] This meaning is hard to distinguish from "life"; as in 1 K. 17:21 f., where the dead child's *nephesh* comes back into him.[26] Other Old Testament passages that speak of delivering the *nephesh* from death are naturally taken by Christian readers as referring to the future life, but in most, if not all, such cases the meaning is simply preserving a person's life.[27] This is true especially of Ps. 16:10 (*v.i.* on Acts 2:27, 31).[28]

Postbiblical Judaism was acquainted with the idea of the soul as the immortal part of man; so not only Hellenistic sources, which use *psyche* in this sense,[29] but also rabbinic literature, where, however, the word used is usually not *nephesh*. It is reasonable, therefore, to expect this use of *psyche* in the New Testament. In fact, it is used of the souls of the martyrs in Rev. 6:9; 20:4. Acts 2:27, 31 apparently takes Ps. 16:10 to mean that Christ's soul had gone to Hades but was not allowed to remain there. Paul never uses *psyche* in contrast to flesh or with reference to the future life. Jn. 12:25 speaks of hating one's *psyche* in this world and saving it to eternal life (*zoe*). Here the English versions ren-

[21] Eph. 6:6.
[22] Gen. 23:8; Dt. 18:6, A.V.; 28:65, A.V.; 1 S. 2:35; 1 Chr. 28:9; Ezek. 23:17, A.V.
[23] Phil. 1:27, A.V. and R.S.V.
[24] So especially A.S.V.
[25] Gen. 35:18; Job 11:20.
[26] V. 17 has a different word for breath, the one used for the breath of life in Gen. 2:7 and for the immortal soul in later Jewish sources.
[27] Ps. 33:19; 56:13; cp. Josh. 2:13; 1 S. 19:11, where the word is translated "life."
[28] Cp. also Ps. 30:3; 49:15; 86:13; 89:48; Prov. 23:14; Is. 38:17; Job 33:18, 22, 28, 30.
[29] W.S. 3:1 ff.; 8:19 f.

der both Greek words by " life "; in the synoptic parallels [30] the Authorized Version wavers between " soul " and " life," while the American Standard Version and the new revision read " life " throughout. In these passages, and in others that speak of saving the soul (or souls), it is hard to tell how much more is meant than saving one's life or oneself.[31] In general the Bible does not use *nephesh* or *psyche* in the sense of the immortal soul which is delivered from future punishment, but expresses that idea by the word " spirit " (s. 47).

46. Heart, Mind, Conscience

The main biblical term for the seat of feeling, will, and even thought is " heart," often used interchangeably or in parallelism with " soul." [1] The heart is regarded as the seat of the will and of good and evil intentions and attitudes,[2] of conscience,[3] and of thought, intelligence, or mind.[4] It is also frequently mentioned as the seat of such emotions as joy and sorrow, as in modern Occidental usage. New Testament usage follows that of the Old Testament.[5] Other terms for the emotions are the Hebrew and Greek words for the bowels [6] and the kidneys.[7]

There are Hebrew words for thinking and thought, also others meaning insight, understanding, and the like, used especially in the wisdom literature. The Greek language, however, has more words than Hebrew for the concepts " mind " and " conscience." In Mk. 12:30, quoting Dt. 6:5, a Greek word for mind (*dianoia*) is inserted. The word for " heart " in the original already included this idea; in fact, the Septuagint often translates it by the very word added here. The same Greek word is used also elsewhere in the New Testament. It is translated sometimes " mind," [8] sometimes " understanding," [9] sometimes " imagination." [10]

---

[30] Mk. 8:35 ff., etc.
[31] *V.s.* and cp. Heb. 10:39; Jas. 1:21; 5:20; see also Ezek. 18:4, 27 f.
[1] Dt. 4:29; 6:5.
[2] Ex. 4:21; 35:5, 21 f.; 2 Chr. 12:14; Prov. 26:23, and often.
[3] 1 S. 24:5.
[4] 1 K. 3:12; Prov. 10:8; 14:33; 15:28; 16:9.
[5] Mk. 7:21; Acts 5:3 f.; 8:21 f.; 11:23; Rom. 1:21; 5:5; 10:9 f.; 2 Cor. 1:22; 4:6; Gal. 4:6.
[6] Is. 16:11; Jer. 4:19; 31:20; Lam. 2:11; 2 Cor. 6:12; Phil. 1:8; 2:1; Col. 3:12; Phmn. 7, 12, 20; 1 Jn. 3:17 — A.S.V. and R.S.V. avoid translating these terms literally.
[7] Job. 19:27; Ps. 7:9; 16:7; 26:2; 73:21; Jer. 11:20; 17:10; 20:12; in the New Testament only Rev. 2:23.
[8] Col. 1:21; Eph. 2:3; Heb. 8:10; 1 P. 1:13; 2 P. 3:1.
[9] Eph. 4:18.
[10] Lk. 1:51.

Paul uses frequently another word for mind (*nous*), which is rare in the Septuagint and elsewhere in the New Testament. It designates the inner man in general, especially as spiritually renewed in the Christian.[11] In speaking with tongues the *nous* is unfruitful.[12] (Phil. 2:5 has no noun meaning " mind " in the Greek; it reads literally, " Think this in you which also in Christ Jesus.") A distinctly Greek word for " conscience " (*syneidesis*) is sometimes used by Paul[13] and later New Testament writers.

47. *Spirit*

The same Hebrew and Greek words that are used for the Spirit of God (s. 27) are used also for an element of man's nature. Sometimes in the Old Testament " spirit " is practically the equivalent of " soul,"[1] but " spirit " is not ordinarily used, as " soul " is, of the vital functions which man shares with the animals.[2] The Greek word *pneuma*, as applied to the human spirit, like other designations, is often used of man's higher nature.[3]

The basic meaning of " wind " or " breath " makes it natural that the spirit should be connected with the breath of life breathed into man at his creation, and the use of " spirit " in Gen. 6:3 is noteworthy in this connection (s. 48). Job 33:4 uses " the Spirit of God " and " the breath of Shaddai " in parallelism, with reference to the creation and life of the individual man. In Ps. 104:29 *ruah* is used for man's breath, the loss of which means death. In Lk. 23:46 (a quotation of Ps. 31:5, where the meaning is not clear) the separation of body and spirit seems to be contemplated.[4] The same idea may be implied also in 1 Cor. 5:3.

Sometimes " spirit " means, as in English, the attitude or disposition, especially with reference to pride or humility.[5] The Hebrew word is used particularly of thinking and willing;[6] cp. such expressions as " spirit of wisdom," " spirit of understanding."[7] In such connections " spirit " is practically interchangeable with " heart " or " kidneys." " Heart " and

[11] Rom. 7:23, 25; 12:2; 1 Cor. 2:16; cp. Eph. 4:23.
[12] 1 Cor. 14:14 ff.
[13] Especially 1 Cor., chs. 8 and 10.
[1] Job 12:10, where *ruah* is translated " breath "; Is. 57:16.
[2] Yet cf. Eccl. 3:21; also Gen. 7:22, though the Septuagint here omits " spirit."
[3] Mk. 14:38.
[4] Cp. Acts 7:59.
[5] Prov. 16:18 f., 32; Mt. 5:3, but cp. Lk. 6:20.
[6] Is. 29:24; Ps. 77:6.
[7] Dt. 34:9; Is. 11:2; cp. Ex. 31:3, 6.

" spirit " are also used together in connection with divine renewal or regeneration.[8]

The relation between the human spirit and the Spirit of God in the Old Testament is sometimes obscure, and the translator is uncertain whether the word should begin with a small letter or a capital. This is equally true in the New Testament,[9] and here the problem is complicated further by the idea of the Spirit of Christ.

Aside from Acts 7:59 (mentioned above), *pneuma* is not used in Acts, chs. 1 to 12, as the name of an element of man's nature. Paul uses the word much less often in this sense than with reference to the Spirit of God or Christ, and only once is it quite clear that he means the spirits of men in general, including non-Christians.[10] Frequently it is uncertain whether he means the human spirit or the divine Spirit in the Christian; in fact, Paul thinks of the Christian's spirit as being so completely possessed by the divine Spirit that they are almost identified (s. 82). Sometimes " spirit " like " soul " practically means the whole person or self; more often the total personality is designated as " body and spirit " or " flesh and spirit," [11] and once " your whole spirit and soul and body." [12] Frequently, as noted in s. 44, flesh and spirit are sharply contrasted. Paul also speaks of his spirit as being present where he is not present, as we say, in person,[13] but whether he means this in the sense in which we use the same words or in a more realistic sense is uncertain.[14]

The fourth gospel uses the word " spirit " to represent the divine as against the human and also the universal as against the local and national.[15] The spirit as a part of man's nature is mentioned in chs. 11:33; 13:21 (both referring to Jesus). Nothing distinctive is found in the rest of the New Testament. The synoptic evangelists reproduce Old Testament usage.[16] In Rev. 17:3; 21:10 either the divine Spirit or the human spirit may be meant, but cp. ch. 1:10.[17]

In general, the use of all these terms throughout the Bible is popular, not scientific or technical. Various terms often overlap or are used interchangeably. The underlying conception of personality is a unity of

---

[8] Ps. 51:10; Ezek. 11:19; 18:31; s. 63.
[9] Cp. Rom. 8:9–11.
[10] 1 Cor. 2:11; cp. 2 Cor. 7:13.
[11] 1 Cor. 7:34; 2 Cor. 7:1.
[12] 1 Th. 5:23.
[13] 1 Cor. 5:3 f.
[14] Cp. 2 Cor. 12:1–5.
[15] Jn. 4:23 f. (cp. Is. 31:3) ; see also ch. 6:63.
[16] Lk. 1:46 f.; Mt. 27:50; cp. Mk. 15:37 and Lk. 23:46.
[17] See also Heb. 12:9, 23; Jas. 2:26; 4:5 (cp. Gen. 6:3) ; 2 Tim. 1:7; 4:22.

body animated by soul (life), and with a higher nature (spirit) which may be possessed by the Spirit of God. In the Old Testament God gives men his Spirit or a spirit of wisdom, etc.; in the New Testament Paul especially stresses the union of the Christian's spirit with the Spirit of God or Christ.

48. *Man's Place in the Universe*

The creation narratives of Gen., chs. 1 f. (s. 39), express in different ways the fact that man is a part of nature. In P the creation of man is not only a part of the whole creative process; it takes place on the same day as the creation of animal life in general. J represents man as formed of earth,[1] as the animals were.[2] Modern scientific conceptions of man's relation to nature make this emphasis in the Bible especially significant.

The fact of his earthly origin is used elsewhere in the Old Testament to keep man humble, reminding him of his weakness and mortality.[3] The idea of man as clay in the hands of a potter may be related to this conception of his creation.[4] Paul contrasts Adam's creation from the earth with Christ's heavenly origin.[5] Stress on man's imperfection, weakness, liability to suffering, ignorance, and mortality, and on the general futility of his life, is by no means unusual in the Bible.[6]

Yet man is sharply distinguished from the rest of creation by his unique relation to God. P says man was made in God's image.[7] J expresses man's relation to God by saying that God breathed into man's nostrils the breath of life.[8] This is not stated regarding the creation of the animals,[9] though ch. 7:22 apparently includes the animals in the expression " all in whose nostrils was the breath of the spirit of life." In ch. 6:3 Yahweh says that his Spirit (s. 27) shall not remain in man forever.[10]

In Acts 17:25 Paul says that God has given to all life and breath. Vv. 28 f. introduce a different idea, that man is God's offspring, which

---

[1] Gen. 2:7.
[2] V. 19; cp. ch. 3:19, 23.
[3] Ps. 103:14; Eccl. 12:7.
[4] Is. 29:16; 45:9; 64:8; Jer. 18:6; cp. Rom. 9:20 f.
[5] 1 Cor. 15:47.
[6] Job 5:7; 8:9; 11:12; 28:12 f.; Ps. 39:4 f.; 49; 62:9; 78:39; 89:48; 90; 103:14; 144:4; 146:3 f.; Prov. 16:25; Eccl., chs. 1 f.; 8:17; 12:7; Is. 40:6–8; 1 Cor. 1:20; 8:2; Jas. 4:14.
[7] Gen. 1:26 f.; 5:1, 3; 9:6; cp. Ps. 8:5; Col. 3:10; Eph. 4:24; Jas. 3:9.
[8] Gen. 2:7.
[9] V. 19.
[10] Cp. Job. 27:3; 33:4.

is supported by a verse of Greek poetry. It would have been hard to find support in the Old Testament for the idea that man is by nature God's child. The king and the chosen people may regard him as Father (ss. 26, 33), but in both cases the relationship is one of adoption, not of nature: God chooses Israel, and the king in particular, to be his sons. This remains true in the New Testament also, with the exception of Acts 17:28 f. In Jn. 8:44 Jesus even tells his opponents that their father is the devil. The idea of the universal Fatherhood of God and brotherhood of man comes from Stoicism rather than the Bible. God is man's Creator; he loves men like a father; men are also of one common origin and descent (s. 109), and are made in God's image. The terms " Father " and " son," are used in the Bible of a relation which is potential for all men but realized only by those who receive the divine adoption (s. 62). This distinction, however, is not sharply drawn. (The implications of Mt. 5:45 in this connection are uncertain.)

In both P and J the unique relation of mankind to God is shared by man and woman. P expresses this most strikingly,[11] but J conveys the same idea by representing man as unable to find companionship among the animals and as finding it in her who was made of his own bone and flesh.[12] Undue stress by commentators on woman's subordination to man in Gen., ch. 2, has obscured the more basic point of their common elevation above the animals. Paul, to be sure, uses the creation story to keep woman in her place.[13] Truer to the original intention, however, is the allusion to Gen. 2:7 in Mal. 2:15, condemning divorce. Jesus actually combines Gen. 1:27 and ch. 2:24 to the same intent.[14]

God's purpose in man's creation is expressed in P by the command to multiply and to subdue and rule the rest of creation.[15] J again expresses the same idea in a different framework and order of events: man is made before the plants or animals, and everything else is done for his sake; he is also put in the garden to take care of it, and the animals are brought to him to be named.[16] Thus, as we have already seen (s. 39), the idea of the universe is distinctly anthropocentric.[17] Man's dominion over creation is, of course, limited and subject to God's commands. In Gen. 1:29 f. all seed-bearing fruits and vegetables are given to men and

---

[11] Gen. 1:27; 5:2.
[12] Ch. 2:18–24.
[13] 1 Cor. 11:7–9.
[14] Mk. 10:6 ff. (Mt. 19:4 ff.).
[15] Gen. 1:28–30; cp. 9:1, 7; Lev. 26:9; Ps. 8:6.
[16] Gen. 2:4–9, 15, 18–20.
[17] Cp. Ps. 104:14 f.; Acts 14:16 f.; but contrast Job, chs. 38 to 42, especially ch. 38:26.

animals alike for food, but nothing is said of eating meat; ch. 9:3 f. adds " every moving thing " except " flesh with the life thereof, which is the blood thereof." In ch. 2:16 f. (J) the fruit of every tree but one is given to man, and ch. 3 tells the dire results of man's failure to abide by this limitation. Man's highest good, according to P, is to " walk with God." [18]

The growing conquest of nature by modern science adds significance to the biblical doctrine of man's dominion over creation subject to God's will. Religion has too often resisted progress in this respect. The Bible does not, to be sure, encourage unqualified pride in man's achievements. His failure to control himself while controlling nature is exposed and condemned.[19] But the purpose of man's creation as presented in Genesis affords the basis for a religious interest in the growth of man's understanding and control of nature.

49. *Group and Individual*

The conception of a social organism, a group having a sort of individuality and personality of its own, is familiar to us, but it was much stronger and more real to ancient man. Anthropologists emphasize the strong sense of social solidarity and the relative weakness of individual self-consciousness among primitive peoples. The idea of " corporate personality " was especially characteristic of Hebrew thought. The Old Testament narratives often individualize and personify groups.[1] The same habit of mind appears in the treatment of tribes and peoples as individuals in the genealogies of Genesis.[2] In part this is doubtless a mere literary convention, but the common conception of peoples and nations as persons made such a method of stating ethnic and geographical relations natural if not inevitable. An example of the same method in Greek literature reads: " Reigning over the Egyptians Epaphus married Memphis, daughter of Nile, founded and named the city of Memphis after her, and begat a daughter Libya after whom the region of Libya was called." [3]

The stories of the patriarchs similarly combine individual and tribal elements, often quite inextricably.[4] With the individual Hagar and her son Ishmael,[5] for example, compare the Hagarites and Ishmaelites in

[18] Gen. 5:21–24; 6:9; cp. Mi. 6:8.
[19] Gen. 11:1–9; Eccl. 7:29; Jas. 3:3 ff.
[1] Num. 20:14–21; 21:1–3; Ju. 1:1–4, 17.
[2] Gen. 9:18; 10:15 f.
[3] Apollodorus, *The Library*, II. 1. 4 (Loeb edition, p. 135), with more of the same sort.
[4] Cp. Gen. 25:30; 32:28; 36:8.
[5] Gen., ch. 16.

Ps. 83:6.[6] Etiological stories are told to explain the names and relationships of peoples. Thus the hostility between Israel and Edom, in spite of their close kinship, and the achievement of supremacy by Israel, although Edom had been established earlier in its territory, are given three explanations: (1) the oracle to Rebekah before the birth of her sons, (2) the sale of the birthright by Esau to Jacob, and (3) Jacob's fraudulent obtaining of his father's blessing.[7]

The idea of the efficacious blessing forms the basis of a distinctive Hebrew type of poem, illustrated in the first and third of the explanations just cited and before that in Gen. 9:25-27. Highly developed poems of this type are found in Gen., ch. 49; Num., chs. 22 to 24; and Dt., ch. 33 (s. 31). By means of this literary form the conditions and relations of tribes and peoples in the writer's time are explained as the consequence of blessings (or curses) uttered by some patriarch or seer on the eponymous ancestors of the groups in question. Whether or to what extent the Israelite patriarchs were historic individuals may be an insoluble question. The later poets of Israel doubtless thought of them as such, yet the poems are concerned, not with the individuals, but with the personified groups. Here again the literary convention is derived from the older folk-psychology.

A very primitive manifestation of the idea is the assumption of collective responsibility for the offenses of any member of a group. In the Old Testament this appears chiefly in connection with the family. The revolt of Korah, Dathan, and Abiram,[8] and the trespass of Achan[9] are striking examples. In both cases the destruction of the guilty family is regarded as necessary to prevent the destruction of the whole nation, as an infected finger may necessitate the amputation of the hand or arm to save the person's life. The solidarity of the family is further illustrated by the primitive institution of blood-revenge and the function of the go'el: this Hebrew noun is translated " avenger," " kinsman," and " redeemer," the cognate verb being rendered " redeem." [10] The later laws of the Pentateuch often treat the village rather than the family or clan as the unit of corporate responsibility.[11]

Another expression of corporate personality is the idea of the king as

6 Cp. 1 Chr. 5:10.
7 Gen. 25:23, 27-34; 27:1-40.
8 Num., ch. 16.
9 Josh., ch. 7.
10 Lev. 25:25 ff.; 27:13 ff.; Num. 5:8; 35:12; Dt. 19:6, 12; Josh. 20:3, 5, 9; Ru. 2:20; 3:9, 12 f.; 4:1-8, 14.
11 Dt. 21:1-9.

the embodiment of the nation, who speaks and acts for the whole, and for whose deeds the whole group is held responsible. The story of David's census [12] illustrates this conception. It exemplifies also the punishment of whole nations for the crimes of their kings, as often in 1 and 2 Kings. In keeping with the whole conception of corporate personality judgment and salvation in the Old Testament are largely concerned with nations rather than individuals (ss. 60 f.).

Perhaps the most striking expression of the Hebrew idea of corporate personality is Second Isaiah's picture of Israel as the Suffering Servant of Yahweh (s. 30). The solution of the problem of individual or collective meaning here may be found in this characteristic habit of Hebrew mentality.

Over against all this the distinctly individualistic attitude and ideas of the New Testament are conspicuous. As Fosdick points out, collectivism is now regarded as a modern development, but the Bible exhibits a development away from primitive collectivism to individualism.[13] He also remarks, however, that there is truth in the ideas of social sin and salvation, and in this respect the Old Testament still affords a valuable supplement and even corrective for the individualism of the New Testament.[14]

Before leaving the subject of man, we may note an important fact which will be considered more fully later. All that has been said applies to mankind at large, with no distinction of race or nation. One of the most fundamental elements in the biblical conception of man, perhaps all the more significant because it is usually assumed rather than explicitly stated, is the unity of mankind (s. 109).

[12] 2 S., ch. 24.
[13] *A Guide to the Understanding of the Bible*, p. 97.
[14] *Ibid.*, p. 80, v.i., s. 103.

VII

THE PEOPLE OF GOD

50. *The Chosen People and the Remnant*

The religion of the Old Testament begins as the religion of a family or clan and becomes the religion of a nation. The primary religious unit is therefore the same as the social and political unit. As we observed in s. 49, the group overshadowed the individual in early times, as among other peoples. The earliest Hebrew history was a matter of the family, later the tribe, then the confederation of tribes, and so finally the nation. The geographical unit became important also after the conquest and settlement of Canaan, but in general it coincided with the tribal and national unit. Even when the fame of a great shrine attracted several tribes to worship there, the result was commonly a federation (s. 21). Thus a process of combination, involving the identification of the various tribal deities with the deity of the shrine, led toward both political and religious unity.

The covenant of Sinai (s. 5) established Israel as a national unit, and thereafter Hebrew religion was the religion of Yahweh's chosen people. The family was still important, but it was more and more overshadowed by the larger, inclusive unit. United Israel was now a holy people.[1] Throughout the complicated and still obscure developments which ensued, Yahwism remained the religion of Israel in spite of many defections and divisions. The conflict with baalism strengthened the sense of religious unity in spite of political disunity, though the latter strongly tended to produce religious disunity also.

The covenant relationship was essentially conditional (s. 5). Both the law and the prophets are full of warnings of national doom if Israel fails to fulfill her part of the contract. Since Israel actually failed to meet the divine requirements, her history is one of only fleeting glory followed by disaster, which was recognized as just punishment.[2]

---

[1] Ex. 19:5 f.; 24:7 f. [2] Ju. 2:1–23; 2 K. 17:7–23; Neh. 9:5–38.

The announcement of impending doom is tempered in Am. 5:15 by the possibility that a repentant remnant of the nation may be spared. This hope was not fulfilled in the northern kingdom, but Isaiah brought forward and stressed the idea in the southern kingdom as one of his most characteristic teachings.[3] Later prophets repeated this hope.[4] Its application to the people left behind in Judah by Nebuchadrezzar led only to disappointment,[5] but it was persistently applied throughout the exilic and postexilic periods to the exiles in Babylonia and elsewhere,[6] and also to the little postexilic community in Palestine.[7]

51. *The Church*

The idea of the righteous remnant as a holy community, distinguished from the nation as a whole, approaches the idea of the church. The author of Deuteronomy already thinks of Israel more as a church than as a nation: what Yahweh desires is a holy people. Jeremiah's promise of the new covenant [1] can apply only to the holy remnant; in fact, the idea of the law as written in the heart opens the way for individualism and complete independence of the national unit, though Jeremiah himself still cherishes the hope of national restoration.

The destruction of the nation in 586 B.C. did not crush nationalism. After the exile the national hope remained strong, with periodic resurgence in great strength (s. 107 ff.). The individualism of Jeremiah and Ezekiel, however, with its distinction between the righteous and the wicked within the chosen people, became a fixed element in Old Testament religion after the exile. The wisdom literature was always and characteristically individualistic and nonnationalistic.

Through all these developments the chosen people were becoming more and more a religious community rather than a nation, though without ever entirely giving up the hope of national independence. Meanwhile, apart from nationalistic aspiration, and largely independent of the official temple organization and worship, the synagogue had arisen and become the real center of Jewish religious life. The origin of the synagogue is unknown; it apparently arose in the Persian period or perhaps even during the exile, and in either case probably in the Diaspora or at least outside of Jerusalem.

The word " synagogue " is a Greek common noun meaning " gather-

[3] Is. 1:9; 7:3; 10:20–22.
[4] Jer. 23:1 ff.; 31:7 f.
[5] Jer. 40:11, 15; 41:16; 42:2, 15, 19; 43:5; 44:12, 14, 28.
[6] Mi. 4:7 f.
[7] Zc. 8:6, 11 f.
[1] Jer. 31:31–34.

ing." In the Septuagint it is used to render two Hebrew nouns, both representing the congregation or assembly of Israel, especially in the Pentateuch. The same two Hebrew words are also occasionally rendered by the Greek *ekklesia,* meaning " assembly." Prov. 5:14 has both Hebrew nouns, and the Septuagint reads, " In the midst of the *ekklesia* and the *synagoge.*" The latter Greek noun came later to be used as the regular designation of the Jewish organization and place of worship, while the former became the standard designation of the Christian church, but the Hellenistic Jews and early Greek-speaking Christians found both words used interchangeably in their Greek Bible for the congregation of Israel. Hence Stephen speaks of Moses as being in the *ekklesia* (E.VV., church) in the wilderness.[2] In short, the church is historically a continuation and successor of the Old Testament congregation, just as the synagogue is. In other words, the congregation of Israel split into the synagogue and the church. Jas. 2:2 actually speaks of a Christian *synagoge* (A.S.V., synagogue; A.V., R.S.V., assembly).

In Mk. 12:9, concluding the parable of the wicked husbandmen, Jesus says that the lord of the vineyard will destroy the husbandmen and give the vineyard to others. If the vineyard represents Palestine, this may be a reference to the destruction of the Jewish nation by the Romans. Luke follows Mark here, but Mt. 21:41 says that the owner " will let out the vineyard unto other husbandmen who shall render him the fruits in their seasons," and v. 43 adds a specific application: " The kingdom of God shall be taken away from you, and shall be given to a nation bringing forth the fruits thereof." This " nation " can mean only the Christian church, regarded as having taken the place of the Jewish nation as God's chosen people. That Jesus actually expressed this idea is possible, though by no means certain. The allegorical character of the parable arouses suspicion, yet it may be authentic. A similar idea is implied in Lk. 12:32, without any such sharp distinction between Jesus' followers and the Jewish people. In general, the Old Testament idea of the remnant seems closer to what Jesus taught.

The word *ekklesia* occurs only twice in sayings attributed to Jesus, both passages being in Matthew. On the assumption that Jesus applied to his followers an Aramaic term having the Old Testament associations indicated above for the Greek word *ekklesia,* Mt. 16:18 may be taken to mean " my congregation," corresponding to the ancient congregation of Israel. Mt. 18:17 may be similarly interpreted. If Jesus, however,

2 Acts 7:38.

used the current Aramaic word for the synagogue, Mt. 16:18 would presumably refer to his synagogue as over against the Jewish organization, and in that case Mt. 18:17 might mean either the group of disciples or the local Jewish synagogue. Conceivably Mt. 18:17 might even refer to the council of village elders. The authenticity of both passages, however, is very doubtful: ch. 16:18 reflects the later rivalry of different ecclesiastical groups and the claims made for the primacy of Peter, while ch. 18:17 reflects the development of church discipline. The use of any such term as " church " by Jesus is therefore not well attested. The idea of a community of disciples is rooted in his life and teaching, but not an organized institution.

The early Palestinian church was at first hardly distinguished from the Jewish people. Separate synagogues may have been organized by the disciples, since any ten men could organize a synagogue, but there is no positive evidence for this. The disciples evidently worshiped in the temple with other Jews. Gradually, however, the sense of being a distinct group increased. The admission of Gentiles contributed to this development (s. 102). The gospel was still regarded as the true Judaism and believers as the true Israel, yet the nation as a whole rejected it. The frequent use of the word " church " in Acts, chs. 1 to 12, doubtless reflects the growing importance of the group of disciples. How soon an organized body entirely separate from the synagogue emerged is unknown (aside from the provisions for the distribution of goods to the poor, Acts, ch. 6; cp. s. 90), but the group was at any rate achieving a consciousness of itself as a new social and religious unit.

For Paul salvation is primarily an individual experience, but all Christians share this experience, which therefore makes them a community. Paul uses the word *ekklesia* both of local congregations and also of the church as a whole,[3] which is " the Israel of God." [4] He thinks of this universal church as a building,[5] a temple.[6] Paul's most characteristic idea in this connection, however, is that of the church as Christ's body.[7] The individual believer thus has *koinonia* (fellowship, sharing, community) both with Christ and with his fellow Christians (s. 82). The main point in Paul's use of the figure of the body is unity in diversity. Both the unity of the church and its purity were very im-

[3] 1 Cor. 12:28.
[4] Gal. 6:16.
[5] 1 Cor. 3:9.
[6] 1 Cor. 3:16 ff.; 2 Cor. 6:16 — in 1 Cor. 6:19 the individual believer is a temple.
[7] Rom. 12:4 f.; 1 Cor. 12:12; Col. 1:18; cp. Eph. 1:23; 4:12.

portant for him.[8] Similar ideas are elaborated in Eph., ch. 4. The conception of the church as the bride of Christ, already suggested by 2 Cor. 11:2, appears explicitly in Ephesians [9] and Revelation.[10]

In the gospel and epistles of John the word *ekklesia* does not occur, but Christians are sharply distinguished from the world, which hates them and to which they do not belong.[11] The idea of the church appears also in the stress laid on unity.[12] Universal scope, unity, and separateness from the world are thus the main emphases in the Johannine conception of the church. Individual churches are probably meant by the " elect lady " and her " elect sister " in 2 Jn. 1, 13.[13] The stress laid in 3 John on the authority of the elder (s. 90) over a group of churches reflects the tendency toward centralization and standardization to counteract heresy.

The development of a church-consciousness is further shown by Matthew, which, in addition to being the only one of the gospels to use the word *ekklesia*, evinces a pronounced interest in problems of membership and discipline. The parables of the tares and the dragnet are explained [14] as referring to the presence of unworthy members in the church (evidently what Matthew means in this connection by the kingdom of heaven); the man without a wedding garment is added to the parable of the great supper; [15] the church is built on Peter, to whom is given the power of admission and exclusion; [16] and disputes between disciples are referred to the church.[17]

In Rev. 1:6 and 5:10 the idea of Israel as a kingdom of priests [18] is applied to the church, as also in 1 P. 2:5, 9. The emphasis in Hebrews on the idea that the new covenant has superseded the old implies that the church has taken the place of Israel. The idea of the church is highly developed in the pastoral epistles; indeed, the stress on orthodox doctrine as a qualification of church officials brings us practically to the Catholic conception of the church.[19]

---

8 1 Cor., chs. 1 ff.; Phil., chs. 1 f.
9 Eph. 5:22-33.
10 Rev. 19:7; 21:2, 9; 22:17.
11 Jn. 7:7; 8:23; 14:17; 17:9.
12 Chs. 10:16; 11:51 f.; 12:32; 17:20 f.
13 Cp. 1 P. 5:13, " she that is in Babylon."
14 Mt. 13:24-30, 36-43, 47-50.
15 Ch. 22:1-14.
16 Ch. 16:18; cp. ch. 18:18.
17 Ch. 18:15-17; *v.s.* and cp. Lk. 17:3 f.
18 Ex. 19:6.
19 1 Tim. 3:15.

52. *Divisions and Sects*

The divided condition of the Christian church in our time constitutes such an urgent problem that one naturally turns to the Bible for light on its causes and the way out of it. A state religion like that of ancient Israel, in which ritual and organization are more prominent than belief, is not subject to divisions of the same kind as those which have been both the bane and the salvation of Christianity. Reform movements, of course, may arise within such a religion. The prophetic movement in Israel was one of the most outstanding examples of this in the history of religion; it neither sought nor produced, however, a separate religious organization.

Special groups with distinct characteristics within the main body of the religion, comparable to the monastic orders in the Roman church, are exemplified in Hebrew religion by the Nazirites and Rechabites. The Nazirites represent the nearest approach to monasticism in Israel. They were individuals especially consecrated to Yahweh for life, even before birth, as Samson and Samuel were,[1] though the latter is not called a Nazirite. In Gen. 49:26 Joseph is called " separate [*nazir*] from his brethren," indicating the primary meaning of the term " Nazirite." The vow of abstention from wine suggests an anti-Canaanite interest (cp. the Rechabites, *v.i.*). Am. 2:11 f. charges the Israelites with giving the Nazirites wine and forbidding the prophets to prophesy. The law for the Nazirites is given in Num. 6:2, 13–21. They evidently had no organization or official status. Their only lasting religious significance is in the fact that they exemplify the practice of vowing children for religious service.

For our knowledge of the Rechabites we are indebted entirely to Jer., ch. 35. Apparently this group was not a sect or organization but a family, the descendants of Jonadab the son of Rechab,[2] though the category of father and sons does not necessarily indicate literal kinship. At any rate, the Rechabites were devoted to the stern nomadic ideals of ancient Israel, and showed their devotion by rigid abstention from the two most conspicuous marks of Canaanite civilization: living in houses and the cultivation of the vine. They stand as a pathetic symbol of the futile effort to stop the clock of human progress and the fallacy of identifying religious purity with an idealized past stage of civilization.

The beginnings of what may be called an unorganized Puritanical

---

[1] Ju. 13:7; 1 S. 1:11.   [2] Cp. 2 K. 10:15 f., 23.

tendency appear in postexilic references to the " godly " or " saints " (*hasidim*), who are pictured in many of the later psalms as poor and oppressed but devoutly keeping the law and trusting God to deliver them. From this group came the followers of the Maccabees at the close of the Hellenistic period.

During the time of the Hasmonean kings we begin to hear of the Pharisees, whose devotion to the law and opposition both to Hellenistic customs and to political entanglement with the Gentile powers mark them as the spiritual descendants of the earlier *hasidim*. The name Pharisee means " separated." Whether it originally designated separation from Hellenism and worldliness, withdrawal from the Maccabean movement when it went on from the achievement of religious liberty to seek political independence and power, or general dissent from the policies of the Sadducean aristocracy, is still a matter of speculation and debate. In the Roman period the Pharisees were a small but influential group of zealous students and strict observers of the law, including the oral traditions. They believed in the resurrection of the dead and in angels. Trusting God for the deliverance of Israel, they disparaged political or military resistance or revolt. As religious leaders they came into their own when Israel ceased to exist as a nation.

The Sadducees were less a party or sect than a social class, the wealthy aristocrats, among whom were the priests. They interpreted the law literally, not accepting the traditions of the scribes, and rejected the new beliefs in angels and the resurrection. Appeasers and collaborators under the Roman empire, they were dominant in Jewish politics until the destruction of the temple and the extinction of the nation left them without power or influence.

Minor Jewish sects or movements are mentioned by Josephus and Philo, but they have no significance for biblical theology, being historically important only as demonstrating the existence within Judaism of the ascetic and mystical tendencies characteristic of the Hellenistic and Roman periods in other religions.

The New Testament period was hardly long enough for the institutional ossification and corruption which provoke movements of reform and sectarian divisions. Personal rivalries, however, began very early to threaten the unity of the church, and aberrations of faith and practice soon led the leaders of the church to condemn various groups. Such an incident as that of Mk. 9:38–40 is symptomatic. Paul rebukes those at Corinth who set themselves apart as followers of Cephas, Apollos, or himself.[3] The stress on unity in Ephesians and John and the exhortations to respect church officials in the pastoral epistles betray the growth of divisive tendencies toward the end of the apostolic age. Jude and 2 Peter, the Johannine epistles, and the letters to the churches in Rev., chs. 2, 3, mention several heretical groups, never sharply defined. It was the effort to counteract these that led to the emphasis on orthodox belief in the latest books of the New Testament (s. 79).

Aside from this later counsel of desperation, which was in effect a retreat from Christian freedom to a theological legalism, the appeal for unity in the New Testament is based on the principle of Christian love. What is urged is not that all Christians should be of the same opinion, but that they should be of the same mind in the sense of sharing the attitude and spirit of Jesus himself.[4] In the great intercession of Jn., ch. 17, Jesus prays for all his followers that they shall be one as he and the Father are one, that the world may believe in him.[5]

As our study of the church indicates (s. 51), there is nothing in the New Testament that would require a single, united ecclesiastical organization. Unity of spirit is essential, but the degree and kind of union and the degree and kind of diversity desirable are, like all other questions of organization and method (ss. 86–91), matters to be determined only on the basis of effectiveness in promoting the purpose of the church.

[3] 1 Cor. 1:10–17; 3 f.; 11:18 f.
[4] Rom. 12:16; 15:5; 1 Cor. 1:10; 2 Cor. 13:11; Phil. 1:27; 2:2 ff.; 4:2; 1 P. 3:8.
[5] Jn. 17:20 f.

VIII

THE DIVINE REQUIREMENT

53. *Obedience and Retribution*

The first concern of biblical religion, we have seen, is what God requires of man (s. 5). For two reasons, a lower and a higher, the controlling aim of man's life must be to do God's will.

The first and lower reason is that man's own safety and welfare demand obedience to the will of God. In the Bible this consideration is presented chiefly under the category of retribution: obedience is rewarded and disobedience is punished. In return for obedience to his commands God promises all the good things men need and crave, and at the same time he gives warning that failure to do what he requires will bring disaster and death. This is the essence of the covenant-idea (s. 5).

This aspect of biblical religion, characteristic of the Old Testament, corresponds to the fact that in practice, the world over and through all the ages, religion is often merely one of the ways by which men seek to get what they want. So long as natural means (from primitive hunting and fishing to the most elaborate contrivances of modern science) suffice to satisfy men's desires and avoid the dangers they fear, men are not religious. When their efforts to achieve their ends by such means prove inadequate, they turn for aid to superhuman powers.

The Bible, in common with the history of religions in general, gives many examples of such low-aiming, self-seeking religion. Jacob, facing the hazards of a long journey and the uncertainty of achieving its purpose, bargains with God for protection and success.[1] Jephthah makes a rash vow to secure victory in a military campaign.[2] The prominence of vows and votive offerings is illustrated by many of the psalms (s. 95). In fact, the blessings and curses attached to the covenant between Yah-

---

[1] Gen. 28:20–22. [2] Ju. 11:30 f.

weh and Israel fall almost entirely under the head of physical safety and welfare.[3]

From this point of view the primary motive for obedience, aside from the basic desires that are presupposed, is fear. It is no accident that the regular term for religion in the Old Testament is " the fear of Yahweh," though this means much more than merely being afraid of God (s. 81). Other motives also, however, are involved. The Old Testament makes much of gratitude as a motive of obedience: " I am Yahweh, thy God, who brought thee out of the land of Egypt, out of the house of bondage." [4] Closely connected with this is the motive of trust in God's superior wisdom, goodness, and power, for it is the experience of his blessings which induces such confidence.[5]

Here we meet also a further consideration (noted in s. 6 as a basis of God's authority), which goes deeper than mere retribution in the sense of extraneous rewards and punishments. Trust in God's goodness and wisdom carries with it the assurance that his commands are not arbitrary or unreasonable. He knows better than we do what is good for us, and what he demands of us is what we should do in our own interest if we had his wisdom. In this confidence we may commit ourselves wholeheartedly to his sovereign will without anxiety for our own earthly welfare, trusting that he knows what we need and will care for us.[6]

While the dependence of earthly welfare upon obedience is not the highest reason for seeking to do God's will, it would be quite erroneous to suppose that such lowly ends are to be despised. They have a permanent and rightful place in all true religion; asceticism has no place in the religion of the Old Testament or the New (ss. 104 ff.). Over and above all such worldly and personal considerations, however, there is another and much higher reason for making God's will the chief end of life.

54. God's Sovereignty and Glory; the Hallowing of His Name

The will of God is the supreme good because it is his will, and he is God. The religion of the Bible, while including and sanctioning human, this-worldly objectives, subordinates them to God's sovereign will. It does not stop even with the eternal salvation of human beings, but puts God's will above the very highest human good. God's interest is not limited to man, nor is the goal of man's endeavor limited to what is good

---

[3] Lev., ch. 26; Dt., chs. 27 to 30.
[4] Ex. 20:2, and often, especially in the Deuteronomic writings.
[5] Ps. 103.
[6] Mt. 6:25–34; 1 P. 5:7.

for himself or for the race.[1] God's sovereignty is absolute and must be accepted without condition or limit. While the Christian trusts God for what he needs, he must at the same time be prepared and willing to make any sacrifice for the kingdom of God.[2]

Another way of expressing this is that man's chief end is the glory of God. The Old Testament lays great stress on this conception. Sometimes, to be sure, it is presented in such naïve fashion as to be amusing to us, but when Yahweh appears to be moved merely by the desire to show what he can do, as though he were a celestial bully, this impression is doubtless in part the result of men's having projected into their idea of his attitude and purpose the concern for his glory which they recognized as the right motive for their own service.

The same motive also takes the form of exalting God's " name " (i.e., fame, reputation), which must not be profaned but sanctified (hallowed).[3] This conception is especially prominent in the Holiness Code,[4] the prophets,[5] and also the psalms.[6] Rabbinic literature repeatedly exalts glorifying God and sanctifying the Name as the highest motives for obedience to the law. In full agreement with this characteristic Jewish attitude Jesus gives as the first petition of his model prayer for the disciples, " Hallowed be thy name." [7] The two following petitions, " Thy kingdom come " and " Thy will be done," go with the first, all three together being modified by the words, " As in heaven, so also upon earth." The idea of the kingdom of God as the supreme object of the Christian life is expressed also in Mt. 6:33 (Lk. 12:31); Mt. 13:44 ff.; and ch. 19:12. It is exemplified by Jesus' own prayer in Gethsemane.[8] For the follower of Jesus, as for the ancient Hebrew or the later Jew, doing God's will for his sake is the supreme object of all endeavor. In the New Testament this complete, self-forgetting consecration is sometimes expressed as acting for the sake of Christ and his gospel.[9]

---

[1] Job 38:26; Is. 45:9; Jer. 18:6; Rom. 9:21.

[2] Mk. 8:34-37; Mt. 10:34-39; Lk. 9:57-62; 14:26-33.

[3] For typical expressions see Ex. 9:16; 14:17 f.; 33:18 f.; 34:5; Lev. 10:3; Num. 14:11-23; 20:12 f.; 27:12-14 (Dt. 32:48-51); Josh. 7:8 f.; 1 S. 12:22; 1 K. 8:41 f. (2 Chr. 6:32 f.); 9:7.

[4] Lev. 18:21; 19:12; 20:3; 21:6; 22:2, 32.

[5] Is. 8:13; 29:22 f.; Jer. 14:7, 21; Ezek. 20:9, 14, 22, 39, 44; 28:22, 25; 36:22 f.; 38:16, 23; 39:13, 21, 27; Is. 40:5; 42:8, 12; 43:6 f.; 48:9; 66:5, 13 f.; Mal. 2:2.

[6] Ps. 23:3; 25:11; 29:1-3, 9; 31:3; 72:19; 79:9; 96:8; 97:6; 102:15 f.; 104:31; 106:8; 109:21; 143:11; 145:5.

[7] Mt. 6:9; Lk. 11:2.

[8] Mk. 14:36.

[9] Mk. 8:35; 10:29 f.; cp. Phil. 3:7 f.

At this level the supreme motive of biblical religion becomes evident. Fear, gratitude, and trust grow and blossom into love. The first great expression of this ultimate motivation of worship and service is Dt. 6:5, which Judaism has adopted as a part of its basic confession of faith, named from the first Hebrew word of Dt. 6:4 the " Shema." Jesus quotes this passage as the first and greatest of all the commandments.[10]

The connection between love and gratitude is obvious. According to the biblical conception, love for God is a glad, free, humble response to God's love for man, manifested above all in the cross of Christ (s. 75).

55. *The Problem of Rewards*

Since the whole matter of judgment and salvation appears in the Bible primarily under the category of retribution, there is a certain paradox in the insistence on unselfish devotion to God's will and the frequent emphasis on salvation as God's gift rather than man's achievement. In connection with the question of God's justice we have already seen how impossible it proved to carry through consistently the idea of retribution (s. 25). Yet Jesus himself has a good deal to say of the rewards his disciples may expect.[1] This is not inconsistent with his exhortation to seek first God's kingdom and righteousness, for the rewards are promised to those who act, not for the sake of the reward, but for the sake of Christ and the gospel.[2] He who seeks his own life will lose it, but he who loses his life in service will find it.[3] Paradoxical this may be, but it is not contradictory. In fact, it is constantly confirmed by experience.

Some of the difficulty involved in the idea of expecting rewards while not seeking them disappears when we recall that what are described as rewards and punishments are often in reality the direct consequence of the action in question. As we have observed in another connection, what God commands is what man's own welfare requires (s. 6). But Christian discipleship does not guarantee personal safety and success (s. 56). So far as the individual is concerned, the rewards promised to Jesus' followers do not consist of worldly power and prosperity. To take literally such sayings as Mt. 5:5 or Mk. 10:30 would indeed make the gospel contradict itself, for Jesus warns those who follow him that they must expect hardship and hatred and perhaps death.[4]

It is only for the community or for mankind at large that the Chris-

---

[10] Mk. 12:29 f., and parallels.
[1] Mt. 5:3–12; Mk. 10:29 f.
[2] Mk. 10:29.
[3] Mk. 8:34–37; cp. ch. 10:45.
[4] Mk. 8:34; Lk. 9:57–62.

tian way brings earthly welfare. This is what he who loves his neighbor really wants. Yet in the last analysis, whatever may be the cost, that which is good for others is good for oneself. Paul's figure of the body and its members [5] reminds us of the essentially social nature of personality and the consequent fact that the ultimate good of all is the ultimate good of each. So the Christian loves his neighbor, not instead of himself, but as himself. Here if anywhere is to be found the explanation of the promise in Mt. 6:33, " All these things shall be added unto you." [6]

Another consideration that helps to resolve the paradox of doing God's will without regard to rewards, while still confidently expecting to be rewarded, is that man cannot possibly render such service as to put God under any obligation to him. The debt is all the other way, even when we have done our utmost.[7] All men, being sinners before God (s. 59), can really deserve no reward at all. What is called the reward of their righteousness, therefore, is always in reality a free gift of God.

In this connection another problem and a possible solution must be mentioned. It is a striking and puzzling fact that Paul, who more than any other biblical writer insists that salvation is a work of free grace apart from works (s. 62), also says that the Christian must look forward to a final judgment according to his works.[8] This apparent inconsistency may be explained, and is explained by some interpreters, by the supposition that Paul thought of graded rewards within the community of the saved. Only by grace through faith may one be delivered from wrath and have peace with God, but the Christian justified by faith will still be rewarded or punished according to his conduct. On this, as on many other points of Pauline theology, we cannot hope to attain certainty, because nowhere in his extant writings does Paul bring together the two aspects of his thought and explain the relation between them. Lacking such certainty, we must at least regard this explanation as possible.

56. The Law

What, then, is the will of God, and how is it to be known? This is the function of the law and the reason for its existence: in the law God makes known to Israel what must be done to gain his approval and blessing (s. 5). The law is often called the word or words of Yahweh

---

[5] Rom., ch. 12; 1 Cor., ch. 12.
[6] Cp. Mk. 8:35; 10:29 f.
[7] 1 Chr. 29:11–16; Ps. 50:9–12; Lk. 17:10; Acts 17:25.
[8] Rom. 14:10; 2 Cor. 5:10.

(s. 12); it is also designated by several special nouns: law, statute, precept, ordinance, judgment. The word usually translated " law " (Hebrew, *torah*) has been mentioned in s. 14 as being derived from a root meaning both " cast " and " teach." It usually, but not always, refers to the Mosaic legislation. Before the revelation at Sinai it rarely appears.[1] It is used of the commandments written on the stone tablets[2] and often thereafter of particular laws, especially in Leviticus and Numbers. Deuteronomy uses it of the law as given on the plains of Moab.[3] In Psalms it designates the law in general, usually with clear reference to the written law;[4] cp. also Lam. 2:9. In Is. 8:16 it apparently means the prophet's own teaching. It is used also of Ezekiel's new law[5] and of the law to be given in the future,[6] also of the law to be written on the heart[7] or now cherished in the heart.[8] Elsewhere in the prophetic books the reference is usually to the Mosaic law, though sometimes it is more general or uncertain. The wisdom literature uses the word *torah* of direct divine guidance,[9] of parental instruction,[10] and of training in the wisdom of the sages,[11] and also in a general and somewhat obscure way.[12] Later Jewish sources and the New Testament usually mean by the law the laws of the Pentateuch, yet Judaism also uses *torah* of revelation in general. The Greek word *nomos* is used also in the New Testament in other senses as well as to render Hebrew *torah* or its Aramaic equivalent. In general the force and associations of the Hebrew word might be better conveyed if it were everywhere translated " teaching " or " guidance." As was remarked in s. 29, it would not be inappropriate to take the exclamation of those who heard Jesus at Capernaum[13] as meaning that he was giving them a new torah.

The desire to know exactly what God required, and so to be sure of fulfilling his requirements and securing his blessing, led to the formulation of the Old Testament law codes (s. 5). After the completion and canonization of the Pentateuch the same motive produced the oral tradition (s. 10). The motive was wholly laudable, but the result was inevitably legalism, casuistry, and even sometimes hypocrisy. The most vital moral and social requirements were put on the same level with the whole system of traditional ritual practices, including even the irra-

[1] Ex. 12:49; 13:9; 16:4.
[2] Ex. 24:12.
[3] Dt. 1:5; 4:8, 44.
[4] Ps. 1:2; 19:7, and often, especially in Ps. 119.
[5] Ezek. 43:12.
[6] Mi. 4:2; Is. 2:3; 42:4; 51:4.
[7] Jer. 31:33; cp. 2 Cor. 3:3.
[8] Ps. 37:31; 40:8; Is. 51:7.
[9] Job 22:22.
[10] Prov. 1:8; 6:20 ff.
[11] Prov. 3:1; 7:2; 13:14.
[12] Prov. 28:4, 7, 9; 29:18; 31:26.
[13] Mk. 1:27.

tional primitive elements in it. The radical rejection of this point of view by the prophets and their insistence on the ethical as alone essential constitute perhaps the most distinctive development in Old Testament religion. In this respect the prophets were followed by Jesus. He denounced the scribes who laid heavy burdens on men's shoulders and would not move a finger to lift them.[14] By their traditions, he said, they had nullified the word of God.[15] He did not, however, abandon the basic conception of religion as doing the revealed will of God. When the rich man asked him what he must do to inherit eternal life, Jesus replied at once, "You know the commandments."[16] According to Mt. 5:17, he said that he had come not to destroy the law but to fulfill it.

Meanwhile, along with the development of legalism there had also been a growth of inwardness, with the conception that not only correct conduct but a loving attitude toward God was required. The classic expression of this in Dt. 6:5 has been noted in s. 54. The Holiness Code likewise demands love for one's neighbor.[17] Jesus, agreeing with some of the leading rabbis, puts these two commandments above all the written and oral law. He differs from Deuteronomy and all the rabbis, however, in regarding these two basic commandments as making unnecessary any detailed, specific prescriptions. For him the inner disposition takes precedence over the specific act,[18] though to be sure the right disposition also produces right acts and is judged accordingly. This is also the teaching of Paul, who repeats what Jesus said about love as fulfilling the law [19] and insists on Christian freedom, showing that the Christian is free from the law precisely because he is ruled by the spirit of love and therefore needs no law.[20] Practically the same conception of Christian freedom is expressed also in Jn. 8:32–36. Matthew and James, as we have seen (s. 29), present Christianity as essentially a new law, yet James calls it a law of liberty [21] and calls the commandment to love one's neighbor the royal law.[22]

All this is important for understanding the nature of Jesus' teaching. If religion is obeying God's will, but not in a legalistic sense, what is the will of God, and how is it to be known? Jesus left no code of directions for particular moral situations, but a basic ideal which his followers must apply for themselves to all situations. To regard the gospel as

14 Mt. 23:1–4.
15 Mk. 7:1–13.
16 Mk. 10:19.
17 Lev. 19:17 f.
18 Mt. 5:21 ff.; Mk. 7:14–23.

19 Rom. 13:10; Gal. 5:14.
20 Gal. 5:23.
21 Jas. 1:25.
22 Ch. 2:8.

merely a new law, superseding that of Moses but not essentially differ-ent, destroys the whole point of Jesus' ethical teaching.

To many today, as to the devout Jew of the first century, this seems to leave the believer with no positive moral guidance at all. All decisions as to what is right and what is wrong seem to be left to the individual. And so they are.[23] It is quite true, as Bultmann says,[24] that Jesus taught no ethics. He not only gave no code of duties; he gave no system of val-ues, though in some important respects his keen sense of relative values is clearly enough indicated. He went no farther in pointing out the prac-tical implications of the law of love than the quite general principle commonly known as the Golden Rule.[25]

Instead of precepts or a philosophy of values, Jesus taught a single basic attitude. Yet that attitude provides a positive ethical ideal, with implications affecting vitally every department of human conduct. Not mere good intentions in general but doing the will of God in specific sit-uations is what he demands: the tree is known by its fruits.[26] So Paul, in rejecting legalism, is careful to repudiate also the antinomianism with which he was charged by those who misinterpreted his idea of jus-tification by faith.[27] Christian love means to do good as Jesus did; [28] to serve instead of being served, as he did; [29] to be a good neighbor to any person in need of help,[30] not only one who loves us or can repay us but even an enemy.[31] It involves forgiveness and reconciliation, without re-sentment or any attempt at retaliation.[32]

If this still seems to leave too much to the individual, it must be ac-knowledged that the individual cannot know by his own unaided natural judgment what is God's will. Conscience gives all men some knowledge of the law of God,[33] and Jesus rebuked those who did not judge of them-selves what was right,[34] but Paul reminds us that to establish what is the good and perfect will of God men must be transformed by the re-newing of their minds.[35]

Of what use, then, is the law of the Old Testament? Paul endeavors to answer this question in Rom., chs. 3 to 7 and Gal., chs. 3 f., and his ve-hement, rather tortuous argument shows that the problem was a real one for him as well as for his readers. The essence of his answer is that

[23] Cf. Rom. 8:14; 2 Cor. 3:17 (cp. Ps. 119:45); Gal. 5:1.
[24] R. Bultmann, *Jesus and the Word*, p. 84.
[25] Mt. 7:12; Lk. 6:31; cp. Tobit 4:15.
[26] Mt. 7:15–27.
[27] Rom. 3:8; 6.
[28] Acts 10:38.
[29] Mk. 10:41–45.
[30] Lk. 10:29–37.
[31] Mt. 5:44; Lk. 6:27.
[32] Mt. 5:38–42.
[33] Rom. 2:14 f.; s. 15.
[34] Lk. 12:57.
[35] Rom. 12:2.

the law had performed a good but temporary function. Historically it had exposed the sinfulness of human life and the need of redemption, and so had prepared the way for Christ. For the individual it still served the same purpose: it brought the knowledge of sin, which would otherwise reign unrecognized over men's lives and destroy them. But in so doing it only made men wretched, for it had no power to overcome the sin which it brought to light.

While much of the Old Testament law is wholly irrelevant for our lives, there is also much in it that may still be used to bring home to men the realization of their sinfulness. For this purpose it must be read with the saying in mind that to enter the kingdom of God we must be not less but more righteous than the law requires.[36] In other words, the righteousness of the law is a minimum righteousness. He who obeys the two great commandments of love for God and love for man cannot fall below the standard set by the Old Testament. If he is not far above it, he has fallen short of what God requires.[37]

Accepting the responsibility of applying Jesus' ideal to present-day situations, we must face the question whether such an application is possible. Some interpreters deny that Jesus intended his teaching to be applied to normal social relationships in this world. The eschatological emphasis in his proclamation of the kingdom of God has given rise to Schweitzer's theory that Jesus taught an " interim ethic," intended only for the brief interval before the coming of the kingdom.[38] It is true that Jesus did not contemplate a long duration of the present order (s. 73), and therefore did not give instructions for living in such a situation. On the other hand, his ethical teaching was by no means a mere temporary *modus vivendi* pending the parousia: it was concerned with the attitudes and relationships which would obtain permanently in the kingdom itself, and which would have to be realized meanwhile in the lives of those who were to participate in the eternal kingdom. Some of his demands, such as selling all and giving to the poor, may have been intended only for the immediate situation, and not necessarily for all his followers even then, but on the whole he required of his disciples in the present life what would be completely realized in the coming age. In other words, Jesus' ethical teaching was neither an interim ethic, intended to be applicable only for a brief period and under abnormal conditions, nor a

---

[36] Mt. 5:20.

[37] Cp. s. 18 on the permanent validity of the Mosaic legislation.

[38] Albert Schweitzer, *The Quest of the Historical Jesus*, pp. 352, 364; *The Mystery of the Kingdom of God*, pp. 94–105.

visionary ideal for the coming age only, to be held in abeyance and re-garded as inapplicable to the conditions of this life.

Since the kingdom of God did not come as soon as Jesus expected and has not come yet, we must still ask whether his ideal is actually prac-ticable in the world as we know it. To this question we can confidently reply on the basis of all human experience, not only that the Christian way of life works, but that it is the only way which will. To understand what this means, however, four points must be borne in mind.

a. The ideal of Jesus will not work in the sense of accomplishing ends which it was never intended to accomplish. It is not to be judged by its power to bring worldly success. Its end is not the attainment of any good by the individual or group at the expense of others. What it is in-tended to achieve and does achieve is more abundant spiritual life here and eternal life in the world to come (s. 72), and as a means or a by-product better material and social conditions for mankind at large (s. 103). For the individual it may mean a cross (s. 55).

b. To say that the ethical teaching of Jesus is practicable does not mean that it can be enacted into legislation and enforced on people who are not followers of Jesus. The church must always proclaim and dem-onstrate an ideal far above what can be enforced by law, the ideal which would be realized without any laws if all people were Christians.

c. What Jesus demands is not an emotion but an attitude of the will. Christians themselves sometimes complain that the commandment to love our neighbor is too hard, because our feelings are not subject to our control. But love for God, as Jesus taught and exemplified it, is not mere feeling; it is active devotion (s. 81). And love for man is " like unto it." To love one's neighbor is not to feel affection for him but to wish and seek his good. Such service almost inevitably begets a feeling of love for those who are served, but feeling is secondary and not essential.

d. What Jesus demands is that we do what love requires in each given situation. The ideal is not impossible, because it requires no more and no less than the best that is possible under the circumstances. It remains always beyond us because we have not practiced it, not because we can-not. We are sinners because we have done what we could have refrained from doing and have left undone what we could have done.

What is involved is not perfection, either in an absolute, indefinable sense or in the legalistic sense of completely fulfilling every detailed ob-ligation. He who makes the law his standard is obligated to perform all its precepts,[39] for to break one commandment is to break the law. He who lives by faith and love is not judged on that basis, but by a standard infinitely higher and at the same time more attainable.

The form of Jesus' saying in Mt. 5:48, " Be ye therefore perfect even as your heavenly Father is perfect," has created and still creates untold confusion for earnest Christians. Two facts must be observed to set this matter straight. In the first place, the meaning of the word " perfect " here is to be defined by the context. Jesus has been speaking of love for enemies as well as friends, and has pointed out that God is good not only to the just but also to the unjust. The conclusion is that to be a true son of the heavenly Father one must be thoroughgoing in the exercise of love, as God is, without reservation or discrimination. He must not, like the scribe of Lk. 10:29, try to justify himself by saying, " Yes, but who is my neighbor? " If Jesus said what Matthew here reports, he must have used an Aramaic word capable of this interpretation.

But, in the second place, it is extremely doubtful that he used any word accurately represented by Matthew's " perfect " (*teleios*). Instead of this word Lk. 6:36 reads " merciful." This might conceivably, of course, be merely Luke's interpretation of the difficult idea of perfection, which Greek readers would be likely to misunderstand. But the possibility that it is Matthew who has substituted a different word for the one Jesus actually used becomes a distinct probability, little short of certainty, when we note that the same word appears again in Mt. 19:21, " If thou wouldst be perfect," but not in either Mk. 10:21 or Lk. 18:22. What Jesus demanded was impartial love like God's for all men.

The more clearly all this is understood, the more evident is it that all men stand condemned and subject to God's righteous condemnation, " for all have sinned and fall short of the glory of God." [40]

---

[39] Gal. 5:3.   [40] Rom. 3:23.

IX

SIN

57. *Nature of Sin*

Two conceptions of the nature of sin are combined in the Old Testament without any clear statement of the distinction. One, of less permanent significance but important because of its consequences, is an impersonal idea belonging to the general category of the taboo. Under this head come three related ideas, indicated by three different terms though without clear distinctions in meaning:

(1) The idea of the " unclean " is that of an almost material defilement which renders a person unfit for participation in worship until it is removed. Unclean foods, defilement from touching a corpse, sexual taboos, and the like are applications of this concept. (2) The idea of the " accursed " or " devoted " (*herem*) is understood in the Old Testament as applying to what is set apart as belonging exclusively to Yahweh and not to be used by men, especially the spoils of war,[1] or anything voluntarily dedicated to God and thus withdrawn from ordinary human use. In spite of this connection with a personal deity, the idea may well have belonged originally to the impersonal category of taboo. (3) Closely related is the idea of the " holy " when applied to what is set apart for religious purposes (s. 25).

These concepts become connected with the idea of sin because violations of the limits imposed by them incur dire consequences. According to the primitive way of thinking, the consequences are automatic and quite independent of good or evil intentions or social effects (recall the case of Uzzah, noted in s. 25). Violation of the *herem* brings calamity to the whole people until the perpetrator is eradicated.[2] Uncleanness is apparently less serious, since it may be removed by appropriate ceremonies, especially ablutions.[3] Hebrew law and ritual included much that

---

[1] Josh. 6:17 f.; 7:1, 11–15.   [3] Lev., chs. 11 ff.
[2] Josh., ch. 7; cp. 1 S. 14:24–45.

was based on these ideas, thus retaining a mass of requirements having no ethical, social, or rational significance along with the most important moral and social ideals. The conception of the law as the revealed will of God put all these things on the same level of importance and obligation and made the elimination of even the most irrational elements in the tradition almost impossible. Only the radical attitude of the prophets and Jesus could extricate religion from this confusion (*v.i.* on Mk. 7:14–23).

Over against such impersonal ideas is the far more characteristic personal conception of sin as disobedience to the will of God. This is already implied in the story of Adam and Eve and underlies the whole idea of the covenant and the law. While more congenial to our ways of thinking, it is not necessarily less primitive or later in origin than the impersonal conception. At the root of this idea of sin as an offense against a personal deity lies the naïve assumption of primitive man that any harm he suffers must be the result of a deliberate act by an offended power. The offense may of course be purely religious in the sense that it has no moral or social implications. Man may not even know what he has done to bring wrath on himself. Israel, however, has the law and knows what the Lord requires (s. 5). Sin is therefore disobedience to the revealed will of God.

The specific content of the idea of sin, when conceived in this personal fashion, depends upon the character of God. Since Yahweh is a righteous and gracious God, concerned not merely for his own glory but also for the welfare of his people, what he demands is what is best for man himself (s. 6). Thus, while primarily and essentially an offense against God, sin is also an offense against man; or rather, offenses against man are also sins against God. Everything approved by custom and public opinion thus tends to receive the sanction of the divine will. Since the traditional and irrational taboos discussed above are sanctioned by custom and group approval, they too come to be reinterpreted as divine demands. Hence the confusion already noted. The idea that David's census was sinful and was therefore punished by pestilence [4] is probably to be explained by this process. The impersonal and personal conceptions of sin thus come to be combined and confused, but in Yahwism the personal conception is decidedly dominant, especially in the religion of the prophets.

This is equally true of postbiblical Judaism. Since all religion was

[4] 2 S., ch. 24.

subsumed under obedience to the law, and the whole law was inspired, the tendency to regard all requirements as equally obligatory, and thus to put moral and ritual laws on the same level, continued. Some rabbis, however, whose insight was better than their logic, actually distinguished between more and less important laws.

In the New Testament the impersonal conception of sin has dropped out entirely, and with it the traditional conceptions and practices related to it. Jesus, quoting the commandments to the rich man who has asked what he must do to inherit eternal life, names only the ethical commandments.[5] Jesus' freedom in the use of the law has been noted in s. 20. The prominence of stories of controversies on such matters in the gospels shows that the early church had to answer much Jewish criticism in this regard. Such disputes are not stressed in Acts, chs. 1 to 12, perhaps because the apologetic purpose of the book leads to smoothing over controversies; yet Peter's vision at Joppa [6] implies the abrogation of the laws of clean and unclean. Paul opposes on principle any compromise on such matters.[7] In Col. 2:16 he condemns regulations regarding food and drink and the observance of special days. In 1 Cor., ch. 8, however, he counsels consideration for the scruples of weaker brethren who do not know that such things are unimportant, and according to Acts 21:18 ff. he himself underwent ritual purification in the temple to show that he obeyed the law.

Jesus never speaks of sin in the abstract, but always of specific sins. The word " sin " occurs in the singular only once in the synoptic gospels,[8] and even there the meaning is not " all sin " but " every sin." [9] Sins are called " debts," [10] as often in Jewish sources. The content of Jesus' conception of sin differs from that prevalent in Judaism only as his conception of the will of God differs from the current conception. His interpretation of the will of God in terms of love for God and one's neighbor makes his idea of sin more searching and strict than anything in the Old Testament or in Judaism.[11] Sin is any failure to realize the ideal of being worthy children of the Father, as perfect in love as he is.[12] Hence not simply the act but the purpose is involved; the inner attitude is fundamental.[13] Good intentions without action, however, are not sufficient.[14]

[5] Mk. 10:19, and parallels.
[6] Acts 10:9–16.
[7] Gal. 2:11 ff.
[8] Mt. 12:31.
[9] Mk. 3:28, " all sins."

[10] Mt. 6:12.
[11] Mt. 5:20; cp. s. 54.
[12] Mt. 5:43–48; but cp. s. 56.
[13] Mt. 5:21 f., 27 f.; Mk. 7:21 ff.
[14] Mt. 7:15–27; cp. Jas., ch. 2.

Paul has a new and distinctive idea of the nature of sin. Like Jesus, he speaks of " sins "; [15] he also uses the Old Testament words " transgression " and " trespass." In sharp contrast to Jesus, however, he often and characteristically speaks of sin in the abstract, as an alien power resident in the body.[16] Paul's idea of the law (s. 56) is involved here: salvation cannot be achieved by the works of the law, but it could be if anyone could actually obey the law. There is a law or principle of sin in the flesh which prevents man from doing right even when he wants to; hence the law can only show what sin is, and in doing this it gives a further incitement to sin.[17] This whole set of ideas is an extraordinary example of effort to integrate personal experience and inherited conceptions. It gains new significance from our growing recognition of the irrational bases of conduct.

The rest of the New Testament presents no distinctive ideas on the nature of sin. The Johannine literature speaks of sin as walking in darkness.[18] In general the fact of sin is assumed as the basis of the need for salvation, but without any discussion of its nature. The prevailing conception throughout is obviously that of disobedience to the revealed will of God.

58. *Origin*

The Old Testament has no doctrine of the fall of man. Sin, as disobedience, simply began when the first man and woman disobeyed God. In Gen., ch. 3, the origin of sin is no more stressed than any of the other etiological elements in the story (s. 38); furthermore the story plays no part in any discussion of sin in the rest of the Old Testament. The identification of the serpent with Satan has caused much misunderstanding. Actually the idea of Satan is much later than this story (s. 41). The psychological origin of sin, however, is cleverly portrayed in the present form of the story. The feeling that freedom has been limited, doubt regarding the threatened consequences of the act, desire for what is to be gained by it, and the wish to bring another person into it when the act has been performed are presented as successive stages of temptation. The whole story presupposes the existence of divine commandments and the freedom to obey or disobey.

Various ideas regarding the source or cause of sin are stated or implied by the prophets. What we should call selfishness, materialism, and

---

[15] I Cor. 15:3.
[16] Rom. 5:12 to 8:10.
[17] Rom. 7:7–24; Gal. 3:19, 21 f.
[18] Jn. 3:19; I Jn. 2:11.

secularism are stressed by Amos, Hosea, and Isaiah. Hosea emphasizes especially lack of the knowledge of God, leading to paganism.[1] Jeremiah speaks repeatedly of the evil heart as the source of sin.[2] Judah's sin is graven upon the tablet of the heart,[3] as the law will be under the new covenant,[4] when God will give his people a heart to fear him and put the fear of him in their hearts.[5]

The idea of sin as instigated by Satan appears in 1 Chr. 21:1 (s. 41). Later Judaism made much of this idea, as popular Christianity does to the present time. The idea of original sin is approached in some of the discussions of the consequences of Adam's sin.[6] Rabbinic theology has a characteristic doctrine of the " evil impulse," which is regarded sometimes as identical with Satan's instigation to evil, sometimes as something resident in human nature which the tempter arouses to activity. The origin of evil desires and the knowledge of sin are also sometimes explained by the story of Gen. 6:1–4 (s. 39).

Jesus, like Jeremiah, regards the heart (including mind and will, s. 46) as the source of sin.[7] Against his critics he quotes Is. 29:13.[8] No further indication of the origin of sin is given, unless it is implied in the temptation narrative, if this is to be taken as autobiographical;[9] or in the ambiguous references to " evil " or " the evil one " (s. 41). The place taken by Adam in late Jewish and Christian theology is nowhere suggested in any saying of Jesus, whose ideas and attitude with regard to sin are always practical rather than theoretical, Hebrew rather than Greek.

Paul has distinctive ideas regarding the origin as well as the nature of sin, though they appear only incidentally in the exposition of justification by faith (s. 62). Sin entered the world through Adam and has been active ever since, but only when the law came was sin known.[10] The serpent's beguiling of Eve is mentioned once.[11] Paul simply assumes the traditional idea of Adam's trespass, however. His interest is in the deliverance by God's grace in Christ; and by way of contrast he indicates his idea of the origin of sin. From Rom. 5:15 it is possible to infer that the power of sin in the flesh was a result of Adam's trespass, but Paul does not actually say this. His meaning may be simply what is stated in

[1] Ho. 2:8, 20; 4:1, 6; 6:3, 6; 8:2; 13:4.
[2] Jer. 7:24; 11:8; 16:12; 18:12; 23:17.
[3] Ch. 17:1.
[4] Ch. 31:33.
[5] Chs. 24:7; 32:39 f.; cp. Ezek. 11:19.
[6] 2 Esdr. 3:4–9, 20–22; 4:30; 7:46–48.
[7] Mk. 7:21–23.
[8] Mk. 7:6 f.
[9] Cp. Lk. 22:31.
[10] Rom. 5:12–21.
[11] 2 Cor. 11:3.

4 Ezra,[12] that Adam had an evil heart and sinned, and so do all his descendants. In 1 Cor. 15:45–48 Paul contrasts Adam as " natural " and " earthy " with Christ as " spiritual " and " heavenly." Ever since Adam's transgression, human flesh has been the seat of sin, but Paul does not explain how or why. While he gives the suggestion from which the doctrine of original sin was later developed, he does not himself formulate the doctrine or make clear how close his own thought comes to it.

The Johannine literature indicates only that sin is the work of the devil.[13] The devil is referred to also in 1 P. 5:8 and Jas. 4:7, but Jas. 1:13–15 and ch. 4:1 f. attribute temptation to man's own desires. In general, whatever incidental allusions are made to Adam or Satan, the New Testament assumes that sin is an act of man's free will in disobedience to God's law. Only Paul (aside from the suggestion of Mk. 14:38) distinguishes inner consent and outer weakness. The stress laid by later theology on the fall of man as necessitating redemption is not found in the New Testament. This does not, of course, make sin unreal or redemption unnecessary. The reality of sin and the need of redemption are no more dependent upon any theological doctrine than they are on the truth or falsehood of any scientific theory of evolution. They are facts of experience which a realistic theology must take into account.

59. *Extent and Prevalence*

The degree to which human nature is dominated by sin is not stated in the form of a universal proposition in the Bible. The ability to choose and do either the right or the wrong is commonly assumed (s. 76). Judaism holds that there is a good impulse as well as an evil impulse in man. While the rabbis sometimes say that a man cannot overcome his evil impulse without divine aid, this means simply that he must resist it and pray for help. Jesus and all the New Testament writers except Paul, as already noted, assume the sinner's ability to repent and to " go and sin no more." [1] Even Paul at his most helpless says, " To will is present with me." [2]

The idea of total depravity, in the sense of such a complete corruption of human nature that no man can either will or do what is right without redemption by divine grace, is thus unsupported by the Bible. Even in the sense that every part or division of human nature is tainted by sin the doctrine of total depravity is nowhere stated in the Bible, and texts

---

[12] *V.s.*, note 6.
[13] Jn. 8:44; 13:2; 1 Jn. 3:8.

[1] Jn. 8:11.
[2] Rom. 7:18.

can be cited to support it only by pushing them beyond their real meaning. The only sense in which the Bible teaches total depravity is that all men are sinners, and even this is not without exception. The antediluvian generation is condemned as wholly inclined to evil,[3] and apparently the statement still holds good after the flood,[4] yet Noah is approved as righteous.[5] In Ps. 51:5 the psalmist says he was conceived and born in sin, but does not generalize about the whole race. Ps. 58:3 says that the wicked are so from their mothers' wombs; it does not say that all men are wicked. Ps. 14:1–3 (Ps. 53:1–3), however, is inclusive enough, and Paul takes it with other quotations from the Psalms to show that all men are sinners.[6] Other statements apply specifically to Israel at a particular time, or to Israel's enemies, or to the wicked or the personal enemies of the writer. The psalmist claims to be blameless in Ps. 18:20–24 (2 S. 22:21–25); cp. Job 33:9 (though ch. 14:4 says no man is so perfect that God cannot find some fault with him).[7] Even Jeremiah, who condemns his contemporaries in Israel in strong and varied language, gives no generalization about the sinfulness of all men.

Jesus calls the men of his generation evil and adulterous.[8] All men are at least potentially sinners,[9] but Jesus also regards all men as at least potentially sons of God (s. 62), with the resurrection in view. He sees the best possibilities in all individuals and seems to regard none as hopeless except the self-righteous and insincere. His interest in defective personalities and the underprivileged is remarkable. The term " sinner " was applied in that day by Jews to Gentiles, by Pharisees to Sadducees, and by the self-satisfied religious people to the poor and meek, the " people of the land "; Jesus sometimes uses the word similarly, as though in quotation marks, in parallelism with publicans and the like, but in this sense Jesus associated himself with the " sinners." In any case, his conception of sin (s. 57) makes all men sinners.

As noted above, Paul emphatically states the universal sinfulness of mankind.[10] Only Christ is without sin.[11] Even the statement that all men are sinners, however, is a statement of fact for which men are under

[3] Gen. 6:5.
[4] Ch. 8:21.
[5] Chs. 6:9; 7:1.
[6] Rom. 3:9–20, 23.
[7] Cp. also Job 4:17–19; 9:2; 15:14, 16; 25:6.
[8] Mk. 8:38; 9:19; Mt. 12:34 f.; 16:4; 17:17; 23:33; Lk. 9:41; 11:9 ff.; cp. Acts 2:40.
[9] Lk. 13:1–5; cp. Jn. 8:7.
[10] Rom. 3:9–20, 23; Gal. 3:22.
[11] 2 Cor. 5:21; so also Heb. 4:15; 7:26; 1 Jn. 3:5.

judgment and summoned to repentance. Universal sinfulness is not inherently and necessarily true of human nature as a result of Adam's sin. In the same way what Paul says about the power of sin in the flesh is a statement of experience, not a theory. It is an observed and undeniable fact that all men are sinners, and therefore subject to the righteous judgment of God.

X

JUDGMENT AND SALVATION

60. *Judgment*

The biblical conception of judgment requires some explanation, though the basic idea is clear enough. The Hebrew root meaning " to judge " and the words derived from it have a wider meaning than the corresponding English words: they include not only the pronouncement of sentence but also its execution. The essence of the idea is setting right what is wrong, restoring the rights of those who have been wronged and punishing the wrongdoers — in short, establishing justice. The object of the verb " to judge " may be the wronged party whose rights are restored [1] or the wrongdoer who is punished.[2] The noun " judge " means one who establishes justice. The heroes of the book of Judges were not merely magistrates who adjudicated disputes, though some of them did this,[3] but warriors who delivered Israel from oppression and punished the oppressors. The noun " judgment " accordingly means the act by which justice is done; it also means that which is right, whether custom,[4] the rights of an individual or group,[5] the right in general,[6] or simply justice.[7] It is also used as the name of a particular type of law dealing with civil justice.[8]

With reference to those who have been wronged, judgment means deliverance and is thus the same thing as salvation (s. 61); with reference to the wrongdoer it means condemnation and punishment. We are here concerned with it in the latter sense. In the Old Testament, since Israel is God's people, the enemies of Israel are *ipso facto* God's enemies;

---

[1] E.g., the fatherless and the oppressed, Ps. 10:18.
[2] E.g., the Egyptians who oppressed Israel, Gen. 15:14.
[3] Ju. 4:4 f.; cp. Ex. 18:26; 1 S. 4:18; 7:15–17.
[4] Ju. 18:7.
[5] Ps. 9:4; Jer. 5:28.
[6] Gen. 18:25.
[7] 1 S. 8:3; Ps. 72:2; Am. 5:24.
[8] Ex. 21:1.

Israel's victories are therefore divine judgments,[9] God's "righteous acts."[10] This idea was applied not only to the exploits of the judges but also to the whole history of the establishment and growth of the kingdom. The divine vindication of Israel might take the form of a miraculous overthrow of the enemy.[11] But every victory was Yahweh's doing;[12] in fact, all history was the sphere of his judgments (s. 18). An outstanding example of exultation in the overthrow of a dreaded enemy by Yahweh is the book of Nahum.[13]

In later hopes for the future this idea takes such forms as Yahweh's destruction of the great army from the north (s. 66). The New Testament point of view leaves no place for such a conception of judgment on the enemies of God's people as such, though the old idea flares up again under Roman oppression in Revelation.[14]

Meanwhile the chosen people enjoyed no exemption from judgment. As obedience assured freedom from the fear of enemies, so disobedience forfeited any claim on Yahweh's protection; indeed, Yahweh not only left his people to their foes but even summoned other nations to punish them.[15] This is proclaimed by Amos[16] and the other prophets. First Assyria and then Babylonia are regarded as Yahweh's instruments of judgment on sinful Israel.[17] The same warning which is underlined by the Deuteronomic framework of the book of Judges is inserted also at critical points in the other historical books.[18] It is reiterated in the Holiness Code[19] and with bitter ferocity in late additions to Deuteronomy.[20] It appears even in the New Testament.[21]

The emergence of individualism in Hebrew religion (s. 49) involved the application of the idea of divine judgment to the individual. All life was thought of as governed by the principle of retribution: the good prospered and the wicked suffered as they deserved. Something of the

---

9 Ex. 6:6; 7:4; 12:12; Num. 33:4.

10 Literally, "righteousness," Ju. 5:11; 1 S. 12:7-11.

11 Ex. 14:21-31; Josh., chs. 6; 10:11, 13; Ju., chs. 4 f.; 1 S. 7:7-11; 2 K. 6:8-20; 7:6; 19:35.

12 1 Chr. 11:14.

13 See further s. 108.

14 Rev. 17:1, 3, 9, 18; 18:2, 6-8.

15 Ju. 2:13 f.; 3:7 f., and throughout the Deuteronomic framework of the book of Judges.

16 Am. 3:11 f.; 5:27; 6:14; 7:9.

17 Ho. 9:1-3; 11:5; 13:16; Is. 2:10-21; 5:26-30; 7:17-25; 8:5-8; 9:8-12; 10:28-34; Jer. 25:8-11, and often.

18 Note especially 2 K. 17:6 ff., 20-23.

19 Lev. 26:17, 25, 31-39.

20 Dt. 28:25 f., 31-34, 36 ff., 47-57, 64-68.

21 Lk. 19:41-44; 21:20-24.

history of this idea and the trouble it caused has appeared in s. 25. The religion of both Old and New Testaments is dominated by the conviction that every life is subject to judgment, here or hereafter. Sooner or later, in one way or another, the wicked are punished and the righteous rewarded, for God is the righteous Judge of all the earth.[22] Only by divine deliverance from sin itself can there be any escape from God's righteous judgment.

But judgment is not merely a matter of just retribution, and its result is not necessarily destruction or everlasting punishment. As applied to God's people, judgment is not in the first place retributive but redemptive in its purpose; only where the stubbornness of the people prevents the achievement of this purpose does the punishment become retributive. The idea of disciplinary and redemptive judgment appears already in Am. 4:6–11, but it is Hosea who first makes it primary.[23] Lev., ch. 26, similarly regards the purpose of judgment as redemptive; [24] no such idea appears in Dt., ch. 28,[25] but it emerges in ch. 30:1–10. The book of Lamentations regards the nation's calamity as a just punishment which will be remitted if the people repent and turn to Yahweh.[26]

Even retributive or penal judgment may be limited and temporary, in which case it ceases when the sinner has worked out his complete sentence.[27] Temporary discipline does not imply the loss of God's favor; it is to be accepted as the chastening of the loving Father and taken to heart as a warning against repeating the offense which incurred it.[28] Here there is no question or need of salvation.

But when once the law of loving devotion to God and man has been comprehended, it is clear that no man can claim to have satisfied its requirements. Even one who has observed the whole law from his youth finds that he still lacks something vitally necessary.[29] Paul, who exceeded his countrymen in the righteousness of the law,[30] still found that he could not do the good that he wanted to do but was helpless and in need of deliverance.[31]

[22] Gen. 18:25; Ps. 96:13; 98:9; Acts 17:31.
[23] Ho. 2:14–23; 5:15; 7:13, 15; 11:11.
[24] Vv. 18, 23 f., 27.
[25] Cp. vv. 61, 63.
[26] Lam. 1:18; 2:17; 3:21–25; 38–42; 4:22; 5:21 f.
[27] Is. 40:2.
[28] Job 5:17–27; Prov. 3:11; Heb. 12:5–11.
[29] Mk. 10:20 f.; cp. Mt. 19:20 f.; Lk. 18:21 f.
[30] Gal. 1:14.
[31] Rom. 7:14–24.

61. *Salvation*

In the preceding section it was noted that for those who have been
wronged judgment means salvation. So it is said in Ju. 2:18 that Yahweh " raised them up judges . . . and saved them out of the hand of
their enemies." So also the noun " salvation " is used for various instances of judgment in the sense of righting wrongs, deliverance from
oppression, and the like.[1]

Four meanings of salvation are to be distinguished.

a. All the good things men commonly hope to secure through religion have a double aspect, positive and negative: the achievement of
every good means also deliverance from some evil suffered or feared.
Thus health means being saved from sickness; life means being saved
from death, etc. In its most general sense, therefore, salvation means
the sum total of all the rewards of righteousness. For Israel this means
all the benefits of keeping the covenant; for the individual it includes
safety, health, prosperity, and all the particular blessings expected from
God (ss. 104 ff.). Both the Old Testament and the New Testament often speak of salvation in this broad sense, using also such synonyms as
deliverance, redemption, and the like. Hebrew nouns derived from the
root meaning " save " are translated not only " salvation " but also
sometimes, in one or more of the English versions, " health," [2]
" safety," [3] " victory," [4] or " welfare." [5] Security, prosperity, and welfare were all included in a comprehensive idea expressed by the Hebrew
word usually translated " peace," the primary meaning of which is
" wholeness " (cp. English " health "). The breadth of meaning covered
by this term is shown by the fact that it is sometimes in our English versions represented by the word " health," [6] sometimes by " prosperity," [7]
and sometimes by " welfare." [8]

b. When men fail to meet the conditions set by God, they incur punishment. Salvation now acquires further meaning. Sin and judgment
would leave man hopeless and helpless if he could not hope for divine
mercy. Disciplinary punishment and limited retribution (s. 60) require

[1] Ex. 14:13; 1 Chr. 16:35; 2 Chr. 20:17; Ps. 144:10; Lk. 1:71.
[2] Ps. 42:11; 43:5; 67:2.
[3] Ps. 33:17; Prov. 11:14; 21:31; 24:6.
[4] 1 S. 19:5; 2 S. 19:2; 23:10, 12; 2 K. 5:1; 13:17; Ps. 98:1; Prov. 21:31.
[5] Job 30:15.
[6] Gen. 43:28; 2 S. 20:9.
[7] Job 15:21; Ps. 35:27; 73:3; Jer. 33:9; cp. Zc. 8:12.
[8] Gen. 43:27; Ex. 18:7; 1 Chr. 18:10; Ps. 69:22; Jer. 38:4.

no salvation unless it is a matter of escaping the penalty altogether or having the sentence remitted before it has been suffered in full. When the punishment is retributive and permanent, however, only a cancellation of the sentence can give release. The divine wrath or determination to punish must be changed to mercy or willingness to remit the penalty; i.e., God must be appeased or propitiated. In much of the Old Testament, as in primitive religions, the naïve assumption that all misfortune indicates divine wrath, which must be allayed by entreaty or some act or gift to win good will, evokes first spontaneous efforts and later elaborate systems of propitiatory rites (s. 75). Thus salvation means deliverance from incurred misfortune through appeasing the wrath of the God who has inflicted it. This conception of salvation, like the first, is still prominent in the Bible. Both the nation and the individual may be delivered by divine mercy from the calamities their acts have deserved. For the nation the deliverance takes the form of restoration to Palestine after the exile (s. 107); for the individual it means forgiveness and the remission of whatever punishment has been imposed, i.e., atonement (s. 75).

c. The New Testament, with some foreshadowing in the Old Testament, shows also a further aspect of salvation, corresponding to a development in the conception of sin. Man requires not only the forgiveness of his past offenses but also emancipation from the power of sin itself by the infusion of a new power and an inner transformation (s. 63).

d. For both Old and New Testaments the completion of salvation, individual and social, is a matter of the future, involving deliverance from all the consequences of sin and all the evils and limitations of this life (ss. 64 ff.).

For the last three of these aspects of the concept of salvation the term "redemption" (literally, "buying back") seems especially appropriate, though it is actually used in the Bible with much the same range of meaning as "salvation." The English words "redeem" and "redemption" represent the verbal and nominal forms of two different Hebrew roots in the Old Testament and two Greek roots in the New Testament. One of the Hebrew roots (*pdh*), with its derivates, is used for redeeming the first-born; [9] the other (*g'l*) is used for the redemption of property to prevent its alienation from the family,[10] and also for blood revenge.[11]

---

[9] Ex. 13:13; 34:20; Num. 18:15 ff.
[10] Lev. 25:25 ff.; Ru., ch. 4; Jer. 32:6–15.
[11] Num. 35:12; Dt. 19:6, 12; Josh. 20:3, 5, 9.

Both words are applied also to the divine deliverance of Israel from the Egyptians and other foes and the individual's deliverance from sickness, oppression, and other evils. The Greek words used in the New Testament have similar connections and also a more specific association with emancipation from slavery and the ransom of captives; they are applied by the New Testament writers, however, especially Paul, to the believer's salvation from sin.

The implications of the religious usage of these terms in the Bible must be discussed more fully in subsequent sections. The point of the present section is that the biblical terminology of salvation is varied and is used very broadly. While the basic idea of deliverance remains fairly constant, and the deliverance is always a divine act, no hard and fast doctrine or set of ideas can be found in the use of the words denoting salvation. At the same time, certain aspects of the subject are of much greater importance than others. Our task is to select and clarify these most important aspects of salvation.

62. *Forgiveness, Justification, Reconciliation, Adoption*

Since salvation means deliverance from sin and its penalties, the content of the idea of salvation is in part determined by the nature and consequences of sin. Not only does sin incur punishment; it also interrupts or destroys the relationship between the individual or group and God.[1] The literature of the Babylonian exile, for example, is full of mourning because Yahweh has withdrawn his presence and hidden his face from Israel. The psalms repeatedly utter the same complaint from individuals. The New Testament also presents this conception of the estrangement produced by sin.[2]

Since it is man's sin that breaks his communion with God, the restoration of the relationship requires God's forgiveness. This major theme of the whole Bible is expressed in many ways. Various metaphorical expressions are used for God's dealing with men's sins: he heals them,[3] removes them or puts them far away,[4] puts them behind his back,[5] conceals or covers them,[6] lifts or takes them away,[7] wipes them away or

---

[1] Is. 59:2; Ps. 51:10 f.
[2] Rom. 1:18–32; Eph. 2:12.
[3] Ps. 103:3.
[4] V. 12.
[5] Is. 38:17.
[6] Ps. 32:1; 85:2.
[7] Translated " forgive," Ps. 32:1; 85:2; " pardon," Mi. 7:18.

blots them out.[8] The usual Hebrew word for pardoning sin means, literally, " overlook " or the like; [9] in the Old Testament it is used only with God as subject, though modern Hebrew uses it as a general word for pardon. In the Pentateuch it is applied to particular sins; [10] so also Am. 7:2 and often in the Deuteronomic writings, especially 1 and 2 Kings. In Jeremiah it is used three times for the complete pardon of all sin.[11] Some of the same passages also use the verb " cleanse."

In many of the foregoing passages there is no suggestion of winning forgiveness by any act of atonement or even by repentance. The Hebrew verb which ordinarily means " make atonement " (s. 75) is sometimes used with God as subject and sins as object, where we might expect the subject to be the priest or the sinner; i.e., God himself " makes atonement " for man's sins. The meaning of the verb in such cases can only be " cover up " or " wipe out " in the sense of " pardon." [12] Here there is no suggestion of any sacrifice or other means of expiation; it is God who takes the initiative in forgiving. His constant readiness to forgive is often expressed in other places also.[13] The sense of man's need of forgiveness and confidence that God will forgive are voiced by many of the psalms; others rejoice in the experience of forgiveness.[14]

All this carries over into later Judaism, which places great emphasis on God's readiness to forgive. Jesus too teaches his disciples to pray for forgiveness, adding that they cannot expect it unless they forgive their own debtors.[15] God's readiness to forgive is illustrated by the parables of Lk., ch. 15. In a number of particular instances Jesus assures individuals that their sins are forgiven.[16] The preaching of the early Palestinian church stresses " the remission of sins." [17] In John forgiveness is not mentioned; [18] the evangelist's interest lies elsewhere. The synoptic evangelists, however, show their interest by the prominence given to the question of Jesus' right to forgive sins.[19] Matthew assigns to the

---

[8] Is. 43:25; Ps. 51:1, 9.

[9] Cp. 2 K. 5:18.

[10] Ex. 34:9; Num. 14:19 f.

[11] Jer. 31:34; 33:8; 50:20.

[12] Ps. 65:3; 78:38; 79:9 — A.V. translates " forgive " in one of these places, A.S.V. in all three.

[13] See especially Ezek., chs. 18; 33.

[14] Note especially Ps. 32 and 51; cp. Lamentations.

[15] Mt. 6:12, 14 f.

[16] Mk. 2:5; Lk. 7:48.

[17] Acts 2:38; 10:43; cp. ch. 3:19; Lk. 1:77.

[18] But cp. 1 Jn. 1:9; 2:12.

[19] Mk. 2:1-12, and parallels.

church the power to bind and loose.[20] Revelation [21] speaks of releasing from sins and of washing robes white in the blood of the Lamb.[22] Many references to the death of Christ throughout the New Testament imply the forgiveness of sins as its result.[23] The problem of renewed forgiveness after falling away from the faith under persecution is one of the important points in Hebrews; in ch. 6:4–6 the possibility of a second forgiveness is denied (cp. the Shepherd of Hermas and the pentitential system). Forgiveness is referred to in Jas. 5:15 (cp. v. 20); 2 P. 1:9, and often elsewhere under various forms of expression. It is a basic element in the biblical conception of salvation, growing out of the conception of sin as disobedience, offending the God of righteousness.

With Paul the idea of forgiveness has a distinctive form, very important for later theology, especially in Protestantism. Like much else in his thinking, it was molded by his own experience, both in conversion and in subsequent controversy. The problem of the Christian's relation to the Old Testament law was central for Paul. His solution seems to us involved and obscure, partly because of the difficulty of translating his terms satisfactorily. His most characteristic word in this connection is commonly translated "justification." It is the regular Greek word for justice or righteousness, and is often so translated. Paul himself often uses it with these meanings, especially in speaking of God's justice, but he also uses it in the special sense of being free from guilt, absolved or acquitted of a charge, pronounced innocent and so exempt from punishment.[24]

Paul had been an earnest, zealous student of the law, taking it very seriously and trying to obey it perfectly.[25] Unlike the average pious Jew, who delighted in the law,[26] Paul was so extremely conscientious that he felt he had broken the law and incurred God's just wrath if he failed to observe every precept.[27] But he found this impossible: not only did he sin through ignorance or negligence, but the very knowledge of the law only made him want to do what he might not have thought of otherwise, and while he wanted to obey the whole law in the bottom of his heart, there was something in him which blocked and thwarted his efforts at righteousness (s. 44). Thus he was frustrated and helpless.[28]

When he accepted the crucified Jesus as his Lord, all this burden of

---

[20] Mt. 16:19; 18:18; cp. Jn. 20:23.
[21] Rev. 1:5.
[22] Ch. 7:14.
[23] Cp. s. 75.
[24] Cp. 1 K. 8:31 f.

[25] Gal. 1:14.
[26] Ps. 1:2; 119:14, 45, 97.
[27] Gal. 3:10; 5:3.
[28] Rom. 7:24.

guilt and frustration was lifted; Paul felt himself a new man, at peace with God and with himself, and overflowing with joy and a sense of unlimited power.[29] This is what gives Paul's conception of " justification " its permanent importance, not only for the history of theology but for the religious life of all times. Paul alone, among the writers of the Bible, meets the needs of the " twice-born " type of personality and experience, the divided self which wants and seeks righteousness and cannot find it.

Paul's doctrine is expounded principally in Romans and Galatians.[30] Being justified, as Paul uses the term, does not mean having adequate and valid reasons for acting, and so really being right; it means being accepted as righteous, acquitted at the bar of divine judgment. Since man has actually been unrighteous, this obviously involves forgiveness. Paul himself only rarely uses that term,[31] but in Rom. 4:7 f. he quotes Ps. 32:1 f. to support his idea of justification. To the much discussed question whether justification means imputed or imparted righteousness the answer is that it means the former. Paul also believes that righteousness is imparted (s. 63), but this is not what he means by justification, which is the canceling of all previous offenses and the acceptance of the sinner as righteous by a free and unmerited divine act. Man is helpless under God's wrath, but God is not only just in condemning and punishing sin; he is so completely just that he also provides a means of deliverance from sin, giving freely what man could never achieve for himself.

To support this radical doctrine, which seemed to overthrow the whole revelation of the Old Testament, Paul mustered logical and exegetical arguments which must have been dug out by painful study during the years following his conversion and in the heat of later controversy. The law itself, he claims, teaches that man cannot win salvation by obedience but can only receive it by faith (s. 79). This raises for Paul the problem of the significance of the law. He answers, as we have seen (s. 56), that its purpose was temporary, to prepare for the revelation and redemption in Christ by exposing sin and showing the need of salvation.[32]

Evidently Paul's conception was not accepted or perhaps understood

---

[29] Rom. 7:25; 8:1 f.
[30] See especially Rom. 1:18, 32; 2:1 f., 6–13; 3:9–12, 19 f.; Gal. 3:21 f.; Rom. 3:21–25; 4:16, 20–25; 5:1; 6:23.
[31] Col. 1:14; 2:13.
[32] Rom. 7:7; Gal. 3:21–24.

by the apostolic church as a whole. Its importance in Protestant theology makes its neglect in the rest of the New Testament seem surprising. Even where Paul's language is echoed, his characteristic ideas are not in evidence,[33] except in writings distinctly under Pauline influence.[34] Jas. 2:14–26 attacks what must have been a common misunderstanding of Paul's doctrine. On the whole the other writers of the New Testament find no such difficulty as Paul does in salvation by repentance and obedience.

The relationship between God and man assumed by the idea of justification is the forensic relation of judge and criminal. Useful as this is for Paul, it does not do justice to his experience of salvation, and he uses other ideas to supplement it. Salvation involves not merely the cancellation of past offenses, but also a new, rich, and intimate relation to God which can only be expressed as that of a child to his father. Paul follows the usage of Jesus and the earlier apostles in speaking of God as Father (s. 26), but he thinks of the Christian's sonship as one of adoption rather than birth.[35] A somewhat different idea appears in Galatians: under the law one is like a child under the control and discipline of guardians and trustees, but the Christian is a son who has come of age and entered into his inheritance.[36]

Much the same basic idea, from a slightly different point of view, is expressed under the concept of reconciliation. Here again the relation presupposed is not that of a criminal before his judge so much as that of a child estranged from his father. Furthermore, Paul's conception of justification represents God as offended and forgiving, whereas his idea of reconciliation is not that God has been alienated and must be reconciled to man, but that man is estranged and must be reconciled to God.[37] The connection between justification and reconciliation is shown by 2 Cor. 5:19b: justification is God's forgiveness; reconciliation is man's acceptance of it.

Still another relationship is presupposed by Paul's use of the term " redemption." This does not rest on the frequent use of the words " redeem " and " redemption " in the Old Testament, but on the redemption of a slave as practiced in the Hellenistic world and exemplified by a fa-

---

[33] Heb. 11:7; Jas. 5:15.
[34] Titus 3:4–7; Eph. 2:8.
[35] Rom. 8:14–17.
[36] Gal. 4:1–7.
[37] 2 Cor. 5:14, 18–20; cp. Rom. 5:10; Col. 1:19–20a, 21–22a; contrast Heb. 2:17, where A.V. renders " reconciliation " but A.S.V. rightly " propitiation."

mous group of inscriptions at Delphi.[38] For the idea without the word
see 1 Cor. 7:22 f. (cp. ch. 6:20).[39]

It should be emphasized that for Paul all these concepts represent
one and the same experience. As Deissmann has shown, justification, reconciliation, redemption, adoption, and forgiveness are not five different doors through which one enters into life, but one door with five
names.[40]

63. Regeneration, Sanctification

The aspects or phases of salvation thus far considered have to do
with the remission of the penalties of sin and the restoration of a favorable relation to God. Ordinarily it is assumed that a life of obedience
will follow; otherwise salvation would have to take place not once but
repeatedly (as it does in the case of the nation in Judges). For Paul,
however, the initial difficulty or inability to do the will of God as he
wished means that salvation must include not only the remission of past
offenses but the power to avoid repeating them. It must involve victory
over the power of sin in the flesh, and this necessitates a transformation in human nature. Hence the Christian has not only a new position
and relationship; he is a new creature.[1]

The Old Testament has very little to say about this, assuming on the
whole that the individual or nation has sinned freely and can stop sinning with equal freedom. Some passages, however, express an approach
to the sort of experience with which Paul deals. In speaking of forgiveness we have noted that the Old Testament sometimes refers to God's
" cleansing " the sinner. Generally this seems to mean the same as wip-
ing away or blotting out the guilt for past offenses, i.e., forgiveness. So
Ps. 51:1 f., 9, but in vv. 5–7, 10, the psalmist feels that he is so completely sinful that he needs an internal cleansing and renewal. The idea
of a new heart appears also in 1 S. 10:9, an especially striking instance
because the passage is part of a very ancient narrative of the beginning
of the monarchy. The account seems to indicate a real conversion — not
merely the enthusiasm of the ecstatic prophets whom Saul meets, but
also an inner spiritual experience which fits him to rule as Yahweh's

---

[38] Rom. 3:24; 1 Cor. 1:30; Gal. 3:13; 4:5; Col. 1:14 (cp. Eph. 1:7). See Deissmann,
Light from the Ancient East, pp. 324 ff.

[39] Paul also uses the word " redemption " for the completion of salvation after death,
s. 72.

[40] Cf. *Paul, A Study in Social and Religious History,* Chap. VI. *The Religion of Jesus
and the Faith of Paul,* pp. 207–221.

[1] 2 Cor. 5:17.

anointed. Jeremiah says that under the new covenant the law will be written on the hearts of the people.[2] Ezekiel develops this further,[3] though elsewhere he assumes the sinner's freedom to amend his ways at will.[4] Is. 1:18 does not imply more than this; [5] in fact some commentators take it as a question, implying a negative answer. What is promised in both Jeremiah and Ezekiel, in fact, is not an experience open to individuals now, but an eschatological experience of the whole people, part of the national restoration, like the outpouring of the Spirit in Joel 2:28.[6]

Judaism does not carry this idea farther: freedom of choice between good and evil is always assumed (s. 76). Jesus also assumes that a man can stop sinning if he will. The petition in the Lord's Prayer, " Lead us not into temptation but deliver us from evil " (or " the evil one "), implies no more than the need of divine aid to avoid or overcome temptation, as in Judaism. The sermons of the early church in Acts, chs. 1 to 12, add to the remission of sins the gift of the Holy Spirit, regarded as a characteristic and necessary part of Christian experience (s. 82), but this is not connected anywhere with moral renewal or the struggle against sin; it is rather an ecstatic experience which attests the remission of sins and perhaps also guarantees future salvation.

Paul's idea comes out in his refutation of objections to justification by faith. Objections based on the significance of the law have already been considered (s. 62), but one difficulty was more than theoretical. There was a danger of misinterpretation which evidently had to be met at once. If one need not obey the law to be accepted as righteous, why not just go on sinning and rely on God's merciful forgiveness? With exasperation Paul replies that the very question evinces a complete misunderstanding of the whole matter. The Christian does not desire freedom to sin; what he has been craving is freedom from sin. Salvation involves not merely exemption from the consequences of sin but deliverance from slavery to the power of sin itself. Justification does not mean that God does not care how much we sin; it presupposes an earnest desire to overcome that " law of sin and death " [7] which prevents us from doing the good we want to do.

This second phase or aspect of salvation is as distinctive of Paul's thought and as directly derived from his own experience as his idea of

---

[2] Jer. 31:31–34.
[3] Ezek. 11:19 f.; 36:25–27.
[4] Chs. 18; 33.

[5] Cp. vv. 16 f.
[6] So Dt. 30:6, 8.
[7] Rom. 8:2.

justification. Traditional Protestant theology uses the term " sanctification " to distinguish it from justification, but Paul's own terminology is not so clear-cut or systematic. From his unfettered and varying use of several expressions it is evident that for him the experience of salvation meant both the cancellation of past sins and the power to overcome sin from then on. The word " regeneration " would have expressed the idea of a new creature, and it is so used in Titus 3:5, but Paul himself does not use it. Its only other occurrence in the New Testament, in fact, is the eschatological application in Mt. 19:28.

As Rom., chs. 3 to 5, expounds Paul's idea of the free gift of God's forgiveness, chs. 6 to 8 present his conception of the mastery of sin in the flesh. Unlike the removal of guilt and estrangement, this victory over sin itself is not won immediately. Paul is honest and realistic: sin is still present, the flesh still wars against the spirit.[8] So long as we remain in the body the struggle will continue.[9] But the Christian is no longer helpless; he has in him a new power, the power of the Spirit, the power of Christ, who lives in him.[10] One who yields to the power of sin is still subject to judgment, but the Christian is able to overcome. Still in the flesh in the ordinary sense of the phrase,[11] he is no longer living in the flesh in Paul's special sense.[12] He is no longer " according to the flesh " or " carnal " or " natural " but is " according to the spirit " and " spiritual." [13] He has newness of life in Christ; he is crucified to the world and the world to him.[14]

Thus salvation for Paul is threefold: past, present, and future. The believer *is* already saved; he has been forgiven, justified, adopted, reconciled, delivered from the fear of judgment (s. 62). He *will* be saved; in the life to come he will be free altogether from the power of sin in the flesh (ss. 69, 72). Meanwhile he is *being* saved: in Christ he is overcoming the power of sin in himself. Paul himself does not make these distinctions in so many words, but they are implicit in what he says.

The present experience of deliverance from the power of sin is, or may be, progressive. Often Paul seems to assume that by the power of Christ the Christian not only can but will overcome his sinful impulses; yet his frequent exhortations show that he realized the failure of most Christians to do so. Paul also admits that he himself is not yet perfect.[15]

The conception of sanctification gives the final explanation of Paul's

---

[8] Gal. 5:17.
[9] Rom. 8:22 f.
[10] Rom. 8:1–5, 10–13.
[11] Phil. 1:22, 24.

[12] Rom. 8:9.
[13] 1 Cor. 2:14 to 3:3.
[14] Rom. 6:3 f.; 2 Cor. 4:10; 5:17; Gal. 2:19 f.; 6:14 f.
[15] Phil. 3:12–14; cp. 2 Cor. 4:16.

attitude to the law and his idea of Christian freedom. The Christian is
not under the law because he is above it. He is not subject to it because
he does not want to do anything it forbids. The Spirit produces fruit in
his life which makes the law inapplicable to him.[16]

Nothing exactly like this is found elsewhere in the New Testament,
but there are ideas closely related to it. Deliverance from the power of
sin is implied in a sense in the petition, " Deliver us from evil " (or " the
evil one "; v.s.). So in Jn. 17:15 Jesus prays that his disciples may be
kept from the evil one. In 1 Jn. 1:7, 9, cleansing from sin may mean
simply forgiveness, as in the Old Testament, but in ch. 3:6–10 it is said
not merely that the Christian does not sin but that he cannot, because
God's seed is in him. This clearly suggests the idea of regeneration in
the sense of a mystical transformation of human nature. The distinctive Johannine conception of salvation, in fact, is that of a change of nature by the infusion of " life " through union with Christ.[17] The idea of
a new birth has its classic expression in Jn. 3:1–10 (the Greek word may
mean either " again " or " from above," and its use here may be a deliberate word-play). Rabbinic sources speak of conversion to Judaism as
a new birth, but with the idea of a new beginning rather than a transformation of nature. The latter idea is found in the mystery cults (rena-
tus in aeternum or in XX annos), but there the result is immortality instead of power over sin. Jn. 5:24 speaks of passing from death to life.
This involves the Johannine idea of eternal life as a new quality of life
beginning here and now for believers (s. 72), but the particular reference in this passage seems to be to deliverance from the fear of judgment, corresponding to Paul's idea of justification.

The epistle to the Hebrews speaks of Christians as partakers of
Christ and of the Holy Spirit, who have " tasted the powers of the coming age." [18] The term " perfected " (used in the mysteries for the final
stage of initiation) occurs also: Jesus was perfected by learning obedience.[19] Christians are " sanctified " in the Old Testament sense of being consecrated, set apart.[20] The author's idea seems to be that the ideal
of the perfect man is realized first in Jesus and through him in his followers, involving both completion and consecration.[21]

1 P. 1:2 mentions " sanctification of the spirit " along with obedience
and sprinkling of the blood of Jesus Christ, and the following verse in-

---

16 Gal., ch. 5; Rom. 13:10; cp. Mk. 12:29–31.
17 Jn. 10:10; ch. 15.
18 Heb. 3:14; 6:4 f.
19 Chs. 2:10; 5:8 f.; 7:28.
20 Ch. 2:11.
21 Cp. Jn. 17:19; Eph. 4:13.

troduces the idea of regeneration.[22] Salvation from sin itself rather than judgment is implied by ch. 1:18,[23] but the nearest approach to Paul's idea is perhaps ch. 5:10. In general the object of Christ's death seems to be thought of in 1 Peter as moral cleansing rather than legal acquittal, but the ideas are not sharply defined or elaborated.

Jas. 1:18 says that God " brought us forth by his own will " (using a verb applied in v. 15 to sin's bringing forth death, and not used elsewhere in the New Testament). Nothing else in the epistle suggests the idea of regeneration or moral transformation. The pastoral epistles use several expressions echoing Paul's language or ideas, with a suggestion of development in the direction of sacramentalism.[24] Jude 24 says that God can keep the Christian from stumbling, and v. 19 speaks of schismatics as " not having the Spirit." Several expressions in 2 Peter imply deliverance from sin as defilement and as an evil power, but how far Paul's idea is adopted is not clear.[25]

In any case the conception of victory over the power of sin by the indwelling power of Christ is characteristic of Paul and most clearly expressed in his letters. It was fundamental in his experience, but not so for all Christians. Something like it is involved in the Johannine conception of salvation, and of course the whole New Testament assumes a change of life and character, but the idea of a transformation of nature to make Christian living possible is hardly more than suggested outside of Paul's letters and the gospel and epistles of John.

Thus far we have been concerned with salvation in the present life. But the New Testament is also and even more concerned with the life to come. Paul even goes so far as to say that if our hope in Christ is confined to this life we are the most miserable of men.[26] The possession of the Spirit is not only a power for overcoming sin in this world; it is also an " earnest " of the complete redemption still to come (s. 72). In fact, hope is one of the great blessings of the Christian life (s. 83). We must therefore proceed to the consideration of salvation in its otherworldly aspect.

---

[22] Cp. also v. 23.
[23] Cp. chs. 1:5; 2:2.
[24] 2 Tim. 1:7, 14; 2:1; 3:5; 4:18; Titus 2:13 f.; 3:5; cp. ss. 97 f.
[25] 2 P. 1:4; 2:20; 3:18.
[26] 1 Cor. 15:19 — the translation adopted in R.S.V. is compatible with the Greek but is not supported by the context.

XI

ESCHATOLOGY AND THE FUTURE LIFE

64. *Present and Future Manifestations of the Kingdom of God in This World*

Jesus' teaching regarding the future is given under the head of the kingdom of God, but before considering the eschatological implications of that concept we must understand its relation to the power of God as manifested in the present world. In s. 23 we saw that the basic meaning of the kingdom of God is the eternal divine sovereignty. As such it includes all the ways in which God rules the world and the life of mankind.

Theoretically the Hebrew monarchy was a concrete expression of God's rule, a theocracy, the king being God's representative (s. 31). The Messianic hope of Israel was at first directed to a future assertion and establishment of the divine sovereignty in this world. From this point of view the kingdom or kingship of God was regarded as still future, because his chosen people still suffered oppression, and righteousness did not prevail in the world. The Jewish prayer book contains petitions that God may speedily establish his kingdom, that his kingdom may be revealed and be seen, and that he alone may reign over his people. The pictures of God's sovereignty in some of the psalms may have this future reference.[1]

Some of Jesus' sayings indicate that the kingdom of God is in some sense present, not simply as the divine sovereignty that has existed from the beginning, but as something that has just recently come to pass, something new. In view of the prevalent confusion and difference of opinion on this subject, it seems best to consider the most important sayings in some detail.

A crucial passage is Mt. 12:28 (Lk. 11:20). If this is an authentic saying of Jesus, which there is no reason to doubt, it must mean something consistent with the sayings that speak of the kingdom as still fu-

1 Ps. 47; 93; 96; 97; cp. s. 23.

ture (s. 73). Jesus is here replying to the charge that his miracles are wrought by the power of Beelzebul. In that case, he says, Satan is fighting against himself, and therefore his kingdom cannot stand.[2] This implies that over against the kingdom of God there is a kingdom of Satan (s. 41), but that it is doomed. But, Jesus continues, if the demons are cast out by the power (or finger) of God, the kingdom of God has " come upon " Jesus' hearers and accusers. The Aramaic verb probably used by Jesus in this saying means primarily to arrive or reach, also to befall or happen to a person.[3] Jesus' statement then means, in effect, " what has happened to you is the kingdom of God," i.e., God's sovereign power has made itself evident in this event. Here the kingdom of God is present as the cause of Jesus' conquest of the demons.

Mark does not have this saying but in the same connection gives a parable implying the same idea. The plundering of the strong man's goods [4] must mean the casting out of the demons, depriving Satan of the possessed victims who have been under his power. The fact that this has happened, Jesus implies, proves that the strong man has been bound, i.e., that Satan has been rendered helpless.

In all three gospels, therefore, Jesus' reply to his accusers represents the kingdom of God as a power already at work in the world and manifest in the miracles of healing. But since the demons are still present and active, Satan's kingdom has not yet been completely overthrown; the complete establishment and triumph of God's kingdom is thus still in the future, though so near that its power is already felt in the world.

Lk. 17:20 f. may have any one of three meanings: (1) It may refer to the rule of God in the individual's heart and life. But the context in which Luke presents it is distinctly eschatological, and the phrase translated " within you " may well mean " in your midst." The saying may therefore mean (2) that the coming of the kingdom will be unpredictable and sudden but unmistakable when it occurs: to paraphrase, " Even while you are looking about for signs of its approach, all of a sudden here it is in your midst, like a flash of lightning filling the whole sky." The meaning may, however, be (3) the same as that of Mt. 12:28: " You are looking about for signs, but the kingdom is already here in the midst of you." The context favors the second of these interpretations.

Equally difficult are the sayings about " entering " the kingdom of God. Some of these are clearly eschatological (s. 73), but there are oth-

---

[2] Mt. 12:26; Lk. 11:18.   [3] Cp. Dan. 4:24, 28.   [4] Mk. 3:27.

ers which imply the possibility of entering the kingdom here and now. Mk. 10:23–25 and ch. 12:34 suggest that by taking one more step the person in question might be in the kingdom. Mt. 11:11 (Lk. 7:28), which speaks of people already in the kingdom, is probably not authentic, but expresses the later idea that the kingdom is the church. Lk. 16:16 (Mt. 11:12) is undoubtedly authentic but also undoubtedly corrupt, as shown by the difference between the forms given by Matthew and Luke. Unlike Mt. 11:11, it places John the Baptist within the new order or dispensation of the kingdom. Some reference to contemporary events is obviously implied, but of several possible interpretations none is certain. Mt. 22:1–13 (Lk. 14:16–24) is connected with the kingdom of God by the introductions in both Matthew and Luke. The original story (without Matthew's and Luke's additions) refers to the failure of the Jewish leaders to accept the invitation to the kingdom of God, and the ready response and entering in of the outcasts. Mt. 21:31 states this even more clearly. The idea of a present entering is implied also in Mt. 23:13 (Lk. 11:52); cp. Mt. 16:19, though this is hardly authentic. All this evidence indicates that Jesus spoke not only of entering the kingdom of God hereafter but also of entering it immediately in this life. This can only mean entering into the relationship of a loyal subject to the divine King, thus becoming a member of the group in which the power of the kingdom is already manifest, and which is ready for the final, complete coming of the kingdom.

Another group of sayings represents the kingdom as a valuable possession to be sought at any cost. Mt. 6:33 (Lk. 12:31), already noted in s. 54, suggests something of this idea, but the chief examples are the parables of the treasure in the field and the pearl of great price.[5] The supreme value of the kingdom as worthy of any sacrifice appears also in Mt. 19:12. The idea of possessing the kingdom is implied by Mt. 5:3, 10 (Lk. 6:20) and Mk. 10:14 and parallels, but in these cases the meaning may be a right of possession or citizenship in the future establishment of the kingdom, just as Daniel[6] predicts that the saints of the Most High will receive and possess the kingdom in the sense of coming into power. Something like this may be implied even in the idea of entering the kingdom in this life; in short, all these sayings, while referring to something that happens in the present life, are capable of an interpretation in keeping with the view that the kingdom-concept of Jesus was primarily eschatological.

[5] Mt. 13:44 f.   [6] Dan. 7:18, 22.

Three parables suggest the idea of a growth of the kingdom in the world. They are the parable of the seed growing of itself [7] and the parables of the mustard seed [8] and the leaven.[9] The first clearly means that the power of the kingdom, already at work in the world, will of itself, without dependence on any human effort, produce the final complete triumph over evil. Any implication regarding the time required for this, or the process by which it will come about, need not be looked for. The successive stages of growth mentioned suggest a progressive manifestation, but they may be simply a part of the picture without special significance. The conception of the kingdom in this parable seems to include all three aspects of it as eternally real, as now at work, and as still to come with power. The parables of the mustard seed and the leaven stress the contrast between a small beginning and a great outcome, referring presumably to the present working of the kingdom in the conquest of the demons and the preaching of the gospel, as contrasted with the greatness of its final manifestation at the end of the age.

The parables of the tares [10] and the dragnet [11] are followed by an explanation which arouses suspicion because of its allegorical character, which is foreign to the nature of Jesus' parables on the whole, and also because it reflects a situation in the later church with which Matthew is especially concerned, when the presence of unworthy members raised the problem of excommunication. The statement that the angels will gather such members out of the kingdom at the last judgment makes the kingdom equivalent to the church.[12] The parables themselves, however, may be genuine, in which case they belong with those already considered as indicating a present working of the kingdom with a future consummation.

The idea of a gradual process, undoubtedly suggested by some of these parables when taken by themselves, is excluded by the clear evidence of other passages that Jesus expected the end very soon (s. 73). Moreover, the present working of the kingdom, however conceived, is contrasted with the future manifestation. Whether the latter will be the direct outcome of the present working of God's power in the world, or added to it, cannot be inferred from the parables themselves.

Other sayings which clearly refer to a future coming of the kingdom of God do not make clear whether it is to be an event within the present

---

[7] Mk. 4:26–29.
[8] Mk. 4:30–32, and parallels.
[9] Mt. 13:33; Lk. 13:20 f.

[10] Mt. 13:24–30, 36–43.
[11] Vv. 47–50.
[12] Cp. ch. 11:11.

world-order or one belonging to the sphere of eschatology. The coming of the kingdom prayed for in the Lord's Prayer is explicitly located on earth, but that may be true of either the prophetic or the apocalyptic type of hope. The summary of Jesus' Galilean preaching in Mk. 1:15 indicates that the kingdom is near but not yet present.[13] While the Greek verbs used here and in Mt. 12:28 (Lk. 11:20) seem to have contradictory meanings (nearness and arrival), they may actually represent the same Aramaic verb, though of course it is also possible that Jesus used the literal Aramaic equivalents of both. Mk. 1:15 suggests that a long period of waiting is now ended. What is meant by the "time" that is now "fulfilled" is suggested by a saying in the apocryphal conclusion of Mark in the Freer manuscript at Washington: "Fulfilled is the limit of the years of the authority of Satan." By itself Mk. 1:15 might mean that the promise of the kingdom's coming is already or is about to be fulfilled in the ministry of Jesus himself (C. H. Dodd's "realized eschatology"[14]), but in the light of other undeniably authentic sayings it must mean rather that the full, eschatological manifestation is near.

In Mk. 9:1[15] the phrase "with power" may be merely adverbial (i.e., "powerfully"), or it may imply a contrast with the present working of the kingdom in weakness.[16] Matthew's substitution of the parousia of the Son of Man for the coming of the kingdom of God raises the question of the relation between these events in the thought of Jesus and the evangelists, which will be considered in s. 73. But before taking up the eschatological aspect of the kingdom of God we must consider the future life of the individual.

65. *The Future Life of the Individual: Sheol and Immortality; the Intermediate State and Judgment at Death*

While the Hebrews never thought of death as the end of existence, early Hebrew religion had no conception of judgment or salvation after death. The future life was supposed to be merely a reduced, weakened, undesirable kind of existence to which all alike must come eventually, but which was to be avoided as long as possible. The widespread practices of leaving useful and valuable objects in tombs and making offer-

---

[13] Cp. Mt. 3:2; 4:17 — Luke omits the statement in ch. 4:14, but in ch. 10:9 has its equivalent; cp. Mt. 10:7.

[14] *The Parables of the Kingdom*, pp. 50 f.

[15] Cp. Mt. 16:28; Lk. 9:27.

[16] Cp. the use of the same phrase in Rom. 1:4; s. 33.

ings to the dead,[1] as also perhaps such idiomatic expressions as " gathered to his fathers " and " slept with his fathers," point to the idea of the grave itself as the continued abode of the dead. Like other ancient peoples, however, the Hebrews had also the idea of a subterranean cavern in which the dead lived on in gloom and misery. It was called Sheol, perhaps from the verb meaning " ask " in the sense of inquiring of the dead.[2] The psalms often refer to deliverance from Sheol in the sense of being preserved from death (s. 45). In the Septuagint and the New Testament, Sheol is represented by the Greek word " Hades," and the Greek idea of Hades closely resembles the Hebrew idea of Sheol.[3] The most effective pictures of Sheol in the Old Testament are in Job 3:17–19; Is. 14:9–11; and Ezek. 32:17–32, all relatively late.

The modern mind thinks of the future life, if at all, in terms of the immortality of the soul. The Hebrew conception of personality makes no such sharp division between body and soul (ss. 44 ff.), and the idea of Sheol involves the immortality, not of the soul, but of the whole person, though in a relatively lifeless and weak state. When the idea of a blessed future existence finally appears in the religion of the Old Testament, it takes the form of the resurrection of the body (s. 69), not of the escape of the immortal soul from its fleshly prison.

Hellenistic Judaism adopted the Greek idea of the immortality of the soul instead of the resurrection of the whole person. The denial of either hope in Ecclesiastes [4] shows that there were skeptics, and a fine literary expression of such skepticism is given in words attributed to the wicked in the Wisdom of Solomon.[5] The writer of the book himself, however, does not share this point of view but shows his own faith by a beautiful statement of the hope of immortality.[6] The belief is expressed also in 4 Maccabees.[7] Epitaphs on Hellenistic Jewish gravestones often express no faith beyond resignation to death as inevitable or longing for it as rest from life's troubles.

Some passages in the New Testament suggest a tendency in the direction of the Greek type of hope. According to Luke, Jesus spoke of the dead as going immediately to their reward.[8] He said that in the

---

[1] Dt. 26:14.
[2] As in 1 S., ch. 28, though Sheol is not mentioned by name.
[3] Cf. *Odyssey*, Bk. XI.
[4] Eccl. 3:19–21; 9:4–6, 10; cp. 12:7.
[5] W.S. 2:1–5.
[6] Chs. 3:1–5, 8 f.; 5:15 f.
[7] 4 Macc. 7:19; 16:25; cp. Mk. 12:26 f.; Rom. 14:8.
[8] Lk. 16:19–31; 23:43.

future life men would be " like the angels." [9] The spiritualized resurrection of John [10] and Paul's conception of the spiritual body point in the same direction. In general, however, the New Testament is too close to the Old Testament and Palestinian Judaism to make the transition from the resurrection of the body to the immortality of the soul.

Throughout Christian history both conceptions have been retained. Orthodox faith combines them, applying the conception of the immortality of the soul to the intermediate state and the idea of the resurrection to the eschatological consummation of salvation. The same combination was made also in Jewish theology and may have been accepted by Jesus and the apostles. Paul, like Stephen,[11] thinks of death as departing and being with Christ [12] and speaks of the Christian's citizenship in heaven, though at the same time he cherishes the common eschatological hope.[13] The writer of Hebrews likewise thinks of heaven as a present reality, the true tabernacle into which Jesus has already gone as our High Priest, passing within the veil, where our hope is securely anchored.[14]

It is now commonly assumed by Christians that the dead go at once to their reward, yet the idea of a final resurrection and judgment still persists. When the belief in a resurrection of the dead first arose, the logical consequence was that Sheol became merely a temporary abode of the dead pending the resurrection, with no moral distinctions. While the Old Testament has nothing to say on this subject, there is at least no evidence of any other conception.

Later Judaism, however, was no more content than Christianity has been to leave the departed in such an indiscriminate state until the final judgment. Since God needs no eschatological session of the heavenly court to determine who are righteous and who are wicked, the idea of a division at death soon emerged, with separate abodes for the good and evil in the intermediate state. The book of Enoch has a divided Sheol, providing places for the righteous and for two or three different types of sinners.[15] Rabbinic literature from about the end of the first century A.D. presents the idea of an immediate judgment at death, and this ultimately prevailed in Jewish thought. Some sources even imply that the righteous and the wicked will be taken at once to their final abodes (ss. 71 f.), making a final judgment unnecessary and anomalous. The rab-

---

9 Mk. 12:25; cp. Lk. 20:36.
10 Jn. 11:25 f.
11 Acts 7:59.
12 Phil. 1:23.

13 Phil. 3:20 f.
14 Heb. 6:19 f.; cp. chs. 11:13–16; 12:22–24.
15 I Enoch, ch. 22 — the details are obscure.

binic literature sometimes even applies to the state of the righteous immediately after death the common expression for the eschatological consummation of history, " the coming age " (s. 72). The idea of a shadowy place where the righteous merely await the resurrection is still found, however, in 4 Ezra (2 Esdras) 7:88–101, 120.

References to Hades in the New Testament have the background of the Old Testament conception of Sheol. In sayings of Jesus (or attributed to him) the term occurs in only three passages.[16] In Revelation, Death and Hades are personified; at the last judgment both will be cast into the lake of fire.[17] In Lk. 16:19–31 a separation of the righteous and wicked immediately after death is clearly indicated.[18] According to John the judgment does not even wait for death but takes place in this life.[19]

66. *The Messianic Woes and the Antichrist*

The Old Testament prophets, in warning Israel and the nations of the coming judgment, often picture the dire calamities that will accompany it: clouds and thick darkness,[1] invading armies,[2] or a combination of both ideas.[3] These conceptions reach their fullest development in the Old Testament in the picture of the invasion of Gog.[4] Later Judaism carried them still farther as a part of the preliminary Messianic kingdom (s. 68).

The same chapters in Ezekiel provide also the Old Testament basis for the later idea of the Antichrist. The rabbinic literature pictures Gog as a monstrous incarnation of all the enemies of God and his people. The idea of a last, desperate revolt against God is connected with predictions of unprecedented calamities just before the advent of the Messiah and the divine deliverance, and such passages as Ps. 2:2 f. are adduced to support it. This conception of the " Messianic woes " (often pre-Messianic) corresponds psychologically to the general feeling that the darkest hour is just before the dawn; and the idea of a being in whom all the powers arrayed against God are personified expresses the human tendency to pick out one person upon whom can be focused all hatred of what he represents.

The preaching of Jesus and the early church is notably free of such ideas, since the end of the age was expected immediately without apoc-

---

[16] Mt. 11:23; 16:18; Lk. 16:19–31.
[17] Ch. 20:14.
[18] Cp. Lk. 23:43; Acts 7:59.
[19] Jn. 3:19; 5:25; but see further ss. 69 f.

[1] Am. 5:18–20; Zp. 1:14 f.
[2] Is. 5:26–30; 8:5–8; Jer. 1:13–15.
[3] Joel 2:1–11; 3:9–16.
[4] Ezek., chs. 38 f.

alyptic preliminaries or signs.[5] At the same time these ideas are the background of elements that appear in some New Testament passages, particularly the eschatological discourse.[6] While this discourse may be made up in part of authentic sayings of Jesus, commentators are fairly well agreed that much of it is secondary and incompatible with the teaching of Jesus. The specific situation calls for a pronouncement on the destruction of Jerusalem,[7] but the form of the disciples' question in Matthew and the bulk of the discourse in all three gospels identify the fall of Jerusalem with the end of the world and the second coming of Christ. The warning of wars and rumors of wars as the beginning of the woes [8] corresponds to this identification, and the description of terrible distress in Judea fits both the situation during the war of revolt against Rome in A.D. 66–70 and also the apocalyptic expectation of the woes.[9] But all this is inconsistent with Jesus' repeated warning that the end will come quite unexpectedly.[10] The statement that only the Father knows the day and hour [11] may have been Jesus' original reply to the question when Jerusalem would be destroyed,[12] and everything intervening may have been composed by a Christian apocalyptic writer in the crisis of A.D. 39–41, when the emperor Caligula ordered his image set up in the temple.[13]

In 2 Th. 2:1–12, Paul presents a similar idea, apparently a part of his inherited Christology and eschatology. The passage is extremely obscure. Some elements in it doubtless have a mythological and eschatological background in traditional ideas current at that time but now lost. We cannot determine with certainty the meaning of " that which restrains " (v. 6), " he who restrains " (v. 7), or " the man of sin " (v. 3) or " lawless one " (v. 8). The restraining power may be the Roman government. The lawless and impious being who will try to usurp the place of God when this power is taken away (vv. 4, 7), but will be destroyed by Jesus at his coming (v. 8), corresponds to the common Jewish and early Christian conception of the Antichrist, though Paul does not use that term. A reference to emperor worship is probable.

---

[5] Lk. 17:20–30.
[6] Mk., ch. 13; Mt., ch. 24; Lk., ch. 21; and scattered parallels elsewhere.
[7] Mk. 13:1 f.
[8] Mt. 24:8.
[9] Cp. Dan. 12:1; Joel 2:2.
[10] Mk. 13:33–37; Mt. 24:36–51; 25:1–13; Lk. 12:35–48; 17:20–30; 21:34.
[11] Mk. 13:32.
[12] V. 4; cp. Acts 1:7.
[13] Cp. v. 14, based on Dan. 11:31; 12:11.

The chief importance of the whole passage for us is the impressive demonstration it gives of the large amount of ancient Oriental cosmology, mythology, and eschatology in the thinking of Paul and his contemporaries.

As Paul has the idea of the Antichrist without the word, so 1 John has the word without the idea. The current belief is deliberately reinterpreted and spiritualized as referring to heresy.[14] Pseudo christs (so the Greek) are mentioned in Mk. 13:22, together with pseudo prophets.

The book of Revelation shows the furthest development of these ideas in the New Testament. Preliminary events in heaven and earth, including the seven seals and the plagues (chs. 4 to 6), the sealing of the redeemed (ch. 7), the seven trumpets (chs. 8 f.), and the vision of the strong angel, the little book, and the two witnesses (chs. 10 f.), are followed by the war with the dragon in heaven and on earth and the appearance of the two beasts (chs. 12 f.). The first beast[15] comes out of the sea[16] and makes war on the saints, receiving power and authority from the dragon, i.e., Satan;[17] the second beast[18] exercises the authority of the first. While the identification of all the elements in this symbolism is difficult, it is clear that the idea of the Antichrist is involved, and that the author sees it incarnate in the Roman empire of his day. In later chapters[19] a false prophet is associated with the beast, and in two instances[20] the false prophet seems to take the place of the second beast. Perhaps this prophet is not a historic individual but a personification of the priesthood of the imperial cult.

The clue to the whole passage is given for the initiated in ch. 13:18 — the number of the beast is a man's number, 666. Such a symbolic use of numbers is a regular feature of the apocalyptic tradition, based on the fact that the letters of the alphabet were used as numerals in both Hebrew and Greek.[21] Attempts to interpret the 666 of Rev. 13:18 on the basis of the Greek alphabet have not succeeded, but in the Hebrew alphabet the numerical values of the letters in the name *Neron Kesar* (Emperor Nero) total 666. The reference in ch. 13:3 reflects the legend of *Nero redivivus*.

---

[14] 1 Jn. 2:18, 22; 4:3.
[15] Rev. 13:1–10.
[16] Cp. Dan. 7:2 f.
[17] Rev. 20:2.
[18] Ch. 13:11–18.
[19] Chs. 16:13; 19:20; 20:10.
[20] Chs. 19:20; 20:10.
[21] See *Sibylline Oracles,* Book V, 1–50, for an elaborate example.

The religious value of this whole cycle of ideas is questionable. They may serve, however, to remind us that no easy progress to a Utopia may be expected in human history, yet wars and disasters can never invalidate the Christian hope.

67. *The Second Coming of Christ*

For Judaism, of course, what Christianity expects as the second coming of the Messiah is still awaited as his first coming. Only once in the New Testament is it explicitly called Christ's appearing " a second time." [1] Elsewhere the first coming is taken for granted and the second is called simply the " manifestation " or " appearance " or " arrival " (Greek, *parousia*).

The Messianic prophecies of the Old Testament (ss. 29 ff.) either speak of the Messiah as being born [2] or refer to his coming in the same general terms used with reference to any king. Zc. 9:9 is a notable exception in giving a specific indication of the way in which the King will come. All these passages, however, are commonly taken by Christian interpreters as referring to the incarnation rather than the second coming of Christ.

Old Testament references to the coming of Yahweh himself in judgment afford a partial background for the later expectation of the Messiah's coming. [3] An especially vivid picture, later applied to the parousia of Christ, is Zc. 14:3 f. The most influential of all Old Testament passages in this connection is the description of the judgment of the Ancient of Days and the appearance of the " one like a son of man " in Dan. 7:9–14, 26 f. Originally this did not refer to the Messiah, but in the pseudepigraphic Book of Enoch it is the basis of the idea of judgment by the Son of Man from heaven (s. 32).

The prophetic hope of a Messianic king (s. 31) was confined to the sphere of human history. Supernatural elements were always more or less involved, however, and in late postexilic times, as the hope of political deliverance and independence faded, belief in a supernatural transformation of the world and a new divine age, including the resurrection of the dead (s. 69), became popular. This is the essence of the hope expressed in the apocalyptic literature, represented in the Old Testament canon by the book of Daniel and in postcanonical Jewish literature by such works as Enoch and 4 Ezra.

The identification of the " one like a son of man " of Dan. 7:13 with

---

[1] Heb. 9:28.   [2] Is. 9:6.   [3] Ps. 96:13; 98:9.

the Messiah was a part of this development. The result was no little confusion. The later rabbis were puzzled, e.g., by the apparent contradiction involved in taking both Zc. 9:9 and Dan. 7:13 as referring to the coming of the Messiah. A third century rabbi suggested that if Israel was faithful the Messiah would come on the clouds, but if Israel was unfaithful he would come in humility, riding on an ass.

Jewish sources record many efforts to calculate the time of the Messiah's coming, even to the month. The only point on which all agree is that it would be soon. Many signs were discussed, particularly the woes (s. 66) and an unprecedented prevalence of wickedness. Much was made also of the idea of the forerunner, derived from the prediction of Elijah's return in Mal. 4:5 f. The gospels show that this idea was applied by Jesus to John the Baptist [4] and by some of his hearers to Jesus himself.[5] Consequently the church has not connected the expectation of a forerunner with the second coming of Christ.

Corresponding to the various forms of Messianic and apocalyptic hope, there were many different ideas regarding the work of the Messiah in the Judaism of New Testament times. In some sources the Messiah does not appear at all in connection with the end of the age and the divine judgment; in others he plays an unimportant part. His function and the point in the eschatological program at which he appears vary according to the presence or absence of the idea of a preliminary Messianic kingdom before the final consummation (s. 68).

The sayings of Jesus on this subject frequently echo the language of Daniel (the Son of Man coming on the clouds), and sometimes that of Enoch (the holy angels, the throne of his glory).[6] From all the material it is clear that Jesus expected the parousia within a generation, but warned that the exact time could not be known in advance. Apart from the use of the imagery of Daniel, no indication is given of the manner of his coming, and we cannot tell how literally Jesus himself understood the idea of coming on the clouds. Comparison with Jewish and early Christian apocalyptic literature in general throws into relief the reticence of Jesus on such questions. He was convinced of the reality and nearness of the parousia, but his concern was with readiness for it, not with speculation about its form or nature.

For the early church the expectation of Christ's return was central.

[4] Mk. 9:11–13; Mt. 11:14; Lk. 1:17.
[5] Mk. 6:14 f.; 8:28; and parallels.
[6] The most important sayings are Mk. 8:38; 14:62; Mt. 24:44 (Lk. 12:40); Mt. 10:23; 25:31; Lk. 18:8. Cp. ss. 32, 73.

Apparently the disciples' ideas regarding the Messiah and the kingdom of God had not been changed much by their association with Jesus, and his death had merely postponed what they expected him to do as Messiah, " restore the kingdom to Israel." [7] He was now in heaven and must remain there until the time of the " restoration of all things," [8] when he would return as he had ascended.[9] Judging by the eschatological discourse (s. 66) and Matthew's interpretations of the parables of the tares and the dragnet,[10] we may regard it as likely that the church very soon added considerable apocalyptic coloring to the simple teaching of Jesus.

Paul's conception of the second coming is given in 1 Cor. 15:22 ff.[11] Its nearness is expressed by the Aramaic watchword quoted in 1 Cor. 16:22, *Marana tha*, " Our Lord, come." Probably Rev. 22:20, " Come, Lord Jesus," echoes this common watchword.[12] Other references, including 1 Cor. 11:26, show how central the parousia remained for Paul.

The importance and persistence of the expectation is shown by its prominence in the synoptic gospels and by numerous references in the pastoral and general epistles.[13] Even Hebrews, though mainly interested in the present experience of salvation, retains the characteristic early Christian hope.[14] In spite of the strongly apocalyptic character of Revelation, the idea of the parousia is not clearly expressed anywhere in the book, though implied in some sense in the concluding chapters.[15]

The fourth gospel characteristically reinterprets the idea of the second coming, spiritualizing it and apparently identifying it with the gift of the Spirit. Many statements in chs. 14 to 16 apparently mean that Jesus will come to the individual Christian at death to take him to heaven; others, such as ch. 14:16-18, connect the coming of Jesus with the coming of the Paraclete (s. 27).[16] In 1 John, however, the idea of the parousia is apparently still taken literally.[17]

In the church at large the hope of a personal return of Christ was never given up. The problem raised by its delay and the efforts to answer objections are exemplified by 2 P. 3:1-13. Popular Christianity still takes the hope of the second coming very seriously and very literally. It is much stressed in all forms of Fundamentalism. On such points a min-

---

[7] Lk. 24:21; Acts 1:6.
[8] Acts 3:21.
[9] Ch. 1:11.
[10] Mt. 13:36-43, 49 f.
[11] Cp. s. 69; 1 Th. 4:14-17; 2 Th. 1:7.
[12] Cp. Rom. 13:11; Phil. 4:5.

[13] 1 P. 1:7, 13; 5:4; Jas. 5:7 f.; 1 Tim. 6:14 f.
[14] Heb. 9:28; 10:25.
[15] Recall Rev. 22:20.
[16] Cp. Jn. 20:19-23.
[17] 1 Jn. 2:28; 3:2.

ister trained in a modern world-view often feels that conservative Christians really have a different religion from his own, but if he is to preach to people brought up in that tradition he must at least understand their position and appreciate the values it has for them. This applies equally to the subjects of the next few sections.

68. *The Intermediate Messianic Kingdom* (*Millennium*)

The combination of the Messianic hope of the prophets and the apocalyptic hope of a new world produced, we have observed, considerable variety and confusion in Jewish faith. Some sources represent the prophetic Messianic hope without any further eschatological conclusion to history; some express the apocalyptic hope instead; still others combine the two in what has been called a two-act drama, with a Messianic kingdom on earth preceding the eschatological consummation. This combination became the most common type of hope.

The first act of the drama, generally called in rabbinic literature " the days of the Messiah," takes place within the present world-order, corresponding to the hopes of the earlier Old Testament prophets. The two types of hope and the two acts of the drama are not always kept entirely distinct. Supernatural elements borrowed from the apocalyptic hope sometimes appear in accounts of the Messianic kingdom. One of the most prominent features of the Messianic age is the emancipation and return of the Jewish exiles in all lands. The majority of the Jewish people in the Roman period did not live in Palestine, but the national restoration was hardly conceivable anywhere else. The complete obedience of Israel to the law and the renewal of worship in the temple were important features also. Different views as to the place of the Gentile peoples in the days of the Messiah are expressed (s. 102), but the final rebellion of the nations against the Messiah and the war of Gog (s. 66) are frequently placed in the Messianic age, which reaches its climax in the overthrow of the enemy, clearing the way for the second act of the drama.[1] The duration of the Messianic kingdom is variously estimated in different sources, ranging from forty to a thousand years. Later rabbis made it two thousand years, following two thousand years of chaos and two thousand years of the law, constituting altogether the world-week of six millennia, to be followed by the eternal Sabbath (*v.i.*).

Jesus and the early church were not interested in the this-worldly features of the Messianic kingdom. Their vivid expectation of the pa-

---

[1] So also Rev. 20:7–10 (*v.i.*).

rousia and the kingdom of God left no room for an intermediate Messianic kingdom. Paul speaks of a kind of intermediate kingdom of Christ, but it is the present age, in which Christ is reigning and overcoming his enemies.[2] It will come to an end with the resurrection of the dead, when Christ has overthrown his last enemy, death.[3]

Only in Rev. 20:1–6 does the New Testament have anything corresponding directly to the Jewish hope of an intermediate Messianic kingdom. As in some Jewish sources, the period will last a thousand years; hence it has come to be called the millennium. It will belong to the resurrected martyrs, who will sit on thrones, exercising judgment,[4] and will live and reign with Christ. The fact that the coming of Christ is not definitely mentioned in this sole account of the millennium in the New Testament has made possible the agelong controversy between premillennialism and postmillennialism. The postmillennialists identify the millennium with the present age of the church.[5] Some have made use of the idea of a world-week with days of a thousand years.[6] But in Rev. 20:4, 6 the martyrs reign with Christ. If the parousia is not to occur until the end of the millennium, this reigning with Christ must take place in heaven, but in that case the expressions " live " and " first resurrection " are strange.

Such difficulties exist only for the interpreter who assumes that all the New Testament writers had the same conception of things to be. The problem is all the greater when the attempt is made to reconcile the idea of a millennium with predictions of the coming of Christ and the kingdom of God within the generation in which Jesus lived, and to combine both with the signs of the end described in the eschatological discourse of the synoptic gospels. Some commentators identify the imminent parousia of the synoptic predictions with the coming of the Spirit at Pentecost, others with the destruction of the temple and the Jewish nation in A.D. 70 (which is more in keeping with the context in Mk., ch. 13, and parallels). The statement that the gospel must first be preached to all nations [7] is met by the assumption that it had been sufficiently preached throughout the Roman empire by A.D. 70 to give the Jews of the Dispersion an opportunity to accept or reject it. But since

[2] 1 Cor. 15:22–28.
[3] V. 26.
[4] If that is the meaning of v. 4 " judgment was given to them "; cp. Mt. 19:28.
[5] Cp. 1 Cor. 15:22–28.
[6] Cp. 2 P. 3:8.
[7] Mk. 13:10.

most of such interpreters still look for Christ's coming again at the end of the world, this view involves a third as well as a second coming, both a premillennial and a postmillennial parousia. Sound exegesis makes no such attempt to force all the ideas of the New Testament writers into one mold, and a sound understanding of revelation does not demand the assumption that the inspired writers all thought alike. It is hard enough to make each book consistent in itself without trying to make it consistent with all the others.

The importance of the idea of the millennium for modern theology is that it shows once more how pre-Christian and sub-Christian ideas survived in the faith of the early church, and demonstrates again the fact that literalism is incompatible with a true historical interpretation of the Bible. The minister who has to deal with people holding a literal view of such passages as Rev. 20:1–6 should stress more important things in his preaching, but he should also know the facts and take a clear, unequivocal position when the question comes up. By an inductive use of biblical evidence and a Socratic method of discussion he can show the impossibility of taking all eschatological passages literally and at the same time making them agree.

69. *The Resurrection of the Dead*

As we have seen, the emergence of any hope for the individual after death was a relatively late phenomenon in Old Testament religion. The earliest forms of Israel's hope for the future were national rather than individual; the individual Israelite could participate in the coming salvation only if he lived to see it. Otherwise his only hope was for his descendants. The growth of individualism (s. 49) made this less and less satisfying, and the repeated disappointment of the hope of national restoration after the exile encouraged a shift of emphasis. The national hope on the plane of history gave way to the apocalyptic hope of a divine, miraculous intervention and a new world-order. Later the two types of hope were combined (s. 65). Apparently contact with Zoroastrianism, the religion of the Persian empire, supplemented these tendencies and supplied the pattern for the Jewish hope of resurrection and judgment after death.

Recent writers have tried to demonstrate an earlier Hebrew and even Canaanite hope of resurrection, but without success. Ho. 6:1–3 refers to national restoration, not individual resurrection. An allusion to the cult of the dying and rising vegetation god is possible, but the worshipers of such deities did not expect resurrection for themselves. Ho. 13:14 refers to deliverance from death in the sense of being kept alive. If Ezek. 37:1–14 was written in the Greek period, the writer doubtless knew of the belief in resurrection, but what he was talking about here was clearly national restoration. Job 19:25 f. is hopelessly obscure; but ch. 14:7–12 denies any hope of a resurrection (vv. 14 f. are a contrary-to-fact condition, as in A.S.V.), and even if such a hope is involved in ch. 19:25 f., it does not reappear thereafter in the book as affording a solution of Job's problem.

The idea of resurrection is clearly expressed in Is. 26:19, part of an apocalyptic document (chs. 24 to 27) which is commonly dated in the Greek period. This is probably the earliest expression of the hope in the Old Testament. The first definite and datable statement, however, is Dan. 12:2, at the very end of the Old Testament period. In postbiblical Judaism, except for its Hellenistic variety (s. 65), belief in the resurrection of the dead was generally accepted and much stressed. One of its most striking expressions is 2 Macc. 7:9–11, 14, 22 f., 29. The rabbinic literature designates the resurrection by a Hebrew expression meaning literally " the making alive of the dead." God is often called " He who makes alive the dead." Naturally the hope is especially prominent in apocalyptic writings, such as Enoch, 4 Ezra, and 2 Baruch. The Sadducees denied the resurrection,[1] but after the fall of Jerusalem and the destruction of the temple in A.D. 70 the Sadducees disappeared, and Pharisaic beliefs prevailed. The Mishna says that the resurrection can be deduced from the Torah, and anyone who denies this has no part in the life to come. Elaborate logical and exegetical proofs of the doctrine were devised by the rabbis.

Jesus agreed with the Pharisees against the Sadducees on this point. Mk. 9:1 implies that most of Jesus' hearers will die before the kingdom of God comes; hence they can participate in it only by resurrection. The resurrection is mentioned in Lk. 14:14 and implied in Mt. 8:11 (Lk. 13:28) and Mt. 12:41 f. (Lk. 11:31 f.). The chief reference to the subject is Mk. 12:18 ff., and parallels, where the argument Jesus uses (s. 20) is less important than the fact that he defends the belief but interprets it as involving a mode of existence essentially different from this life.

The resurrection was a prominent part of the preaching of the apostles.[2] Paul apparently neglected this subject somewhat in his preaching

---

[1] Mk. 12:18–27; Acts 23:6 ff.   [2] Acts 4:2; 23:6.

at Thessalonica, for he has to explain in 1 Th. 4:13–15 that death does not exclude the believer from the coming glory. True to his Jewish heritage, Paul thinks in terms of resurrection, but not resurrection of the flesh. The Christian awaits with groaning his deliverance from the flesh by the redemption of the body.[3] At the parousia (s. 67) those Christians who are still alive will be transformed into bodies of glory, and the dead will rise with spiritual bodies.[4]

John makes the resurrection a present possession, corresponding to Paul's conception of rising to newness of life,[5] though there is a puzzling series of references to the future resurrection also in chs. 5 f. The traditional view of the resurrection of both righteous and wicked for judgment is clearly stated in ch. 5:28 f. Whether we have here a group of interpolations by an orthodox scribe who was not wholly satisfied with the evangelist's idea of the resurrection as a present spiritual experience, or whether the evangelist himself combined his own distinctive idea with the traditional belief — by no means a rare phenomenon — we cannot tell.

The interest of the synoptic evangelists and of the circles they represent is shown by the stress on the resurrection of the dead in the book of Acts.[6] Revelation has a unique idea of two resurrections (v.i.). Heb. 6:2 names the resurrection of the dead among the rudiments of Christian faith and ch. 11:35 says that the heroes of faith died to " obtain a better resurrection."

As an event in the eschatological drama the resurrection is a prerequisite for the judgment of the dead and their admission to or exclusion from the final rewards of the righteous. A resurrection of both good and evil is thus required, and this is distinctly stated in Dan. 12:2 (though for " many " rather than all). When the parousia is thought of as primarily a coming for judgment, the resurrection naturally follows it immediately. Only when there is an intermediate Messianic kingdom is this not the case, and even then there is some confusion; e.g., it is said that Elijah, who will come just before the Messiah at the beginning of the Messianic kingdom, will have a part in raising the dead. Revelation solves the difficulty by having two resurrections and two judgments.[7]

---

[3] Rom. 8:23.
[4] 1 Cor. 15:35 ff.; Phil. 3:20 f.; cp. 2 Cor. 3:17 f.; 5:1–10; Col. 3:10; for a partial parallel to this conception see 2 Baruch, chs. 50 f.
[5] Jn. 11:23–26; Rom. 6:4–11.
[6] Acts 17:18, 31 f.; 23:6–9; 26:6–8.
[7] Rev. 20:4–6, 11–15.

No saying of Jesus explicitly connects the resurrection of the dead with the parousia or the judgment, though in Mt. 12:41 f. (Lk. 11:31 f.) the men of Nineveh will " rise in the judgment " and the queen of the South will " be raised in the judgment " (so the Greek). We can infer, in any case, that Jesus thought of the resurrection and judgment as occurring together, because (1) they went together in Judaism and in later parts of the New Testament, (2) they belong together logically, and (3) the presence of the dead seems to be assumed in Jesus' sayings regarding the judgment. The apparent anomaly in Paul's ideas at this point will be treated in s. 70.

70. *The Last Judgment*

The background of all the biblical conceptions of the day of judgment is the idea of the Day of Yahweh in the prophetic books of the Old Testament, beginning with Am. 5:18, 20. Proclaiming judgment on the sinful nation, Amos denounces those who desire the Day of Yahweh, expecting it to be a day of light. Apparently this refers to a current hope of divine judgment in the sense of national triumph over all the enemies of Israel and Israel's God, based on the assumption that Yahweh's power and his favoritism for his chosen people guaranteed victory regardless of moral worthiness or unworthiness.

On the background and specific content of this popular hope, its relation to the official cult, and the place of the official court prophets in its development and propagation, we have many theories but little evidence. In its earliest form the hope doubtless involved divine aid with regard to such natural phenomena as the weather and the fertility of the soil, as well as military security and aggrandizement, especially if Canaanite influence had a part in its origin. The presence of both natural and political elements in later eschatology favors this hypothesis. In short, what was hoped for probably included all the benefits associated with the covenant, but with insufficient attention to its moral and social conditions. Since the national life was rotten with oppression and injustice, Amos declared that the Day of Yahweh would be darkness and not light.

Through the later prophetic and apocalyptic writings the idea of darkness is enhanced by references to thick clouds and smoke and even such celestial portents as the turning of the moon into blood.[1] How far all this is symbolism and how far it involves the expectation of super-

---

[1] Zp. 1:14-16; Joel 2:31 f.; Zc. 14:6.

natural phenomena is not clear, but since Yahweh was God of both nature and history, and the accounts of his judgments on Israel's enemies
in the past included miraculous events in nature,[2] it is not unlikely that
the powers of nature were expected to be arrayed with the human agents
of Yahweh's judgment in the future. The promise of national restoration in Second Isaiah involves marvelous features in such a way that
we cannot tell where realism ends and symbolism begins. This is equally
true of the later prophetic and apocalyptic visions. Joel 2:30 f. is included in the quotation in Acts 2:16-21, although there is no indication
of convulsions of nature on the Day of Pentecost. The psalms refer to
Yahweh's coming to judge the earth in terms which leave it uncertain
whether the judgment is to be historical or eschatological.[3]

True to the basic Hebrew conception of judgment (s. 60), the eschatological visions of the Old Testament combine the idea of punishment
by war with the conception of a court in which judgment is pronounced.
The former idea is sometimes expressed in terms of a great sacrificial
meal at which beasts and birds as Yahweh's guests devour his slaugh-
tered enemies.[4] The conception of the eschatological war appears also
in Joel and Zechariah.[5] The climax of the development of the idea comes
in Ezek., chs. 38 f. (cp. s. 66). In Joel 3:12-14, however, the idea of a
forensic judgment scene appears to be involved also.

With the rise of the apocalyptic hope and belief in the resurrection
of the dead, the final judgment becomes the permanent separation of
righteous and wicked for their eternal reward or punishment (ss. 71 f.).
The first definite attestation of this idea is Dan. 12:2. When this hope
is combined in later Judaism with the idea of an intermediate Messianic
kingdom (s. 68), the judgment by war tends to be placed before the
resurrection, and the final judgment then becomes a forensic pronouncement of the divine sentence on the good and the evil.

When the final judgment is considered in Jewish sources as the condemnation and punishment of sinners, there is often a nationalistic emphasis. When it is thought of as the separation of the righteous from the
wicked, the point of view is more universalistic (s. 102). Sometimes God
is the Judge, as in the Old Testament; sometimes, especially in the apocalyptic literature, the Judge is the Messiah. The terrifying phenomena
of the Day of Yahweh are still more or less combined with the picture
of a trial in court. To the latter conception belong the idea of a book in

[2] Ex. 14:21-31; Ju. 5:20 f.   [4] Zp. 1:7 f.; Jer. 46:10; Ezek. 39:17-20; Is. 34:1-7.
[3] Ps. 96:13; 98:9.   [5] Joel 3:9 ff.; Zc. 14:3, 12.

which men's deeds are recorded, or in which the names of the righteous are inscribed,[6] and the idea of testimony by angelic witnesses. The mathematical accuracy of the judgment is expressed in rabbinic sources by the idea of the balance.

Several sayings of Jesus refer to the coming judgment. The idea of a forensic trial appears both in Mt. 12:41 f. (Lk. 11:31 f.) and in Mt. 25:31–46. In the latter case those who are condemned protest, and those who are approved express surprise. Two questions arise in connection with this passage: (1) How much of it is authentic? (2) How literally is the account to be taken? In view of the perennial debate regarding the relative importance of the ethical and the eschatological in the teachings of Jesus, it is worth noting that one of the great texts of the social gospel occurs in the midst of this distinctly apocalyptic passage.[7] Assuming the authenticity of the whole account, the fact that Jesus elsewhere uses somewhat different imagery and the fact that he says the resurrection life will be like that of the angels [8] indicate that the picture as here given is not to be taken too literally. Matthew's explanations of the parables of the tares and the dragnet present a different picture: at the parousia the Son of Man and his angels will gather up the wicked and cast them into the fire.[9] While these verses are probably secondary, Jesus may at times have presented the idea of the judgment in this form. The sayings on confessing and denying before the Father those who claim to be his disciples fall into the general category of the forensic judgment.[10]

In the early church stress was laid on the idea that Jesus himself would be the judge.[11] Mt. 25:31–46, discussed in the preceding paragraph, may in part represent the tradition of the Palestinian church. Paul's accounts of the parousia and resurrection in 1 Th., ch. 4, and 1 Cor., ch. 15, contain no judgment scene, since the unsaved apparently have no part in the resurrection at all but simply stay dead; yet 2 Th. 1:7 ff. says that the persecutors of the Christians will suffer vengeance and punishment, and in ch. 2:8 the lawless one is slain by the breath of the Lord's mouth at the parousia. The former statement, to be sure, may refer to the wicked who are still living when Christ comes. Paul's refer-

---

[6] Called the book of life in Enoch 108:3; the books of the living in ch. 47:3.
[7] Mt. 25:40, 45.
[8] Mk. 12:25.
[9] Mt. 13:41 f., 49 f.
[10] Mk. 8:38; Mt. 10:32 f.; Lk. 9:26; 12:8 f.; cp. Rev. 3:5; 2 Tim. 2:12.
[11] Acts 10:42; cp. 17:31.

ences to a final forensic judgment for Christians [12] have been discussed in s. 55. In 1 Cor. 6:2 f. Paul says that the saints will judge the world and even the angels. Perhaps in his own mind Paul could reconcile all these ideas, but what we find in his letters suggests that he had not thought through his conception of the last judgment. Not improbably he would have brushed aside such questions as unimportant.

The fourth evangelist, in keeping with his spiritualization of eschatology in general, treats the judgment as a present, automatic process. The word " judgment " (Greek, *krisis*) is one of the prominent words of the gospel, indicating the separation of believers and unbelievers by virtue of the very fact of their belief or unbelief. The unbeliever is already condemned; [13] the believer has passed from death to life and will not come into judgment.[14] All judgment is committed to the Son,[15] who came into the world for the purpose of judgment,[16] though elsewhere it is said that he came not to judge but to save.[17] The judgment in the last day is mentioned in ch. 12:48.[18] In ss. 67 and 69 we note the possibility that the evangelist did not reject the traditional ideas of the parousia and resurrection, but simply added to them his own spiritual reinterpretation. This may have been so with regard to the judgment also. At any rate, if there was to be a future judgment, its result was already determined by the individual's previous acceptance or rejection of Christ.

Rev. 20:4 speaks of judgment as given to the martyrs in the millennial kingdom (s. 68). After the millennium will come the loosing of Satan, followed by the war of Gog and Magog and their destruction by fire from heaven, and then the casting of the devil into the lake of fire and brimstone where the beast and the false prophet have already been cast.[19] Then a great white throne will be placed, the dead will be given up by the sea and by Death and Hades and will stand before the throne, books will be opened, the dead will be judged by their deeds, and all not named in the book of life will be cast into the lake of fire.

Further references to the judgment, without anything new or specific, are found in other books of the New Testament.[20]

---

[12] Rom. 14:10; 2 Cor. 5:10.
[13] Jn. 3:18.
[14] Ch. 5:24.
[15] Ch. 5:22–27.
[16] Ch. 9:39.
[17] Chs. 3:17; 12:47.
[18] Cp. 1 Jn. 4:17.
[19] Cp. Rev. 19:20.
[20] Heb. 6:2; 9:27; 10:27; 13:4; 1 P. 4:5; Jas. 5:9.

71. *The Final State of the Wicked*

On the ultimate doom of those who are condemned in the last judgment the Old Testament has no clear teaching. The judgment of the wicked is most commonly presented in terms of death and destruction, but complete annihilation of the individual person is hardly contemplated. Death itself means going down to Sheol (s. 65), which is punishment enough. In Dan. 12:2, where resurrection and judgment first appear clearly, the wicked are committed to " shame and everlasting contempt."

As in other matters, the Old Testament provides ideas and imagery which were later reapplied to the punishment of the wicked after the final judgment, but were not so intended by the writers. Perhaps the most influential passage of all in this respect was Is. 66:24, which seems to imply eternal punishment in the flesh. The idea of punishment by fire appears also in Is. 30:33, where judgment on the Assyrian emperor (cp. v. 31) is proclaimed in the form of a sacrifice by fire on the altar. As shown by 2 K. 23:10, Topheth was a place in the valley south of Jerusalem where children were sacrificed by fire.[1] From the name of the valley in which child-sacrifice was performed, " the valley of the sons of Hinnom " or " the valley of Hinnom " (Hebrew, *ge' hinnom*), comes the common name of the place of eternal torment in later Jewish sources and in the New Testament, " Gehenna." The name was also taken over by Islam in the form *Jehinnam*.

The lack of clear teaching on this subject in the Old Testament is reflected in the later Jewish sources. Rabbinic literature records a variety of opinion among the rabbis on the nature of Gehenna, including even the view that there is no such place. Some of the Apocrypha speak of the destruction of the wicked by fire and sword; in others the wicked simply disappear without any indication of what happens to them. Where Gehenna is recognized, the rabbis differ as to whether it is eternal, some regarding it practically as the equivalent of purgatory. The prevailing idea, however, is that of eternal punishment in Gehenna for all who are condemned in the judgment. Many vivid descriptions of the torments of Gehenna are given, with a variety of imagery, but the idea of fire remains dominant.

Many of Jesus' sayings mention Gehenna. (The Greek text simply

---

[1] Cp. Jer. 7:31 f.; 19:6, 11–15.

transliterates the name; the English versions translate " hell.") Like the rabbis, Jesus quotes Is. 66:24 in this connection.[2] The word " eternal " in these passages, as we shall see more fully in connection with eternal life (s. 72), does not mean primarily " endless " but " belonging to the coming age." The idea of infinite duration is implied, however, because the coming age will have no end. Aside from the imagery derived from Is. 66:24, Jesus uses also the effective figure of " outer darkness," [3] with which are combined " weeping and gnashing of teeth." While much of all this is found in Matthew only, there is enough in Mark and Luke to authenticate the main ideas sufficiently. As noted with regard to the judgment, the use of different figures of speech shows that Jesus did not intend any one of them to be taken literally. A unique indication of gradations in punishment is given in Lk. 12:47 f.

It must be noted that there is no basis in the recorded sayings of Jesus for universalism in the sense that all men will ultimately be saved. So far as the evidence indicates, he thought of the punishment of the wicked as eternal. Whether his conception of God logically demands the ultimate salvation of all is a question for systematic theology. It involves the further question whether repentance (s. 78) is ultimately possible for all, and also the question whether universal repentance can ever be certain, since repentance presupposes freedom of choice.

For the early church we have little evidence on the punishment of the wicked, and none of any change in ideas. The preservation and use of Jesus' sayings may be taken as evidence of the persistence of the idea of Gehenna, and if some of the language attributed to Jesus is not authentic, it is primary evidence at least for the conceptions prevalent in the church.[4]

Aside from frequent references to the death of the wicked, Paul practically ignores the question of their final state, with the sole exception of 2 Th. 1:9, which describes the punishment of the wicked (or at least some of them, cp. s. 70) as " eternal destruction from the face of the Lord and from the glory of his might." Whether this implies annihilation, Gehenna, or simply being left in Sheol we cannot be sure. Even more vague is the statement of 2 Cor. 5:10 that we shall all " receive the deeds done through the body." John also has nothing more specific

[2] Mk. 9:43–48, and parallels; cp. also for Gehenna Mt. 5:22; 10:28 (Lk. 12:5) ; 23:15, 33; and for fire (without mention of Gehenna) Mt. 13:42, 50; 25:41 (cp. v. 46).

[3] Mt. 8:12; cp. Lk. 13:28; Mt. 22:13; 25:30.

[4] Mt. 13:40–42, 49 f. and perhaps ch. 25:41, 46.

than the general idea of death, evidently meant in some spiritual sense, because the believer has passed from death to life.[5]

To sum up, throughout the New Testament, where the subject is treated at all, the idea seems to be eternal torment, especially by fire, unless Paul and John contemplate the annihilation of the wicked or perhaps simply exclusion from the kingdom of God.[6] The doctrine of eternal hell-fire has been very important in Christian preaching in the past. Modern theology must face the question of its truth, or of a moral equivalent for it if it is entirely abandoned. The main emphasis should always be on the positive hope of the saved, but the eternal consequences of sin must not be ignored.

72. The Final State of the Righteous; the Coming Age and Eternal Life

In part this subject has already been considered in connection with the ideas of resurrection and immortality (s. 69); in part it is involved also in the subject of s. 73. Thus Dan. 12:2, like many passages in the New Testament, designates the final state of the righteous as eternal life, while v. 3, which pictures the glory of the righteous, is echoed by Mt. 13:43 with an added reference to " the kingdom of their Father."

Negatively, the final state of the righteous is one of freedom from condemnation or any fear of future judgment. For Paul it means also the final deliverance from the flesh and the power of sin.[1] The positive content of the hope of final blessedness is expressed in various forms, including some already noted. In the beatitudes [2] Jesus speaks of being comforted, inheriting the earth, being filled with righteousness, seeing God, and being called sons of God, in addition to possessing the kingdom of heaven. The conception of future blessedness in the presence of God is foreshadowed by a few hints in the Old Testament, especially Ps. 49:15 and 73:23 f., but unfortunately the meaning of these passages is far from clear. The expression, " Great is your reward in heaven," [3] suggests the idea of immortality rather than resurrection.[4] In connection with the intermediate state it was noted that Lk. 16:19-31 and 23:43 may indicate the final rather than the intermediate abode

---

[5] Jn. 5:24; cp. v. 29. For the rest of the N.T. cp. Rev. 14:9-11; 19:20; 20:10, 15; 21:8; 22:19; Heb. 2:2 f.; 6:2, 8; 10:26-31; Jas. 5:1-3; 1 Tim. 1:20; 2 Tim. 2:12; 2 P. 2:4.

[6] Jn. 3:3, 5.

[1] Rom. 7:24; 8:23; 1 Cor. 15:53-57; 2 Cor. 5:2-4; cp. Eph. 1:14; 4:30.

[2] Mt. 5:2-12 (cp. Lk. 6:20-26).

[3] Mt. 5:12.

[4] Cp. also chs. 6:20; 19:21 (Mk. 10:21).

of the righteous, and also that Jesus' conception of the righteous in the resurrection as being like the angels [5] brings the ideas of resurrection and the immortality of the soul very close together (s. 65).

For Paul the climax and completion of salvation will be the " redemption of the body." [6] This hope is for Paul an indispensable part of the gospel.[7] Contemplation of the glories still to be revealed moves Paul to ecstatic joy.[8] Having a spiritual body instead of a body of flesh will mean being, not unclothed, but clothed.[9] To depart and be with Christ is far better than living in the body.[10] The Christian's true citizenship is in heaven.[11] The completion of the parousia and resurrection is expressed in the words, " And so shall we ever be with the Lord." [12]

In John the emphasis on salvation as a present experience overshadows the idea of future salvation, except in ch. 14:1–4, where the Father's house is the final abode of Christ's followers. The references to heaven in Hebrews,[13] and to the assembly in the heavenly Jerusalem, including " the spirits of just men made perfect," [14] have been noted in s. 65. The most elaborate picture of the final blessedness of the saved in the whole Bible is the description of the new Jerusalem which John sees coming down from heaven.[15] Jewish sources present similar ideas of Paradise, i.e., the garden of Eden, as existing now in heaven and to be brought down to the temple mountain at the end of this age. The details of the highly developed symbolism of Revelation are less important than the presence of God and the Lamb and the end of all sorrow and pain. Although now commonly applied to heaven as believers enter it at death, the description is obviously intended to be eschatological.

The meaning of the adjective translated " eternal " (or " everlasting "), as applied to the punishment of the wicked and the blessedness of the righteous, has been mentioned in s. 71. Its use in Jewish sources and the New Testament follows the pattern of Dan. 12:2. The Hebrew there means literally " the life of eternity," but the noun meaning " eternity " has considerable range of meaning. Sometimes, especially in later Jewish usage, it means " world " or " universe "; it is used especially, however, for the eschatological distinction between the two ages, this age and the coming age. The favorite term for salvation in the rabbinic literature is " the life of the coming age " (or " a share in the life of the coming age ").

[5] Mk. 12:25.
[6] Rom. 8:23.
[7] 1 Cor. 15:19.
[8] Rom. 8:38 f.
[9] 2 Cor. 5:1–8.
[10] Phil. 1:23.
[11] Phil. 3:20.
[12] 1 Th. 4:17.
[13] Heb. 6:19 f.; 11:16.
[14] Ch. 12:22 f.
[15] Rev., chs. 21 f.

In this sense the Hebrew noun is represented by the Greek *aion*, which is used frequently in the New Testament in the same way that the Hebrew word is used in rabbinic literature. Thus blasphemy against the Holy Spirit will not be forgiven in this *aion* or in the *aion* which is to be.[16] Matthew has several times [17] an expression meaning literally " consummation of the age." [18] From this noun is derived the adjective *aionios* (translated " eternal "), which is used by the Septuagint to render the Hebrew phrase of Dan. 12:2, and by the New Testament in the same sense. Both noun and adjective appear together in Mk. 10:30, " and in the coming *aion* life *aionios*."

The use of the word " life " for salvation has a long history. The Old Testament often speaks of salvation in terms of life as against death, the meaning varying from mere longevity to comprehensive welfare and abundance.[19] The verb " live " is used also in the same way. The life of the coming age therefore means not merely existence in the eschatological order but full participation in its blessings.

In accordance with Jewish usage the gospels sometimes speak of salvation as " inheriting " (or, rather, " coming into possession of ") eternal life. The rich man in Mk. 10:17 and parallels and the lawyer in Lk. 10:25 ask what they must do to inherit eternal life. When the rich man turns away, Jesus says that it is hard for the rich to enter the kingdom of God,[20] indicating that to inherit eternal life and to enter the kingdom of God (ss. 64, 73) are identical. The interchangeability of the two expressions is even clearer in Mk. 9:43–48.

The early church continued to use " life " as a general term for salvation.[21] The fuller expression, " eternal life," does not occur in Acts, chs. 1 to 12, but it is used in ch. 13:46, 48. Paul frequently speaks of salvation as " eternal life," [22] and also simply as " life." [23] Nothing in the context shows just what is meant by these expressions, but there is no reason to suppose that they mean for Paul anything other than what they mean in Judaism and in the teaching of Jesus, the life of the coming age.

---

16 Mt. 12:32.
17 Mt. 13:39 f., 49; 24:3; 28:20.
18 E.VV., " end of the world "; cp. Heb. 9:26, " consummation of the ages "; 1 Cor. 10:11, " ends of the ages."
19 Cp. Dt. 30:19 f.; 32:46 f.; Prov. 4:13, 20–23; 8:35.
20 Mk. 10:23.
21 Acts 2:28 (quoting Ps. 16:11); 11:18.
22 Rom. 2:7; 5:21; 6:22; Gal. 6:8.
23 Rom. 5:17 f.; 11:15; 2 Cor. 2:16; 5:4; Gal. 3:21; Phil. 2:16; 4:3; Col. 3:4.

In John " eternal life " (sometimes " life " alone) is the principal term for salvation. It expresses the object of Jesus' coming [24] and of the writing of the gospel.[25] But just as the fourth evangelist spiritualizes the ideas of the parousia, resurrection, and judgment, so eternal life is no longer the life of the coming age but a present possession of the believer.[26] It is defined as knowing God and Christ.[27] This resembles Paul's idea of life in Christ, but whereas Paul looks beyond this life for complete redemption, in John there is no suggestion that salvation will ever be more complete than it is now. Except for the puzzling references to the last day noted in s. 69, eternal life begins now and continues in the hereafter, death being an unimportant incident.

The rest of the New Testament frequently uses the word " life " for salvation,[28] usually with a clear eschatological reference. In short, throughout the New Testament, with the exception of the gospel and first epistle of John, " eternal life " means the life of the coming age. Endless duration is implied, but the primary meaning of the adjective is the reference to the coming age as over against this age. In other words, eternal life is not merely a state of unending bliss for the individual by himself, but participation in the cosmic, eschatological redemption (s. 73).

73. *The Final Consummation of the Kingdom of God*

We have seen that in Mk. 9:43–48 entering into life and entering into the kingdom of God are identified, and that " eternal life " means the life of the coming age (s. 72). This suggests that the kingdom of God and the coming age are closely related, if not identical. The very essence of the idea of the coming age is in fact the complete establishment and exercise of God's sovereignty throughout the universe.

This was clearly what Jesus had in mind in those sayings which imply the presence of the righteous dead in the kingdom of God. Thus Mt. 8:11 (Lk. 13:29) speaks of the Hebrew patriarchs as being joined by many from all quarters in the kingdom. While this might conceivably refer to heaven as a place in which the righteous dead already abide, the use of the traditional conception of the Messianic banquet in-

---

[24] Jn. 3:15 f.; 10:10.
[25] Ch. 20:31.
[26] Jn. 3:15 f., 36; 5:24; 6:47; 1 Jn. 5:13.
[27] Jn. 17:3; cp. 1 Jn. 5:11 f.
[28] For " eternal life " cf. 1 Tim. 1:16; 6:12; Titus 1:2; 3:7; Jude 21.

dicates an eschatological reference. Mk. 14:25 points to a reunion of Jesus with the disciples in the kingdom after his death. This could refer either to heaven or to the coming age after the parousia. Luke's form of the saying [1] explicitly supports the latter interpretation, while Lk. 22:15 f., if authentic, would fit either view. In Mk. 10:23–25, whatever is meant by entering the kingdom (s. 72), it is explicitly connected with the coming age (vv. 17, 30).

In s. 67 we noted the fact that in Mt. 16:28 the coming of the Son of Man in his kingdom [2] takes the place of the coming of the kingdom of God in Mk. 9:1. In all three gospels the context implies that these events are identical, and Mk. 13:30 says the same thing about the parousia that ch. 9:1 says about the kingdom of God. In Lk. 17:20–24 (cp. s. 64) the coming of the kingdom is discussed together with " the days of the Son of Man " without any suggestion of a distinction between them.[3] The kingdom of the Son of Man and the kingdom of the disciples are connected in Mt. 19:28 and Lk. 22:29 f.[4] In the eschatological discourse, which is a primary source for the views of the evangelists if not for the teaching of Jesus (s. 66), Lk. 21:31 reads " the kingdom of God is nigh " for " he [or it] is nigh." [5] Matthew and Luke follow this with several parables stressing the imminence and unexpectedness of the parousia, but also referring more or less explicitly to the kingdom of God.[6] Evidently the identity of the parousia and the coming of the kingdom, while nowhere explicitly stated, is assumed by the evangelists. There is no reason to suppose that this misrepresents the thought of Jesus. The sayings regarding both subjects are most naturally interpreted on the assumption that they are the same.

Our conclusions regarding Jesus' conception of the kingdom of God may now be summed up in seven propositions: (1) The basic meaning of the concept is the eternal sovereignty of God, and in a few cases this is the meaning Jesus has in mind (s. 64). (2) God's sovereignty is fully realized and effective in heaven, but not yet on earth; hence the kingdom of God is still to come. (3) Its final coming will be eschatological, involving the parousia, the resurrection, and the judgment, and inaugurating the coming age; hence in many sayings the kingdom of God

---

[1] Lk. 22:18.
[2] Cp. Mt. 10:23; 19:28; 25:31.
[3] Cp. also Lk. 23:42 for the Son of Man coming in (or into) his kingdom.
[4] Cp. Mt. 5:3, 10; 25:34; Lk. 12:32.
[5] Mk. 13:29; Mt. 24:33.
[6] Mt. 25:1; cp. Lk. 19:11, introducing the parallel to Mt. 25:14 ff.

means the coming age. (4) The expulsion of demons shows that Satan's power is inferior to God's and therefore doomed, and thus that the power of the coming kingdom is already at work in the world. (5) Jesus' followers are already in the kingdom in the sense that they accept God's sovereignty, that its power is manifest in their lives, and that they have the assurance of participation in its final consummation. (6) Jesus did not mean by the kingdom of God a Christianized social order in this world, but every advance in the direction of such an order is, like the expulsion of demons by him and his disciples, a demonstration of the power of the kingdom. (7) For Jesus the kingdom of God thus represents the sum total both of individual salvation and of the divine cosmic redemption of all creation.

74. *The Truth of Jesus' Eschatological Teaching*

We must now face the question raised in s. 18 and postponed to this point. If Jesus taught, as the evidence indicates, that the kingdom of God would come within the generation in which he lived, and if what he meant by the coming of the kingdom included the end of this age, the parousia of the Son of Man, the resurrection of the dead, the judgment, and the inauguration of the coming age, he was obviously mistaken. These things did not happen then and have not happened yet. But the announcement of the nearness of the kingdom was the very heart of his message. Is not his whole teaching invalidated and our faith in him as the supreme revealer of divine truth undermined if he was wrong at this crucial point? The answer can only be summarized here in a series of concise statements.

a. So far as we have any reliable evidence of Jesus' teaching, honest historical criticism cannot avoid the conclusion that he expected the eschatological consummation of the kingdom of God within his generation; we must therefore admit that at this point he was mistaken.

b. Jesus thought in terms of such knowledge as was available for a real person in Palestine in the first century, which did not enable him to foresee the long stretches of history still ahead.

c. The truth of his teaching on other matters and the validity of his ideals of life are quite independent of the accuracy of his predictions regarding the time of the kingdom's coming.

d. The limitations of his world-view do not necessarily invalidate his spiritual insight regarding the ultimate outcome; indeed, the " prophetic foreshortening " of his hope may have been caused by the very keenness and immediacy of his perception of the inevitable triumph of God's will.

e. Possibly, as Acts 1:7 suggests,[1] what Jesus taught was that the kingdom was near and might come at any moment if Israel accepted it, but that God reserved the sovereign authority to postpone or withhold it until his people showed themselves ready for it. (A view like this appears two or three centuries later in rabbinic theology.)

f. If God is the Lord of heaven and earth, as Jesus taught, his righteous, loving will cannot be defeated. Individuals may perhaps exclude themselves permanently from his kingdom by their stubborn disobedience (s. 71), but while he does not desire that any should perish,[2] the inexorable operation of laws which he has ordained does not impair his sovereignty. The ultimate question is therefore whether Jesus was right in proclaiming, with all the prophets, the kingship of God. That question, of course, cannot be answered by knowledge, but only by faith.

g. Granting God's power to accomplish his purpose, we must leave to him the manner as well as the time of its achievement. Whether there will ever be a complete end of all resistance to his rule, a veritable eschatological coming of his kingdom in full power, must perhaps remain uncertain. What may be called a commutation of eschatology begins already in the New Testament with the explanation of the delay of the parousia as due to God's patience.[3] Even 2 P., ch. 3, still insists that the Day of the Lord will come, but a final, complete establishment of God's sovereignty by power, no matter how remote, would actually defeat his purpose unless all the creatures to whom he has given freedom finally yield to the persuasion of his love, or those who have not yielded are so hardened and corrupted by their own stubbornness that God knows even his love can never redeem them. Any end which implies a loss of patience on God's part is out of the question. A Scriptural precedent for the complete commutation of eschatology in which some modern theologians have taken refuge is afforded by the spiritualization of all eschatological concepts in the fourth gospel.[4]

h. However interpreted, the eschatological expectation cannot be regarded as merely a " mythological " expression of God's eternal sovereignty. It at least embodies three inescapable facts: (a) for every individual the end of this world is coming and may come at any moment; (b) for every people and civilization there will be a sure doom if it fails

---

[1] But cp. R.S.V. and Mk. 13:32.
[2] Ezek. 33:11; 2 P. 3:9.
[3] 2 P. 3:9.
[4] With exceptions noted in s. 69.

to obey God's laws; and (c) the end of physical existence on earth must come eventually, and no hopes dependent upon the continuance of this world-order can be permanent.

The stern cry of the prophets, " The end is coming," holds good for us and all later generations. But beyond the inevitable doom and the inescapable judgment the gospel offers hope and joy. The glory has departed from Christian faith unless " we look for a new heaven and a new earth, wherein dwelleth righteousness," [5] " a city which hath foundations, whose builder and maker is God," [6] that eternal city in which " there shall be no curse any more, and the throne of God and the Lamb shall be therein." [7]

A few suggestions regarding the use of this material by the minister may serve to summarize and conclude our discussion of eschatology. (1) Literalism should be met by showing inductively that the Bible presents not one picture of the future but many, which are irreconcilable if taken literally. (2) The precedent of John may be cited for a spiritual reinterpretation in the light of our best knowledge and thought. (3) The main stress should be laid on the basic religious interest of all eschatology, the ultimate triumph of the justice of God. (4) It should be recognized that this involves more than the achievement of a Christian social order in this world, even if that can ever be expected, because any social order on earth will come to an end, and because justice to the countless generations that have lived and died must be taken into account.

[5] 2 P. 3:13.
[6] Heb. 11:10.
[7] Rev. 22:3; note also Heb. 12:26–29; Lk. 12:32.

XII

THE WAY OF SALVATION

75. *Atonement*

The proclamation of judgment and salvation, both here and hereafter, evokes the questions: " Brethren, what shall we do? " " What
must I do to be saved? " " What shall I do that I may inherit eternal
life? " [1] We have already found that man could do nothing at all to
save himself if God had not himself provided a way of deliverance, not
by prescribing how man might deliver himself but by performing a divine work of deliverance for man (s. 61). This fundamental conception
appears in the Bible under many forms. God's work of redemption may
be considered first under the head of atonement.

It is not surprising that the idea of atonement is especially prominent
in the priestly legislation of the Old Testament. Here it sometimes still
retains the ancient meaning of ritual purification, corresponding to the
conception of sin as defilement (s. 57). It is expressed by the Hebrew
verb *kpr* and the nouns *kopher* and *kippur*. From this point of view the
rites of atonement have an essentially magical character (s. 93), as
shown by the fact that atonement is sometimes said to be made, not
" to," but merely " before God." [2] The climax of these rites is the ceremony of the Day of Atonement (Yom Kippur) as described in Lev.,
ch. 16. (In later Judaism the Day of Atonement was converted into a
day of penitence and prayer.)

Except for such survivals in the practice and theory of ritual, the
idea of ritual purification is overshadowed in the Old Testament by the
idea of propitiation, appeasing the wrath of the offended Deity. This
corresponds to the personal conception of sin as disobedience (s. 57).
The border line between the two conceptions appears in such cases as
Dt. 21:1–9, the ceremony performed by the elders of a city when a
murder has been committed and the criminal is unknown. The effect of

[1] Acts 2:37; 16:30; Mk. 10:17.   [2] Lev. 19:22.

this rite is that the city is cleansed of defilement and cleared of guilt (literally, " the blood is atoned to them "). In Dt. 32:43 the verb *kpr* is used with God himself as the subject, in the statement that he will " make atonement for his land," i.e., either purify it from defilement or, perhaps, give it satisfaction for what it has suffered.

The propitiation of an angry God is of course something that man undertakes in order to escape punishment and gain salvation. The most characteristic biblical conception of atonement, however, is that of a redemption which proceeds from God himself. The same Hebrew verb used for ritual purification is also used with God as the subject in such a way that it can only be translated " forgive " or the like (s. 62). As a matter of fact, while it can be used of appeasing an angry man with a gift,[3] it is never used in the Old Testament in the sense " appease " or " propitiate " with God as object.[4]

Apart from the use of this particular word, the idea of propitiation appears in the conception of offerings as gifts (s. 94). A gift is a natural means of appeasing an offended person, human or divine, usually in combination with such other inducements as entreaty, flattery, or the intercession of favored individuals. Such conceptions and practices are very primitive and almost universal in the religions of mankind. It is therefore not strange that they are found in the Old Testament. Intercession with offerings is exemplified by Job 42:8 f., without offerings by Gen. 18:23–32; 19:18–22; 20:7, 17. Moses propitiates God by intercession.[5]

Later Judaism has the idea of atonement by suffering, a development of the idea of suffering as discipline. The rabbis put much stress on this, even going so far as to say that death wipes out all sin, though evidently it is not meant that there is no punishment after death. Atonement by suffering and death may even be vicarious. In the Old Testament this finds expression in Is., ch. 53 (s. 30). A famous example in the Apocrypha is 2 Macc., ch. 7.[6] The words of Caiaphas in Jn. 11:50 reflect the same idea.

For the bearing of all this on the significance of Jesus' death it is important to consider whether or how far the atoning sacrifices of the Old Testament were substitutionary. As a gift, a sacrifice or offering may

[3] Gen. 32:20; cp. 2 S. 21:3; Prov. 16:14.
[4] In Ex. 32:30, where the meaning implied by the context is averting the wrath of God by intercession, no object is expressed.
[5] Ex. 32:30; *v.s.*, note 4; cp. also Am. 7:1–6; 2 Chr. 30:18; but contrast Ezek. 14:14, 20.
[6] Cf. especially vv. 37 f.

simply be a means of pleasing the Deity and so appeasing his anger and averting injury or death at his hands. An example of this is Noah's sacrifice after the flood.[7] Here there is no idea of substitution. The idea of a sacrificial victim as a substitute for the sinner himself, however, appears clearly among peoples closely related to the Hebrews. In the Old Testament the idea of substitution is most clearly expressed in connection with the redemption offering.[8] The Hebrew root used for such redemption is used in Arabic for substitutionary offerings. Incidentally, the substitution of one victim for another is by no means the same as the payment of an equivalent value, as in the commutation of blood revenge or capital punishment by a pecuniary payment. A substitutionary offering is not a means of satisfying exact demands of retributive justice. It is a gift which God is willing to accept in place of what he might otherwise demand. The ram in Gen., ch. 22, was not equal to Isaac in value, but was accepted as a substitute for him.

The interpretations of Christ's death in the New Testament must be seen against this background, though other categories than that of sacrifice are used, such as the redemption price or ransom of a slave (see below). For Jesus' own thought of his death Mk. 10:45 is basic. Assuming its authenticity, we cannot be sure what Aramaic word lies back of the Greek word translated " ransom," but the associations of the Greek word indicate an atoning sacrifice or a redemption offering rather than a slave's or captive's ransom. An allusion to Is., ch. 53, is obvious in any case.[9]

The sayings of Jesus at the Last Supper are important also in this connection. The whole transaction is best understood as a dramatic symbol like the symbolic acts of the Old Testament prophets. Facing his own death, Jesus said in effect, as he poured the wine, " My blood is about to be poured out as this wine is poured out." As he broke and distributed the bread, he said, " My body is about to be broken as this bread is broken." But he looked beyond his death to the kingdom of God, in which he would drink the wine new [10] and the passover would be fulfilled.[11] It is not unlikely that he also said, " As my Father has covenanted to me a kingdom, so I covenant to you that you shall eat and drink at my table in my kingdom." [12] The references to the blood of the covenant, however, are probably not authentic (see p. 224).

(see p. 224)

[7] Gen. 8:20–22.
[8] Ex. 13:13; 34:20.
[9] Note the phrase " for many " and cp. Is. 53:11 f.
[10] Mk. 14:25.
[11] Lk. 22:15 f.
[12] Lk. 22:29 f., Greek.

Just how Jesus believed his death would help others is not clear, except that it was somehow the means of coming into his kingdom and so of mediating it to others. His prayer in Gethsemane suggests that he was willing to accept God's will for him without understanding it, and perhaps we should not expect anything more specific than the conviction that his rejection and death were necessary for the establishment of the kingdom of God.

A clear doctrine of the atonement is still lacking in the sources for the early Palestinian church. The disciples were convinced that the crucifixion was in accord with " the determinate counsel and foreknowledge of God," [13] as foretold by the prophets.[14] Is., ch. 53, was used to show that Jesus' death was a necessary part of God's plan.[15] Remission of sins through faith in Christ is stressed (s. 62), but the connection with the death of Christ is not clearly made. Certainly there is no idea of anything like the businesslike transaction presupposed by Anselm's doctrine. The disciples simply express rather vaguely, using the suggestion of Is., ch. 53, their experience of new life through Jesus and their conviction that his suffering and death were necessary to bring this about.

In Paul's preaching the Cross was central.[16] The incarnation was simply a necessary preliminary to the crucifixion.[17] Christ was sent " that he might redeem them that were under the law " [18] and " condemn sin in the flesh." [19] In Rom. 4:25 Paul connects justification (s. 62) with Christ's death and resurrection.

Paul's conception of the atonement is not expressed in the category of sacrifice. The reference to sacrifice in 1 Cor. 5:7 [20] is merely a passing metaphor.[21] This may be true also of the obscure statement of Rom. 3:25, where the word translated " propitiation " is the noun used in the Septuagint for the " mercy seat " of the tabernacle.[22] If that is the reference intended here, the meaning must be something like " place of access to God." In any case what is meant is not a sacrifice offered to God by Christ or by anyone else: God himself " set forth " Christ.[23] The

[13] Acts 2:23.
[14] Acts 3:18; Lk. 24:25–27, 44–47.
[15] Acts 8:26–35.
[16] 1 Cor. 1:23 f.
[17] Phil. 2:6–11.
[18] Gal. 4:5.
[19] Rom. 8:3.
[20] Cp. Eph. 5:2.
[21] Cp. Rom. 15:16; Phil. 2:17.
[22] So in Heb. 9:5, the only other occurrence of the word in the N.T.
[23] Cp. Rom. 5:8.

idea of propitiation is thus irrelevant.[24] Paul's idea of the atonement can be connected with sacrifice only by supposing that God himself provided the sacrificial victim, as he provided for Abraham's sacrifice the ram in the thicket.[25]

Paul's conception does involve vicarious suffering on behalf of sinners. He frequently says that Christ died " for us " or " for me." Probably for him as for the rest of the apostolic church the background of this was Is., ch. 53. This, indeed, must be the Scripture referred to in 1 Cor. 15:3. The language of Is., ch. 53, is often echoed in Paul's letters.[26] Sometimes he uses the category of purchase, as in the redemption of a slave (s. 61). The " price " to which he refers in this connection is doubtless the death of Christ, but it is unreasonable to look for such an elaboration of the metaphor as would make clear how Christ's death purchases the believer's freedom from sin, or to whom the price is paid. Gal. 3:13 makes use of Dt. 21:23 in a similar way: by dying on the Cross Christ became a curse for us. The conception of the blood of the new covenant may be Paul's idea.[27]

According to 2 Cor. 5:18–21, the result of Christ's death is reconciliation (s. 62), and v. 14 indicates how this is effected: the Cross by demonstrating Christ's love, in which is seen the love of God himself,[28] breaks down the sinner's hostility and evokes his responding love.[29] It does this, however, only because of the interpretation which faith puts upon it: " the love of Christ constraineth us because we thus judge, that one died for all, therefore all died, and he died for all that they that live should no longer live unto themselves but unto him who for their sakes died and rose again." [30] Here we reach the heart of the Pauline doctrine of the atonement and the explanation of Paul's frequent references to Christ's dying for or on account of sin, and for or on behalf of us.

The passage just quoted is to be understood in connection with Gal. 2:19 f. and Rom. 6:3–11; 7:1–6, which show what is meant by the statement that Christ died for all and therefore all died. For Paul, Christ died not as our substitute but as our representative; his death did not make our death unnecessary but brought it about, for in the per-

---

[24] Note the similar ideas and language of 1 Jn. 4:10; v.i.
[25] Gen., ch. 22.
[26] Gal. 1:4; 2:20; Rom. 4:25; 8:32 (cp. Eph. 5:2).
[27] 1 Cor. 11:25; cp. Ex. 24:8.
[28] Rom. 5:8.
[29] Cp. 1 Jn. 4:9, 19.
[30] 2 Cor. 5:14 f.

son of our representative we ourselves died. What made our death necessary was not the satisfaction of an inflexible penal justice; it was our bondage to sin under the law. As long as " the old man " lives in his " body of sin," [31] " the body of this death," [32] he is under the dominion of the law and without power to overcome sin. He is not only under condemnation but under the power of sin in his flesh (s. 57). He can escape only by dying and beginning life again as a new person,[33] and this is brought about by his participating in the representative death of Christ and rising with him to newness of life.[34] In other words, Paul's conception of the atonement is of a piece with his " Christ-mysticism " (s. 82). What is accomplished by the death of Christ is not only justification but also sanctification, which indeed are for Paul quite inseparable (ss. 62 f.). Hence the connection between Christ's death and resurrection, which is sometimes so close as to give the impression that for Paul the Cross is hardly more than a preliminary step to the resurrection.[35]

To judge by the remaining books of the New Testament, Paul's profound but undoubtedly obscure and involved interpretation of Christ's death was not adopted and probably was not wholly understood by the church at large. In John the emphasis is on the incarnation rather than the Cross as the means of salvation. As the incarnation is for John not an emptying but a manifestation of glory and life, so Christ's death is a voluntary throwing off of the partial and temporary limitations of his life in the flesh in order to be lifted up and glorified and to be where he was before.[36] At the same time this deliberate laying down of his life is regarded as the greatest possible demonstration of love.[37] Jesus died for the nation and for all men; [38] he is the Lamb of God, who bears the sins of the world,[39] the true paschal lamb, of which not a bone must be broken.[40] (The Johannine date of the crucifixion may have something to do with this interpretation of the Cross.) Christ's going to the Father enables the disciples to do greater works than his [41] and makes possible the coming of the Paraclete.[42]

The importance attached to the death of Christ in the church at large is shown by the prominence of the passion story in the gospels. It occupies about half of the gospel of Mark. Critics agree that the first por-

---

[31] Rom. 6:6.
[32] Ch. 7:24.
[33] 2 Cor. 5:17.
[34] Rom. 6:4 f.
[35] Rom. 4:25; 8:34.
[36] Jn. 3:14 f.; 8:28; 12:23; 17:5.

[37] Jn. 10:15; 15:13; 1 Jn. 3:16; 4:9 f., 19.
[38] Jn. 11:51 f.
[39] Ch. 1:29, 36.
[40] Ch. 19:31–37; cp. Ex. 12:46.
[41] Ch. 14:12.
[42] Ch. 16:7; cp. s. 27.

tion of the gospel material to achieve a definite, consecutive form was the passion narrative, perhaps because it was used in the observance of the sacrament. Mark stresses the significance of Christ's death as an example for Christian martyrs. Luke makes it primarily a step to Christ's resurrection and ascension to glory.

Revelation refers to the blood of Christ as a redemption price,[43] and says that the saints have washed their robes in the blood of the Lamb [44] — an idea to be understood as symbolism, not imagery. No theory is presented regarding the necessity of the Cross; the writer simply accepts it as axiomatic that Christ's death was indispensable for his triumph and the triumph of his people. 1 Peter quotes Is., ch. 53, with reference to Christ's death.[45] The idea of redemption by the death of Christ appears also in the pastoral epistles.[46] 2 P. 2:1 says that heretics deny " the Master who bought them."

The distinctive idea of Christ as the Priest who offers himself as a sacrifice, as presented in Hebrews, has been discussed in s. 30. The writer lays great weight on the idea that whereas the Levitical sacrifices of the old covenant could not " sanctify unto the cleanness of the flesh," the sacrifice of Christ can " cleanse your conscience from dead works to serve the living God." [47] Consequently, unlike the old, ineffective sacrifices, Christ's offering does not need to be repeated.[48]

In brief, no systematically developed doctrine of the atonement is given in the New Testament, but Is., ch. 53, is much used as affording the solution of the problem of the Cross, even if only as showing that it fulfilled prophecy. Ideas of redemption and ransom appear also from Mk. 10:45 to 2 P. 2:1, in varying senses. The fundamental point throughout is that the death of Jesus was not a defeat and did not disprove his Messiahship, but was in some way necessary as a part of his saving work.

The idea of constraining love [49] is the most specific and satisfying explanation offered. From this point of view the death of Jesus was a " price " or " ransom " for others, not because on the basis of retribution it provided a fund of merit for sinners to draw on, nor because it satisfied the demands of retributive justice, but because, being the result of the sins of others, it revealed the enormity of sin and at the same time

---

[43] Rev. 5:9; 14:3 f.; cp. ch. 1:5.
[44] Ch. 7:14.
[45] 1 P. 1:18 f.; 2:22–25.
[46] 1 Tim. 2:6; Titus 2:14.

[47] Heb. 9:11–14.
[48] Vv. 25 f.
[49] Paul and 1 John.

showed how far God would go to reconcile sinners to himself. Along with this, for those enabled by experience and temperament to appropriate it, Paul's distinctive conception of dying with Christ and rising to a new life with him and in him has the spiritual dynamic of his whole idea of becoming a new person in union with Christ.

76. *Election and Freedom*

In Christ man's redemption has been wrought, but for whom and how is it effective? If the principle of retribution were consistently carried through, salvation could be earned and claimed as the reward of righteousness, but we have seen that for the New Testament, and indeed for much of the Old Testament also, salvation can only be a gift of free grace (s. 55). The ancient Israelite could be sure of salvation by fulfilling the requirements of the law under the covenant, but that covenant itself was a manifestation of the extraordinary grace of God, who had chosen Israel as his people, established the conditions of salvation, and revealed them in the law.

The emergence of individual distinctions within Israel, the extension of God's favor to non-Israelites, the rejection of Israel as God's people, and the establishment of the church as the true people of God have been discussed in other connections (ss. 49–52). Our concern here is to note that it is recognized, through all phases of this development, that whatever man may and must do to receive salvation, he could not be saved at all if God had not made it possible for him. In that sense at least salvation is the result of God's sovereign choice.

Beyond that, the idea that God has also chosen and predestined certain individuals in advance to be saved, limiting the efficacy of the atonement to them, is not clearly stated anywhere in the Bible except in the epistles of Paul and the gospel of John, and even there man's responsibility to work out his own salvation is still maintained, as we shall see presently. For most of the Bible the major emphasis is on responsibility, which implies freedom of choice. The problem of freedom is not felt in the Old Testament. The facts of experience on both sides of the question are presented, and God's sovereignty and man's responsibility are both emphasized. In law, prophecy, the wisdom literature and the historical and poetic writings, the necessity of choice and man's responsibility for his choices are asserted or implied constantly.

The idea of God's overruling control appears in its harshest form in

the statement that God hardened Pharaoh's heart and yet punished him
severely.[1] The same thing is said of Sihon, king of Heshbon; [2] it is said
also of the Canaanites.[3] The idea that God moved David to take a census and then punished him [4] is perhaps a little less harsh, allowing at
least the possibility that David might have resisted the temptation, but
this was hardly in the writer's mind, his conception being that God was
angry with Israel and deliberately created an occasion for punishing
the nation. In Is. 6:9 f. a similar idea is applied to Israel,[5] and in Is.
63:17 Israel's sinfulness is explicitly attributed to Yahweh.

The use of Assyria and other nations as instruments of divine judgment, according to the conception of the prophets and historians, implies God's control of men's actions. Second Isaiah's argument for monotheism makes much of Yahweh's foreknowledge of history (s. 21),
and God knows what will happen because it is he who determines from
the beginning what is to be, calling men and nations to work his will.[6]

Salvation also is his work, as conspicuously shown by the gracious
choice of Israel from all the nations for his special favor (s. 50). In
Dt., ch. 8, Moses tells Israel that the conquest of Canaan is not a reward
for their righteousness; they are a stiff-necked people, and God is
merely using them to punish the Canaanites. Individuals also are chosen
and used for special service not infrequently in the Old Testament. This
idea is applied to kings,[7] and in the case of Cyrus it is at least suggested
by the context in Second Isaiah that the choice was made long in advance.[8] Prophets are divinely chosen also,[9] and Jeremiah is explicitly
said to have been set apart for his work before he was born.[10] In spite of
the individualization of retribution, however, the Old Testament does
not have the idea of a divine choice of individuals in advance for salvation.

Postbiblical Judaism continued to stress both the divine sovereignty
and human freedom to choose between good and evil. Rabbinic theology, with its conception of the evil impulse as the source of sin (s. 59),
held nevertheless that the righteous man could overcome his evil im-

---

[1] Ex. 3:19 f.; 4:21.
[2] Dt. 2:30.
[3] Josh. 11:20.
[4] 2 S., ch. 24.
[5] Cp. Mk. 4:12; Jn. 12:37–41.
[6] Is. 41:1–4, 8–16, 21–27; 44:24–28; 45:1–7; 48:12–15.
[7] 1 S. 9:15 f.; 2 S. 7:8.
[8] Is. 44:28; 45:1; cp. ch. 48:15 f.
[9] Am. 7:15.
[10] Jer. 1:5.

pulse by the help of God. At the same time the idea of predestination was accepted by some of the rabbis, and efforts were made to reconcile it with freedom. Sometimes human freedom and divine justice were guarded by the assertion that predestination was based on God's fore-knowledge of each man's merits.[11] Josephus defines the difference be-tween the Jewish sects of the Roman period in terms of their positions on this question: the Sadducees, he says, sacrifice destiny to freedom; the Essenes put no limits to destiny; the Pharisees harmonize the two. While these groups were not philosophical schools, as Josephus sug-gests, they may actually have held the positions he attributes to them (s. 52).

Jesus speaks often of God's will, not merely as what he wishes or de-mands from men, but as his immutable purpose. Rarely if ever does he suggest, however, that the choices and acts of individuals are predeter-mined, though a few sayings may be taken to imply that the salvation of certain persons has been divinely ordained.[12] The expression " the elect " occurs in the eschatological discourse; [13] elsewhere the word ap-pears only in Mt. 22:14,[14] and there it means that many in the church will be rejected at the final judgment, not that only a few are predes-tined to be saved. The parable of the sower [15] suggests that Jesus ex-plained the failure of many hearers to accept his gospel, or to persevere if they accepted it, on the ground that they had not been given the abil-ity to do so; more probably, however, it means that the trouble is not in the gospel but in the hearers, who could accept and follow it if they would. The nearest approach to a definite statement of individual pre-destination in a saying of Jesus is Lk. 10:20.[16] Jesus' conception of his own mission as fulfilling prophecy [17] may or may not imply that what had been foretold could not be changed.[18] The statement in the eschato-logical discourse that God knows the time of the end [19] does not neces-sarily mean that God himself may not change the time if he sees fit.

The early church made much of the argument from prophecy to sup-port the Messiahship of Jesus (ss. 18, 31).[20] There is nothing in the book of Acts, however, to show that individuals were believed to be foreor-

---

[11] Cp. Rom. 8:29; v.i.
[12] Mt. 18:14; 25:34; Lk. 12:32.
[13] Mk. 13:20, 22, 27; Mt. 24:22, 24, 31; Luke omits.
[14] Some mss., followed by A.V., insert it in ch. 20:16 also.
[15] Mk. 4:3-9, and parallels.
[16] Cp. Phil. 4:3; Rev. 3:5; 13:8; 17:8; 20:15; 21:27.
[17] Mk. 14:21; Mt. 26:24; cp. Lk. 22:22.
[18] Cp. Mk. 14:36; Lk. 24:26.
[19] Mk. 13:32; Mt. 24:36; cp. Acts 1:7.
[20] Cp. Acts 2:23; 10:43.

dained to salvation or damnation, until ch. 13:48, which says that when Paul and Barnabas preached at Antioch in Pisidia, " as many as were ordained to eternal life believed." This verse proves at least that the idea of predestination was not unknown in the Hellenistic church, to which Luke belonged. A more general expression, not necessarily implying individual predestination, occurs in Acts 17:26. The divine appointment of individuals for special missions is asserted in chs. 17:31 and 22:14.

With Paul predestination is an important article of faith. In addition to general references to the will or pleasure of God, and to the gospel as a divine mystery " foreordained before the worlds," [21] we find the statement that Paul himself was set apart for his mission before he was born.[22] The question of predestination became concrete for Paul in connection with Israel's rejection of the gospel, which he explained as the result of a divine hardening until the Gentiles should be won.[23] But Paul goes farther and makes the acceptance or rejection of individuals a matter of foreordination, using many terms to express the idea.[24] Nevertheless he still insists on man's responsibility and often seems to assume freedom of choice.[25] True to his Jewish training and to common human experience, Paul sees no contradiction between God's working in us and our working out our own salvation.[26] In Rom. 8:29 he makes foreordination dependent upon foreknowledge.

In the fourth gospel Jesus tells his disciples that they have not chosen him, but he has chosen them.[27] In spite of the fact that each person by his response to the gospel enters into life or judgment,[28] that response depends upon God rather than man.[29] The idea of election is apparently assumed in Rev. 17:14. The dependence of the Christian upon God's working in him is implied by the benediction in Heb. 13:20 f., but of course this does not imply foreordination. 1 Peter reflects a more highly developed idea of election.[30] James refers to the gift of wisdom [31] and to

[21] 1 Cor. 2:7; cp. Rom. 11:25; Col. 1:26 f.; 2:2; 4:3; also Eph. 1:9; 3:3, 4, 9; 5:32; 6:19.
[22] Gal. 1:15; cp. Jer. 1:5.
[23] Rom., chs. 9 to 11.
[24] See specially Rom. 8:29 f.
[25] Rom. 1:18, 20, 24, 26, 28, 32; 2:1–12; 11:22 f.; 2 Th. 2:10 f.
[26] Phil. 2:12 f.; cp. Eph. 2:8.
[27] Jn. 15:16.
[28] Chs. 3:18 f.; 5:24.
[29] Chs. 6:37, 44; 8:47.
[30] 1 P. 1:1 f.; 2:4, 8 f.; 5:10.
[31] Jas. 1:5.

God's choice of the poor rather than the rich,[32] but in general regards salvation as a matter of voluntary good works. General references to calling and election and the eternal purpose of God occur in the pastoral epistles.[33] Election and voluntary effort are again combined in 2 P. 1:10.

The same Hebrew and Greek words used for God's will are also applied to human choice and action throughout the Bible, but in a way which clearly indicates wish, purpose, and the like rather than the power of volition. Freedom of choice is implied, however. Verbs of willing, wishing, deciding, and the like, are used also with no difference of meaning. No distinct conception of what we call the will as volitional effort is apparent in either the Old or the New Testament. Perhaps the nearest approaches to it are the use of the verb " choose," as in Josh. 24:15, and Paul's use of the verb " to will " in Rom. 7:18.

There is thus no clear, consistent biblical teaching on the question of freedom versus predestination. Perhaps that is why it has aroused such hot controversy and even split Christian churches. The language of passages dealing at all with the subject is often ambiguous, and it is not always clear whether groups or individuals are in view. No explanation of the relation between foreknowledge and predestination is given. Only Paul and the fourth evangelist have clear statements of predestination, though it often seems to be implied elsewhere, especially in the latest books of the New Testament. All the writers consistently assume freedom and responsibility in any case. The primary, constant appeal to repentance and faith and the frequent references to judgment presuppose freedom of choice and action.

Paul, to be sure, has also his idea of a hopeless struggle with the lower nature, with inability to do what is right even when it is chosen and desired.[34] Freedom of action is for Paul not a condition but a result of salvation (s. 83).[35] This sense of the divided self and moral frustration, however, is peculiar to Paul, and even he assumes that a man is free to will the good if not to do it.

The motives underlying the idea of election as applied to Israel in the Old Testament and to the individual Christian in Paul's letters and the fourth gospel should be recognized. One of them is of course the emphasis on God's sovereignty, especially as guaranteeing the fulfillment of his promises. Equally important is the humble sense of gratitude for unearned and undeserved blessings. The experience of reaping where

---

[32] Ch. 2:5.
[33] 2 Tim. 1:9; 2:10; Titus 1:1.

[34] Rom., ch. 7.
[35] Cp. s. 59 on the effect of sin on freedom.

others have sown [36] and the sense of unworthiness and privilege [37] have always given a strong impulse to the belief in a divine choice for God's own reasons and purposes. Comparison of self with others less favored stimulates the reflection, " There, but for the grace of God, go I." A third motive is the difficulty of explaining the strange blindness of men who reject the truth when it is presented to them, which seems comprehensible only on the assumption that they have been denied the power of recognizing truth when they see it.[38] Thus the belief in a divine election is not a basis for pride and complacency but for a high sense of responsibility.[39] Election to privilege implies election to service.

Perhaps the conception which best does justice to the biblical representation as a whole is that the possibility of salvation, including all the historical and social media by which it comes to the individual, is God-given; but the individual is left free to accept or reject and to act accordingly, and is held responsible for his choice.

77. Calling and Conversion

Many passages in the New Testament, especially in the letters of Paul, mention the believer's " calling " or being " called " as a phase or step in his salvation. The Greek verb translated " call " has much the same range of meanings as the English word. The same may be said of the corresponding Hebrew verb in the Old Testament. Both are used frequently in the sense of " summon " or " invite " in a wide variety of connections, including a divine summons to special service (s. 89).

Somewhat closer to the characteristic New Testament usage is the designation of the chosen people in Second Isaiah as " Israel my called." [1] In many of the New Testament references there is a close connection between calling and election.[2] The clearest, most specific statement of Paul's idea of the Christian's calling is Rom. 8:28–30, already noted as a locus classicus for his doctrine of election (s. 76). Here foreknowledge, predestination, calling, justification, and glorification are named in turn, apparently as successive steps in the work of salvation. From this fact and the basic meaning of the word it seems fair to infer that what is meant by the calling of the Christian is the divine summons

---

[36] Jn. 4:38.
[37] 1 Cor. 15:8–10.
[38] Is. 6:10; Mk. 4:11 f.; Rom. 9:15–18; 11:7 f., 25–32.
[39] Gen. 12:3; Is. 49:6; 53; Am. 3:2; Acts 9:15.
[1] Is. 48:12.
[2] Rom. 8:28; 9:11, 23 f.; 2 Th. 2:13 f.; 2 Tim. 1:9; 2 P. 1:10; cp. Mt. 20:16; 22:14.

which brings election to bear immediately upon the individual. Having chosen those who are to be saved, God at the proper time issues his royal summons to each of them. This seems to be the implication of other references in the New Testament also.[3]

The same conclusion may be drawn from passages that speak of that from which and that to which the believer is called. Where Jesus says, according to Mark and Matthew,[4] that he has come to call not the righteous but sinners, Luke adds the phrase " to repentance." [5] Elsewhere Christians are said to have been called from darkness into light,[6] into salvation,[7] life eternal,[8] an eternal inheritance,[9] eternal glory in Christ,[10] the fellowship of Christ,[11] God's own kingship and glory.[12] They are called to be saints,[13] not for uncleanness but in sanctification.[14] They are called for freedom [15] and peace,[16] but also for patient suffering.[17]

In 1 Cor. 7:17–24, where Paul, in view of the nearness of the end of this world, urges Christians not to seek any change in their social status (s. 105), being called evidently means simply becoming a Christian, both the divine summons and the individual's response being assumed. All this confirms the interpretation of the call as God's summons to the individual to respond to the gospel.

The result of the divine calling is conversion. Literally conversion means simply turning, the same Hebrew and Greek verbs being translated sometimes " turn " and sometimes " convert." [18] In this active sense conversion is the equivalent of repentance, hearing the call and responding to it (s. 78); but ordinarily the word conversion indicates the passive rather than the active aspect of salvation, the experience rather than the act, being turned rather than turning.[19]

The necessity of a definite, conscious, and remembered experience of

[3] Acts 2:39; cp. Jn. 6:44.
[4] Mk. 2:17; Mt. 9:13.
[5] Lk. 5:32.
[6] 1 P. 2:9.
[7] 2 Th. 2:13 f.
[8] 1 Tim. 6:12.
[9] Heb. 9:15.
[10] 1 P. 5:10.
[11] 1 Cor. 1:9.
[12] 1 Th. 2:12.
[13] Rom. 1:7; 1 Cor. 1:2.
[14] 1 Th. 4:7.
[15] Gal. 5:13.
[16] Col. 3:15.
[17] 1 P. 2:20 f.
[18] Cp. A.V. and A.S.V. in Is. 6:10 (quoted Mt. 13:15; Mk. 4:12; Jn. 12:40); Mt. 18:3.
[19] Ps. 19:7; 51:13; 80:3, 7, 19; 85:4; Jer. 31:18; Dan. 12:3; Lk. 1:16 f.; Jas. 5:19 f.

conversion is often emphasized in evangelical Protestantism. Examples of such experiences occur in both Old and New Testaments. Jacob's wrestling with God [20] is a possible but doubtful instance. Saul's new heart [21] is a clearer case. The outstanding example in the New Testament is Paul's conversion.[22]

The principal texts cited for the necessity of such an experience are Mt. 18:3 and Jn. 3:5. The former has already been mentioned [23] and will be considered again in s. 78; the latter has been discussed in s. 63. While the idea of a supernatural transformation, as a part of the meaning of salvation rather than a prerequisite for it, is clearly taught in the New Testament, especially by Paul and John (s. 63), for biblical theology in general and for the religion of Jesus in particular it may be said with assurance that what is essential is not experience but conduct, not what happens to a man but what he does, not being converted but repentance and faith. That back of these lie the divine initiative and action is of course true, but the fact that a person receives and responds to the call is sufficient evidence that God has done his part. Experience is not a condition but a contributing factor, where it is not a consequence, and it does not always or necessarily conform to a particular psychological type. Certainly the Bible does not emphasize the way a person feels. What it does stress is a definite decision and self-committal.

Our common use of the word " conversion " to indicate a change from one religion to another appears only once in the Bible.[24] Of course, such changes are referred to in various other ways, including the use of the verb " turn " both actively and passively.[25]

78. Repentance

Since all men are sinners (s. 59), salvation necessarily involves forgiveness (s. 62), and the first condition of this is repentance. The Hebrew verb most commonly translated " repent " in the Old Testament means " be sorry," and the Greek word for repentance in the New Testament means literally " a change of mind." The act of repentance in the sense of turning from sin to God, however, is represented by the same Hebrew verb meaning " turn, turn back, return," which has been

---

[20] Gen. 32:24–32.
[21] 1 S. 10:9.
[22] Acts 9:1–9; 1 Cor. 15:8; Gal. 1:15–17.

[23] V. s., footnote 18.
[24] Acts 15:3.
[25] Acts 14:15; 26:18.

pointed out in s. 77 as the word used for being converted.[1] In Lk. 22:32, where the Authorized Version reads, " When thou art converted," the Greek verb is in the active voice; the American Standard Version, followed by the Revised Standard Version, rightly reads, " When once thou hast turned again," i.e., repented. This word became the regular term for repentance in Judaism, and it was undoubtedly the word used in the original Aramaic preaching of Jesus and the apostles. In Acts 3:19 the Greek uses two verbs, " Repent and turn again." In short, repentance involves not only a change of mind but a change of behavior.

In the Old Testament repentance is the only condition of salvation. The prophets and the later rabbis in general take this position. Even when various means of atonement are recognized, it is often emphasized that they are of no avail without repentance. This is the position of John the Baptist also.[2] Matthew summarizes Jesus' preaching in Galilee in the same words as John's preaching; [3] Mark adds belief,[4] but in any case repentance is the first requirement.[5] The early church in Palestine continued to stress repentance,[6] as did also the Hellenistic churches.[7]

Paul seems strangely silent on this subject. Aside from Rom. 2:4 f., he speaks only of the repentance of Christians who have done wrong. New Testament scholars sometimes draw unwarranted inferences from this fact; actually the rabbis also say little or nothing of repentance in connection with proselytes, putting in its place the idea of rebirth.[8] Furthermore Paul's whole thought of salvation presupposes conviction of sin and a desire to be free from it, so that we may say he takes repentance for granted. His conception of being reconciled to God (s. 62) also involves the change from alienation and disobedience to acknowledgment and obedience which is elsewhere called repentance.

The gospel and epistles of John ignore the subject of repentance, not because a change of conduct is unnecessary,[9] but because salvation is thought of primarily as regeneration (s. 63), with faith as the primary

---

[1] Dt. 4:30; 30:10; 1 K. 8:33, 35, 47; Ezek. 14:6; 18:30.
[2] Mt. 3:2; Mk. 1:4; Lk. 3:3.
[3] Mt. 4:17.
[4] Mk. 1:15.
[5] Cp. Lk. 13:5.
[6] Acts 2:38.
[7] Acts 17:30; 26:20.
[8] Cp. Mt. 18:3, where both ideas appear together, *v.s.*
[9] Cp. 1 Jn. 1:6 f.; 3:3–10.

condition (s. 79). Revelation makes much of repentance, both for back-sliding Christians [10] and for non-Christians.[11] Heb. 6:1 names " repentance from dead works " as the first of the rudiments of Christianity. The possibility of a second repentance after falling away is denied.[12] Repentance is mentioned in 2 Tim. 2:25 but nowhere else in the pastoral epistles and not at all in 1 Peter, James, Jude, or 2 Peter, though it is doubtless assumed everywhere.

79. Faith

According to Mk. 1:15, Jesus began his mission with the proclamation of the kingdom and the summons, " Repent and believe the gospel." This makes faith a condition of entering the kingdom of God. Elsewhere the necessity of belief in Jesus and his message as a condition of salvation is implied rather than expressed, except in the statement that only those who confess Christ before men can expect to be acknowledged by him before the Father.[1] Confession without conduct, of course, will not be accepted.[2]

Faith in the sense of confidence in Yahweh's power and his fidelity to his promises is exalted throughout the Old Testament.[3] Isaiah was the first of the prophets to make explicit the importance of faith, condemning the kings and people of Judah for their lack of confidence in Yahweh and their foolish reliance on the help of other nations.[4] For Habakkuk faith gives the answer to the problem of theodicy (s. 25). Faith in times of distress and persecution is often expressed in the Old Testament, especially in Psalms. The Messianic and apocalyptic hopes and the whole area of eschatology should be recalled in this connection as important manifestations of religious faith.

Postbiblical Judaism exalts faith in the sense of confidence in God's promises and self-committal to Providence without anxiety. The Talmud says, " He who has a piece of bread in his basket and says, ' What shall I eat tomorrow? ' is of the little in faith." Faith that remains true in trial, assured that everything God does is good, is praised by the rabbis. Abraham is often cited as an example of such faith.

---

[10] Rev. 2:5; 3:3.
[11] Chs. 9:20 f.; 16:9, 11.
[12] Heb. 6:4-6; 10:26-31.
[1] Mt. 10:32 f.; Mk. 8:38; Lk. 9:26; 12:8 f.
[2] Mt. 7:21; 25:41-45.
[3] Note especially Gen. 15:6 and Hab. 2:4, Paul's favorite proof texts for justification by faith.
[4] Is. 7:9; 28:16; 30:15.

Jesus not only demands faith as a condition of entering the kingdom of God; he also makes it prerequisite for his miracles of healing,[5] and repeatedly rebukes his disciples for their lack of it.[6] He stresses its importance also in connection with prayer.[7] The eschatological aspect of faith as belief in the good news of the kingdom is prominent in the teaching of Jesus, and also the lack of anxiety regarding personal needs when God's kingdom and righteousness become the supreme end in life.

The early church strongly emphasized belief in Christ and confession of him as Lord as a condition of salvation.[8] The history of the early church is full of examples of faith regarding both the present and the future. Putting all one's property into the common fund (s. 106) was no mean act of faith. The eschatological expectation, which was evidently strong and vivid, was doubtless often misguided and even fanatical, but it was at least a faith that enabled the disciples to meet persecution and martyrdom triumphantly.

Paul makes faith the primary and sole condition of salvation. By faith he means not only trust in God but also belief in Christ, yet not in the sense of merely accepting certain theological propositions about him, but rather confidence in him and devotion to him, unreserved self-committal to him, and grateful acceptance of the free gift of salvation through union with him. Faith is the bond of this union as well as the initial act of acceptance. It is a constant, active attitude.[9] Righteousness comes from faith and leads to faith.[10] Faith is the very life of Christ in the Christian.[11] The future aspect of faith also is important for Paul, though he more often speaks in this connection of hope (s. 83). With faith goes also confession.[12]

In John also, while the intellectual element is perhaps more prominent relatively than with Paul, faith means self-committal and devotion as well as belief. Insistence on the necessity of believing specified propositions about Christ, however, was increasingly strong in the church, not only for the sake of distinguishing Christians from Jews but also as

---

[5] Mt. 9:28; Mk. 9:23; Lk. 8:50.
[6] Mk. 4:40; 5:36; Mt. 6:30; 8:26; 14:31; 16:8; 17:20; 21:21; Lk. 8:25; 12:28; 18:8; 22:32, 67; cp. ch. 24:25.
[7] Mk. 11:23 f.
[8] Acts 4:12; Mk. 16:16; s. 31.
[9] Gal. 5:6b.
[10] Rom. 1:17.
[11] Gal. 2:20.
[12] Rom. 10:9 f.

a means of counteracting heresies which were already threatening to denature the gospel. The Johannine epistles clearly exemplify this tendency.[13] We find also in John the stress on faith in God and Christ with regard to the hereafter [14] and the characterization of faith as the victory that overcomes the world.[15]

Hebrews treats faith as the " substance " (*hypostasis*) of things hoped for, giving a long roll call of heroes of faith leading up to Jesus.[16] This implies a conception of faith as trust and fidelity. In ch. 11:6 the faith that is necessary to please God is simply such an assurance of his existence and his help as will induce a man to come to him. James 1:6–8 stresses the need of unwavering faith in prayer.

The bitter condemnation of heresy in Jude and 2 Peter [17] and the stress on sound words and fidelity to tradition in the pastoral epistles [18] show the growing stress on orthodoxy at the end of the New Testament period.

The sense in which and the degree to which faith is a condition of salvation are important questions today for evangelism and the missionary enterprise. Confusion and loss of conviction at this point have been largely responsible for the decline of interest in evangelistic and missionary work. Both modern thought and the spirit of Jesus would seem to put devotion to his way of life above correct belief. Both also make it difficult to believe that salvation is denied to any person because of erroneous belief, to say nothing of lack of conformity to traditional orthodoxy. False belief is unfortunate, but it is fatal only if it leads to wrong conduct or to failure to accept what God offers. Fidelity to the highest ideals and the fullest truth one knows is the surest way of gaining greater insight into spiritual truth.[19]

80. *Church Membership; Sacramental Grace*

Under the Old Testament conception of the covenant between God and Israel the individual's salvation depends upon his membership in the chosen people, normally a matter of heredity. The relations of individual and group have already been considered (s. 49); the conflict

---

13 1 Jn. 2:22; 4:3; 2 Jn. 7.
14 Jn. 14:1 ff.
15 1 Jn. 5:4 f.
16 Heb., chs. 11 f.
17 Jude 3 f., 10–13, 19; 2 P. 2:1–3, 12; 3:3 f.
18 1 Tim. 1:6 f., 19 f.; 4:1, 6; 6:3–5, 20 f.; 2 Tim. 1:13 f.; 2:14–18, 23; 3:14; 4:3 f.; Titus 1:3, 10–14; 2:1, 3–9.
19 Cp. Jn. 7:17.

between particularism and universalism will be considered in some detail later (s. 102). In the New Testament the church takes the place of Israel as the people of God, as we have seen (s. 51). It is nowhere indicated, however, that joining the church is a condition of salvation; in fact, this way of putting the matter is quite incompatible with the New Testament conception of the church. From the point of view of the whole New Testament, the church is not an institution entrusted with the means of salvation and therefore able to communicate saving grace to its own members, all others being excluded. The church is simply the community of those who have met the conditions of salvation and received God's free gift of justification and adoption, and who by virtue of being in Christ are members of his body. In other words, the conception of the church as an organization, which individuals join by a voluntary act distinct from their acceptance of salvation, is foreign to the New Testament.

Only in the gospel of Matthew is there any exception to this general point of view. In Mt. 16:19 Jesus promises to give Peter the keys of the kingdom of heaven with the power of binding and loosing on earth and in heaven. In ch. 18:18 the power of binding and loosing is given to the disciples. In line with the characteristic emphasis on the church in Matthew (s. 51), this can mean only that the church in the person of the apostles has the power of admitting or excluding persons who wish to enter the kingdom of heaven, i.e., to be saved. Since there is nothing corresponding to this in the other gospels, and it is contrary to the most basic teaching of Jesus regarding the individual's relation to God, we can only regard these passages in Matthew as historical evidence of a tendency in the early church away from the original gospel and the prevailing conceptions of the New Testament as a whole.

Some branches of historical Christianity have stressed membership in the church as a condition of salvation on the ground that the saving grace of God comes through the sacraments, which are administered by the church. We shall discuss the nature and the significance of the sacraments later under the head of public worship (ss. 97 f.). It will be seen there that in such places as Acts 2:38 and Mk. 16:16 the sacrament of baptism is assumed to be at least normal, if not essential, for those who accept the gospel. Paul's idea of dying and rising with Christ is presented in Rom., ch. 6, in connection with baptism, calling to mind the initiation rites of the mystery cults and the experience of mystical union with the deity of the cult in such rites. Since Paul elsewhere lays no stress on baptism,[1] it is difficult to believe that he thought of the experience of union with Christ as bound up with the rite of baptism. To judge by the narrative in Acts 9:1–18, it had not been so in his own case. It is possible, indeed, that in Rom. 6:3 f. Paul refers to the inner experience of " baptism into death " and not at all to the ceremony. In any case what Paul says repeatedly about circumcision [2] applies with equal force to baptism as a condition of salvation.

That salvation depends upon taking the sacrament of the Lord's Supper is not even suggested anywhere in the New Testament. The discourse on the bread of life in the fourth gospel [3] is probably a deliberate polemic against the sacramentarian view of the Lord's Supper, which undoubtedly arose very early in the church.

Regardless of particular texts, to make any rite essential for salvation is contrary to the whole spirit and purport of the teaching of Jesus.

[1] Cp. 1 Cor. 1:13–17.   [2] See especially Gal. 5:2–12.   [3] Jn. 6:48–63.

XIII

THE CHRISTIAN LIFE

81. *Fear and Love*

The experiential and devotional aspects of religion, which have been considered only incidentally thus far, are essential, not only for Christianity, but for all religions. Even on its most primitive level religion may be said to originate in experience rather than in thought or action. On the one hand, experiences of frustration, helplessness, and dependence on powers beyond one's control impel a man to seek the aid of a divine being or to avert his wrath. On the other hand, experiences of the " numinous " compel men to recognize something beyond what they can see and touch in the world about them. Religion also brings its own new experiences, either as the result of religious acts or apart from them.

The experience of the numinous comes to expression, as already noted, in the Hebrew conception of holiness (s. 25). It is reflected also by the regular term for religion in the Old Testament, " the fear of Yahweh." The element of the awe-inspiring and fearful has been observed also in connection with the majesty of God (s. 23). The sense of the numinous is especially prominent in such narratives as Abraham's vision,[1] Jacob's dream at Bethel,[2] and the theophanies at Sinai.[3] The belief that to see God was dangerous (s. 12) and the occasional references to trembling in the presence of God [4] attest different forms of the same basic conception.

Generally, however, the word " fear " as applied to the right attitude toward God indicates reverence and obedience rather than dread. In 2 K. 17:28 it is said that the pagans who were imported into Samaria from other parts of the Assyrian empire after the fall of the kingdom of Israel suffered calamities because they did not know how to fear Yahweh, and a priest was sent to teach them. The close connection between fear and obedience is apparent in Dt. 5:29; 6:2, and often; it is implied also in

---

[1] Gen. 15:12.
[2] Ch. 28:17.
[3] Ex. 19:24; 20:18; 24:1 f.
[4] Is. 2:10; Jer. 5:22; Ps. 2:11; Ezra 10:3.

the frequent statement of the wisdom literature that the fear of Yahweh is the beginning of wisdom.[5] Prov. 8:13 defines the fear of Yahweh as hating evil.[6]

The command to love Yahweh does not appear until Dt. 6:5 (s. 56), and the idea of loving God is not common in the Old Testament outside of Psalms.[7] Christians have often supposed and said that Judaism was inspired by fear rather than love, yet the devout Jew recites twice daily the Shema, beginning with Dt. 6:4 f. Jewish sources sometimes treat the fear and the love of God as practically identical; where they are distinguished, fear is regarded as an inferior motive for the religious life. The Talmud says that the righteous show their love for God by accepting suffering as his loving chastisement.

Jesus quotes the Shema in reply to the question about the first commandment (s. 56); he also teaches reverence and even awe.[8] His emphasis on God's Fatherhood, however, excludes trembling dread. Acts 9:31, in quite Hebraic fashion, speaks of the early church as " walking in the fear of the Lord and in the comfort of the Holy Spirit." While the word " love " does not occur in Acts, the whole atmosphere of the life of the early church is one of radiant joy and fellowship (ss. 83 f.).

Paul speaks several times of the fear of God and even tells the Philippians to work out their salvation with fear and trembling,[9] yet he also speaks of loving God.[10] Love for God is especially stressed in 1 John, together with the insistence that it presupposes love of the brethren.[11] 1 P. 2:17, however, says, "Love the brotherhood, fear God." James speaks of the crown of life and the kingdom which God has promised to those who love him.[12] In general the attitude toward God commended by the New Testament may be characterized as reverent love.

82. *Communion; Prayer; Mysticism*

Over and above all temporal blessings, and even the hope of salvation hereafter, the sense of divine approval and the experience of communion with God came to be valued in Israel for their own sake. As even a child craves not only material gifts but recognition, approval, and fellowship, so the presence of Yahweh in the midst of Israel was a source of pride and confidence, not merely as a guarantee of protection and help but as good in itself. Israel's sin made God's presence dangerous and destruc-

---

[5] Ps. 111:10; Prov. 1:7; 9:10.
[6] Cp. the parallelism in Job 28:28.
[7] Ps. 18:1; 31:23; 97:10; 116:1; 145:20.
[8] Mt. 10:28; Lk. 12:4 f.

[9] Phil. 2:12.
[10] Rom. 8:28; 1 Cor. 8:3.
[11] 1 Jn. 4:18–21.
[12] Jas. 1:12; 2:5.

tive,[1] but the priestly legislation provided for ritual purification in order that Yahweh might dwell in the midst of Israel.[2] This is even given as the reason for the sanitary regulations of Dt. 23:9–14. The climax of the promises in Lev. 26:11 f. is that God will dwell among his people. Israel's pride in the temple was connected with this feeling,[3] though both Micah and Jeremiah warned the nation against false assurance based on Yahweh's being in their midst.[4] God's presence with his people was also a prominent part of the later eschatological hope.[5]

Not only the nation as a whole but the individual Israelite also valued the presence of God, once the primitive fear of him had been outgrown, though the primacy of the national unit made the individual's personal relation to God less immediate in early Israelite religion than it was later (s. 49). In Genesis, God talks with Abraham as a master with his trusted servant; in later sources Abraham is called the friend of God.[6] Moses is described as one with whom God spoke face to face as a man speaks with his friend.[7] David is portrayed as having a close personal relationship with God.[8]

Jeremiah values close personal communion with Yahweh as a recompense for all his affliction, and suffers when it is interrupted.[9] Job's experience and testimony are notable also.[10] Hosea finds the root of Israel's sin and judgment in failure to know God (s. 58), and Jeremiah looks for the time when all God's people shall know him.[11] The Deuteronomic requirement of love for God (s. 81) makes inward devotion rather than outward observance the essence of religion, though, of course, obedience is still the chief expression of love, as it remains for the New Testament (s. 53).

The postexilic tendency to make God more and more transcendent (s. 22) increased the difficulty of a personal relationship, as did also the development of the cultus and the legalistic tendency, yet Nehemiah evinces an intense consciousness of such a relationship,[12] and it is in the

---

[1] Ex. 33:5.
[2] Num. 5:1–3.
[3] Ps. 46:4 f.; Is. 12:6; Jer. 14:9.
[4] Mi. 3:12; Jer. 7:4, 11–14.
[5] Ezek. 39:7; 43:7, 9; Joel 2:27; Zp. 3:15, 17; Zc. 2:5, 10 f.; 8:3.
[6] Is. 41:8; 2 Chr. 20:7; Jas. 2:23.
[7] Ex. 33:11, but cp. chs. 33:12 to 34:28.
[8] 1 S. 30:6.
[9] Jer. 10:23 f.; 12:1–4; 15:15–18; 20:7–11.
[10] Job 42:5 f.
[11] Jer. 31:34.
[12] Neh. 1:4; 2:4, 8, 12; 5:19; 6:14; 7:5; 13:14, 22, 29, 31.

psalms, which were collected and used and in many cases written after the exile, that personal religion comes to its fullest and finest expression.[13] Joy and comfort in the presence of God are often, but not always, associated with the temple.[14] Many of the psalms are so personal in tone as to seem out of place in corporate worship, though some of the most popular Christian hymns are even more intimate and egocentric. Commentators have debated the meaning of the " I " of these psalms, some holding that the nation rather than the individual is meant. It seems probable that some of the psalms were originally written as expressions of private devotion and later adopted as hymns for public worship, as has happened with many of our own hymns. The fact that the psalms were used in the temple makes it all the more remarkable that in them forgiveness and divine favor are often represented as dependent, not on sacrifice, but on confession and prayer.[15]

Postexilic and postbiblical Judaism have often been charged with " arid legalism " and a loss of devotional immediacy. The rabbinic literature makes an impression of mechanical legalism and externalism, but that is due largely to the subject matter and purpose of this literature. Other sources, especially the Testaments of the Twelve Patriarchs, Jubilees, Sirach, and, above all, the prayer book, are full of fine expressions of a profound devotional spirit. Prescribed daily prayers and blessings exemplify the legalistic interest in fulfilling definite obligations for the sake of merit, but in addition to these the devout Jew offers voluntary prayers which follow no prescribed form. The prayers recorded in the sources are marked by simplicity, trust, and devotion.

The gospels refer often to Jesus' prayers, some of which are quoted. These evince the qualities required by his sayings on prayer: directness, simplicity, and childlike trust. Jesus commends persistence in prayer.[16] As an expression of faith, this involves no inconsistency with the condemnation of vain repetitions and wordiness, which show a lack of faith. Christian prayer, however, is always subject to God's will.[17] Prayers of the early church are mentioned and quoted in Acts, and the rest of the New Testament abounds in references to prayer.

To communion with God the New Testament adds communion with Christ, which with Paul means a spiritual union and identification. The Christian can overcome sin because he is in Christ and Christ is in him,

---

[13] Ps. 23:6; 27:4; 42:1 f.; 73:26.
[14] Ps. 11:7; 16:11; 17:15; 42:1 f.
[15] Ps. 6; 32; 38; 51; 90; 130.

[16] Lk. 11:5–8; 18:1–8.
[17] Mk. 14:36; s. 43.

or, as Paul also puts it, because he is in the Spirit or has the Spirit (s. 63). This idea runs all through Paul's letters. He uses the expression " in Christ " (or " in Christ Jesus " or " in the Lord ") more than two hundred times. The Christian's oneness with his Lord is also called *koinonia* (participation, sharing, communion, fellowship), as in 1 Cor. 1:9.[18] In speaking of this relationship Paul uses interchangeably the terms " Christ," " Lord," and " Spirit." [19] In 2 Cor. 3:17 he identifies Lord and Spirit, but whether " Lord " here means Christ or God is by no means certain.

As the background of Paul's conception of the Spirit and the exalted Christ the Stoic conception of spirit has been adduced, indicating that he thought of the Spirit or Christ in spatial and material terms, like an atmosphere in which the Christian lived (s. 27). Paul's idea of union with Christ, however, was " the oneness which unites persons who love one another." [20] Paul's exalted, spiritual Christ was still the real person who had very recently lived in Galilee. This fact constitutes also a basic difference between Paul's faith and the mystery cults, whose deities were mythical beings supposed to have lived in the remote past, not real persons remembered by many people still living, as Jesus was in Paul's day.

Oneness with Christ is the means of gaining moral power (s. 63), but it is not only that; it is itself the supreme content of Christian salvation, the Christian's highest good, so far as the present life is concerned.[21] To die and be with Christ would be better still, but in this world to live is Christ.[22] Paul also connects the possession of the Spirit with the future completion of salvation (s. 72). The working of the Spirit in the Christian's life is the " first-fruits " of the final redemption of the body,[23] an " earnest " (i.e., a part payment guaranteeing full payment in the future) of what is to be received hereafter.[24]

The Old Testament has nothing like this, the nearest approach to it being the joy in the presence of God expressed by some of the psalms or Jeremiah's " they shall know me " (*v.s.*). The Judaism of the inter-Testamental period and New Testament times also, as represented by the Apocrypha and Pseudepigrapha and the rabbinic literature, has nothing comparable to Paul's " Christ-mysticism." There is no reason

[18] Cp. 2 Cor. 13:14.
[19] Rom. 8:9–11; Gal. 2:20; 2 Cor. 13:5; Col. 1:27.
[20] F. C. Porter, *The Mind of Christ in Paul*, p. 290.
[21] Phil. 3:7–9a.
[22] Phil. 1:21 ff.
[23] Rom. 8:23.
[24] 2 Cor. 1:22; 5:5; cp. Eph. 1:14.

to believe that Jesus included in his conception of salvation anything like Paul's idea of life in the Spirit. The evidence is equally negative for early Palestinian Christianity. The whole conception is clearly new and distinctive with Paul.

The gospel and epistles of John are closer to Paul in this matter than any other part of the New Testament. The disciples must abide in Christ as the branch in the vine.[25] Eternal life is defined as knowing God and Jesus Christ whom he has sent.[26] Jesus prays that his disciples may be one with him and with one another as he and the Father are one.[27] In the first epistle of John the sufficiency of the simple Christian's experience is stressed as against the claims of heretics to superior enlightenment.[28] Perhaps this Gnostic claim accounts for the fact that the noun "knowledge" is not used in the fourth gospel, though the use of the verb "know" shows the importance of the idea for the evangelist. In general, while the idea of union with Christ in the Johannine writings resembles Paul's idea, it is relatively lacking in personal warmth.

The question whether or in what sense biblical religion involves mysticism is a matter of definition. Absorption-mysticism of the Hindu type is nowhere found in the Bible, but a vivid sense of close personal communion is constant and characteristic from the time it first emerges. Ecstatic experience appears in Hebrew prophecy (s. 12), and the experience of the prophets was sometimes thought of as possession by the Spirit. Joel expects "all flesh" to share this experience in the future,[29] but it is not regarded as the normal religious experience of all Israelites in the present world. Religious ecstasy appears also in the charismatic worship of the early church (s. 91). Its most extreme instance in the Bible is probably 2 Cor. 12:1–4. Paul's "Christ-mysticism," however, is not ecstatic experience. He recognizes and values such experiences,[30] but his basic conception of being in Christ means that the Christian is always possessed by Christ's Spirit, as shown by the fruit of the Spirit in his life.

Hellenistic Judaism, as exemplified by Philo, valued very highly the experience of mystical illumination. In both Old Testament religion and early Christianity, however, as in Palestinian Judaism, the controlling

---

25 Jn. 15:4.
26 Ch. 17:3.
27 Ch. 17:21, 23.
28 1 Jn. 1:3, 6 f.; 2:3–6, 24, 27 f., 3:6, 24; 4:12 f., 15 f.; cp. 1 Cor., chs. 1 to 3.
29 Joel 2:28.
30 1 Cor. 14:18.

conception of the individual's relation to God is not that of absorption into the Absolute and the loss of separate identity, but that of the relation between two persons, subject and King, servant and Master, child and Father, disciple and Lord.

83. *Freedom, Joy, and Hope*

Joy is an outstanding characteristic of the spiritual life throughout the Bible. Hebrew religion on the whole was decidedly joyful. The great annual festivals were times of rejoicing, though there were also days of penitence and fasting (s. 99). The psalms are full of expressions of joy and gratitude, with repeated summons to the worshipers and even to all creation to make a joyful noise to the Lord. Even the bitter complaints of some of the psalms often give way to joyful thanksgiving.[1] The characteristic stress of the Old Testament on obedience to the law produces no sense of constraint but rather one of freedom and joy.[2] This remains true in later Judaism. Paul's experience of frustration and despair in the effort to obey the law was clearly exceptional.

The almost overwhelming sorrows of the exile and the postexilic period were relieved by promises of deliverance and exhortations to rejoice, especially in Second Isaiah.[3] From Second Isaiah comes the characteristic New Testament term for the message of Jesus and its proclamation: it is good news (*euangelion,* gospel), and the preaching of it is declaring good news (*euangelizesthai*). The wretchedness of the people of Palestine under Roman rule, of which the gospels give us hardly more than a hint, must have made the assurance that God lived and reigned and would establish his kingdom in the world good news indeed. This helps to explain the enthusiasm and radiance of the early Christians.

For Paul deliverance from the slavery of sin and death meant, not only freedom from the law, but also a joyful sense of relief and emancipation through the resolution of his inner conflict and the achievement of integration instead of division and frustration.[4] Paul rejoices not only in his present freedom but also in hope as one of the Christian's blessings.[5] This is connected with his idea of the possession of the Spirit as an " earnest " of full redemption hereafter (s. 82). Later books of the New Testament emphasize hope as giving strength to endure persecution. In Revelation the eschatological hope is the primary content of

---

[1] Ps. 124; 126.
[2] Ps. 1; 19; 119 (note especially v. 45).
[3] Is. 40:9; 52:7; 61:1.
[4] Rom. 11:33; 1 Cor. 15:57.
[5] Rom. 8:24 f., 35–39; 15:13; Col. 1:27.

faith, as in the eschatological discourse of the synoptic gospels.[6] Hebrews calls hope the anchor of the Christian's soul.[7] In 1 Peter hope is stressed almost to the point of taking the place occupied by faith in Paul's thought, and with practically the meaning that faith has in Hebrews.[8]

84. *Fellowship in the Church*

Salvation, especially in the Old Testament, is an affair of both individual and group, and the individual's salvation comes to him in part as a member of the group (s. 49). It is enriched by the fact of being thus shared with others. In the Old Testament the group is primary, the emergence of the individual being gradual and incomplete, and this remains largely true of later Judaism. In the New Testament the main stress is on the individual, yet even here the individual is never thought of as being saved entirely by himself apart from the community of the saved. Although Jesus did not establish a church in the sense of an institution (s. 51), the fact that he addressed his disciples together in the plural implied that they shared with one another the life of the kingdom of God; indeed, the idea of the kingdom includes the community of those who enter into it, the " little flock " of Lk. 12:32 (s. 64).

The sense of sharing, having in common the blessings of Christian salvation and the Christian life, is expressed in the New Testament by the same word used by Paul for the Christian's fellowship with God and Christ, *koinonia* (s. 82). This noun and its cognates are used in various connections, both for the idea of participating and for the idea of sharing with others, e.g., making contributions.[1] In 2 Cor. 8:4 the word has both meanings, sharing in the work and sharing with others. The sense of Christian fellowship is exemplified by many passages.[2]

85. *Christian Attitudes and Virtues*

Something of what love means as the fulfillment of the law has been presented in s. 56. Its application to various personal and social relationships will be considered further in Chapter XVII. We are here concerned with Christian love as the chief fruit of the Spirit,[1] one of the results of regeneration (s. 63), and with the other Christian attributes and

---

6 Mk., ch. 13, and parallels.
7 Heb. 6:19.
8 1 P. 1:3, 13; 3:5, 15; cp. ch. 5:6 f., 9.
1 Rom. 15:26; 2 Cor. 9:13; Heb. 13:16.
2 Acts 2:42; Gal. 2:9; Phil. 1:5; 2:1; 1 Jn. 1:3, 7.
1 Gal. 5:22.

virtues that come with it. Nothing is more distinctively characteristic not only of the New Testament but of the Bible as a whole than the constant insistence that right living is the outcome of right character and attitudes.[2]

When we ask what particular virtues are commended in the Bible, it is not surprising to find that there is a large area of agreement with the current standards of the ancient world. The fact of general revelation should lead us to expect this (s. 15). Certain general concepts of right and wrong are in the nature of the case practically universal, though their specific content and applications may differ. Such terms as " just," " upright," and even " perfect " (cp. s. 56), for example, are hardly more than synonyms of " good " and " righteous "; [3] in fact, our words " justice " and " righteousness " are to a large extent merely variant translations of the same Hebrew word in the Old Testament and the same Greek word in the New Testament, though the Hebrew also has another word meaning " justice " or " judgment " (s. 60).

The Old Testament naturally puts considerable stress on what may be called the peasant virtues. The solid dependability of a Boaz and the shrewd, sensible competence of a Naomi may be cited as examples, while both Boaz and Naomi, as well as Ruth, exemplify also family loyalty and the kindness that goes beyond duty. Faithfulness is highly esteemed in the Old Testament.[4] Jesus also praises fidelity to a trust.[5]

The strong emphasis on industry in the wisdom literature falls in the same category.[6] Industry is commended and slothfulness condemned in the New Testament also, especially by Paul.[7] Covetousness, however, is condemned by both the Old and the New Testaments.[8] The Christian must be content with what he has.[9]

Among these homely, everyday virtues is honesty. The apparent approval, or at least lack of strong disapproval, with which Jacob's shrewd but rather shady dealings are narrated suggests that this virtue was not always so highly prized as it might have been.[10] Some growth in moral sensitivity in this matter may be seen between the J and E accounts of

---

[2] Dt. 6:5; 1 S. 16:7; 1 Chr. 28:9; 29:17; Ps. 139:23; Prov. 4:23; 23:7; Mt. 5:21 f., 27 f.; Mk. 7:14–23; 2 Cor. 10:5.

[3] Gen. 6:9; Job 1:1, 8; 2:3.

[4] Neh. 9:8; 13:13; Prov. 20:6; 28:20.

[5] Mt. 25:14–30; Lk. 12:35–48; 19:12–27.

[6] Prov. 6:6, 9; 10:26; 12:24, 27; 13:4, and often; Eccl. 10:18.

[7] Rom. 12:11; 13:8; Eph. 4:28; Col. 3:23; 1 Th. 4:11; 1 Tim. 5:8; Heb. 6:12.

[8] Ex. 20:17; Eph. 5:3.

[9] Phil. 4:12; Heb. 13:5; 1 Tim. 6:6–10; cp. s. 106.

[10] Gen., chs. 27; 30:25–43.

Abraham's representing Sarah as his sister.[11] Certainly the Bible as a whole strongly emphasizes honesty. While our English versions often use the word "truth" in the Old Testament where the meaning is really fidelity or reliability, truthfulness also is repeatedly praised in both Testaments, and lying and falsehood are emphatically condemned.[12] Sincerity is of course closely related to honesty. Jesus strongly denounces hypocrisy, and the same note echoes through the epistles.[13] Not only lying but also malicious, corrupt, and foolish speech are frequently censured.[14]

Such virtues as sobriety and chastity will be discussed later (ss. 104 ff.), but purity in a wider sense is a quality of Christian character,[15] and one of the fruits of the Spirit is self-control.[16]

All the world honors courage. Throughout the Old Testament a high esteem for physical and military courage is naturally evident, but there is evident also an appreciation of moral courage, especially in the form of steadfast fidelity to one's convictions under persecution. One of the best examples of such courage is Jeremiah.[17] The stories of Daniel and his companions afford further examples.[18] The "saints" of the psalms are sometimes apparently the chosen people in general but sometimes more particularly those who even under affliction persevere in their devotion to God and his laws.[19] The apocryphal writings of the inter-Testamental period give further instances of fearless persistence.[20] The New Testament frequently urges endurance and faithfulness under persecution.[21] A true follower of Jesus accepts persecution and injury without even trying to prevent it.[22]

Christian endurance, however, is not Stoic insensibility, nor is it

11 Gen. 12:13; 20:2, 12; cp. ch. 26:9.

12 Ex. 20:16; Ps. 15:2; 24:4; and often; Prov. 6:17; 8:7; 12:17, 19, 22; 19:5, 9; 30:8; Is. 65:16; Zc. 8:16; 13:3; 1 Cor. 5:8; Eph. 4:15, 25; Phil. 4:8; Col. 3:9; 1 Tim. 4:2; Jas. 3:14; 1 Jn. 2:21; Rev. 21:27; 22:15.

13 Mk. 8:13–21; 12:38–40; Mt. 6:5 f., 16 f.; 16:5–12; 23:1–7, 13–36; Lk. 11:37–52; 12:1; 20:45–47; Rom. 12:9; Jas. 3:17; 1 P. 2:1.

14 Job 27:4; Ps. 34:13; Prov. 10:8, 10, 14; 14:3; 15:2; 17:20; Eph. 4:29; 5:4; Col. 4:6; Jas. 3:2–12; 1 P. 2:1; 3:10.

15 Mt. 5:8; Phil. 4:8.

16 Gal. 5:22 f.

17 Jer. 26:14 f.

18 Dan. 1:8; 3:16–18; 6:4–10.

19 Ps. 30:4; 31:23, and often.

20 1 Macc. 1:62 f.; 2:23–38; 2 Macc. 6:18–31; ch. 7.

21 Mt. 5:10–12; Mk. 13:11–13; Rom. 12:12; 1 Cor. 16:13; 2 Cor. 11:23–27; Phil. 1:27–30; Eph. 6:10 ff.; 2 Tim. 2:3 f.; Heb. 11:32–40; 12:1–4; 1 P. 2:19 ff.; 3:14, 17; 4:1; Rev. 2:10 f., 26; 3:5, 10, 12, 21.

22 Mt. 5:25 f., 38–41; see further s. 108.

mere helpless submission. It is an expression of love, which includes even enemies and not only endures but forgives and returns good for evil.[23] This is in strong contrast with the vindictive spirit expressed by some parts of the Old Testament; [24] but the Old Testament also has the idea that vengeance belongs to God,[25] and even the ideal of returning good for evil is found both in the Old Testament and in the inter-Testamental literature.[26]

Back of all this is the spirit of humility. Whether Jesus said, " Blessed are the poor in spirit," or, " Blessed are ye poor," [27] a humble spirit is praised throughout the Bible.[28] Not the morbid self-abasement which is only a form of pride and conceit, but an unselfish devotion to others constitutes Christian humility.[29] Simplicity in dress is commended, particularly to women, as an expression of proper humility.[30]

Closely related to humility is the quality designated in the older English versions as " meekness " but more accurately represented by the word " gentleness " or sometimes " modesty." As a matter of fact, the word translated " meek " in the Old Testament is in most cases the same one rendered elsewhere " humble." [31] It is the word applied in some of the passages noted above to those who patiently endure affliction and persecution. The Greek words rendered " meek " or " meekness " in the New Testament have much the same connotation.[32] There are also other Hebrew and Greek words translated " gentle " or " gentleness." [33]

Desire for peace and effort to secure it are an expression of this loving, gentle disposition.[34] Evidently, however, it did not prove easy to

[23] Mt. 6:14 f.; 18:15–17, 21–35; Rom. 12:14, 17–21; 1 Cor. 13:4, 7; 1 Th. 5:15; Eph. 4:2, 32; Col. 3:13; 1 P. 3:9.
[24] Gen. 4:24; Ps. 137:8 f.; Jer. 11:20; 20:12.
[25] Dt. 32:35; 1 S. 25:32 ff.
[26] Ex. 23:4 f.; Prov. 25:21 f.; Testaments of the Twelve Patriarchs: Gad 6:3–7; Zebulon 5:3; Joseph 18:2.
[27] Mt. 5:3; Lk. 6:20, 24.
[28] Ps. 34:2; 69:32; Prov. 3:34; 15:33; 18:12; 22:4; Is. 57:15; Mi. 6:8; Lk. 18:9–14; Rom. 12:10, 16 f.; 15:1 f.; Col. 3:12; 1 P. 3:8.
[29] Mk. 9:33–37; 10:35–45; Mt. 20:20–28; 23:8–12; Lk. 14:7–11; 22:24–27; Jn. 13:1–15; 1 Th. 5:11; Jas. 4:10.
[30] Is. 3:16–24; 1 Tim. 2:9 f.; 1 P. 3:3–5; cp. Lk. 20:46; Jas. 2:1–4.
[31] Num. 12:3; Ps. 22:26; 25:9; 37:11 (cp. Mt. 5:5); 76:9; 147:6; 149:4; Is. 11:4; 29:19; 61:1; Am. 2:7; Zp. 2:3.
[32] Mt. 5:5; 11:29; 21:5 (cp. Zc. 9:9); 1 Cor. 4:21; 2 Cor. 10:1; Gal. 5:23; 6:1; Eph. 4:2; Col. 3:12; 1 Tim. 6:11; 2 Tim. 2:25; Titus 3:2; Jas. 1:21; 3:13, 17; 1 P. 3:4, 15.
[33] 2 S. 18:5; 22:36; Ps. 18:35; 2 Cor. 10:1; Gal. 5:22; 1 Th. 2:7; 2 Tim. 2:24; Titus 3:2; Jas. 3:17; 1 P. 2:18.
[34] Mt. 5:9; Ps. 34:14 (cp. 1 P. 3:11); Rom. 12:18; 1 Th. 4:11.

maintain this spirit even within the church itself. The disciples began with " one heart and soul," [35] but it was not long before they
had to be warned repeatedly against envy, jealousy, anger, strife, and
division.[36]

Another expression of the same basic attitude is submission to both
religious and civil authorities, where it may seem to us that the writers
of the New Testament sometimes went too far.[37] Respect for parents
and for one's elders in general are also manifestations of humility.[38]

Compassion and kindness are valued highly throughout the Bible. As
we have previously observed, the Hebrew word commonly rendered
" kindness " or " loving-kindness " means primarily " loyalty," but it
often implies also a beneficence which exceeds anything the recipient
has a right to expect. A kind, sympathetic attitude toward others, especially when they are suffering or in need, is one of the most fundamental qualities of Christian character.[39] Both kindness and humility
require a charitable judgment of others.[40] Not only a feeling of benevo-
lence but practical helpfulness is demanded.[41] Hospitality, always
highly esteemed in the Orient, is explicitly enjoined in the New Testament.[42]

Christian love should be especially fervent and deep within the fellowship of the church.[43] The sense of community is strengthened by the
responsibility of being God's holy people, his chosen and loyal saints.[44]
This involves worthy living which will command the respect and ad-
miration of those outside the church.[45] The expectation of Christ's im-

[35] Acts 4:32.
[36] Rom. 13:13; 14:19; 1 Cor., chs. 1 to 3; 13; Gal. 5:22; Col. 3:8; Eph. 4:3 ff., 26, 31;
Phil., ch. 2; 1 Th. 5:13; Jas. 3:14, 16; 1 P. 2:1.
[37] Rom. 13:1-7; 1 Th. 5:12 f.; Titus 3:1; Heb. 13:17; 1 P. 2:13 ff.; see further s. 107.
[38] Ex. 20:12; Lev. 19:32; Dt. 5:16; Prov. 23:22; Mk. 7:9-13; Eph. 6:1 f.; Col. 3:20;
1 Tim. 5:1 f.
[39] Job 6:14; Ps. 35:13; Prov. 3:3; 11:17; Ho. 6:6 (cp. Mt. 9:13; 12:7); Mi. 6:8; Zc.
7:9; Mt. 5:7; Mk. 1:41; 6:34; Lk. 6:36 (cp. s. 56); Rom. 12:15; 15:1; 2 Cor. 11:29; Gal.
6:2; Eph. 4:32; Phil. 2:1; Col. 3:12; Heb. 13:3; Jas. 2:13; 1 P. 3:8.
[40] Mt. 7:1-5; Rom. 14:3 f., 10-13; Jas. 4:12.
[41] Mt. 25:35 ff.; Mk. 9:41; Lk. 10:30-37; 11:41; 12:32; Acts 9:36; 10:2, 4, 31; Rom.
12:13; Heb. 13:3, 16; Jas. 1:27; 2:15 f.; 1 Jn. 3:17.
[42] Rom. 12:13; Heb. 13:2; 1 P. 4:9.
[43] Jn. 13:34 f.; Acts 2:44 f.; 4:32, 34 f.; Rom. 12:10; Eph. 3:18; Heb. 13:1; 1 P. 4:8;
cp. s. 84.
[44] Ex. 19:6; Lev. 11:44 f.; 19:2; 20:7, 26; Dt. 7:6; 14:2, 21; 26:19; 28:9; Ps. 30:4;
85:8; 89:7; 97:10; Is. 62:12; Dan. 7:18, 21 f., 25, 27; Acts 9:13, 32, 41; 26:10; Rom. 1:7;
16:2; 1 Cor. 1:2; 6:1 f.; Eph. 1:4; 2:19; 4:12; 5:3; Col. 1:12, 22; 1 Th. 3:13; 5:27; Heb.
3:1; 1 P. 1:15 f.; 2:5, 9; 2 P. 3:11; Rev. 13:10; 14:12; 19:8.
[45] Mt. 5:16; Rom. 12:17; Eph. 4:1; Phil. 4:8; Col. 4:5; 1 Th. 4:12; 1 P. 2:12.

minent return afforded the early church a strong motive for constant vigilance and adherence to their ideals.[46]

Underlying and undergirding the whole Christian life is the earnest hunger and thirst for righteousness which issues from complete dedication to God's kingdom, according to the pattern given by Jesus himself.[47]

[46] Mk. 13:33–37; Mt. 24:42–44; Lk. 21:34–36.
[47] Mt. 5:6; 8:21 f.; 10:37; Mk. 8:34 ff.; 10:21; Lk. 14:26.

XIV

SPECIAL OFFICES AND FUNCTIONS

86. *Priests*

The origins of the Hebrew priesthood are obscure, but much development is discernible within the Old Testament. The elaborate organization which finally emerged confined the priestly office to the tribe of Levi, which may have originated as a professional guild rather than an ethnic group, though that is not certain. Within the tribe only the descendants of Aaron were priests, the rest being simply Levites, with minor functions in the temple worship. At the head of the organization was the high priest. Both priests and Levites were divided into courses, which served in turn for a specified period. There was also considerable specialization of function. The whole system is attributed to Moses and Aaron by P; the Chronicler makes David the author of most of it. David, however, actually made some of his own sons priests, though he did not belong to the tribe of Levi.[1]

The priests were teachers of the law, and much of the composition and editing of the Old Testament books was probably done by them, but their primary duty was the conduct of worship in the temple. This fact naturally produced a tendency to overemphasize the ritual element in religion. The prophets often condemn the priests as corrupt, though it should be remembered that they condemn other prophets also (*v.i.*). Jesus does not condemn the priests of his day, but sends a leper to the priest for cleansing;[2] at the same time the part played by priest and Levite in the parable of the good Samaritan is not flattering to either group,[3] and Jesus' cleansing of the temple and prediction of its destruction show that the system of worship was not basic or essential for him. The early church was persecuted by the priestly authorities.[4] Jn. 7:32 regards the priests as leaders in the opposition to the gospel.

[1] 2 S. 8:18 — the E.VV. mistranslates here and in ch. 20:26.
[2] Mk. 1:44.
[3] Lk. 10:31 f.
[4] Acts, chs. 4 f., but cp. ch. 6:7.

There is no priesthood in the religion of the New Testament. The whole system is treated in Heb., chs. 7 to 9, as a type of the ministry of Christ (s. 30). Ex. 19:6 is applied to the church in the New Testament.[5] Rev. 20:6 makes the martyrs priests in the millennium.

87. Prophets

The Hebrew word translated " prophet " means one who speaks for another: it is applied to Abraham as an intercessor [1] and to Aaron as Moses' spokesman.[2] Other words, such as " seer," were applied to the prophets also.[3] Prophecy was known among the Canaanites, and the origin of Hebrew prophecy was in some way connected with this institution, though perhaps mainly as a reaction against its influence. Popular forms of divination and clairvoyance (s. 14) lie back of Hebrew prophecy also.[4] Groups called " the sons of the prophets " appear in the stories of Elijah and Elisha,[5] recalling the companies of prophets mentioned in 1 S. 10:5, 10; 19:20. Groups of prophets frequenting the royal courts of Israel and Judah and the temple appear occasionally.[6] Recent research has shown that prophets had a regular part in the temple cultus. A striking instance of prophetic utterance by a Levite is given in 2 Chr. 20:14–17, and it is not unlikely that some of the psalms were composed and recited by temple prophets.

The great canonical prophets, however, were independent individuals, unpopular, rejected by kings, priests, people, and other prophets alike. They received their office by direct individual experience, not by birth or appointment, and were independent of the cultus and the official religious organization. They bitterly condemn the " false prophets " as subservient men-pleasers.[7] Their characteristic and consistent message is a championship (1) of the sole worship of Yahweh as against paganism and idolatry, (2) of ethical religion as against ritualism and institutionalism, and (3) of the rights of the common people as against exploitation by the rich and powerful.

After the exile, prophecy lost much of its vitality, with a few great exceptions. Postbiblical Judaism on the whole regarded it as a thing of

---

5 Rev. 1:6; 5:10; 1 P. 2:5, 9.
1 Gen. 20:7.
2 Ex. 7:1 f.
3 1 S. 9:9.
4 Num. 11:24–29; 24:3 f., 15 f.; 1 S. 10:5–13; 19:18–24; 2 K. 3:15.
5 1 K. 20:35; 2 K. 2:3, 5, 7, 15; 4:1, 38; 5:22; 6:1; 9:1.
6 1 K., ch. 22; Jer., chs. 26 to 28.
7 Mi. 3:5–7 Jer. 5:30 f.; 6:13 f.; 8:9–11; 14:13–18; 23:9–40; Ezek., ch. 13.

the past, to be restored only in the Messianic age (s. 12). The scribes and rabbis (s. 88) did not speak by revelation but preserved and transmitted tradition. Yet 1 Macc. 4:46 and 14:41 indicate the possibility that a prophet might appear at any time, and Josephus claims that the gift is still exercised by some, including himself.

Christianity begins with the spoken word of a new Prophet (s. 29), whose teaching came with immediate, divine authority.[8] Prophecy was a common practice in the early church. Several examples are given in the book of Acts.[9] Paul values prophecy above speaking with tongues.[10] The author of Revelation calls his message prophecy.[11] But the liberty of prophecy [12] entailed the danger of false prophecy. False prophets are mentioned explicitly.[13] The reaction of the church against heresy evidently quenched the spirit of free prophecy, its final flare-up in the early church being Montanism. Like Judaism before it, the church more and more fell back upon more easily standardized ways of knowing the word of God, in particular the established tradition and the written Scriptures (s. 10).

88. *Sages, Scribes, and Rabbis*

Jer. 18:18 names along with the priests and prophets the " wise " or sages. These are not elsewhere referred to as a special class or group except in the wisdom literature which they produced, though celebrated sages of the east are named in 1 K. 4:31. When the tradition of wisdom was incorporated into the main stream of Jewish tradition and wisdom was identified with the law of Moses,[1] the honorable title " the wise " was applied to the scribes with much the connotation of our word " scholar."

The first of the scribes on record was Ezra, who was also a priest.[2] The account of his work clearly embodies the Chronicler's conception of the ideal scribe. The emergence of the scribes in Judaism was a result of the canonization of the law, which necessitated the interpretation of the old laws and their application to new situations (s. 10). The scribes were the professional experts in the law and the custodians of the tradi-

---

8 Mt. 5:21 ff.; Mk. 1:14 f., 22; 13:31; cp. Jn. 6:63; 14:10, 24; 17:8, 14.
9 Acts 11:27 f.; 13:1; 15:32; 21:9 f.
10 1 Cor. 14:1–19.
11 Rev. 1:3; 22:7, 10, 18 f.
12 2 Cor. 3:17.
13 1 Jn. 4:1; 2 P. 2:1; Mk. 13:22; cp. Rev. 2:20; 19:20.
1 Ecclus. 24:23; s. 13.
2 Ezra 7:1–6, 11 f.

tional interpretations. The New Testament sometimes calls them law-yers. In the gospels " the scribes of the Pharisees " are mentioned par-ticularly. Not all the scribes were Pharisees, but many naturally were, because it was the Pharisees who especially cultivated the oral tradi-tions (s. 52).

The rabbis were the leaders of the scribes, the most prominent teach-ers of the law. The title " rabbi " is used informally and unofficially in the New Testament, sometimes of Jesus; its more specialized application developed somewhat later. The rabbis of the New Testament period were not ordained ministers or official leaders of organized worship, but teachers and interpreters of the law. Their authority was that of scholarly knowledge.

89. *Apostles, Evangelists, Teachers, Ministers*

The first specifically Christian religious leaders in anything like an official capacity were the apostles. The word " apostle " is from the Greek verb meaning " send," and is thus the exact equivalent of the Latin word " missionary." Mk. 3:14 uses the verb (Lk. 6:13 has the noun), and in ch. 6:30 the twelve are called " the apostles " without further explanation.[1] The purpose of their appointment was being with Jesus and being sent out to preach and cast out demons.[2] The term may have been used informally during Jesus' ministry for those whom he sent on preaching missions. In the early church the twelve continued as leaders of the group with the prestige naturally conferred by Jesus' choice of them. Their position was practically official, and the choice of Matthias indicates that even the number twelve was regarded as inal-terable.[3] Their function was giving witness to the resurrection,[4] the min-istry of the word.[5] Paul speaks in Gal. 2:9 of James and Cephas and John as "those who were reputed to be pillars " at Jerusalem. In ch. 1:19 he apparently calls James, the brother of Jesus, an apostle. Paul considered himself an apostle and jealously defended his right to the title.[6] So far as the New Testament indicates, he was the last to be so called.

The preaching of the apostles, like that of Jesus himself, is designated by the Greek verb euangelizesthai," " bring good news " (s. 83.) The per-son who thus proclaims good news might appropriately be called an

---

[1] Cp. Mt. 10:2.
[2] Mk. 3:14 f.
[3] Acts 1:15 ff.; cp. Mt. 19:28.

[4] Acts 1:21 f.
[5] Ch. 6:2, 4.
[6] 2 Cor., chs. 11 f.

" evangelist." This noun is not applied to the apostles in the New Testament, but it appears a few times as a term for a person who was not an apostle but apparently an itinerant missionary. Thus Philip is called " the evangelist " in Acts 21:8. In Eph. 4:11 evangelists are mentioned after apostles and prophets, and in 2 Tim. 4:5 Timothy is exhorted to " do the work of an evangelist." Whether the word indicated an official position, with formal ordination, we do not know.

Teachers also are mentioned as a recognized group in the early church, though again we know nothing specific about their position or work. There were teachers as well as prophets in the church at Antioch.[7] The lists in 1 Cor. 12:28 f. and Eph. 4:11 include teachers, and the function of teaching is mentioned with others in Rom. 12:6 f. (The reference to teachers in Jas. 3:1 seems to have in view, not an official position, but rather a self-imposed responsibility for others which shows a lack of humility.) The fact that the Jewish rabbis were primarily teachers, and even more the fact that Jesus was considered a teacher and the word " disciple " means literally " pupil," would tend to exalt the position of the teacher in the church.

In Eph. 4:11 pastors also are mentioned, but this term seems not to have achieved any official status in the apostolic church. The English word, in its literal sense " shepherds," is used by the Authorized Version in Jer., ch. 23, for the unfaithful kings of Israel. In Eph. 4:11 it translates the same Greek word used elsewhere of Jesus as the Good Shepherd.[8] The idea of the shepherd, without the word, is applied in 1 P. 5:2 f. to the elders (s. 90).

Our use of the word " minister " in the Protestant churches has no exact Scriptural precedent. Acts 6:4, as already noted, speaks of the work of the apostles as " the ministry [*diakonia*] of the word." Jesus says that he who would be first among the disciples must be their " minister " (R.S.V., " servant ").[9] The Greek word used here, *diakonos,* is the one from which our word " deacon " is derived, and in the New Testament it is sometimes rendered " deacon." Possibly the " deacons " mentioned by Paul in Phil. 1:1 were more like the ministers than the deacons of our churches (s. 90). Paul often applies this word to himself and his associates as servants of God and Christ and dispensers of the

---

7 Acts 13:1.
8 Jn. 10:11, 14; Heb. 13:20; cp. 1 P. 5:4; Rev. 7:17.
9 Mk. 9:35; 10:43.

gospel.[10] Sometimes " minister " represents a different Greek word meaning " attendant," " assistant," or " servant." [11] A third Greek noun, used occasionally in the New Testament and translated " minister," [12] is used by the Septuagint for a Hebrew word often applied in the Old Testament to the priests, and regularly translated " minister " in our English versions.[13] The New Testament church, however, had no regular ordained pastor known as its " minister."

90. Deacons, Elders, Bishops

In the preceding section something has already been said concerning the use of the Greek word *diakonos* in the New Testament. Aside from its literal and figurative use in the gospels in the sense of " servant," [1] the application of the word to a specific Christian function is perhaps foreshadowed in the appointment of " the seven " in Acts, ch. 6. What seems to be contemplated here is merely a temporary committee for a special emergency, necessitated by the " communism " of the group (s. 106) and the friction between Hebrews and Hellenists regarding the distribution of goods. The apostles feel that this distracts them from the ministry (*diakonia*) of the word in order to wait on (*diakonein*) tables; hence the seven are selected for the " daily ministration " (*diakonia*), though they are not actually called deacons (*diakonoi*) in the text. Strangely enough, they always appear in the subsequent narrative as preachers. The title " deacon " occurs first in Phil. 1:1 (cp. s. 89); thereafter deacons do not appear again until the pastoral epistles, where they are clearly ecclesiastical officials with specified requirements and duties like those of the deacons in our churches now.[2]

The first reference to elders as appointed officials of the church is in Acts 14:23. In the Old Testament and in Judaism the elders are simply the older men of the community, like the Arab *sheikh* (literally, " old man "), and in this sense they are often mentioned in the gospels and Acts along with the priests. Sometimes the New Testament uses the term

---

[10] 1 Cor. 3:5; 2 Cor. 3:6; 6:4; 11:23 (cp. v. 15); Col. 1:7, 23, 25; 4:7 (Eph. 6:21); 1 Th. 3:2; cp. 1 Tim. 4:6.

[11] Cp. Lk. 1:2; 4:20; Acts 13:5; 26:16; 1 Cor. 4:1.

[12] Rom. 13:6; 15:16; Heb. 1:7 (R.S.V., servants); 8:2.

[13] Ps. 103:21; 104:4; Is. 61:6; cp. Jer. 33:21; Ezek. 44:11; 45:4 f.; 46:24; Joel 1:9; 2:17. Other forms of the Hebrew verb are used more than fifty times for the priests' service in the sanctuary.

[1] Mk. 10:43; Jn. 2:5.

[2] 1 Tim. 3:8-13.

in the literal sense as contrasted with younger men: 1 P. 5:1–5 seems to have both the literal and the official meanings in mind. In Acts 20:17–38 Paul bids farewell to the elders from Ephesus at Miletus. In his epistles, however, Paul never mentions elders. The requirements and duties of the office are described in the pastoral epistles,[3] where the term has become definitely an ecclesiastical title.

Bishops, like deacons, are mentioned first in Phil. 1:1, and here the word may still have its primary meaning "overseer" (Greek, *episkopos,* the equivalent of the Latin word "superintendent"). In Acts 20:28, Paul tells the elders of Ephesus that the Spirit has made them *episkopoi* of the flock, making each elder of the local congregation a "bishop." 1 P. 2:25 speaks of Christ as the Great Shepherd and Overseer (Pastor and Bishop) of our souls. The requirements of the office of bishop are stated in 1 Tim. 3:1–7. Elders are mentioned separately in ch. 5:1, 17–19, but Titus 1:5–9 seems to identify elders and bishops. While the developments here reflected are by no means clear, there was evidently no "monarchical episcopate" in the New Testament church, though a tendency in that direction is perceptible. Later ecclesiastical tradition makes James the first bishop of Jerusalem and Peter of Rome.

91. *Spiritual Gifts*

Both worship and organization in the early church were at first governed by the direct guidance of the Spirit. The choice of Matthias to succeed Judas was made by casting the lot after prayer, the Spirit being given a choice between two nominees of the church.[1] In Acts 13:2 the Spirit takes the initiative and does the nominating. No such guidance is indicated in the choice of the seven (s. 90), but other instances of direction by the Spirit in the missionary work of the church are given.[2]

Lists of special spiritual gifts (*charismata*) are given by Paul,[3] though not in such a way as to suggest that they were intended to be exhaustive. In addition to some of the functions already considered, they include administration, healing, and apparently any special aptitude. Speaking with tongues and the interpretation of tongues, for example, are treated as spiritual gifts. 1 Cor. 12:7 and ch. 14:26 suggest that all Christians had such gifts. Their relative value and honor are masterfully discussed by Paul in 1 Cor., chs. 12 to 14: all, he says, are honorable, but none is of any value without love, and those which edify

---

[3] 1 Tim. 5:17–19; Titus 1:5 f.   [2] Acts 8:29; 10:19; 11:12.
[1] Acts 1:15–26.   [3] Rom. 12:6–8; 1 Cor. 12:8–10, 28; cp. Eph. 4:11.

others are to be preferred above those which the individual can only enjoy by himself. A radical departure is made by Paul's declaration that for the sake of decency and order those who speak with tongues and those who prophesy must await their turn, only two or three of each group being allowed to speak, and that those who speak with tongues must keep silence unless an interpreter is present. This inevitably meant the doom of the free gifts of the Spirit.

Perhaps the outstanding point in all this, and the one of most importance for church organization and Christian unity in our own day, is that the offices and organization of the apostolic church were not divinely ordained once for all, but developed gradually under the guidance of the Spirit to meet specific situations and needs as they arose.

XV

PUBLIC WORSHIP

92. *Historical Background and Basis of Christian Worship*

The task of the church may be found summarized in the purpose for which Jesus appointed the twelve apostles, as summarized in Mk. 3:14 f.: " That they should be with him, and that he might send them forth to preach, and to have power to heal sickness and to cast out demons." This suggests a twofold commission, including worship and service. Worship is the cultivation of our relationship with God and Christ — " that they should be with him." Service is the expression and application of that relationship in our relations with our fellow men.[1] Worship gives power for service: in Lk. 24:49 Jesus tells the disciples to wait for power from on high before undertaking their mission to the world.[2] Service completes worship by putting the power to work: " faith working through love." [3]

A large part of the Old Testament is concerned with directions for public worship. As law these have no force or relevance for the Christian church, but they cannot be ignored by biblical theology. Since they are still a part of the Scriptures accepted by the church, they at least call for some explanation, if only to prevent their misuse. A more positive value lies in the fact that they contain much material that can still be used with spiritual profit in Christian worship, even though much sifting of the wheat from the chaff is needed to make them available for this purpose. The literature of Hebrew worship, of course, includes the psalms, which are much used and could be more effectively used than they are in the church. The ritual of Old Testament religion is significant also for the understanding it gives us of the origins and background of Christian worship.

During the lifetime of Jesus the temple was still in its glory, and the cultus was carried on in all its elaborate magnificence. Zacharias was

---

[1] Cp. Mk. 12:29–31.   [2] Cp. Acts 1:4–8.   [3] Gal. 5:6.

performing his priestly office at the altar when he received the angelic announcement of the fact that he was to have a son who would be great in the sight of the Lord.[4] Jesus and his disciples attended the temple worship, as Joseph and Mary had done in his childhood.[5] Jesus revered the temple [6] and with righteous indignation drove out the money-changers who desecrated it.[7] He seems to have approved and observed the ritual forms of Judaism, provided they were backed up by righteous living,[8] though he swept aside all traditions that made void the word of God.[9] In fact, apart from the worship of the temple and synagogue, public worship of any kind by Jesus and his disciples is not recorded in the gospels.

When the church became separated from Judaism, the whole ritual law came to be regarded as superseded, though the party of James in Jerusalem long resisted this tendency. The epistle to the Hebrews draws a sharp contrast between the whole Levitical system, as the shadow of things to come, and the new covenant (s. 30).

The background of Christian worship, in general, is to be found not so much in the temple ritual as in the services of the synagogue. After the destruction of the temple in A.D. 70 some features of the temple worship were carried over into the ritual of the synagogue, especially in the liturgies for the festivals (s. 99), and the beginnings of this process may have been as early as the lifetime of Jesus. From Mk. 1:21 on the attendance of Jesus and the disciples at the services of the synagogue is frequently noted. According to Acts, Paul made it his practice on his missionary journeys to seek first his own people at their synagogues.[10] It is not improbable that the first church organization was simply a new synagogue (s. 51); indeed, Jas. 2:2 still speaks of the synagogue of the Christians.

93. *Magic and Religion*

The elaborate system of ritual presented in the Old Testament was evidently the result of a long process of development from very primitive beginnings. While the later priestly law carries the whole system back to Aaron and Moses, the actual origins of the rites were both earlier and later — later, because the system was certainly elaborated after the conquest, under the kings, and even after the exile, but also earlier,

4 Lk. 1:8 ff.
5 Lk. 2:22 ff., 41 ff.
6 Mt. 23:16–21.
7 Mk. 11:15–17.

8 Mk. 1:44; Mt. 5:23 f.; 23:23 f.
9 Mk. 7:1–23.
10 Acts 13:5, 14; 14:1.

because some practices must have been inherited from the early ancestors of the Israelites. The stories of the offerings of Cain and Abel, the
building of altars and offering of sacrifices by Noah and Abraham, and
the institution of such a rite as circumcision,[1] all reflect a consciousness
of the primitive beginnings of Hebrew ritual.

In its earliest stages the ritual of the Semitic ancestors of the Hebrews
clearly involved much of what we should now call magic rather than
religion. Since ritual always tends to be strongly conservative, some elements of the later cult practices can be understood only by reference to
their origin in magic. The distinction between magic and religion, of
course, was not drawn by the early Hebrews themselves. It is not drawn
by all modern scholars in the same way or at the same point. For our
present purpose the term " magic " may be used to designate practices
supposed to control automatically the operations of nature, however
conceived, while religion seeks to gain its ends by winning the favor of
a personal deity or deities.

Belief in the existence of personal beings that can aid or hinder man
is presupposed by some forms of magic as well as religion, but magic assumes that these beings are subject to human control, provided one
knows and follows the proper procedure. In other words, the beings with
which magic deals are infrahuman, not superhuman, though, like modern man's machines, they can do some things man cannot do himself.
The powers with which religion deals cannot be coerced by man; they
can at most be persuaded, and if what is sought is contrary to their
wishes, it may be denied. Man is therefore dependent upon their favor,
which he tries to gain and hold by doing what he believes will please
them.

Obviously the line between religion and magic, as we have drawn it,
is a thin one, sometimes quite imperceptible, because the ideas underlying primitive practice are not so clear and specific as to be always
obvious in the act itself. Primitive religion always tends to stress ritual
as a technique of direct dealing with the deities or even of the direct control of natural forces; in other words, it tends to be essentially magical.

Religion is not only closely allied to magic in its beginnings; it is always in danger of degenerating into magic. Even in the most sophisticated modern church two worshipers may sit side by side in the same
pew and repeat the same words and acts, and for one these may be religious, for the other magical. The Lord's Prayer is often recited more as

[1] Gen. 4:3–5; 8:20; 12:7 f.; 13:18; 17; 22.

a magical charm than as a Christian prayer. Indeed, prayer itself has been defined, with pious blasphemy, as " the lever that moves the arm that moves the world." What such a degeneration of religion into magic means is that the sense of God's sovereign majesty has degenerated to such a point that he can be thought of as subservient to man's ends and subject to man's control.

Fortunately the opposite tendency is always at work also, and it was this that produced those elements in the Old Testament cultus with which we are here concerned. An act originally conceived and performed as magic may be preserved but transformed by reinterpretation into a religious act of worship. For example, religious ceremonies often involve the dramatization of myths. Anthropologists have shown that in actual origin these rites precede the myths, which arise as interpretations of them. In the later stages of religious development, however, this fact has been quite forgotten. The act is now performed as a solemn commemoration of what is believed to have occurred in the past, stimulating and expressing religious attitudes and aspirations. An excellent instance of this is the passover (s. 99).

For biblical theology the final interpretation is much more important than the origin of a rite. The latter is significant only as a means of understanding how such an act came to be performed, since in many cases this could never be inferred from the later reinterpretation. The ritual system of Old Testament religion was completely and definitely lifted out of the realm of magic by the priestly legislators and historians through the application of the covenant idea. All the complicated rites of the cultic tradition were subsumed under the dominant idea that this was what God required, the way of atonement and access to communion with him which he himself had ordained. The original intent and specific nature of the particular act thus became irrelevant. The performance of every rite was an act of obedience to the revealed will of God, the Holy One of Israel. It was a means of being holy as God is holy.[2]

Our evaluation of the rites, therefore, both in general and in particular, must be governed by their fitness to express and cultivate a worthy spiritual life. As with the social legislation of the Old Testament, we cannot and need not pronounce any sweeping judgment concerning their having been, or not having been, what God actually desired at any time in the past. What he requires of us, we know, is worship in spirit and truth,[3] by whatever forms best achieve their purpose.

[2] Lev. 19:2.   [3] Jn. 4:24.

94. *Sacrifice and Offerings*

The basic rite of Hebrew worship is sacrifice. One of the most spontaneous and primitive ways of dealing with gods, as with men, is the
presentation of a gift to appease wrath and secure favor.[1] Votive thank
offerings are an equally natural and practically universal expression of
human feelings. Other conceptions also enter into the practice of sacrifice. The primitive idea of feeding the deity to keep him alive is barely
echoed in the Old Testament in the expression " the bread [i.e., food]
of God." [2] The conception of a communion meal is much more important
for Semitic religion and was certainly involved in early Hebrew sacrifice, though it developed into the idea of eating before God rather than
with him. (If the idea of eating the god himself ever existed among the
Hebrews, no trace of it survives in the Old Testament.) The thought of
a sacrifice as a festive social occasion is prominent not only in Ju. 9:27
(with reference to Canaanite religion) but also in 1 S. 9:12 f., 22–24.[3]
It still survives in the celebration of the passover.

Gen., ch. 22, suggests that animal sacrifice was a substitute for human
sacrifice, which was certainly practiced in later times though condemned
by the religious leaders, and may once have been sanctioned by Yahwism.[4] The practice of sacrificing children to Moloch by fire is regarded
by the prophets and historians of the monarchic period as apostasy from
Yahweh.[5]

The offering or redemption of the first-born son in Ex., chs. 22 and 34,
comes under the same category as the offering of first fruits, acknowledging Yahweh's right to everything and the worshiper's dependence
upon him for life. Tithing also serves the same purpose, like paying rent
for the use of another's property (cp. s. 106). The classic expression of
this idea is 1 Chr. 29:14. It becomes more important as the realization
grows that God does not need gifts. The prophets even say that he does
not want them.[6] The later priestly legislators, however, do not even ask
why sacrifice is necessary. Being commanded in the law, it needs for
them no further justification.

It is hard to realize how prominent the sacrificial ritual was in Hebrew religion and how important it seemed, though the interest in ritual

---

[1] Prov. 18:16; Ex. 23:15; 34:20.
[2] Lev. 21:6, 8, 17, 21 f.; 22:25.
[3] Cp. also for condemned pagan rites Am. 2:8; Ho. 4:18 (note A.S.V. margin).
[4] Cp. Ex. 22:29 f. with ch. 34:19 f.
[5] Lev. 18:21; 20:2–5; 2 K. 23:10; Jer. 32:35; Am. 5:26.
[6] Am. 5:21–25; Ho. 6:6; Is. 1:11–17; Mi. 6:6–8; Jer. 7:21–23; cp. Ps. 50:9–13; 51:16.

in some forms of Christianity should help us to understand this. Jesus carried on the prophetic tradition in this as in other respects. His cleansing of the temple and his quotation of Is. 56:7 on that occasion show that he condemned the commercialization of worship, but not necessarily the whole practice of sacrifice.[7] Sacrifices were never offered by the church; they had never been offered in the synagogue. The destruction of the temple in A.D. 70 brought to an end the whole sacrificial cultus. Orthodox Judaism still looks for its resumption in the days of the Messiah, but for Christianity it has been forever superseded.

One aspect of the system of sacrifice and offerings under the old covenant may be regarded as fulfilled in the offerings made in Christian worship. Like the ancient offerings of animals from the flocks and fruits from the fields, these are an expression of dependence upon God and obligation to him and a practical implementation of Christian love. They are not treated in the New Testament as a part of public worship, but their use in this way is quite in accord with the spirit of New Testament religion.

95. *Prayers, Liturgies, Hymns, and Other Forms of Worship*

The offerings in the temple were usually accompanied by prayer; perhaps it would be more accurate to say that the offering supplemented and reinforced the prayer. Examples of public prayer are given at several points in the Old Testament narratives.[1] Gradually, fixed forms of prayer developed. Prayer was a prominent part of synagogue worship; in fact, the synagogue may have arisen from informal gatherings primarily for the purpose of prayer. Some of the prayers still used in the synagogue were already in existence during the New Testament period. Jesus and his disciples were undoubtedly familiar with some of them. In Mt. 6:5 f. Jesus condemns ostentation and wordiness in prayer, but not necessarily all public prayer. The fact that some of his prayers are quoted in the gospels suggests that he prayed alond. He at least pronounced the customary blessing at his last supper with his disciples.[2]

The early church met for prayer and the teaching of the apostles.[3] The liturgical expansion of the Lord's Prayer in some manuscripts of

---

[7] Cp. Mt. 5:23 f.
[1] 1 Chr. 29:10–19; 1 K. 8:22–53; Neh. 9:5–38.
[2] Mk. 14:22 f.
[3] Acts 1:14; 2:42.

Matthew [4] is an example of the way in which fixed forms of prayer developed in the early church.

The temple worship included hymns, accompanied by instrumental music, which is often mentioned in Psalms.[5] (It is an interesting example of historical irony that some churches which use no modern hymns but only the psalms in their worship are at the same time opposed to the use of musical instruments.) The structure of the psalms and the occasional explicit references to antiphonal performance indicate something of the manner of their use in the temple. Reiterated responses, as in Ps. 136, and the successive summons to different groups to praise God, as in Ps. 135:19–21, are examples of what is meant. (It is unfortunate that the responsive reading of the psalms in our churches usually follows the mechanical and arbitrary division by verses instead of the original metrical structure.) Special classes of singers are named by the Chronicler and in the titles of many of the psalms.

Jesus and the disciples sang a hymn at their last supper together.[6] Paul refers to "psalms and hymns and spiritual songs."[7] Examples of early Christian hymnody are probably quoted at several points in the New Testament.[8]

Other rites described or mentioned in the Old Testament may be briefly mentioned here. Am. 5:26 refers to ritual processions, condemning them as idolatrous. They are probably alluded to in some of the psalms.[9] Sacred dances are indicated also.[10] Elaborate rites of purification are prescribed in the law (s. 75).

As has been noted in s. 91, the worship of the early churches in Gentile territory was at first free and charismatic, but Paul's condemnation of the unregulated exercise of spiritual gifts paved the way for fixed forms of worship, which probably developed first in connection with the sacraments (ss. 97 f.).

---

[4] Mt. 6:13, followed by A.V. but not A.S.V.
[5] Ps. 33:2; 57:8; 71:22; 81:2 f.; 92:3; 98:5 f.; 144:9; 149:3; 150:3–5.
[6] Mk. 14:26.
[7] Col. 3:16.
Phil. 2:6–11; 1 Tim. 3:16.
[8] So perhaps Lk. 1:46–55, 68–79; 2:29–32; 1 Cor. 2:9 (cp. Is. 64:4; 65:17); Eph. 5:14;
[9] Ps. 24:7–10; 48:12 f.; 68:24 f.
[10] Ex. 15:20; 32:19; Ju. 21:19–21 (in later Judaism there was dancing in the vineyards in connection with the feast of tabernacles) ; 2 S. 6:14; Ps. 149:3; 150:4.

96. *Scripture Reading and Preaching*

The public reading and interpretation of the law by Ezra [1] illustrates what was probably a common practice in later Old Testament times.[2] Much of the Old Testament may have been composed originally for reading or recitation in public worship: so perhaps the P accounts of the creation, flood, etc. The dramatic representation of such narratives, especially at the festivals, is not unlikely, being common in Egyptian and Babylonian religion (cp. s. 93).

The services of the synagogue included the reading of the law and the prophets, and later the psalms also. This practice was doubtless taken over by the early church, especially in view of the search for Messianic prophecies fulfilled by Jesus. Paul refers to the public reading of his letters in the churches.[3] In Rev. 1:3 a blessing is pronounced on reader and hearers.

The antecedents of Christian preaching may be seen both in the exposition of the law by the priests and in the speeches of the prophets, though the latter were not a part of public worship. Informal expository preaching was a regular part of synagogue worship, probably from the beginning. Visitors might be invited to speak in this way.[4] Jesus' preaching, for the most part, was occasional, like that of the prophets. The teaching of the apostles [5] was probably much like that of the rabbis in the synagogues. Meanwhile evangelistic preaching apart from the services of worship continued as the primary means of the missionary extension of the gospel.[6]

97. *Circumcision and Baptism*

In the religion of the Old Testament, and in Judaism ever since, circumcision has been much emphasized as a distinctive rite. The P document connects it with Abraham.[1] When and how it was actually adopted by the Hebrews we cannot tell,[2] but it was a primitive and widespread practice. The church retained it as long as the connection with Judaism was preserved, but Paul vehemently insists that to require it is contrary to the very essence of the gospel, making the Christian subject to the law.[3]

[1] Neh., ch. 8.
[2] Cp. Dt. 31:9-13.
[3] Col. 4:16.
[4] Lk. 4:16-30; Acts 13:14 ff.
[5] Acts 2:42.
[6] Rom. 10:11-15.
[1] Gen., ch. 17.
[2] Cp. Ex. 4:24-26; Josh. 5:2-9.
[3] Rom. 2:25-29; 4:9-12; Gal. 2:3-10; 5:2-12; 6:12-15.

The place of circumcision, as a rite of initiation into and membership in the holy community, was taken by baptism, though the latter undoubtedly came into use before circumcision was abandoned. The baptism of proselytes was practiced in Judaism along with circumcision; the antiquity and the nature of the rite, however, are still disputed. In the New Testament baptism appears first with John the Baptist as a " baptism of repentance unto remission of sins." [4] Jesus accepted baptism at the hands of John, but apparently did not practice the rite himself.[5] It may have been introduced into the church through the influence of John's followers; at any rate it appears already in Acts 2:38. Thereafter it is frequently mentioned in Acts.

Paul accepted the rite as a part of the tradition of the church and seems to have regarded it as necessary, or at least normal, though he rarely administered it himself.[6] He interprets it as connected with the believer's dying with Christ and being raised with him to new life, though it is not clear just how he thought of the relation between the ceremony and the inner experience.[7] John alludes to baptism only incidentally and, apart from ch. 4:1-3, indirectly.[8] In 1 P. 3:21 it is compared with the flood. Titus 3:5 calls it " the washing of regeneration " (if baptism is actually here in mind). The " great commission " of Mt. 28:19 and Mk. 16:15 ff. assumes the practice as usual and essential.

The mode of administration is nowhere prescribed or clearly described, though immersion seems to be implied by some passages. The significance of the rite and its place in the scheme of salvation remain at best obscure.

98. *The Lord's Supper and Ordination*

The importance of the observance of the Lord's Supper in the early church is shown by the prominence of the accounts of Jesus' last supper with his disciples. While the present forms and variations of the narrative reflect at some points developments in the liturgy, the story is by no means a mere cult legend. The significance of what Jesus said and did has been considered already in s. 75. The accounts do not indicate that he intended to institute a rite, yet in a very real sense the experience was for him and for the disciples a sacrament, in which the disciples were consecrated to the kingdom and it was convenanted to them.

---

4 Mk. 1:4.
5 Jn. 4:1-3.
6 1 Cor. 1:13-17.

7 Rom. 6:4; 1 Cor. 6:11; 12:13; Gal. 3:26 ff.; cp. s. 80.
8 Jn. 3:5; 19:34; 1 Jn. 5:8.

In Acts, chs. 1 to 12, the breaking of bread is referred to repeatedly, but without any clear indication of a formal rite. Paul gives in 1 Cor. 11: 17–34 an account of the institution of the sacrament, with an interpretation of it as a memorial of Christ's death and a testimony of the hope of his coming again. The references here to the body and blood of Christ introduce ideas recalling some of the Hellenistic mystery cults, in which the initiates drank the blood and ate the flesh of the cult deity. 1 Cor. 10:16–21 sounds decidedly sacramentarian, and ch. 11:29 f. even magical, but we cannot tell how Paul would reconcile such ideas with his conception of salvation through faith alone (cp. s. 80). His directions regarding eating at home prepare the way for the development of a separate service, quite different from such a real meal as the Corinthians had evidently enjoyed together.

John omits the account of the institution of the supper and in ch. 6 stresses the spiritual meaning of the idea of eating Jesus' flesh and drinking his blood, perhaps thus seeking to counteract a tendency toward superstitious sacramentarianism among converted Gentiles. Nowhere in the New Testament is there anything approaching the idea of transubstantiation or the repeated sacrifice of the mass. The significance of the observance for the early church seems to have been much like that of the passover in Judaism: it was a solemn memorial and a common testimony nourishing the faith of the group.

Ordination for special missions and offices by the laying on of hands with prayer was a common practice in the early church.[1] In Acts 8:17–19 the laying on of hands is the means by which the Holy Spirit is given to believers, constituting, so to speak, a second baptism. It may be compared, perhaps, with the later sacrament of confirmation, but it is not the same thing. As a rite of what may be called apostolic succession, ordination has a precedent in the laying of Moses' hands on Joshua.[2] Elijah's casting his mantle on Elisha may be recalled also in this connection.[3]

Nowhere is ordination called a sacrament, but neither is baptism or the Lord's Supper. The very concept " sacrament " never clearly appears in the Bible. The word " sacrament " is the Latin equivalent of the Greek word " mystery," which the eastern churches still use for the sacraments, but this usage is derived from pagan precedents, not from

---

[1] Acts 6:6; 13:3; Heb. 6:2; 1 Tim. 4:14; 2 Tim. 1:6; cp. 1 Tim. 5:22, though a reference to ordination here is doubtful.

[2] Num. 27:18–23; Dt. 34:9.

[3] 1 K. 19:19–21.

the New Testament. Only by inference from the actual practice of the church is the idea of a sacrament to be found in the Bible, if at all.

In general it must be said that the New Testament gives no pattern of Christian worship. The questions often hotly debated among Christian bodies — liturgical versus nonliturgical services, the use of instrumental music, hymns versus psalms, vestments, images, etc. — are not to be settled by any legalistic use of Scripture. The New Testament requires sincerity, simplicity, dignity, and freedom in public as in private worship.[4]

The rich resources of material for public worship in the Bible cannot be discussed here. Bearing always in mind the primary requirements just mentioned, one may draw upon a wealth of material in both Old and New Testaments for prayer and praise. Recent studies of the psalms as liturgical compositions reveal possibilities which the church has hardly begun to realize (s. 95).

99. Sacred Times

The observance of special festivals is a characteristic feature of Old Testament religion. Probably the most ancient Israelite festival was the passover, which seems to have been even pre-Mosaic.[1] It probably originated as a celebration of the birth of the lambs in the spring and the consecration of the flock for the year, with rites to ward off malevolent spirits and a communion feast to strengthen the bond between the Deity and the group. After the exodus it came to be regarded as a memorial of the deliverance from Egypt.

Three annual festivals are prescribed in Ex. 23:14–17 and 34:18, 22 f. The first is the feast of unleavened bread, occupying seven days at the same time of year as the passover, and later combined with it. Originally it was a solar, agricultural festival, while the passover was lunar and pastoral. While already connected with the exodus as a memorial in Exodus, the agricultural significance of the feast of unleavened bread is still clear. It celebrated the completion of the barley harvest,[2] and the elimination of leaven was probably intended originally to avoid anything that might contaminate the new crop.

The second annual festival is the one called the feast of weeks or Pentecost, because it was observed fifty days after the beginning of the

---

4 Mt. 6:5–8; Jn. 4:23 f.; 1 Cor. 5:7 f.; 14:39 f.   2 Dt. 16:9.
1 Ex. 5:1.

feast of unleavened bread. It is called the feast of harvest in Ex., ch. 23, the first fruits of wheat harvest in ch. 34. (The barley harvest in Palestine is ready about the first of April, the wheat harvest a few weeks later.) The agricultural connection of this festival was retained throughout the Old Testament, though later Judaism reinterpreted it as a commemoration of the giving of the law.

The third annual festival was the feast of ingathering, or tabernacles (Sukkoth), at the end of the year, i.e., the grape vintage in the fall. The Jewish New Year is still observed in the fall, but the Old Testament shows the interplay of two calendars, beginning in the spring and fall respectively. The name "tabernacles," though not appearing until Dt. 16:13–16, may be based on ancient practice, apparently connected with fertility rites and perhaps taken from the Canaanites.

Other festivals appear in later sources. The feast of dedication (Hanukkah), also called the feast of lights, commemorates the rededication of the temple by Judas Maccabeus in 165 B.C. Its date, the 25th of Kislev (Nov.-Dec.), may have influenced the date of Christmas. The feast of Purim celebrates riotously the deliverance narrated in the book of Esther, though its actual origin is disputed. There are also days of fasting and penitence, especially a day of mourning for the destruction of the temple and the Day of Atonement (Yom Kippur, cp. s. 75). The latter is the most solemn day of the Jewish year, coming at the end of ten days of penitence after the New Year's celebration in the fall.

The observance of the new moon was probably very ancient, connected with the lunar calendar mentioned above. Am. 8:5 indicates that business was suspended at the new moon. Frequently mentioned together with this observance, and doubtless related to it as a lunar observance, is the sabbath, the origin of which is unknown. The connection with the creation in Gen. 2:2 f. is an etiological myth (s. 38). The practice may be Mosaic or earlier; it is commanded not only in the decalogue but also in Ex. 23:12; 34:21. It is especially stressed, however, in the postexilic literature (P; Nehemiah; Third Isaiah). Later Judaism valued it highly as a mark of separation from the Gentiles. It was observed as a day of joy and rest. Detailed and rigorous laws regarding it were developed by the scribes.

While Jesus and his disciples observed the passover and probably the other Jewish festivals, and even Paul was eager to celebrate Pentecost in Jerusalem according to Acts 20:16, no specifically Christian annual observances appear in the New Testament. Easter and Christmas both developed later, evidently as substitutes for the spring and winter festivals of Judaism and paganism.

Jesus observed the sabbath with great freedom, making it subordinate to human welfare.[3] The early church followed this precedent, and the prominence of the sabbath controversies in the synoptic tradition probably reflects the continuance of disputes with the Jews on this subject. Paul treats the observance of all special days, along with the dietary regulations, as a matter of the individual's conscience.[4] There is no indication of any special day of Christian worship in the New Testament unless Acts 20:7 implies the observance of the Lord's Supper at a regular time; cp. also the expression " the Lord's day " in Rev. 1:10. Paul's reference to the first day of the week in 1 Cor. 16:2 has nothing to do with worship or a sacred day.

The use of Sunday as a special day for Christian worship may have begun within the New Testament period, but it is not clearly attested. Doubtless it developed in a Gentile environment, after the observance of the sabbath by Christians had fallen into abeyance. The application of the sabbath laws of the Old Testament to the Christian use of Sunday is a relatively modern invention, symptomatic of that legalistic distortion of the gospel to which the Puritans were especially susceptible.

100. *Sacred Places and Objects*

Sacred places require no extended discussion here. Their place in the achievement of Israelite monotheism and national unity has already been pointed out (ss. 21, 50). As centers of pilgrimage for the observance of the festivals [1] they played an important role in Hebrew religion. To all who know Old Testament history the very names of such places as Sinai, Bethel, Dan, Beersheba, Shiloh, and Jerusalem are sufficient to recall their part in the religion of the Old Testament. The central position held by Jerusalem even in eschatology will come to our attention later (s. 107). When the Samaritans seceded from Judaism, they put Mt. Gerizim in the place of Jerusalem (s. 21). This is the basis of the Samaritan woman's attempt to distract Jesus' attention from her affairs by drawing him into a doctrinal debate in Jn. 4:20–24; his reply makes Christianity forever independent of any local attachment. Further discussion of sacred places is therefore unnecessary for the purposes of biblical theology.

Much the same may be said regarding sacred objects. Having no place

---

[3] Mk. 1:21–25; 2:23–28; 3:1–6.   [1] 1 S. 1:3; Lk. 2:41.
[4] Rom. 14:5 f.; Gal. 4:8–11; Col. 2:16, 20–23.

in New Testament religion, they call for only such explanation as may be needed by Christian readers who find them in their Bible. The rite of sacrifice requires an altar. Noah, Abraham, Jacob, and Moses built altars at various places.[2] After the conquest we read of the erection of altars by Gideon and Samuel.[3] Saul, in an emergency, used a rock as an altar.[4] The Book of the Covenant declares that altars must be made of earth or unhewn stone, not of cut stone and not with steps.[5] The later altars of the tabernacle are described in considerable detail, including a great altar for burnt offerings and a smaller one for incense.[6] The altars of Solomon's temple and the postexilic temple are not so fully described, and the details are obscure.[7]

Sacred objects of the Canaanites are frequently mentioned in connection with the destruction of Canaanite shrines. They include the stone pillar,[8] the wooden *asherah* (commonly supposed to have been a tree or post, but more probably an image of the goddess Asherah),[9] and idols of stone and bronze, which were strictly prohibited in the worship of Yahweh.[10] The Israelites themselves for some time used images called teraphim, but their nature and significance are unknown.[11] The climax of the prophetic condemnation of idolatry is reached in the bitter satire of Second Isaiah.[12]

A mysterious object often mentioned in the Old Testament is the ephod.[13] In a few passages ephods are said to have been made of gold or silver and used idolatrously.[14] Elsewhere, when the context gives any indication of its nature, the ephod is a part of the priestly garments, perhaps an apron or the like supporting the breastplate or pectoral with its twelve gems.[15] It may have had a pocket for the Urim and Thummim used in casting the sacred lot (s. 14).

The most sacred object of Yahwism was the ark or chest in the inner-

---

[2] Gen. 8:20; 12:7 f.; 13:18; 22:9; 26:25; 33:20; 35:1, 3, 7; Ex. 17:15; 24:4–6.

[3] Ju. 6:26; 1 S. 7:17.

[4] 1 S. 14:33.

[5] Ex. 20:24 f.; cp. Dt. 27:5 f.; Josh. 8:31.

[6] Ex. 27:1–7; 30:1–3.

[7] 1 K. 6:20–22; cp. ch. 8:64; Ezra 3:2 f.; cp. Ezek. 43:13–17.

[8] Dt. 16:22; Ho. 3:4; 10:1 f.; 2 K. 23:14; cp. Gen. 28:18–22; 31:45, 51 f.; Ex. 24:4.

[9] Ex. 34:13; Dt. 7:5; 12:3; 16:21; Ju. 3:7; 6:25–30; 1 K. 14:15; 16:33; 2 K. 13:6; 17:10, 16; 18:4; Jer. 2:27.

[10] Gen. 35:2, 4; Ex. 20:4–6; 32; but cp. Ju. 17:2–4; 1 K. 12:28 f.; 2 K. 10:29; 17:16; Ho. 8:5 f.

[11] Gen. 31:19, 30–35; Ju. 17:5; 18:14–20; 1 S. 19:11–17; Ho. 3:4.

[12] Is. 40:18–23; 41:6 f.; 44:9–20; 46:1–7.

[13] Ex. 25:7, and often; Lev. 8:7; 1 S. 2:18, and often; 2 S. 6:14; Ho. 3:4.

[14] Ju. 8:24–27; 17:5; 18:14–20; cp. 1 S. 21:9.

[15] See especially Ex. 28:6–12.

most shrine of the tabernacle and temple.[16] It was destroyed when Jerusalem fell to the Babylonians in 586 B.C., and the second temple had no ark. The significance of the ark is obscure, having evidently undergone some reinterpretation in the course of Israel's history. Alongside the tradition that it contained only the tables of the law [17] there is another to the effect that it contained also the pot of manna and Aaron's rod.[18] Upon it was the *kapporeth* (" mercy seat "; cp. s. 75), with the cherubim.[19] In general the ark represented the presence of God in the sanctuary.

Various other objects and sacred vessels used in the tabernacle and temple require no discussion here.[20]

[16] Ex. 25:10–22; 37:1–9; Num. 10:33, 35 f.; Josh., chs. 3; 8:33; Ju. 20:27; I S. 3:3; 4:1 to 7:2; 14:18; 2 S., chs. 6; 15:24–29; I K. 3:15; 6:19; 8:1–21; Ps. 132:8; Jer. 3:16.

[17] I K. 8:9; cp. Ex. 25:16, 21; Dt. 10:5.

[18] Heb. 9:4; cp. Ex. 16:33; Num. 17:10.

[19] Ex. 25:20; I K. 6:27; cp. s. 42.

[20] Ex., ch. 25; I K., chs. 6 f.; 2 K. 23:4–14; 25:13–17; Jer. 27:16–22; 28:3–6; Dan. 1:2; 5:2 f.; Ezra 1:7 ff.; 5:14 f.; 6:5; Neh. 10:37–39; 13:5, 9.

XVI

CHRISTIAN SERVICE

101. *Religious Education*

The preservation of continuity and the prevention of a loss of the spiritual heritage of the church require that both children and new converts be instructed and trained in Christian truth and life. For this both Old and New Testaments afford many precedents, some of which may be briefly indicated.

In Dt. 4:9 f.; 6:7; 11:19, the importance of teaching children in the home the religious traditions and observances of Isreal is stressed. An educational responsibility is laid also upon the priests and Levites, including not only ritual but the whole law.[1] The function of the wisdom teachers, often represented as parental instruction and hardly distinguishable from it, is illustrated throughout Proverbs and Ecclesiastes (s. 88).

The ministry of Jesus was in large part that of a teacher (s. 29). His love for children may be recalled in this connection.[2] The apostles also both preached and taught, and teaching was one of the gifts of the Spirit (s. 89). Paul, indeed, exhorts all Christians to teach and admonish one another.[3] The pastoral epistles include teaching among the duties of church officials.[4] The influence of a devout grandmother and mother is recognized in 2 Tim. 1:5.

We have seen (s. 56) that the very word *torah* means literally "teaching." This is true also of our word "doctrine" and the Greek words *didaskalia* and *didache*. At the end of the New Testament period, as we may infer from the pastoral epistles, orthodox doctrine was coming to be the main content of Christian teaching, but it had not always been so and was never so entirely. The process that led in this direction

---

[1] Lev. 10:11; cp. 1 S. 12:23; 2 Chr. 15:3; also Dt. 31:9–13; Neh., ch. 8.
[2] Mk. 9:35–37, 42; 10:13–16.
[3] Col. 3:16.
[4] 1 Tim. 3:2; 2 Tim. 2:24; cp. Heb. 5:12.

cannot be reviewed here; in fact, sufficient evidence to trace it in detail is not available. The teaching of the apostles [5] was probably concerned chiefly with the Messianic interpretation of the Old Testament and with the words and deeds of Jesus. The latter were used both as proof of his Messiahship and as examples and guidance for the Christian life. That much we may infer from the nature of the material preserved in the gospels and the way it is presented; indeed, we undoubtedly owe the preservation of this material largely to the practical use of Jesus' acts and teaching in the church, including, of course, evangelistic preaching as well as religious education. An interest in church organization and discipline appears in Matthew along with doctrinal and moral instruction as motives for the use of Jesus' sayings (s. 51).

Religious education deals with those who are already Christians and their children. That a person may be born a Christian and brought up to recognize himself as such without a definite experience of conversion is a contention which, however sound it may be intrinsically, can be supported more easily from the Old Testament than from the New (ss. 77, 80). Hereditary membership in the people of the covenant is not a New Testament idea. Properly qualified, however, it has still much significance. The conditions of salvation as we have reviewed them in ss. 75–80 make it plain that the aims of religious education must include confronting the individual with the necessity of a conscious choice and decision for himself. Once the decision has been made, religious education must stimulate and guide the execution of the Christian's life purpose.

102. *Evangelism and Missions*

The first kind of Christian work suggested by the commission of the twelve in Mk. 3:14 f. is preaching — literally, " proclaiming " or " heralding," i.e., carrying on Jesus' own work of proclaiming the good news of the kingdom of God and calling for repentance and faith. As we have seen (s. 83), this is the basis of the other word for preaching in the New Testament, from which our English word " evangelize " is derived, meaning literally " telling good news." An evangelistic mission of the twelve is described in Mk. 6:7–13 and parallels; in Mt. 10:5 f. it is explicitly limited to Israel. Luke connects some of the same material with a mission of " seventy others," [1] not mentioned by Mark or Matthew

[5] Acts 5:42.

[1] Lk. 10:1 ff.

and doubtless an expression of the special interest in the Gentile mission which is evident at many other points also in the gospel of Luke.

Concern for non-Israelites, or even willingness to recognize them as eligible for salvation, was not a matter of course for either Israel or the early church. When a clear distinction came to be made between the righteous and the wicked in Israel (ss. 49 f.), the implication that the righteous of other nations would be accepted and rewarded was not at once recognized. A remarkable foreshadowing of such a universalistic conception is found in Is. 19:23–25; cp. also Zp. 2:11; 3:9; and note the international outlook of Is. 2:1–4 (Mi. 4:1–5).

After the exile the struggle for existence brought about a strong emphasis on purity of blood, with a corresponding opposition to intermarriage; [2] note also the prominence of the genealogies in P and Chronicles-Ezra-Nehemiah. Individuals might be taken into the community from outside, but they were simply incorporated as members of the people of Israel.[3] Racial purity, of course, could never be more than fictitious, since Israel was of diverse origins from the beginning. The defensive, artificial nature of the emphasis on the purity of the group is apparent in the bitterness against Moab and Edom which is characteristic of post-exilic literature,[4] though a more liberal attitude also appears.[5]

Monotheism logically implies universalism; it is therefore not surprising to find a universal ideal in Second Isaiah. The repeated declaration that all peoples will see Yahweh's wondrous acts for Israel and acknowledge his power does not necessarily mean that they will become his worshipers on an equality with the chosen people; indeed, many passages suggest rather that they will merely submit and become Israel's servants.[6] At the same time the idea of a missionary function of Israel as Yahweh's servant is clearly present.[7] According to the most probable interpretation of ch. 53 (s. 30), even the suffering of Israel is a means to the salvation of other nations.

Whether Mal. 1:11 and 2:10 imply a universalistic attitude is doubtful, and the promise of Joel 2:28 probably refers only to the Jews.[8] Universalism and the missionary interest, however, appear again in the

[2] Ezra, chs. 9 f.; Neh. 13:23–27.
[3] Gen. 34:15; Ex. 12:44.
[4] Obadiah; Dt. 23:3 f.; Is., chs. 34; 63:1–6.
[5] Is. 56:3, 6 f.; Ruth.
[6] Is. 40:5; 41:5, 8–16; 51:4 f.; 52:10; also chs. 59:17–19; 60:3–7, 10–12, 14–16; 63:1–6; 66:18–20.
[7] Chs. 42:1; 48:20 f.; 49:6.
[8] Cp. Joel 3:1 f., 12, 16 f., 19 f.

magnificent satire of Jonah.[9] The popularity of the wisdom literature in the Persian and Greek periods may indicate an expanding horizon. The use of an Egyptian source in Proverbs (s. 13] may be recalled in this connection. On the other hand, Hebrew wisdom literature itself became more and more nationalized until Sirach identified wisdom with the law (s. 28). Instead of a clear tendency in postexilic times, there was evidently a dialectic tension between particularism and universalism.

Meanwhile other religions of western Asia were becoming less national in character and more individualistic. The Hellenistic period was characterized generally by individualism and cosmopolitanism. Judaism, especially in the Diaspora, developed a missionary movement which stressed monotheistic faith and high ethical ideals and simplified the ritual requirements for converts. The expression, " Ye that fear the Lord," in Ps. 115 and 135, may refer to proselytes. The conservative reaction against all such liberal tendencies appears in the legalistic emphasis, both in the priestly portions of the Old Testament and in the development of the oral law after the canonization of the Pentateuch (s. 10).

The conflict between liberalism and conservatism, cosmopolitanism and nationalism, universalism and particularism, was especially sharp in the Hellenistic period. It came to a head when Judaism for the first time endured active persecution under Antiochus Epiphanes (168 B.C.). The only apocalyptic book in the Old Testament, Daniel, appeared in this crisis. In symbolic visions it presents a scheme of history as a succession of world-empires, to be followed by a divine empire, the eternal kingdom of God (s. 64), and the interpretation given the visions shows clearly that the divine kingdom was also to be the kingdom of " the people of the saints of the Most High." [10]

Postbiblical Judaism was often intensely and bitterly nationalistic, both under persecution and also in the first flush of national triumph under the Maccabees. Some sources indicate that in the coming judgment the Gentiles would be destroyed; others look for a more or less complete conversion of the Gentiles. All assume that the Jews will still be the true sons of the kingdom; Jerusalem will be the capital of the redeemed world, and salvation will be possible for Gentiles only by conversion to Judaism.

That Jewish missionary activity continued in the Roman period is indicated by Mt. 23:15. For Gentiles dissatisfied with paganism Jewish monotheism and the high moral standards of Judaism had a strong ap-

---

[9] Note especially Jonah 4:11.   [10] Dan. 7:27.

peal. The rabbinic literature exhibits varying attitudes toward prose-lytes, but such hostility and suspicion as are expressed are based on sad experience, and when the way of the proselyte is made hard it is obviously with the purpose of making sure of his sincerity. After the destruction of the nation by the Romans and the shameful persecution of Jews when Christianity became the state religion of the empire, Judaism drew into its shell and became inhospitable to converts; but in the New Testament period the attitude was still on the whole favorable.

Jesus was a Jew and found his religious ideas in the Hebrew Scriptures. He regarded himself as sent primarily, if not exclusively, to the Jewish people, though the authenticity of such a saying as Mt. 10:5 f. is open to suspicion. The tradition of Jesus' sayings reflects the controversy in the early church regarding the admission of Gentiles, and some of the sayings may have been selected and colored, if not created, in the interest of one or the other group. The parable of the wicked husbandmen,[11] which may be authentic, indicates that Israel has been rejected as the people of God (s. 51). At the last supper Jesus recalls the idea of the new covenant; again the sayings have undoubtedly suffered some alteration, as their variant forms indicate, but the idea may well have been original (s. 75) .The preference for Gentiles expressed in the sermon at Nazareth, however, evidences Luke's special interest rather than the attitude of Jesus himself.[12]

The stories of the ten lepers,[13] the centurion's servant,[14] and the Syrophoenician woman [15] suggest that perhaps in personal dealings with Samaritans and Gentiles Jesus learned with some surprise what good and worthy people some of them were. Such experiences may have affected his attitude toward non-Israelites in general. Be that as it may, the basis upon which Jesus put participation in the kingdom of God was essentially independent of racial or national limitations and thus at least made possible the extension of the gospel to the Gentiles.

Thus, while the " great commission," which in variant forms concludes our gospels of Matthew and Mark, cannot be taken as an authentic saying of the historical Jesus, it is true to his purpose. Mt. 28:19 instructs the apostles to " make disciples " (so A.V. margin, A.S.V., and R.S.V.) of all nations; Mk. 16:15 bids them preach the gospel to every creature (A.V.) or the whole creation (A.S.V., R.S.V.).[16]

---

[11] Mk. 12:1–12, and parallels.
[12] Lk. 4:24–27.
[13] Lk. 17:11–19.

[14] Mt. 8:5–13; Lk. 7:1–10.
[15] Mk. 7:24–30; Mt. 15:21–28.
[16] See also Lk. 24:47; Acts 1:8.

The book of Acts tells how they proceeded to carry out this commission. (Acts 14:21 uses the two verbs " evangelizing " and " making disciples.") The persecution following the death of Stephen spread the gospel to other lands, leading to the Samaritan and later the Gentile mission; [17] meanwhile the problem of admitting Gentiles to the church arose in Palestine itself.[18] With Paul the distinction between Jew and Gentile is definitely and finally abolished,[19] though not without opposition.[20] Paul's conception of salvation, derived from his own experience, put the whole matter on a basis independent of the law or of anything peculiar to Judaism.

As a loyal Jew, however, Paul was troubled by the fact that the chosen people, to whom the law and the Messiah had been given, had rejected the gospel. His own preaching to Gentiles not only brought upon him criticism from more conservative Jewish Christians; it caused him personal pain also. The result of his pondering is given in Rom., chs. 9 to 11 (s. 76). He also quotes Is. 10:22 f. regarding the remnant, applying it to the church,[21] and similarly 1 K. 19:18 regarding the seven thousand left to Yahweh in the time of Elijah.[22] The idea of the fullness of the Gentiles [23] may be derived from Gen. 48:19. It is closely related to Mk. 13:10 (v.i.). A similar expression appears in Lk. 21:24 but with a different idea, resembling rather Gen. 15:16. Hoping for the final conversion of Israel, Paul warns the Gentiles not to be proud but to beware lest God cut them off as he has cut off Israel. Thus Paul makes Christianity a completely universal religion. Not Abraham's physical descendants but his spiritual descendants are the people of God and heirs of the promise.[24] Not Israel but the Christians are the elect, the saints. This outcome had already been adumbrated by John the Baptist, if he is correctly reported by Luke.[25]

For the evangelists and the remaining writers of the New Testament books the admission of Gentiles has ceased to be an issue. The synoptic eschatological discourse (s. 66) makes the evangelization of the nations prerequisite for the parousia.[26] This is an important source for the belief of the church, though not for the teaching of Jesus; as is also the " great commission " (v.s.). These and other sayings attributed to Jesus may have been originally uttered by prophets in his name (s. 87).

---

[17] Acts 8:1, 4.
[18] Acts, chs. 10 f.
[19] Rom. 3:29 f.; Gal. 3:26–28; Col. 3:11; cp. Eph., ch. 2.
[20] Acts 15:1–35; cp. Gal., ch. 2.
[21] Rom. 9:27.

[22] Rom. 11:4.
[23] Rom. 11:25.
[24] Rom. 2:28 f.; 4:9 ff.
[25] Lk. 3:8.
[26] Mk. 13:10; Mt. 24:14.

Luke's special interest in the Gentile mission has already been pointed out. In addition to the sermon in the synagogue at Nazareth [27] he has the significant addition of the guests brought in from the highways and hedges in the parable of the great supper,[28] and the whole book of Acts is primarily a story of the missionary expansion of the church. The admission of Gentiles is assumed in Rev. 7:4, 9, not to speak of the letters to the seven churches of Asia.[29] The opening verses of James and 1 Peter, though written for Christians, speak of them as the twelve tribes or sojourners of the Diaspora, as though addressing Hellenistic Jews. The pastoral epistles have a strong universalistic note.[30]

There is thus no question that the first responsibility of the church toward the rest of the world is evangelism, including what is now called foreign missions.[31] In s. 79 we have considered the importance of belief and confession for salvation. The work of evangelism and missions, as was there noted, has suffered from confusion and doubt at this point. To what was said previously we may add here that active evangelistic and missionary propaganda need not be inconsistent with a sympathetic, appreciative attitude toward other faiths or other interpretations of Christianity than our own, provided the spirit of the effort is that of free sharing, with open-minded willingness to hear and consider fairly the convictions of others. True tolerance is not indifference but readiness to be shown where we are wrong. To be sure, such tolerance is hardly biblical: the Bible is not a tolerant book. On the other hand, Christian love involves the desire to share with others what we believe is good, including such knowledge and insight as have been given to us. It involves also such respect for the intelligence and sincerity of others as will prevent bigotry.

For us everything important is summed up and made real in the person of Jesus Christ. For other peoples also, including those least attracted by our Western civilization or by our forms of organized Christianity, Jesus has a direct and strong appeal. It is therefore true that our gospel for the world is Christ himself. That is not to be taken, however, as meaning that the essence of the missionary message is Christology. Following Jesus must come before interpretation or even confession, and the best way to get men to follow him is the demonstration of his spirit in unselfish service.

---

[27] Lk. 4:16–27.
[28] Lk. 14:15–24.
[29] Rev., chs. 2 f.

[30] 1 Tim. 2:1, 4; 4:10; Titus 2:11.
[31] Cp. Ps. 51:12 f.; Mk. 1:17.

As to the content of missionary and evangelistic preaching if theological orthodoxy and unanimity are not made primary, we may say that the Christian purpose in life, the Christian spirit, commitment to Christian ends is the most urgent, desperate need of the world now as always. The church must preach for conviction of sin, to convince the world that living for unchristian, sub-Christian, and anti-Christian ends is sin, and the wages of sin is death. Materialism, secularism, nationalism, imperialism, militarism, and all other unchristian " -isms " are lanes in the broad highway that leads to destruction. And when conviction of sin and a hunger and thirst for righteousness have been aroused, the gospel of God's free gift of salvation and the way of salvation must be proclaimed in terms all men can understand, with emphasis on the commitment of heart and will rather than intellectual assent. Obviously this requires home as well as foreign missions. It requires evangelism inside the church as well as outside.

103. *Social Action*

Jesus, as we have seen, was not a social reformer or revolutionist. The use of his idea of the kingdom of God by exponents of the social gospel is now known to be based on false exegesis: man cannot " build " or " bring in " or " establish " the kingdom of God, and the kingdom is not a Christianized social order to be progressively achieved on earth (s. 73).

The teaching of the Old Testament that the nation as a whole will be saved from calamity and injustice is not taken up by the New Testament; indeed the national unit as such is not regarded as capable of salvation (s. 107). Much the same must be said regarding any hope for the salvation of society as a whole or of particular social institutions. The New Testament records no effort or concern for social reform, to say nothing of revolution. The practice of slavery, for example, is assumed and no hint of the possibility of abolishing it is given (s. 106). The New Testament has no hope of converting society or a majority of the individuals composing it, nor does it ever suggest that individuals may be saved by means of a change in the social system. Aside from Paul's hope that Israel will be saved in the end, the hope and purpose of the New Testament church is to pluck individual brands out of the burning.[1]

The reason for this is clearly the eschatological expectation and excitement of early Christianity. Paul clearly expresses this connection

[1] Am. 4:11.

with regard to slavery and marriage.[2] Jesus' lack of interest in the question of tribute to Rome [3] is doubtless to be so explained in part. The New Testament looks for a redemption of all creation, but by an eschatological, supernatural transformation, not by social and political reform.

It does not follow, however, that the church has no responsibility for social welfare and justice. The implications of biblical religion are quite the contrary. While the hope of the kingdom of God as proclaimed by Jesus was not a hope of achieving a Christian social order in this world by human effort, we must not forget that he taught his followers to pray that God's will should be done on earth. He interpreted that will in terms of love for God and man. Love for God demands doing what he wishes, which is the good of all his children. Love for man requires service. While the sharing of goods in the Jerusalem church cannot be taken as a pattern for all ages (s. 106), it is at least commendable as an effort to find social expression for the Christian spirit.

Even evangelism requires not only preaching but demonstration.[4] The Christian life is the most effective evangelism,[5] and the Christian life is the life of service. Medical and educational missions have shown in our day the evangelistic value of social service as a demonstration of the Christian spirit. The twelve were sent out by Jesus, not only to preach, but also to cast out demons and heal the sick.[6] Healing and exorcism are prominent throughout the gospels and Acts. Modern theology, embarrassed by the problem of reconciling the miracle stories with science, has failed to see their significance as demonstrating the power of the kingdom of God in the world. Their modern equivalent is social service, both remedial and preventive.

From this point of view we can appraise the concern of the Old Testament for social values. The hope of Israel's restoration in the Old Testament was not merely or even primarily nationalistic or political. Its basic motive was the demand for justice. The concern of the prophets and lawmakers of Israel for social justice will be studied in connection with the moral and social ideals of the Bible (ss. 104 ff.); here we note only the fact that justice in all social relations was basic not only in their conception of what God required but also in their hopes for the nation's future. The psalms also, in expressing confidence in the triumph of Yahweh on earth often stress his righteous judgment and the establishment

[2] 1 Cor. 7:20 f., 27, 29–31.
[3] Mk. 12:13–17; s. 107.
[4] 1 Cor. 2:4.
[5] 2 Cor. 3:2 f.
[6] Mk. 3:15.

of justice.[7] How far these psalms contemplate a just social and political order on the plane of history and how far their hope is eschatological is not clear. Eschatology itself, for that matter, while sometimes signifying the abandonment of any hope for justice in this world, is essentially an expression of the sense of injustice in the world as it is and the conviction that God is good and his justice must somewhere and somehow ultimately triumph.

Thus, while the Bible as a whole and the New Testament in particular do not explicitly teach what we call a social gospel, active effort for the good of society is involved in the gospel so long as Christians are to continue living in this world. The end is always the spiritual salvation of individual persons, apart from whom society does not exist; they must be saved, however, not as isolated units, but as members of the community of the redeemed. And beyond all human ends the goal of all the work of the church is that God's name shall be hallowed and his will done on earth as it is in heaven. This does not require universal wealth and ease; it does include basic security and health. Love for man is impossible without service.[8] Social action is necessary also to prove to the world that the Christian way of life is practicable, and that the ends it seeks and achieves are superior to those which can be gained in any other way (s. 56).

7 Ps. 22:28; 82; 85:11–13; 94:1–3; 96:10–13; 98:6–8.
8 1 Jn. 3:17.

XVII

MORAL AND SOCIAL IDEALS

104. *Bodily Health and Pleasure*

Since revelation, as presented in the Bible, is concerned first of all with God's will for man, and the Bible has more to say about what man must do than about what he must believe, biblical theology must include the ideals of human life contained in the Scriptures. While the Christian is not under the law, and the Christian life is not one of obeying specific precepts but of a free, spontaneous expression of the spirit of love (s. 56), the Christian's concern for the good of his neighbor makes him welcome help in seeing what this means specifically. Even Paul, uncompromising as he is in rejecting the authority of the law for the Christian, finds it expedient to give some moral guidance in his letters. To this end not only the demands of the prophets but even the requirements of the Pentateuchal legislation offer much that is useful, and all the more so when it is no longer regarded as a blueprint for modern society but as a source of suggestions to be examined and applied according to the needs of our own day. More significant for us than the particular prescriptions are the principles and ultimate social goals underlying the law and the prophets. This is equally true of the wisdom literature and the ethical and social teachings of the New Testament itself.

One of the basic human needs for which men the world over turn to religion is health. This is one of the rewards promised to Israel for obedience to God's law, and disease is one of the punishments for failure to keep the covenant.[1] Man's sense of helplessness and fear in times of sickness, especially before a scientific approach had given some grounds for more assurance, makes this easy to understand; and the best medical knowledge and skill of our age have not made mankind wholly able to contend with disease. Many of the psalms are appeals for deliverance

[1] Lev. 26:16; Dt. 28:21, 27, 35; Am. 4:10.

from sickness or songs of gratitude for such deliverance.[2] In some of the psalms sickness and even death are apparently regarded as the effects of sorcery and curses.[3] Job's supreme test was a loathsome disease. Length of life was one of the great desires of the normal Israelite, and the Old Testament regards it as one of the great rewards of righteousness.[4] An effective and beautiful correction of this conception is given in W. S. 4:8 f.

Health requires adequate nourishment, clothing, and shelter. Jesus tells his disciples not to worry about these, not because they are not essential, but because God knows they are needed and will provide for his people as he does for the flowers and birds.[5] Clearly this does not mean that the righteous will always have comfort and ease, or that they may parasitically rely on the labors of others and hypocritically call their attitude trust in God. Such an attitude is corrected by Paul's anticipation of a Marxian maxim in his statement to the Thessalonians, " If any will not work, neither let him eat." [6] Jesus' promise must be read with his constant warnings in mind that the Son of Man has not where to lay his head, and his followers must be willing to make any sacrifice, even of life itself, for his sake.[7] The complacent statement of a psalmist that in all his long life he has never seen the children of the righteous reduced to beggary [8] is as contrary to the teaching of Jesus as it is to human experience (cp. s. 55).

On the other hand, the Bible does not teach an ascetic attitude to the good things that God has made; they are to be received and used with thanksgiving.[9] The Lord's Prayer includes a petition for " daily " bread.[10] The Christian is not subject to laws regarding food and drink.[11] The Old Testament laws of clean and unclean foods have no force for him as divine requirements.[12] If any of them coincide with the laws of health as scientifically determined, the modern Christian will follow them for that reason, but their sanitary and hygienic values and intent have been exaggerated under the influence of an apologetic interest.

The Son of Man himself, unlike John the Baptist, came eating and drinking, sharing so freely and naturally the normal pleasures of the table with high and low that his enemies called him not only a friend of

---

[2] Cp. Ps. 30; 38; 41; 88; 102; 116; though the reference to sickness is not equally certain in all these cases.

[3] Ps. 6; 56; 64; 109; 140.

[4] Ex. 20:12; Prov. 10:27; Job 42:16 f.

[5] Mt. 6:25-34.

[6] 2 Th. 3:10; cp. s. 106.

[7] Lk. 9:58; Mk. 8:34.

[8] Ps. 37:25.

[9] 1 Tim. 4:3-5.

[10] Mt. 6:11.

[11] Col. 2:16.

[12] Mk. 7:14 ff.; Acts 10:15.

tax collectors and sinners but even a glutton and tippler.[13] The obvious exaggeration of this coarse and prejudiced accusation should not be allowed to obscure the important fact that Jesus was anything but an ascetic. The strange notion that he could have been associated with the Essenes (s. 52) finds here sufficient refutation.

According to the fourth gospel Jesus even, as his first " sign," changed water to wine at a wedding feast.[14] There is certainly no indication in any of the gospels that he ever opposed the use of wine. At his last meal with his disciples, as doubtless throughout their association together, he gave them bread and wine, making the act this time a solemn symbol of his impending death. The practice of substituting unfermented grape juice for the wine in the celebration of the sacrament, harmless and perhaps commendable as it may be, cannot claim any Scriptural basis. Throughout the Bible the use of wine is taken for granted. Timothy is even instructed not to drink water exclusively but to drink a little wine for the sake of his health,[15] unquestionably a wise bit of advice in the ancient Mediterranean world, as in many parts of the world to this day, where it is not safe to drink water without boiling it.

It has been remarked with wondering surprise that many Fundamentalists in the United States are prohibitionists and many prohibitionists are Fundamentalists, whereas on the basis of a consistent Fundamentalist exegesis prohibition can hardly be justified. Apologetic efforts to make some of the Hebrew and Greek words for wine mean something other than wine are futile, if not dishonest. Jotham's reference to " new wine which cheers God and man "[16] may perhaps be ascribed to Canaanite influence, but this can hardly be said of Ps. 104:15. The renunciation of wine and strong drink by the Nazirites (s. 52) no more implies a sweeping condemnation of alcoholic beverages than their long hair implies a basic religious scruple against the use of the razor.[17] Both were forms of special self-denial indicating special consecration. The refusal of the Rechabites (s. 52) to drink wine or cultivate vineyards is to be understood, along with their refusal to build houses or live in them, as an expression of opposition to civilization in general, as exemplified by the Canaanites. For those who have thrown off the fetters of legalism, of course, the question of prohibition or of total abstinence is not to be decided on the basis of exegesis but on the

---

[13] Mt. 11:19; Lk. 7:34.
[14] Jn. 2:1–11.
[15] 1 Tim. 5:23.

[16] Ju. 9:13.
[17] Cp. Num. 6:20.

basis of social welfare and scientific evidence on all the questions involved.

Certainly the Bible does not condone drunkenness or gluttony. He who makes his own belly his god is justly condemned.[18] The prophetic books and the wisdom literature of the Old Testament abound in bitter, scornful castigation of the drunkard,[19] though in one remarkable instance some sympathy is expressed for the wretch driven to drink by poverty and misery.[20] If there is relatively less on this subject in the New Testament than in the Old, it is only because this particular vice was relatively less prominent in the social environment of the apostolic age. The New Testament is by no means lacking in condemnations of drunkenness.[21]

The subject of physical pleasures in general recalls what has already been said in s. 44 regarding man's body and flesh. As was shown in that connection, even Paul's designation of the sinful lower nature of man as " flesh " does not imply the conception of the physical aspect of human life as essentially evil. As for Jesus' attitude, there is good ground for the statement of Henry Drummond that Jesus was less severe toward sins of the flesh than toward sins of the disposition.[22] In brief, the moral teaching of the New Testament is not ascetic (cp. s. 105). Perhaps the nearest approach to an ascetic, dualistic contempt for the flesh as such is the association of the flesh with the world and sin in 1 John,[23] but this book is at the same time the one that insists most strongly on the necessity of acknowledging that Christ came " in the flesh." [24]

Fasting is often mentioned in the Old Testament, not as a regular ascetic practice, but as an expression of sorrow or repentance or in connection with prayer and sacrifice, especially in times of dire calamity.[25] Formal fasting for selfish ends is denounced by Second Isaiah, who declares that the fasting God wants is undoing burdens and freeing the oppressed.[26]

---

18 Phil. 3:19; cp. 1 Cor. 6:13.
19 Prov. 20:1; 21:17; 23:20 f., 29–35; Eccl. 10:17; Is. 5:11, 22; 28:1–8; Am. 6:6; Hab. 2:5.
20 Prov. 31:6 f.
21 Mt. 24:49; Lk. 12:45; Rom. 13:13; Gal. 5:21; Eph. 5:18; 1 P. 4:3.
22 " The Greatest Thing in the World," *Addresses* (1893), p. 43.
23 1 Jn. 2:15–17.
24 Ch. 4:2 f.; cp. 2 Jn. 7.
25 Ju. 20:26; 1 S. 7:6; 31:13; 2 S. 1:12; 12:15–23; 1 K. 21:27; Ezra 8:21, 23; Neh. 1:4; Est. 4:16; Joel 1:14; 2:15; Jonah 3:5.
26 Is. 58:3–6; cp. Jer. 14:12; Zc. 7:5 f.

Jesus is said to have fasted forty days at the time of his temptation.[27] He tells his disciples to do their fasting in secret.[28] Unlike the disciples of John the Baptist, however, Jesus' disciples did not fast, and he defended them on the ground that a bridegroom's party would not fast while he was with them, adding that they would fast when the bridegroom was taken from them.[29] In the church at Antioch fasting as well as prayer preceded the selection of Paul and Barnabas for their mission.[30] Throughout the Bible it is clear that fasting is not commended as a means of mortifying the flesh but as an exceptional act of self-denial, closely related to sacrifice in its motives.

The pursuit of pleasure for its own sake is repeatedly condemned, especially in the New Testament.[31] Biblical religion, however, is by no means a sad affair. At the creation Wisdom rejoiced, the stars sang, and all the sons of God shouted for joy.[32] In God's presence there is fullness of joy,[33] and a contrite psalmist prays God to restore to him the joy of salvation.[34] The psalms abound in exhortations to rejoice in the Lord and shout for joy.[35] The anointed prophet of Is., ch. 61, recognizes it as part of his mission to give " the oil of joy for mourning." [36] The gospel and epistles of John emphasize the joy of Christ, which he gives to his disciples.[37] Jesus endured the Cross for the joy that was set before him, says the epistle to the Hebrews.[38] We have already noted (s. 83) the fact that joy was one of the fruits of the Spirit characteristic of the life of the early church.[39]

With this spirit of radiant joy, even under persecution and in the face of all the hosts of evil, goes the fact that there is more humor in the Bible than is commonly recognized. While Ecclesiastes scorns laughter and mirth,[40] and the epistle to the Ephesians puts jesting in the same

---

[27] Mt. 4:2; Lk. 4:2.
[28] Mt. 6:16 f.
[29] Mk. 2:18–20, and parallels.
[30] Acts 13:2 f.
[31] Is. 47:8; 1 Tim. 5:6; 2 Tim. 3:4; Titus 3:3; Heb. 11:25; Jas. 5:5; 2 P. 2:13.
[32] Prov. 8:30 f.; Job 38:7.
[33] Ps. 16:11.
[34] Ps. 51:12.
[35] Ps. 5:11; 32:11; 35:9, 27; 63:5; 65:13; 66:1; 67:4; 95:1 f.; 96:12; 98:4, 6, 8; 100:1; 113:9; 132:9, 16; 149:2, 5; cp. Is. 49:13; 56:7; 61:10.
[36] Is. 61:3.
[37] Jn. 15:11; 16:20, 24; 17:13; 1 Jn. 1:4; 2 Jn. 12.
[38] Heb. 12:2.
[39] Acts 13:52; 15:3; Rom. 14:17; 15:13; Gal. 5:22; Phil. 1:25; 4:4; 1 Th. 1:6; Heb. 10:34; 1 P. 1:8; Jude 24.
[40] Eccl. 2:2; 3:4; 7:3.

category as filthiness and foolish talking,[41] other parts of the Bible show a less severe attitude. The Old Testament as a whole cannot be called a lighthearted book; its theme is too serious for that. There are light touches now and then, however, and one whole book, the book of Jonah, is pervaded by a delicious spirit of satirical ridicule which must have made its first readers laugh with glee. With a consummate deftness of touch, the author makes Jonah himself and the spirit of exclusive pride he represents thoroughly absurd. The finest humor in the Bible, however, appears in the characteristically Semitic hyperbole of some of Jesus' parables and metaphors.[42] Pedestrian exegesis has done its best to spoil this element in Jesus' teaching, but one who appreciates it can well understand how the great masses of his people must have heard him with delight.[43]

The interest of modern religious workers in recreation is not easily supported by Scriptural precedents. While the Hebrews undoubtedly had their games as other peoples do, the writers of the Old Testament evince no great interest in this phase of the nation's life. What was called playing on one occasion, perhaps with deliberate irony, was very rough sport indeed.[44] But one of the psalmists believed that the Lord was not wholly averse to the spirit of play, for had he not made the leviathan to play in the sea? [45] In the glorious future foreseen by some of the prophets a little child would play safely over the hole of an asp,[46] and the streets of the holy city would be full of boys and girls playing.[47] Jesus had watched children playing and with telling effect used their occasional peevishness to characterize the critical attitude of his contemporaries.[48] Athletic contests are often used in the Bible to illustrate religious ideas, especially in the epistles of the New Testament, which were addressed to people familiar with the Greek races and other sports.[49] A form of recreation frequently mentioned in the Bible is dancing. It is never condemned; in fact, it is often referred to as a form of worship (s. 95).[50]

41 Eph. 5:4.
42 Mt. 5:15; 7:3–5; 23:24 f.; Mk. 10:25.
43 Mk. 12:37.
44 2 S. 2:14.
45 Ps. 104:26.
46 Is. 11:8.
47 Zc. 8:5.
48 Mt. 11:17; Lk. 7:32.
49 Ps. 19:5; 1 Cor. 9:24–26; Gal. 2:2; 5:7; Phil. 2:16; 2 Tim. 2:5; 4:7 f.; Heb. 12:1.
50 Ex. 15:20; Ju. 21:16–23; 1 S. 18:6; 2 S. 6:14; Job 21:11; Ps. 30:11; 149:3; 150:4; Jer. 31:13; Lam. 5:15; Mt. 11:17 (Lk. 7:32); Lk. 15:25.

A word may be added here, though perhaps it is not strictly in order, concerning aesthetic forms of enjoyment. The Hebrews were not without a normal appreciation of beauty in women [51] and in men.[52] The psalms express pride in the beauty of Zion.[53] An association of beauty with goodness appears in the expression " the beauty of holiness " (or " holy beauty ").[54] Such appreciative references to beauty are not in evidence in the New Testament, yet Jesus' reference to the lilies as surpassing Solomon in glory shows a keen sense of beauty in nature.[55]

The cultivation of the plastic arts in Israel was hindered by the abhorrence of idolatry, yet skillful work in carving, metal work, embroidery, and the like was gladly utilized in the construction and equipment of the tabernacle and temple, and the ability to do such work was regarded as a divine gift.[56] The use of music in worship has already been considered (s. 95). References to what may be called secular music occur occasionally.[57] Literary beauty is abundantly manifest in the Bible itself, perhaps all the more so because the books were not written for aesthetic enjoyment, and the art in their composition was spontaneous and largely unconscious. The Bible as a whole is too much concerned with matters of deadly seriousness and urgency to give much encouragement for the leisurely cultivation and enjoyment of the arts. With security, peace, justice, and brotherly love established and assured, the delights of culture could be more fully enjoyed, not by a favored few but by all the people. With this the whole spirit of the Bible would be in hearty accord.

105. Sex, Marriage, and the Family

The treatment of various social relationships in this and the following sections will necessarily be largely historical. Its purpose will be to promote a correct understanding of what is found on these subjects in the Bible and so facilitate its application to our own needs. Such a study should also aid in the attainment of a true historical perspective for judging present situations and meeting present needs.

[51] Gen. 24:16; 29:17; 1 S. 25:3; Est. 2:7; S.S. 1:8; 5:9; 6:1, 4, 10; 7:1-7; but cp. Prov. 6:25; 11:22.
[52] 1 S. 16:12; 2 S. 14:25.
[53] Ps. 48:2; 50:2.
[54] 1 Chr. 16:29; 2 Chr. 20:21; Ps. 29:2; 96:9; 110:3 (all A.V.; cp. A.S.V. for a different interpretation).
[55] Mt. 6:28 f.
[56] Ex. 31:1-11; cp. s. 13.
[57] Is. 5:1; Ezek. 33:32.

In ancient Israel the family was the basic social unit (s. 50). In the early periods this meant the clan rather than the immediate family of husband, wife (or wives), and children. The organization of society was patriarchal.[1] Hebrew conceptions of marriage, the relations of parents and children, and everything connected with the family grew out of this patriarchal form of society. The social basis of marriage was the perpetuation of the family. Gen. 1:28 makes the command to be fruitful and multiply the first commandment of God to man. In later Judaism this commandment remains basic: failure to fulfill it, the rabbis say, is equivalent to homicide.

The Hebrews always valued highly having large families. Childlessness was felt to be one of the worst signs of divine displeasure.[2] The New Testament not only gives no promise of such blessings to the righteous but even warns that following Jesus may mean the sacrifice of all family relationships.[3] How far this fact is bound up with the special situation in Jesus' lifetime, as it plainly is with Paul (s. 103), is not entirely clear.

The Hebrew conception of the purpose of marriage makes it more a concern of the family than of the individual. It is a transaction between families rather than individuals; [4] hence it is arranged by the parents, though some choice is allowed to the young man or woman concerned. The form of the marriage arrangement is therefore that of a covenant between the families of the bridegroom and the bride, brought about and sealed by the presentation of gifts, especially a gift from the bridegroom or his father to the father of the bride. The obvious resemblance between this practice and the acquisition of property by paying a price for it accounts for the common but inaccurate idea that Hebrew marriage was marriage by purchase.

The contrasts between this ancient Oriental conception of marriage and ours should not blind us to the corrections it may suggest for present ideas and practices. Marriage is not an affair of two individuals only, but of their families and of society at large. It has economic as well as social implications and responsibilities. Having children is not the concern of the parents alone. The value placed by the Old Testament on large families throws into relief the modern tendency to avoid or postpone having children. A return to the attitudes and practices of

1 Gen., chs. 13 f.; 46.
2 Gen. 20:17 f.; Job 1:2; 42:13-15; Ps. 127:3-5; 128:3.
3 Mk. 3:31-35; Mt. 10:34-37; 19:10-12; Lk. 12:51-53; 14:26.
4 Gen., chs. 24; 29; 31.

ancient Israel under modern social conditions would not be desirable, nor is unrestricted and irresponsible parenthood to be commended. A greater realization of social responsibility in marriage and parenthood, however, is much needed.

The primacy of the family and the patriarchal organization of society explain many characteristic Hebrew customs and institutions. Polygamy is taken for granted throughout the Old Testament. It was never actually outlawed in later Judaism, though it gradually became less common. By New Testament times monogamy seems to have become the normal type of Jewish marriage. The dangers of polygamy are already recognized in the Old Testament. Dt. 21:15–17, like many Babylonian marriage contracts, guards against favoritism. The unromantic attitude involved in polygamy comes to startling expression in 1 S. 25:42 f., a sad anticlimax for the modern reader. David's family affairs in the latter part of his life afford typical instances of the disadvantages of polygamy.[5] Against this general background it is a striking fact that the creation stories of Genesis seem to contemplate monogamy as the normal form of marriage. Mal. 2:14 f. apparently presupposes monogamy also, as does the description of the ideal Hebrew wife in Prov., ch. 31. The New Testament throughout takes monogamy for granted.

The historical literature of the Old Testament recognizes concubinage as a common practice, though the law codes do not sanction it. In polygamy there was some gradation in the status and rights of a man's wives, and the concubine occupied a place between that of a wife and that of a slave. If concubinage had any social basis, instead of being merely a matter of personal indulgence on the part of those wealthy enough to afford it, the basis was still the perpetuation of the family.

Various other means to this end were legally recognized and socially approved. A barren wife might give her maid to her husband and adopt the child as her own,[6] a practice known among other peoples also. A man with no son to succeed him might take a husband for his daughter into his own family instead of giving the daughter to her husband's family.[7] This was a recognized form of marriage in Babylonia. Once in the Old Testament we read of a man who gave his daughter to one of his slaves to get a son.[8] So great was the importance attached to the preservation of the name that if a man died without leaving a son the law required a levirate marriage.[9] The argument of the Sadducees against

---

[5] 2 S., chs. 13 ff. [7] Gen., ch. 29. [9] Dt. 25:5–10; cp. Gen., ch. 38.
[6] Gen., chs. 16; 30. [8] 1 Chr. 2:34 f.

the resurrection of the dead in Mk., ch. 12, is based on this institution. The story of Ruth attests what was apparently an earlier custom, requiring not merely the husband's brother but any near male relative to beget a son for the dead husband.

Hebrew standards of chastity and marital fidelity naturally followed the basic conception of marriage. Adultery was strongly condemned; [10] in fact it was a capital offense.[11] Virginity was demanded of the bride; rape or seduction of an unmarried girl was punished, a betrothed girl being regarded as married.[12] Questions of property rights were clearly involved in these laws, e.g., the father's right to a normal marriage gift for his daughter, which he could not expect if she was not a virgin. For the man there was no such strict requirement of chastity.

The common practice of prostitution is frankly recognized throughout the Bible. In Gen., ch. 38, it is not even condemned, but is as casually taken for granted as in modern fiction. Usually, however, it is denounced as contrary to the law of God. Contact with the Canaanites had made the Hebrews acquainted with religious prostitution, a characteristic feature of Canaanite as of Babylonian religion, frequently mentioned in the Old Testament (s. 25). There were male prostitutes [13] as well as female. That Hosea's wife was a cult-prostitute is possible, but the tendency to see references to this institution everywhere in the Old Testament has sometimes gone to extremes.

Common commercial prostitution also is recognized even in very early times.[14] That it became very common in the Greek period is indicated by the frequent warnings against it in the book of Proverbs. Greek trade in boys and girls is mentioned in Joel 3:3. The prevalence of this evil in New Testament times is shown by the frequent references to harlots in the gospels, usually together with the despised tax collectors. Jesus says that the harlots and tax collectors are going into the kingdom of God ahead of the religious leaders.[15] This does not condone their sin; it shows Jesus' readiness to recognize sincere repentance wherever he found it, and his sympathy with wretched people who may have been more sinned against than sinning, and in any case now hated their sin.[16] Paul expresses the Christian's disgust with prostitution on the ground

10 Ex. 20:14; Dt. 5:18.
11 Lev. 20:10; Dt. 22:22; cp. Jn. 8:1-11.
12 Dt. 22:13-21, 23-29.
13 E.VV., sodomites.
14 Gen. 34:31.
15 Mt. 21:31.
16 Cp. Lk. 7:36-50 — the parallels say nothing of the woman's being a sinner.

that our bodies belong to Christ.[17] The prevalence of other forms of sexual perversion in the Graeco-Roman world is reflected in Rom. 1:26 f.

A great difference is evident between the Old Testament and the New Testament with regard to sexual relations in general. Law codes, of course, are commonly on a much lower moral level than the ideals or even the actual practices of a people. It must be said also that on the whole the treatment of sex in the literature of the Old Testament, while quite frank, is entirely wholesome, in sharp contrast to the pseudo realism of much recent literature. Even so there is a wide gulf between the best in the Old Testament and the penetrating statement of Jesus in Mt. 5:27 f. This is one of the finest instances of the practical implications of Christian love: to the Christian man every woman is a sister, respected as a person, who cannot be treated or even thought of as a mere instrument of his advantage or pleasure. Jesus' example is even more remarkable than his teaching. His utter purity appears best of all in his complete lack of any fear of pollution or loss of reputation through association with the lowest of sinners, and in the absence of any self-consciousness in his concern for them as persons, potential children of God and citizens of the kingdom.

In this there is no ascetic distrust of the sexual instinct. Jesus says that in the resurrection there will be no marriage,[18] and in this life some may have to forego it for the sake of the kingdom; [19] in fact all family connections may have to be sacrificed.[20] All this reflects Jesus' own experience.[21] But marriage and the family are divinely decreed and sacred. This is evident particularly in Jesus' teaching regarding divorce. Deuteronomy had permitted a husband to divorce his wife for any " uncleanness " he found in her, requiring only that he should give her a certificate of divorce so that she might marry again.[22] Hasty divorce was guarded against by the condition that he could not later take her back if she had married again in the meantime. Malachi had condemned divorce.[23] Jesus repudiates the law altogether,[24] saying that Moses allowed divorce on account of the hardness of men's hearts, but God's intention was that marriage should be permanent. The exception in case of adultery which Matthew adds shows what becomes of an ideal when it is treated as legislation.

By condemning divorce altogether Jesus eliminates the question

[17] 1 Cor. 6:15.
[18] Mk. 12:25.
[19] Mt. 19:10–12.
[20] Mk. 10:28; Mt. 10:37; Lk. 14:26.
[21] Cp. Mk. 3:31–35.
[22] Dt. 24:1–4.
[23] Mal. 2:13–16.
[24] Mk. 10:11 f., and parallels; cp. Mt. 5:32.

whether a wife may divorce her husband. The Old Testament makes no provision for this, but rabbinic law accords liberal rights of divorce to the wife as well as the husband, though the latter still has greater freedom. Both the Old Testament and Judaism give the husband considerable authority over the wife, but Hebrew law does not, like Babylonian and Assyrian law, allow a man to sell his wife to pay his debts. A Hebrew husband had the right of veto over his wife's vows, as a father might veto his daughter's vows before her marriage.[25] The Hebrew wife was distinctly subordinate, but not the property of her husband. Where the tenth commandment, according to Exodus, forbids coveting a neighbor's house, wife, slaves, or cattle, Deuteronomy sets the wife distinctly apart from the property, as though to avoid any possible misunderstanding.[26]

Rabbinic law obligates the wife to obey her husband, and consigns to Gehenna a man who is guided by his wife's advice, as many doubtless were. But the husband is urged to use moderation in ruling his wife, loving her as his own body and honoring her more than his body. The New Testament presents a similar view. Paul tells wives to obey their husbands, and husbands to love their wives and not be bitter against them.[27] Women are to keep silence at church; if they want to learn anything, they must ask their husbands when they get home.[28] They are to keep their heads covered at church, and to let their hair grow long, because man is the head of woman as Christ is the head of man.[29] Marriage is not sinful, but singleness is better.[30] Paul's ideas on these subjects are of historical and psychological interest, and in part justified by the social situation of the time as well as the eschatological tension. At their worst they compare favorably with the ideas of Aristotle or Mohammed, and Paul at least said that in Christ there is neither male nor female.[31]

The general position of woman in Hebrew society was distinctly lower than that of man, though there are instances of women in high positions of influence and authority from Deborah on. Women had less economic freedom in Israel than in Babylonia, but otherwise their position was higher. Jesus treats men and women exactly alike. Paul cannot quite bring himself to this point.

The relations of children and parents in the Old Testament are dominated by the conception of obedience. Long life depends on honoring

25 Num. 30:3–16.
26 Ex. 20:17; Dt. 5:21.
27 Col. 3:18 f.; cp. Eph. 5:28 f.; 1 P. 3:1–7.
28 1 Cor. 14:34 f.

29 Ch. 11:1–16.
30 Ch. 7.
31 Gal. 3:28.

father and mother.[32] The wisdom literature as well as the law puts much stress on obedience to parents.[33] Severe punishments were imposed on disobedient children.[34] The father's authority was great; he might even sell his children as slaves.[35] But the responsibilities of parents were recognized also, especially as regards religious education and discipline.[36]

Judaism and the New Testament follow these precedents. Paul adds the interesting counsel to fathers not to provoke their children, lest the children be discouraged.[37] The highest ideal of parenthood is what is implied in Jesus' conception of God as our Father, though human fathers at best are " evil." [38]

106. *Economic Relations and Institutions*

The Old Testament is much interested in " freedom from want." Abundant rain and bountiful crops are often mentioned in this connection.[1] Disobedience is punished by deprivation of these blessings.[2] So when drought, crop failure, locust plagues, and famine occur, they are attributed to the wrath of God.[3]

The Old Testament laws reflect a simple, democratic economy on an agricultural basis. The historical and prophetic books reveal increasing complications and difficulties, caused largely by commercial expansion. The Canaanites had been great traders; their prosperous commerce was interrupted by the Israelite and Philistine invasions, but Solomon revived it, being aided by the improved means of transportation afforded by the introduction of the camel. Excavation, especially at Ezion-Geber, confirms the biblical account of Solomon's commercial exploits.[4] The visit of the queen of Sheba was probably motivated by economic considerations rather than mere curiosity.[5] The result of this development was much wealth for the few, and therefore a greater difference between rich and poor than had obtained previously. Luxury, materialism and secularism, intemperance, and the oppression of the poor by the

---

[32] Ex. 20:12; Dt. 5:16; cp. Mk., ch. 7.
[33] Prov. 1:8; 4:1; 20:20; 23:22.
[34] Ex. 21:15, 17; Lev. 20:9; Dt. 21:18–21; 27:16.
[35] Ex. 21:7–11; cp. 2 K. 4:1; Neh. 5:5.
[36] Dt. 6:6–9, 20–25; cp. Prov. 13:22, 24; 17:6; 19:18; 20:7; 22:6; 27:5.
[37] Col. 3:20 f.; cp. Eph. 6:1–4.
[38] Mt. 7:9–11.
[1] Lev. 26:3–5, 10; Dt. 28:3–5, 8, 11 f.
[2] Lev. 26:19 f., 26; Dt. 28:16–18, 23 f., 38–40, 42.
[3] Am. 4:6–9; Hg. 1:5 f., 9–11; 2:15–19; Mal. 3:10 f.; Joel, chs. 1; 2:12–14.
[4] 1 K. 9:26–28; 10:11, 14 f., 26–29.
[5] Ch. 10:1–10, 13.

rich were the natural consequences. All this is vividly reflected in the bitter invectives of the prophets from Amos on, continuing the tradition of championship of the poor already notable in Nathan and Elijah.[6]

The old Israelite conception of wealth as a reward of righteousness and of poverty as punishment for sin now gives way more and more to a recognition of the perils of wealth and the superiority of spiritual and moral values, as may be seen on almost any page of the prophetic books and the wisdom literature. The general assumption that prosperity is a sign of divine favor and poverty a punishment, however, remains basic in the wisdom literature.[7] In s. 25 we have seen how this put a strain on Israel's faith in God and how the problem was met. The New Testament does not promise prosperity to the righteous nor threaten the wicked with want. Even Mk. 10:29 f. adds " with persecution " to its promise, which the whole context prevents us from taking literally. Luke's form of the beatitudes promises wealth to the poor and poverty to the wealthy,[8] but the reference is to the coming age (s. 72). In Mt. 6:25–34 Jesus says that his disciples need not worry about food, drink, and clothing, but we have seen that this does not do away with the necessity of sacrifice (s. 104). Paul says flatly that the kingdom of God is not eating and drinking.[9] He himself has learned to be content with either abundance or want.[10] While the conception of poverty as meritorious in itself begins to appear in the New Testament, it is not the original or prevailing idea. Jesus exposes the dangers of wealth, however, and the necessity of putting God first: a man cannot serve both God and Mammon.[11]

The fact that Jesus made no effort to improve economic conditions has been previously noted (s. 103). It is explained in part, as we saw, by his eschatological expectation, but it is due even more to his dominant concern for spiritual values.[12] His understanding and sympathy, however, undoubtedly made him keenly aware of the economic distress of his people; [13] indeed, the temptation to make bread out of stones may symbolize an impulse to devote himself to the alleviation of want.[14] He

---

6 2 S. 12:1–4; 1 K. 21:17 ff.
7 Prov. 13:21, 25; 14:11; Ps. 1; Job 1:1–3; 42:12–17.
8 Lk. 6:20 f., 24 f.
9 Rom. 14:17.
10 Phil. 4:11 f.
11 Mt. 6:19–24; Mk. 4:19; Lk. 12:33 f.; 16:13.
12 Mt. 4:3 f.; Lk. 4:3 f.
13 Mk. 8:2 f.
14 Mt. 4:3; Lk. 4:3.

expected his followers to give to the needy.[15] The statement, " Ye have the poor always with you," [16] is neither an expression of lack of concern for poverty nor an assertion that it is permanent and necessary, but a rebuke to Judas' hypocrisy.

The provisions of the Old Testament laws for economic welfare cannot be considered here in detail, but a few may be selected to indicate the basic attitudes involved. Incidentally we may note that the Hebrew language has two words for " property ": one is the common word for " work "; the other means both " creation " and " acquisition." In the English versions the second word is often translated " cattle," and of course the primary form of wealth in nomadic and seminomadic life is livestock.[17] The early laws include regulations regarding damages to animals [18] and damages to persons by animals.[19] Stray animals must be restored to their owners and overloaded donkeys relieved of their burdens.[20] In the Book of the Covenant the sabbath law is given a humane motivation.[21]

Personal property is guarded by laws regarding deposits,[22] loans, pledges, and interest,[23] and theft.[24] A religious sanction is explicitly attached to many of these laws; to that extent the Old Testament sanctifies the right of private property.

Many interesting institutions and developments appear with regard to the ownership of land. In early seminomadic life what was involved in the use of land was access to water and pasture, with only rudimentary agriculture in a subordinate position.[25] The nomad's contempt for settled life comes to expression in Gen. 4:1–5; 2 S. 7:1–7. It survived among the Rechabites [26] down to the last days of the kingdom of Judah.

But the possession of the promised land was an important item in the covenant; at least it was so regarded when Israel later looked back on the conquest. This involved settled agricultural and village life. Own-

---

15 Mt. 25:35, 40, 42, 45; Mk. 9:41.
16 Mk. 14:7, and parallels; cp. Dt. 15:11.
17 Cp. Job 1:3; 42:12.
18 Ex. 21:33–36; Lev. 24:18, 21.
19 Ex. 21:28–32.
20 Ex. 23:4 f.; Dt. 22:1–4.
21 Ex. 23:12; cp. Dt. 5:14. For other humane laws see Dt. 22:6 f.; 25:4 (cp. 1 Cor. 9:9 f.).
22 Ex. 22:7–13; Lev. 6:1–7.
23 Ex. 22:14 f., 25–27; Lev. 25:36 f.; Dt. 23:19 f.; 24:6, 10–13; cp. 2 K. 4:1; Neh. 5:1–13.
24 Ex. 20:15; 22:1–4.
25 Gen. 13:5–11; 21:25–33; 26:12–23, 32 f.
26 Jer. 35:1–10.

ership was primarily an affair of the tribe, clan, or family, yet the individual as head or representative of the family had rights and responsibilities. According to the later theory (which is more important for us than the actual procedure, expressing as it does the Israelite ideal of the times when the Old Testament was written), the land was assigned to the tribes by lot, the amount received in each case being determined by the size of the tribe.[27]

The allotment to each family was supposed to be inalienable, and permanent sale was forbidden. The religious basis for this was the conception that Yahweh was the real owner, Israel being simply his tenants.[28] Hence the laws against removing ancient landmarks.[29] Evidently this condition could not be maintained, but the ideal persisted.[30] The growth of great estates and the crowding out of the poor are attested and condemned in Is. 5:8–10; a later situation involving similar exploitation appears in Neh. 5:3–5. An effort was made to restore the balance periodically by the law of the year of jubilee.[31] Whether this was ever actually observed is doubtful, but again the ideal is significant.

The use of land was subject to the welfare of the community, including provision for the poor, for widows, and for resident aliens (who had no allotment in Israel). Their support was secured by the laws of gleaning and the like,[32] also the sabbatical year,[33] and the release of debts.[34] The Old Testament does not support the position of the owner of the vineyard in Mt. 20:15. Responsibility even to the land itself is implied by Job 31:38–40.

The general conception of ownership appears in the inheritance laws.[35] Levirate marriage (s. 105) is not merely a matter of keeping the family alive but also of keeping the property in the family. Where there are no sons, the question of inheritance in the female line arises, and this is allowed with the condition that the heiress must marry within the tribe.[36] Inheritance or at least trusteeship by a widow is presupposed by Ru. 4:3 and 2 K. 8:1–6.

---

[27] Num. 26:52–54; 33:50–56; Josh., chs. 13 ff.; cp. Ezek. 45:1–6; ch. 48.
[28] Lev. 25:23.
[29] Dt. 19:14; 27:17; cp. Prov. 23:10; Job 24:2.
[30] 1 K. 21:3.
[31] Lev. 25:8–17 — v. 10 contains the motto on the Liberty Bell.
[32] Lev. 19:9 f.; 23:22; Dt. 23:24 f.; 24:19–22; cp. Ru., ch. 2; Mk. 2:23.
[33] Ex. 23:10 f.; Lev. 25:1–7.
[34] Dt. 15:1–11; cp. Neh. 10:31.
[35] Dt. 21:15–17.
[36] Num. 27:1–11; 36:1–9.

Sale and transfer also are governed by the same basic conceptions. Vivid accounts of such transactions are given in Gen. 23:3–20 and Ru., ch. 4. Jer. 32:9–15, 43 f., attests the use of written deeds. The transaction in this instance illustrates another institution designed to keep property in the family, the institution of redemption by the near kinsman (go'el).[37] A complicated case, involving marriage and inheritance as well as redemption, is presented in Ru., ch. 4.

Among the forms of ownership recognized by Hebrew custom and law was slavery. Within Israel an effort was made to maintain social equality, and a sharp distinction was made between foreign and Hebrew slaves. The Hebrew slave was in a favored position. He could be acquired only for six years, unless at the end of that time he formally asserted his desire to remain permanently in his master's service. The law includes various regulations regarding the family relations of such slaves.[38] Foreign slaves were acquired by capture [39] or by purchase.[40] Under Solomon forced labor is found.[41]

The New Testament as well as the Old Testament takes slavery for granted. Of the two principal words translated " servant " in the New Testament the more common means literally " slave." The frequent figurative use of this word with regard to being slaves of God or Christ or of one another does not necessarily show an unquestioning acceptance of the institution, but it is never actually called in question. Paul also calls the Christian the Lord's freedman.[42] Rather severe treatment of slaves is implied by Lk. 17:7–10. Paul thinks that Christians who were slaves when they were converted should not try to gain their freedom,[43] evidently for the reason that the end of the world was coming soon; so also with marriage.[44] But Paul was convinced that slavery, like race and sex, had no bearing on a person's relation to Christ or to other Christians.[45] Hence he advised slaves to obey their masters patiently.[46] Paul's attitude in the specific case of a runaway slave whose master was a Christian appears in the epistle to Philemon. Paul respects the owner's

[37] Lev. 25:24–34.
[38] Cp. Ex. 20:10; 21:1–11, 16, 20 f., 26 f., 32; Dt. 15:12–18; 23:15 f.; 24:7; Lev. 25:39–43, 47–55; 2 K. 4:1; Neh. 5:5–8; Job 31:13–15; Jer. 34:8–16; Am. 2:6; 8:4–6.
[39] Dt. 20:10–18; Josh. 9:3–27; Ju. 1:28, 30, 33, 35.
[40] Gen. 17:12; Ex. 12:44; Lev. 25:44–46.
[41] 1 K. 5:13–17; 9:15–23.
[42] 1 Cor. 7:22.
[43] 1 Cor. 7:20–24.
[44] Vv. 29–31.
[45] Gal. 3:28.
[46] Col. 3:22 f.; cp. Eph. 6:5–8.

right and leaves to him the decision as to what he should do, though with a rather strong hint. In Eph. 6:9 masters are told to treat their slaves well, remembering that they too have a Master in heaven, and that he has no partiality. 1 Peter urges slaves to obey even cruel and unjust masters — it is in this connection that the example of Christ's patient suffering is adduced and Is., ch. 53, is applied to him.[47]

In spite of the New Testament's lack of concern to abolish slavery, which is explained by the eschatological expectation, a logical application of the Christian principle of love makes the abolition of slavery imperative. It requires also, if carried out consistently, the abolition of present forms of slavery under other names.

Regarding hired labor, the Bible has much to say. The dignity of labor is recognized, implicitly if not explicitly. The law of the sabbath, for example, while requiring rest on the seventh day, requires also labor for the other six sevenths of the week.[48] In the Old Testament hired workers are employed by men who do their own work, or at least supervise it directly,[49] not by absentee owners or corporations. The Israelite judges and the first kings were farmers and shepherds who did their own work; [50] so also were some of the prophets.[51]

Concern for the rights of laborers is frequently expressed in the Bible. Jacob complains that Laban has changed his wages ten times.[52] The law demands that wages be paid promptly, not even held overnight.[53] The purpose of the sabbatical year is to benefit not only the owner of the land but also the slaves, hired labor, and even cattle.[54] Jer. 22:13 calls down woe on him " that useth his neighbor's service without wages, and giveth him not for his work." Mal. 3:5 condemns those who " oppress the hireling in his wages." In the gospels we may note the parable of the laborers in the vineyard (Mt. 20:1–16), which does not express the principle of the minimum wage, as has been thought, but does show that Jesus had observed with sympathy the plight of the unemployed, reminding us at the same time that such evils are not entirely the product of the industrial revolution and modern capitalism. (The chief difficulty of the free worker in the ancient world was competition with slave labor.) So it is only those who *will* not work of whom Paul says that they shall not eat.[55] Employers who exploit their employees

47 1 P. 2:18–25.
48 Cp. 2 Th. 3:10.
49 Gen. 29:15; Ex. 3:1; Ru. 2:4; 3:2.
50 Ju. 6:11; 1 S. 11:5; 16:11.
51 1 K. 19:19; Am. 7:14 f.

52 Gen. 31:7, 41.
53 Dt. 24:14 f.; Lev. 19:13.
54 Lev. 25:6 f.
55 2 Th. 3:10.

are denounced in Jas. 5:1–4, quite in the vein of Old Testament prophecy.

With the increased complexity of the social order, the ancient provisions for the care of the poor (together with orphans, widows, aliens, and Levites, who are usually grouped together in Deuteronomy, Leviticus, and Numbers) now proved inadequate. Charity was still urged, but the prophets demanded fundamental justice.[56] It should be noted, however, that the prophetic ideal is not revolution, nor is any scheme of reconstruction given except in Ezek., chs. 40 to 48. What the prophets desire is the restoration of the ancient social order of Israel, of course somewhat idealized. The wisdom literature continues to exalt thrift and industriousness as the way to wealth.[57]

The New Testament follows the prophetic tradition, but with greater stress on otherworldly ends. The ideal known to us as stewardship is developed also beyond anything found in the Old Testament. Jesus' advice to the rich man to sell all his goods and give to the poor [58] seems not to have been a universal requirement for entrance to the kingdom of God, for Zacchaeus is praised when he gives half of his goods to the poor and repays fourfold what he has wrongly exacted from taxpayers.[59] What is required of all is the readiness to make *any* sacrifice for the kingdom of God. Stewardship, of course, cannot be practiced by a man who has nothing. The story of the good Samaritan is another instance showing that in this matter as in others the gospel gives no legislation but a basic attitude. The commendation of the unrighteous steward [60] is not to be explained as a rhetorical question; it is a case of Jesus' characteristic " how much more." [61] Jesus says that the children of this age are, for their generation, wiser than the children of light, who if equally wise would use their perishable wealth to win friendship, an eternal possession. The parables of the faithful and unfaithful servants [62] and the talents [63] establish the general conception of stewardship as an authentic part of Jesus' teaching. The apparent partiality for the poor in Luke [64] and James [65] is hardly more than the championship of the oppressed

---

[56] Am. 5:24; Mi. 6:8.
[57] Prov. 6:6–11; 10:4 f.; 20:13; 23:20 f.; 24:30–34.
[58] Mk. 10:17–22, and parallels.
[59] Lk. 19:8 f.
[60] Lk. 16:1–12.
[61] Cp. Mt. 7:11; Lk. 11:8 f., 13; 18:6 f.
[62] Mt. 24:44–51; Lk. 12:41–46.
[63] Mt. 25:14–30; " pounds," Lk. 19:11–28.
[64] Lk. 6:20 f., 24 f.
[65] Jas. 2:1–7; 5:1–6.

which we have seen in the Old Testament. More remarkable is the "communism" of Acts 4:32-37, but this seems not to have been imitated elsewhere, and it did not work too well in Jerusalem.[66] The basic principle of concern for the welfare and provision for the needs of all, however, is characteristic of the Bible throughout.

Economic democracy as a pattern of industrial and social organization is not to be found in the Bible, but its basis is given in the conviction of the worth and rights of every man, from peasant to king. Neither in Hebrew nor in early Christian society was the ideal ever realized: here as elsewhere the Bible sets a standard without showing its fulfillment in any human society. The principle of respect for the personality and rights of every human being as such, which the Bible clearly and emphatically teaches, is the indispensable spiritual basis of any true and enduring democracy. It is based on a clear recognition of the common nature and capacities of man, independent of race or sex or any accident of political, economic, or social status (s. 109).

107. *Political Relations*

No pattern for the organization of a Christian state can be derived from the Bible. The efforts of the Puritans to use the laws of Moses as a model for the constitution of a modern state undoubtedly contributed much of permanent value to American law and government, but they were vitiated by the fundamental fallacy of any legalistic use of the Bible. Democracy as a form of government was unknown to the ancient Hebrews, and only at second hand in such Greek cities as those of the Decapolis was it known to the Jews of Palestine in the Roman period. The limited scope of democracy under the Roman empire even in Greek territory is suggested by the episode of the riotous assembly at Ephesus in Acts, ch. 19.

Early Hebrew society was democratic in the sense that there was no hereditary nobility or royalty. The patriarchal social order (s. 105) made the elders of the clan and tribe the natural guardians of order and administrators of justice.[1] The natural leadership of Moses, under divine sanction, united and held together a group of tribes in the wilderness, but more organization proved necessary. The story of the appointment of rulers of thousands, rulers of hundreds, rulers of fifties, and

---

[66] Cp. Acts 6:1; 11:27-30; 24:17; 1 Cor. 16:1-4; 2 Cor., chs. 8 f.
[1] Gen. 14:13-16; Ju. 11:5; 1 S. 30:26.

rulers of tens [2] may be an etiological justification of a later form of organization, but it is equally possible that the arrangement was even earlier than the time of Moses. Elsewhere the word " thousand " is practically a designation of the clan.[3]

The nation originated in the federation of tribes bound together by their common covenant with Yahweh. The covenant was not formulated by a democratic process; it was rather like a constitution voluntarily promulgated by a monarch. Yet it was ratified by the people,[4] and it is possible that the accounts of its ratification reflect an annual ceremony in which the people solemnly renewed their commitment to the covenant. It is fair to say, therefore, that the biblical conception of law and government rests primarily on the divine will but also on popular consent.

After the conquest the city became the main unit of Israelite life, but it was not the feudal city-state of the Canaanites. The affairs of the community were now administered by the elders of the city (often mentioned from Dt. 19:12 to 2 K. 10:1). The congregation and the men of the city appear also as having authority. Dt. 16:18 speaks of local magistrates, but how these were appointed or elected is not stated. The subsequent development of courts and the administration of justice under the monarchy, not to mention postexilic times, make a long story which cannot be told here. Suffice it to say that judging the controversies of his people was always regarded as one of the major responsibilities of the king.[5]

National leaders do not appear after Moses and Joshua until we come to the judges. Their function and the meaning of the word " judge " have been explained in s. 60. Aside from the military function of delivering Israel from oppressors, Deborah judged Israel in the same way that Moses had done,[6] and it was in this sense that Samuel later served as judge.[7]

The monarchy originated in a military emergency.[8] Previous attempts to establish a Hebrew kingdom had proved abortive.[9] Under Saul the government differed little from that of the judges; David, however, followed foreign models in the organization of his administration, and Solomon established administrative districts without regard to the old tri-

---

[2] Ex. 18:13–26.
[3] Ju. 6:15, mg.; 1 S. 10:19.
[4] Ex. 24:3–8; Dt., ch. 27; Josh. 24:1–28.
[5] 2 S. 14:4–11; 15:2–4;.1 K., ch. 3.

[6] Ju. 4:4 f.; cp. Ex. 18:13.
[7] 1 S. 7:15–17.
[8] 1 S., ch. 11.
[9] Ju., chs. 8 f.

bal boundaries.[10] The power of the king was still limited, at least theoretically, by his subjection to the will of God, and Deuteronomy makes this a matter of being governed by the written law.[11] The Hebrew state thus becomes in effect a constitutional monarchy, though here again the constitution was not democratically formulated.

After the destruction of the kingdoms of Israel and Judah and the Babylonian exile, except for a brief period of independence under the Hasmoneans, the Jews were subject to foreign rulers and never had a real state of their own, though a considerable degree of autonomy was sometimes granted them. Civil affairs were administered by the high priest or even, at least in the case of Nehemiah, a Jewish governor. In the New Testament period Herod and his sons ruled as vassals of Rome, until the country came under the direct rule of the procurators. Some local autonomy, vested in the religious authorities, was still allowed by the Romans in matters covered by the Jewish law. Its extent and limits are illustrated by the events connected with the trial and crucifixion of Jesus.

While democracy as a form of government is neither taught nor exemplified in the Bible, there is abundant evidence of the fundamental principle and spirit of democracy. The sacredness and equality of all individuals must be recognized as equally basic for political democracy and biblical religion. The responsibility of all government for the welfare of the people finds interesting expression in the statement that David knew God had exalted him as king " for his people Israel's sake." [12] The constant championship of the common people by the prophets (*v.i.*) and their insistence that the rulers are responsible to God for the performance of their duties as shepherds of his flock [13] point in the same direction. The right of revolution was always assumed in Israel when the king proved unacceptable to God [14] or to the people.[15] In one instance even a revolution in another nation was instigated by a Hebrew prophet.[16] The slogan of the northern tribes when they seceded from the kingdom of Rehoboam [17] echoes the independent spirit of the earlier days. In short, autocracy is condemned throughout the Bible, both explicitly and implicitly. Jesus said that his disciples must not lord it over one another as the rulers of the nations did.[18] The rabbinic liter-

[10] 2 S. 8:15–18; 20:23–26; 1 K., ch. 4.
[11] Dt. 17:14 f., 18–20.
[12] 2 S. 5:12.
[13] Jer. 23:1–6; Ezek., ch. 34.
[14] 1 S. 15:23.
[15] 1 K. 12:16.
[16] 2 K. 9:1–28.
[17] 1 K. 12:16.
[18] Mk. 10:42–45.

ature made a valid use of Scripture in maintaining that tyranny is wrong because all men have a common origin, being made in the image of God. From a different but equally valid point of view, the church fathers held that since all men were sinners none was good enough to dominate his fellows.

Regarding the individual's attitude and relation to the state the Bible has very little explicit teaching, and what it has is often subjected to misinterpretation and abuse. The significance of the religious patriotism of the Old Testament (*v.i.*) for the Christian can be determined only by the importance of national security and welfare for the spiritual good of individuals. An excellent text on civic responsibility may be found in Jotham's fable.[19]

References to the state in the New Testament must be understood in the light of the contemporary situation. The lifetime of Jesus and the apostles was a time of great unrest, which culminated in the disastrous revolt against Rome in A.D. 66–70. Jewish sources of the Roman period express varying attitudes to the empire, from submission to rebellion. Under such circumstances a Christian attitude to a government of the people, by the people, and for the people could not come to expression.

Jesus clearly had no sympathy with armed revolt. The temptation to gain the kingdoms of the world by bowing to Satan is relevant here; [20] so also are the sayings regarding the use of the sword in Mt. 26:52 and Lk. 22:36. Jesus doubtless remembered the punishment visited during his boyhood upon the rebellious city of Sepphoris, only four miles from Nazareth. He knew of the Zealots, who favored armed revolt against Rome; in fact, one of his disciples was a member of this group.[21] Possibly Mt. 11:12 (Lk. 16:16) is a derogatory allusion to the Zealots, though it is impossible to recover the original form of this obscure saying.

The nearest approach to any specific teaching of Jesus on the state is his answer to the question regarding tribute to Caesar.[22] The question was an attempt to trap Jesus, and his answer was a neat evasion of the trap, not a universal proposition intended to be the basis of a Christian doctrine of the state. Its primary implication, however, seems clear

[19] Ju. 9:8–15.
[20] Mt. 4:8 f.; Lk. 4:5–7.
[21] Lk. 6:15; Acts 1:13; cp. Mk. 3:18, where " Cananaean " is a mistranslation of the Aramaic word for " Zealot."
[22] Mk. 12:13–17.

enough: Jesus is concerned with a man's relation to God, not with his relation to the Roman government. In his own ministry he endeavored to avoid political complications (s. 31). It seems ironical that he was put to death as a revolutionist,[23] yet there was some ground for fear of political unrest as a result of his teaching, because the kingdom of God whose near coming he announced meant the end of all human empires.[24]

In the rest of the New Testament the attitude to the state varies with the attitude of the state to the church. Persecution of Christians by the state begins in Acts, ch. 12, though the sanhedrin, which had some civil as well as religious authority, had been persecuting the church for some time. Paul enjoyed on the whole the protection of the Roman authorities against his Jewish opponents; naturally therefore he commended submission.[25] His eschatological hope would have prevented him in any case from taking an interest in revolutionary agitation. A similar attitude, doubtless with direct dependence on Paul, is expressed in 1 P. 2:13-17.

The insistence of the Roman authorities on emperor worship toward the end of the first century made submission impossible for the church. Only by resistance to this demand could the supremacy of spiritual values be established. A new attitude appears in Revelation: Rome is the great harlot, drunk with the blood of the saints and martyrs; [26] the empire is the beast, incarnate especially in the person of Nero.[27] Yet the book is no call to revolt; it teaches steadfast but passive resistance. Faithfulness and endurance in persecution are urged also in Hebrews and in 1 Peter, where no attempt is made to reconcile the counsel of submission in ch. 2:13-17 with the endurance of persecution urged in ch. 4:12-16.

Much in the attitude of the apostolic church to the world and the state may seem unappealing and irrelevant to us, but it has been vitally significant and terribly real to many people in Europe in recent years. The net result of our study on this point is once more that the Bible gives no code or pattern of Christian conduct in relation to the state, but instead provides a basic attitude and principle, the same which must govern all human relationships. The form of a government and the individual's relation to it must depend on what is required by devotion to

---

23 Mk. 15:26.
24 Cp. Dan. 2:44.
25 Rom. 13:1-7; cp. Mk. 12:17.

26 Rev. 17:1-6.
27 Chs. 13; 17:8 ff.; cp. s. 66.

the kingdom of God and the highest welfare of man. It is clearly implied by everything in the Bible bearing on the subject at all that the state is made for man, not man for the state.

The relations of church and state are of vital importance for our world. In Israel religion and the state were closely connected from the beginning. As we have seen, the nation originated in the religious federation of tribes consummated by Moses. Throughout the earlier periods and under the monarchy, while there were religious institutions and a priestly organization, there was no such distinction as we draw between church and state. David made Jerusalem both the political and the religious capital of the nation, bringing the ark there and making his own sons priests (s. 86). Solomon built the temple, confirming David's policy. As the people of Yahweh, Israel now had an official cultus, centered in the royal temple. The significance of this was vividly shown at the division of the kingdom by Jeroboam's adoption of the shrines of Dan and Bethel instead of Jerusalem. Judah now regarded Israel, not without justification, as apostate; the northern point of view, of course, was the opposite.[28] After the destruction of the northern kingdom Jerusalem was the unrivaled center of Yahwism, and more so than ever after the Deuteronomic reform of 621 B.C. Hence even in later visions of the future the center of the redeemed community is Jerusalem, both as the place of the temple and as the capital of the nation.[29] Officially religion was to all intents and purposes a function of government.

The close connection of Yahwism with the state tended to make Yahweh's favor for his chosen people appear to be automatic and permanent. The prophets, however, constantly stressed the conditional nature of the covenant. The monarchy had never been a complete success from the religious point of view, in spite of the theocratic ideal by which the institution was theoretically justified. The first kings had been, like the judges, possessed by the Spirit of Yahweh.[30] The idea of divine adoption was applied to the later kings (s. 33). The king was anointed in the name of Yahweh by a prophet,[31] or later by the high priest.[32] According to one tradition Saul was chosen by lot;[33] popular choice also played a part in the cases of Saul and David.[34] From Solomon on, heredity, with or without nomination by his predecessor, determined who should be king.[35] Through all these varying forms the idea of divine choice and

---

[28] Dt. 33:7.
[29] Is. 2:2 f.; 11:9; Am. 9:11.
[30] 1 S. 10:6, 10; 11:6; 16:13 f.
[31] 1 S. 9:26 to 10:1; 16:1-13.

[32] 1 K. 1:39; 2 K. 11:12.
[33] 1 S. 10:17-27.
[34] 1 S. 11:15; 2 S. 2:4; 5:3.
[35] 1 K. 1:5-53; 2 S. 7:12-16; Ps. 89:3 f., 28-37.

designation remained constant. In theory the Hebrew monarchy was always a theocracy.

From the beginning, however, this theory met with opposition. The double account of the origin of the monarchy in 1 Samuel reflects two opposite views of God's attitude toward it. The unfavorable judgment of one source [36] probably expresses later experience and reflection, but it is quite possible that conservative Israelites had much the same feeling at the time. Samuel and Saul were unable to adjust their respective ideals and ambitions.[37] Subsequent kings by their exploitation of the people aroused the opposition of the prophets, as shown by the relations of Nathan and David,[38] Ahijah and Solomon,[39] and Elijah and Ahab.[40] This prophetic opposition is reflected in the attitude of the Deuteronomic historians and legislators.[41] The responsibility of government to the people is expressed, we have seen, in 2 S. 5:12. Evil kings are freely condemned by Amos, Hosea, Isaiah, Jeremiah, and Ezekiel, and God's judgments on them are narrated in 1 and 2 Kings.

Amos denounced not only the kings but the nation itself, hurling his fierce invective against both Israel and Judah along with the surrounding nations.[42] Hosea also threatened judgment, but with more hesitation and sorrow, presenting it as discipline rather than destruction.[43] The end of the northern kingdom in 721 confirmed the threat of Amos, but Judah still felt secure. Isaiah assured Ahaz and Hezekiah that if they trusted Yahweh he would deliver them from their foes, and events signally confirmed his promise in the case of Hezekiah.[44] Micah, however, in this same period predicted the destruction of Jerusalem itself.[45] In the next century Jeremiah warned against reliance on the temple as a guarantee of national safety.[46] In 586 doom fell on Judah as it had fallen on Israel.[47]

A striking manifestation of the close connection between religion and politics during these times was the relation between national independence and religious purity. The kings of Judah who were subservient to Assyria (Ahaz, Manasseh) were syncretistic and idolatrous in religion, while those who were politically independent were also religious reform-

---

36 1 S. 8:4–22; 10:17–19.
37 1 S., ch. 15.
38 2 S. 12:7–12.
39 1 K. 11:26–40.
40 1 K., chs. 17 to 19; 21.
41 1 S. 8:10–18; Dt. 17:18–20.

42 Am. 2:4 ff.; 3:2; 9:7 f.
43 Ho. 11:8 f.; 13:16; 14:1, 4.
44 Is. 7:1–16; chs. 36 f.
45 Mi. 3:12.
46 Jer. 7:4, 11 f.; ch. 26.
47 Lam. 4:12, 20.

ers (Hezekiah, Josiah). This is in accord with the common ancient conception and practice, as shown by the recognition of a conqueror's gods by conquered kings in ancient treaties.

The prophetic interpretation of history as judgment, including even judgment on the chosen people, made Hebrew religion ultimately independent of the fortunes of the state, so that the destruction of the nation actually enhanced the power of Yahweh and led directly to the clear emergence of monotheism (s. 21). Meanwhile another idea had been introduced which made possible some hope for the future. The nation as a whole had sinned and had now been destroyed, but before this happened a distinction had been made between the wicked and the righteous within the nation, and a promise was held out to the righteous remnant (s. 50). For the nation as a whole the hope of restoration was made possible also by the conception of judgment as disciplinary and redemptive rather than merely punitive (s. 60). The prophetic books consequently have much to say of national restoration, especially after the doom of the nation is obviously inevitable or has actually fallen.

Amos, except for the doubtful possibility that a remnant may still be spared,[48] sees nothing ahead but destruction. The conclusion of the book [49] is clearly a later addition to comfort the people when the blow had fallen. Passages of promise in Hosea may well be authentic in view of his idea of judgment as redemptive.[50] The fact that some statements in Hosea imply complete destruction is to be explained by the prophet's alternation of moods due to his emotional agitation, which he takes to reflect God's own feeling.[51] Apparently what Hosea expected was not a deportation and return, but flight to other nations followed by a gradual return and rehabilitation.[52]

With Isaiah the verb " shall return " does not mean a return from exile; his idea is rather that the destruction of the nation will leave a remnant which will return to Yahweh.[53] The prediction of a return of the dispersed remnant of both Israel and Judah from all lands in ch. 11:11 f. is doubtless a postexilic interpolation. The book of Micah contains promises of restoration, again of doubtful authenticity and to be re-

[48] Am. 5:15.
[49] Ch. 9:8b–9, 11–15.
[50] So Ho. 3:4 f., except " and David their king," which must come from a scribe of Judah.
[51] Ch. 11:8 f.
[52] Ho. 7:11; 8:9; 12:1; cp. 9:3; 11:11.
[53] Is. 1:9; 10:20 f.

garded as expressing the hope of later times, but of course not less important for that reason.[54] The promise of restoration in Zephaniah is also largely, if not wholly, postexilic.[55]

Jeremiah, who most clearly foresaw the destruction of Judah, seems also to have been the first who clearly promised its restoration in the future.[56] Dt. 30:1–5 and Lev. 26:40–45 probably come from the time of the exile itself. Ezekiel, whenever written, contains a great deal concerning restoration to Palestine.[57] A great blueprint of the restored land and community is given in chs. 40 to 48, though unfortunately, like all too many idealistic blueprints, it ignores the realities of both politics and geography to such a degree as to be wholly impracticable. Second Isaiah constantly stresses the restoration of Israel to the holy land, not only from Babylonia but from all quarters, especially Egypt and the isles of the sea, though without any specific reference to political independence.[58]

Ezra tells of the return of the exiles. The restored community was evidently small, poor, and weak. Haggai and Zechariah revived the hope of independence under a Messianic prince, making Yahweh's favor depend only on the rebuilding of the temple. During the Persian period, however, the national hope almost disappeared. For many its place was taken by the ideal of a priestly theocracy. The gradual transformation of Israel from a nation to a religious community has been traced in s. 51. Disappointment and the growth of new ideas promoted hopes of a supernatural, otherworldly redemption of Israel, however, and the hope of national independence still smoldered, occasionally breaking into flame, especially during the persecution under Antiochus Epiphanes and later under the Romans, with the intervening period of actual independence under the Hasmonean kings. The Zealots of the New Testament period agitated and fought for independence from the Romans, but the rebellions of A.D. 66–70 and 132–135 were crushed. From then on Judaism could only hope for an eschatological restoration of the nation until modern Zionism revived the old political hope.

Since the New Testament puts the church in the place of Israel as the people of God (s. 51), the hope of national restoration drops out of the picture, even though some of Jesus' own disciples still cherished

---

[54] Mi. 2:12a; 4:6 f., 10; 5:2 f., 7 f.; cp. s. 31.
[55] Zp. 3:10, 12 f., 19 f.
[56] Jer. 23:1–4, 7 f.; ch. 24; 32:6–15, 36–44.
[57] Ezek. 11:15–18; 17:22–24; 34:11–15; 36:17–24, 28, 34–38; 37:1–22.
[58] Is. 35:1, 6–10; 43:5 f.; 48:20 f.; 49:8–12, 18–22; 54:1–3; 60:4, 9; 66:20.

it.[59] The object of divine solicitude is no longer the nation but the individual. Paul is still concerned for his people and believes that in the end Israel will be saved, but not necessarily as a political entity.[60] Jesus' love for his own people appears not only in such sayings as Mt. 10:6 and 15:24 (if authentic), but even more in his lament over Jerusalem.[61] That he foresaw the fate of Judah at the hands of the Romans seems quite clear.[62]

From this long history some inferences may be drawn regarding the relations of church and state. The dangers inherent in their identification or the domination of either by the other are clearly manifest. The almost ludicrously limited role of the " prince " in the reconstruction program of Ezek., chs. 44 to 46, probably reflects the resentment of the priesthood at the royal domination it suffered before the exile and its determination not to allow such a condition in the future. Biblical history repeatedly illustrates the evils of allowing the state to control religion, especially in the corruption of the priesthood and the official prophets,[63] in the persecution of Yahweh's prophets by Jezebel [64] and the persecution of the church by the Jewish and Roman authorities,[65] and in the refusal of both prophets and apostles to be perverted or silenced by the civil powers.[66] The Cross of Christ is the supreme example of a victory of Caesar over God which was turned into a victory of God over Caesar.

The evils of allowing religious institutions to control or influence government are less apparent in the Bible, because examples of such control are lacking in Hebrew history, and the abundant instances in Christian history are all later than the New Testament period. Samuel's efforts to keep Saul under control were not successful. Jehoiada's intervention in the political affairs of Judah was all to the good as far as it went.[67] It may be, however, that the corruption of the priests and prophets mentioned above was the result not only of their dependence upon the rulers for support but also in part of their power to influence the rulers. The persecution of the early church by Herod Agrippa I [68] may be attributed to his desire to please the Jewish religious authorities; in fact the crucifixion of Jesus was brought about by the political influence of the priesthood and sanhedrin (s. 109).

[59] Lk. 24:21; Acts 1:6.
[60] Rom., chs. 9 to 11.
[61] Lk. 19:41–44.
[62] Mk. 13:2, and parallels.
[63] 1 K., ch. 22; Jer. 5:30 f.
[64] 1. K. 18:4, 13.
[65] Acts, chs. 5; 12.
[66] Am. 7:10–17; Jer., ch. 26; Acts 5:29.
[67] 2 K. 11:1 to 12:2.
[68] Acts, ch. 12.

In our time the only protection against all these evils is the complete separation of church and state, except in so far as the assurance of religious freedom is a function of government. This is all the more necessary in a nation whose citizens belong not to one but to many religions. Hence tolerance is indispensable in any state which can rightly claim Christian approval — tolerance of error as well as tolerance of truth, since each individual and group must be allowed to decide for itself what is truth or error. The fact that the separation of church and state involves an impoverishment of public education must be recognized, and the churches must find a solution for this urgent problem, but the independence of both religion and government must not be compromised.

The separation of church and state does not release the church from its prophetic responsibility to subject all human actions and institutions to judgment according to the will of God. Moral and social issues must be fearlessly brought home to the consciences of citizens and rulers. Direct political action by any church, however, is both a threat to freedom and a sure way to corrupt and secularize the church itself.

108. *International Relations: the Use of Force*

One of the oldest and most fundamental functions of the state is to achieve and maintain security. Prominent among the blessings expected by Israel as a reward of fidelity to the covenant was political and military security, deliverance from enemies and victory over them, " freedom from fear." Yahweh's judgments on Israel's enemies (s. 60) showed his power and his fidelity to the covenant and constituted the first great reward of obedience.[1]

The safety and welfare of the nation of course include the individual citizen's security and opportunity to live his life without fear. Some elements in the promises and warnings addressed to the nation in connection with the covenant are specifically directed to the individual.[2] The value of security to the individual citizen is stressed in a characteristic expression used in describing Solomon's reign [3] and in Micah's form of the prophecy of world peace: [4] " They shall dwell every man under his own vine and under his own fig tree, and none shall make them afraid." Much of the Old Testament represents the point of view of the peasant, who loses most and gains least by war.

Freedom from fear was a vital element in the Messianic hope, which

---

[1] Lev. 26:6–8; Dt. 28:1, 7, 10, 13.　　[3] 1 K. 4:25.
[2] Dt. 28:30–35.　　[4] Mi. 4:4; cp. also Jer. 30:10; Zc. 3:10.

of course was especially cherished in times of foreign domination and oppression. It finds striking expression in the canticle of Zacharias.[5] The New Testament does not promise security or safety any more than it promises prosperity. Jesus assures his followers that the hairs of their heads are numbered,[6] but he warns them that they must be prepared, if need be, even to die with him,[7] being free from fear because they are not afraid to die.[8] The law of love, however, requires concern for the safety of others in the same way and to the same degree that it requires concern for their economic needs and rights.

As a general rule nations have sought security by military power, and this is as true of the Hebrews as of any other people. It has been said that the Bible is concerned with three subjects: war, agriculture, and religion. It is true that much of the Old Testament is occupied with warfare, from the first nomadic conflicts over wells and pastures [9] to the great eschatological war of Gog and Magog.[10] In the period of the exodus Yahweh became Israel's war-god. The conquest of the promised land was a ruthless war of aggression. The book of Joshua represents it as a war of extermination,[11] but Ju., ch. 1, indicates otherwise, and the Deuteronomic editors of Joshua and Judges say that the Canaanites should have been exterminated but were not.[12] This aspect of Israel's relation to Yahweh is not much in evidence in the stories of the patriarchs, except as it is implied in Gen., ch. 14, but in Exodus Yahweh appears as the God of armies (*Yahweh sebaot*), who casts Pharaoh and his army into the Red Sea.[13] Victories over the enemies encountered on the way to the promised land and the conquest of the land itself showed that Israel had made a good bargain and had the right God to give them triumph over their enemies. These victories were celebrated in the Book of the Wars of Yahweh.[14] Much of the Old Testament might be aptly characterized by that title. Later victories under the judges and kings were likewise attributed to Yahweh (ss. 60 f.).

Israel shared with other peoples the ancient view that conflicts between nations were also conflicts between their gods. The emergence of

[5] Lk. 1:71, 74.
[6] Mt. 10:30; Lk. 12:7.
[7] Mk. 8:31–34.
[8] Mt. 10:28; Lk. 12:4 f.
[9] Gen. 21:25–33; 26:12–22; cp. 13:6 f.
[10] S. 66; *v.i.*
[11] Josh. 10:40; 11:14 f., 19 f., 23.
[12] Josh. 23:11–13; Ju. 2:1–3, 20–23; 3:4.
[13] Ex., ch. 15; cp. the angelic captain of Yahweh's army in Josh. 5:13–15.
[14] Num. 21:14.

monotheism modified this conception, making war a divine judgment on Israel as well as other nations. The prophetic and historical books of the Old Testament treat history consistently from this point of view. The importance of a revaluation and reapplication of the truth involved in this fundamental conviction of biblical religion has been pointed out in s. 18.

Whatever part rationalization of the natural human tendency to identify one's own interests with eternal justice may have had in all this, the Hebrew conviction had an ethical basis. The Canaanites and Assyrians, for example, were believed to have been overthrown because they were wicked, not merely because God was partial to Israel.[15] At least the Israelites felt the need for some moral justification of their conquests and victories, though it must be admitted that this is usually true of even the most unscrupulously aggressive nations. The question always is how profound the feeling is and how far it influences conduct.

The apocalyptic idea of the eschatological war may be recalled in this connection. This is not an expression of God's will, however, but the climactic result of all sinful opposition to God (s. 66). Perhaps permanent value may be found in this conception as a reminder of the fact that all hopes for the future must take into account what will be done by men who do not want peace and justice,[16] so that it is futile to say complacently, " Peace, peace," when there is no peace.[17] The idea of the eschatological war reappears in Revelation,[18] but there it is obviously symbolic of the cosmic conflict of spiritual forces.[19]

These ideas bring to mind again the perennial efforts of good but misguided people to calculate in advance the affairs and relationships of nations on the basis of prophecy. All such attempts involve a false view of prophecy (ss. 18, 20) as well as an amazing ability to ignore the failure of every previous effort of the same kind. If God has determined the boundaries of all nations and the periods of their rise and fall,[20] he has given us no ready means of discovering what power or boundaries he has decreed for any particular nation at any particular time.

Over against the bloody element in Old Testament history and religion it should be noted that we find also efforts to limit the brutality of

15 Dt. 8:19 f.; 9:4 f.; Na. 3:1.
16 Contrast Joel 3:9–17 with Is. 2:1–4.
17 Jer. 6:14; 8:11.
18 Cp. Mk. 13:7 f.
19 Cp. Eph. 6:11 f.; 1 Cor. 15:25 f.
20 Acts 17:26.

war.[21] It is only fair to say that the Old Testament as a whole does not glorify war but regards it as a consequence of man's sin. Moreover, the Old Testament holds up clearly a vision of ultimate world peace.[22] If it be asked why God allows war and how long he will allow it to continue, one may point to Jer. 4:19–22, where God asks man how long this has to go on.

The Old Testament also recognizes the limits of what military power can accomplish. Isaiah warned the kings and people of Judah again and again of the dangers and futility of international intrigue and power politics.[23] His wisdom was vindicated by the disastrous results of the frantic alliances of Israel and Judah with Damascus, Assyria, and Egypt in turn during the subsequent century and a half (735–586 B.C.). Jeremiah also warned Judah against relying on Egyptian aid against Babylon, but was not heeded.[24] Ezra's faith in returning from Babylonia to Palestine without a military escort is recorded with obvious approval.[25] The same attitude is urged upon the little postexilic community by Zechariah.[26] The necessity of justice as the only sound basis of peace is strongly stated in Is. 32:13–18.

The root of war in man's selfish cupidity and the generous attitude by which alone concord can ever be achieved between nations or individuals are both illustrated by the story of Abraham and Lot.[27] The importance of rivalry for the control of natural resources as a cause of war appears already here and in the struggles of Abraham and Isaac with Abimelech.[28] An interesting comment on the causes of war is made in Jas. 4:1 f.

We have seen in s. 107 that Jesus refused to take the way of military power to his goal. This raises the whole question of the use of force, which has been postponed to this point because it is most crucial in connection with war, though it affects also other human relationships, from the discipline of children to the treatment of criminals and the problem of social revolution.

There is no question that Jesus told his disciples to suffer personal indignities and injuries without resistance or resentment.[29] Whether he would also have them allow others to be mistreated is another question. The sayings regarding nonresistance are not concerned with wrongs

[21] Dt., chs. 20; 24:5; cp. Am. 1:3, 6, 9, 11, 13; Ho. 1:4; Na. 3:1; 2 K. 21:16; 1 Chr. 22:8.
[22] Is. 2:1–4; Mi. 4:1–4; cp. Ps. 46:9; 68:30d.
[23] Is. 7:1–9; 8:5–8; 20; 30:1–5; 31:1–3.
[24] Jer., ch. 37.
[25] Ezra 8:22.
[26] Zc. 4:6.
[27] Gen., ch. 13.
[28] Gen. 21:25–33; 26:12–22.
[29] Mt. 5:38–41.

done to others or with the prevention of wrongs, but with insult or injury to oneself. They are not applicable to preventive or disciplinary action motivated by love.

On the other hand, the cleansing of the temple does not establish a sanction for violence: Jesus, acting alone, did not expel all the money-changers by force! The incident does, however, show that he would not allow such wrongdoing to go without active protest.

Christian conduct cannot be determined by legalistic considerations (s. 56). If one tries to establish the Christian attitude toward war by a rigidly literal application of Ex. 20:13, for example, he must at least be equally rigid and literal in applying Gen. 9:6; but in both cases he will be violating the basic principle of Jesus' teaching. Only the consequences of action in each particular situation, judged from the standpoint of love, can determine the Christian's duty.

The real point at issue is not force against persuasion, but resentment and vindictiveness against love and forgiveness. For Jesus, not only killing but anger is sinful.[30] For the follower of Jesus, therefore, the real question is whether killing can ever be an act of love, the expression of a sincere desire to seek the real interests, not of one person or group only, but of all concerned. To make force as against other methods the basic issue is like debating whether medicine or surgery is more Christian.

Both Old and New Testaments afford ground for assurance that any people or nation, however sinful, may by repentance and reformation find mercy and redemption, and any nation may be brought to destruction by corruption and injustice. That fact should govern the Christian's attitude to all nations, including his own. This involves neither soft-headed sentimentalism nor unrealistic optimism. The destruction of the world's peace or of civilization itself by nations which are ruled by hatred or greed and do not desire peace or justice must be prevented. To allow criminal or insane individuals or nations to run at large, destroying the helpless and innocent, is not the way of Christian love. We must be harmless as doves and at the same time wise as serpents.[31] With nations, as with individuals,[32] what love requires is fair dealing, based on clear, cool, disinterested judgments, sternly repressing selfish activities which jeopardize the safety of other peoples, but also giving every

---

[30] Mt. 5:21 f. — the best manuscripts do not have the phrase " without cause."
[31] Mt. 10:16.
[32] Cp. 1 Cor., ch. 5; 2 Cor., ch. 2.

opportunity for reformation and recognizing and welcoming it when it is forthcoming. A warning against losing the fruits of victory in such a case through worshiping the gods of the conquered may be found in 2 Chr. 25:14 ff. An interesting basis for discussion of these matters is afforded by the attitude of the other tribes to Benjamin in the story told in Ju., chs. 20 f.

All nations must learn to regard themselves as instruments of the righteous will of God, accepting every privilege as a responsibility and not arrogating to themselves glory and power beyond his purpose.[33] When nations that have committed aggression against others have been restrained, the victorious powers must rigidly observe the difference between just and necessary discipline and unbridled revenge or selfish exploitation. The spirit of pride and self-aggrandizement at the expense of the vanquished may be symbolized by the " eating with the blood " for which Ezekiel denounced those who had taken possession of the waste places of devastated Palestine in the time of the exile.[34] If we in our day inevitably profit by the defeat of Germany and Japan, we need not drink their life's blood.

Wise dealing with other peoples is impossible without sympathetic understanding, and there is enough sin in ourselves to make that possible even for the worst offenders against peace and justice. Feelings and attitudes that we cannot and must not approve can often at least be understood. Portions of the Old Testament that breathe a spirit of bitter vindictiveness and the desire for revenge, such as Ps. 137, may help us to understand the natural human feelings of a vanquished, crushed people, which must be taken into account in our relations with them.

The vital importance of guarding against the inordinate, weedlike growth of international distrust and suspicion, which are among the most potent causes of war, finds expression in Is. 8:12 f.[35]

For the forms and methods of such international organization as may be needed to secure world peace, as for the forms and methods of democratic government in each nation, no specific guidance need be sought in the Bible. Here again we must fall back on the basic Christian attitude and accept the responsibility of working out for ourselves its practical application in our own situation. The question must be what love requires — love for all concerned; i.e., what is best for all, what will best further the Christian ideal.

[33] Is. 10:5–19. [35] Assuming that the Masoretic text is correct; cp. s. 23, note 1.
[34] Ezek. 33:23–29.

Above all it must be constantly recalled and brought to the attention of peoples and governments that no combination of powers, no plan or policy, no world organization can succeed on any other basis than conformity to the known will of God and reliance on his help.[36]

109. *Interracial Relations: the Unity of Mankind*

Very little that bears directly or specifically on interracial relations appears in either the Old Testament or the New Testament, because most of the other peoples with whom the Hebrews and early Christians had to do were fairly closely related in race. A solid basis for all consideration of racial matters is given, however, in the fundamental biblical conception of the unity of mankind. The writers and editors of the Old Testament took pains to stress the fact that mankind is one in origin. Both J and P have not only creation stories but also genealogies showing how the different peoples are related. The name Adam (if it is to be taken as a name at all) is the common Hebrew noun meaning " human being, mankind." In the Hebrew it is used in Gen. 1:26 f. (P) as well as ch. 2:5 etc. (J). While we are not told where Cain got his wife,[1] it must be assumed that a part of the original tradition has been omitted by the editors of Genesis, unless it was simply considered unnecessary to mention the birth of daughters to Adam and Eve.[2] The common origin of all men is recalled in Acts 17:26, where " made from one " probably means " made from one man," i.e., the common ancestor of all nations and races.

The separation of Israel from the other peoples is clearly presented as a matter of divine choice, not of difference in nature or origin. By a series of choices, based only partially on merit or probation, God selected the line of Noah [3] and his descendants through Shem to Abraham.[4] Through all subsequent developments of national pride and exclusiveness, the fact that all men and nations are members of one family was never wholly forgotten. Even the jealous guarding of racial purity after the exile, with its harsh opposition to intermarriage and its cherishing of genealogies,[5] was animated by the fear of religious pollution. The original international and interracial connections of Israel were emphasized even in that very period by the priestly genealogies of Genesis.

---

[36] Ps. 127:1.
[1] Gen. 4:17.
[2] Cp. ch. 5:4.

[3] Gen. 7:1.
[4] Chs. 9:8–11; 12:1–3.
[5] Ezra, chs. 9 f.; Neh. 13:23 ff.; cp. s. 102.

God's purpose in creating man (s. 48) applies, not merely to the chosen people, but to all mankind (note the frequent use of the expression " all flesh "). An original unity of culture as well as descent is suggested by Gen. 11:1–9, and the differences that separate peoples are represented as punishment for sin. Human nature also is seen to be the same in all peoples. The conceptions of body, soul, etc., discussed in ss. 44–47 apply to all peoples alike. Thus the ground is laid in the Old Testament for the New Testament ideal of universalism in religion (s. 102).

The idea of the essential unity of mankind comes to its own in Paul's insistence on the annulment of all distinctions in Christ, whether of sex, economic status, nation, or race.[6] Nowhere does the Bible give any support to theories of racial superiority or of any essential difference in nature or capacity as between races. In fact, they are definitely excluded. There are some things in the Bible that are susceptible to abuse as supporting racial discrimination, and unfortunately are so abused. To use the genealogies of Genesis, the curse on Ham,[7] or the statement of Acts 17:26 that God has determined the times and habitations of peoples, as showing that the Negroes belong in the jungles of Africa merely demonstrates the extremes to which prejudice can go in distorting truth.

One example of such false exegesis in defense of an essentially unscriptural position may be considered in some detail as typical of all. It is stated in Num. 12:1 that Aaron and Miriam spoke against Moses because he had married a Cushite (A.V., Ethiopian) woman. Now if this proved anything, it would support interracial marriages, because Aaron and Miriam are condemned in the sequel (vv. 2–15). As a matter of fact, however, the passage proves nothing whatever with regard to matters of race. If the wife referred to is Zipporah, she was not an Ethiopian woman at all. If another wife is meant, and she was from Ethiopia, she may still have been of Semitic descent. A careful study of the names in the genealogical tables of Gen. 10:6 ff. and 25:1–4 will show that no conclusions whatever regarding racial connections can be drawn from them. Cush is a son of Ham, but so is Canaan. Some of the same names appear among the descendants of Ham,[8] the descendants of Shem,[9] and the descendants of Abraham and Keturah.[10] In short, there is no evidence that Moses' wife was of Negro blood.

Racial and religious prejudice are combined in anti-Semitism. The

---

[6] Gal. 3:28; Col. 3:11; cp. Eph. 2:11–22.

[7] Actually on Canaan; Gen. 9:18–27.

[8] Gen. 10:6 f.

[9] Ch. 10:28 f.

[10] Ch. 25:1–4.

ancient national pride of the Jews has been turned against them in modern times. Anti-Semitism has even exploited hostile statements regarding the Jews in the New Testament, especially the fourth gospel. Jewish writers have responded with pathetic attempts to exonerate their race from responsibility for the death of Jesus. It is therefore important now to stress the fact that Jesus, his disciples, and even Paul, were Jews, and were proud of it. The responsibility for the death of Jesus rests historically neither on the Romans nor on the Jewish people, but on a particular group of Jewish religious leaders whose vested interests were imperiled by Jesus, and on an unscrupulous Roman procurator. The New Testament itself stresses the fact that the leaders were afraid of the popularity of Jesus among the Jewish people, who regarded him as a prophet.[11] Even the " anti-Semitism " of the fourth gospel is more apparent than real, since the evangelist means by " the Jews " the officials who opposed Jesus, as distinguished from " the multitude," who were of course also Jews.[12]

This should be made known by the church, because the misunderstanding of these facts is often and all too easily used to foment intolerance and division. But even if the Jewish people as a whole had been guilty of the death of Jesus, their descendants would not be responsible. If we were all held responsible for the crimes of our ancestors, we should be in a terrible position indeed.

Contempt or condemnation for any group of human beings in the lump is contrary to the Christian attitude as well as to scientific facts. To all who consider themselves racially superior to others it is pertinent to quote Am. 9:7, " Are ye not as the children of the Ethiopians to me? " Mankind is one both in nature and in God's esteem. All are made alike in his image; salvation is freely offered to all alike and all are equally in need of it; [13] what he sees is the heart, which has no color or class or nationality.[14]

11 Mk. 11:18; 12:12; Mt. 21:46; Lk. 20:19.

12 Cp. Jn. 7:11–13.

13 Acts 17:30 f.

14 1 S. 16:7.

XVIII

CONCLUSION

110. *The Nature of Biblical Religion*

The rich variety of the religion of the Bible defies any attempt to catch it in the net of a brief summary or simple classification. There is not only variety but constant change, yet it is not merely kaleidoscopic, but rather the change of a vital, growing organism. The successive stages of growth cannot be reviewed here. Suffice it only to mention the simple tribal cults of the patriarchal period, the federation of tribes in the bond of the covenant with Yahweh, the struggle with baalism in Canaan, the emergence of an elaborate cultus and priestly organization under the monarchy, the vehement protest of the prophets and their insistence on the stern ethical demands of the covenant, the collapse of the nation and its transformation into a religious community, the growth of the wisdom literature and the blossoming of devotional poetry, the decline of prophecy and the rise of the apocalyptic hope; then, after an interval without attestation in our Protestant canon but illuminated by the Apocrypha and Pseudepigrapha, the incarnation of the Word in the person of Jesus Christ, the foundation and spread of the church, the mission of Paul and his translation of the gospel into terms comprehensible to the Hellenistic world, the Johannine expression of mystical thought and devotion and other types of faith in other books of the New Testament, the development of ecclesiastical institutions, and finally the rising cloud of persecution and the steadfast affirmation of faith and hope. In all this there is not a mere unilinear process but an unfolding in many directions, enriched by cross-fertilization through contact with other cultures and religions.

Through it all, however, there is a clearly perceptible continuity and unity, for in it and through it the one God is always speaking to his people. God is the beginning and the ending, the eternal Creator and Ruler of all. In him man lives and moves and has his being.[1] He has made man in his own image and placed him on the earth to replenish and subdue it.[2]

Man is completely dependent upon God. All welfare and safety depend upon obeying his will. Man cannot by his own unaided wisdom find God, but God has made known all we need to know to do his will and have his approval.[3] As the righteous Judge of all the earth,[4] God rewards obedience and punishes disobedience. It behooves all men to flee from his wrath against all transgression of his laws.[5] Yet it is impossible for a man to be so righteous as to put God under obligation to him. All we have comes from him, and he does not need anything we can give him.[6] We are all, in fact, sinners, the best of us falling short of what God requires.[7] The revelation of God's will only makes more glaring man's sinfulness, his selfish, shortsighted use of the freedom God has given him to the end that he might respond to God's love with the love and service which only a free person can give.[8]

Sin alienates man from God and renders him subject to judgment.[9] Neither our wisdom nor our self-control is sufficient to deliver us.[10] But God, being both just and merciful, has provided a way out of our darkness and weakness by sending his Son, Jesus Christ, into the world to make known even through humiliation and death the Father's redeeming love.[11] No man has seen or can see God, but in Christ, the incarnate Word, we behold his glory, full of grace and truth; in the Son we see the Father himself.[12]

Accepting by faith the free gift of eternal life in Christ, we are reconciled, forgiven, justified, adopted, redeemed, and so pass from death to life and are delivered from all fear of judgment.[13] His Spirit in us unites us with him, giving us a new life, making us new creatures, enabling us to overcome the power of sin and bring forth the fruit of the Spirit.[14]

Thus faith overflows into a life of loving service of God and man, and

[1] Acts 17:24–28.
[2] Gen. 1:26–28; Ps. 8:4–8.
[3] Dt. 29:29; 30:11–14; Job, ch. 28; Mi. 6:8; 1 Cor. 1:21.
[4] Gen. 18:25.
[5] Lk. 3:7; 13:3, 5; Acts 17:30 f.; Rom. 1:18.
[6] 1 Chr. 29:10–14; Ps. 50:10–12; Lk. 17:10; Acts 17:25.
[7] Job 4:17–19; Rom. 3:23.
[8] Rom. 3:20; 5:12; 7:12 f.
[9] Is. 59:2; Eph. 4:18.
[10] Rom. 7:18–24.
[11] Jn. 3:16; Rom. 3:21–26; 5:8; 2 Cor. 5:14–21; Phil. 2:5–11; 1 Jn. 4:9 f., 14, 19.
[12] Jn. 1:14, 18; 14:9; 1 Jn. 4:12, 14.
[13] Jn. 5:24; 1 Jn. 4:12–18; Rom. 5:1 f.; 6:23; 8:1, 15 f.; 2 Cor. 5:18.
[14] Rom. 8:2–4, 9 f., 13 f.; 2 Cor. 5:17; Gal. 2:20; 5:22–25.

only so is its genuineness attested.[15] And in the possession of the Spirit we have a foretaste of the powers of the coming world, an assurance of future glory and righteousness beside which the evil and suffering of this world are relatively insignificant.[16] We have not yet attained; we are far indeed from perfection; but we have a high calling, a goal and a prize before us, toward which we press with fervent hope and joy.[17]

As inner experiences and attitudes both faith and love are intensely individual, but they are also shared with others, and only in co-operation with others can they be adequately expressed. Biblical religion is thus the affair of a group as well as of individuals. Under the old covenant the group was Israel, as a nation and as a religious community. Under the new covenant it is the church, a purely religious society, without distinctions of nation, race, sex, or anything that separates one human being from another except the personal commitment of heart and will.[18] Obviously the church still has far to go before this ideal is realized, but it is the biblical conception of the church.

The church itself, however broadly defined, is not the be-all and end-all of God's purpose. As Israel was the servant of the Lord, suffering for the sin of others in order that light might be brought to the nations and all the families of earth might be blessed,[19] so the church exists, not for its own sake, but to be the means of bringing salvation to the world.[20]

Not even mankind is the sole object of God's redemptive will. The corruption of sin has affected the very powers of the universe, and the divine plan of salvation embraces them too.[21] Difficult as it may be for us to conceive what this could mean in terms of modern thought, or perhaps to believe that it can mean anything compatible with what we now know about the universe, there can be no question that it is an integral part of biblical religion. The faith of the New Testament contemplates not merely a relative amelioration of life in this world, but new heavens and a new earth.[22] Whatever may happen to this or any other universe, beyond the utmost possible reach of man's knowledge in this life, Christian faith will always boldly affirm, with the Old and the New Testa-

---

[15] Is. 58:6 f.; Mk. 12:30 f.; Rom. 12:1; 13:10; Gal. 5:6; Jn. 13:34 f.; 15:10, 12; 1 Jn. 4:11 f., 20 f.; Jas. 1:27.

[16] Rom. 8:11, 17–23, 35–39; 2 Cor. 1:22; 5:5; Eph. 1:13 f.; Col. 1:27; Heb. 6:4 f.; 2 P. 3:13.

[17] Phil. 3:12–14.

[18] Rom., ch. 4; Gal. 3:28; Eph. 2:13–18; Col. 3:11.

[19] Gen. 12:3; Is. 42:6; 49:3–7.

[20] Mt. 28:19 f.; Lk. 24:46–48; Acts 1:8; Jn. 10:16; 11:51 f.; 12:32.

[21] Rom. 8:19–22; Eph. 1:10; 3:8–12.

[22] 2 P. 3: 11–13; Rev. 21:1–5.

ments alike, that God's goodness is inexhaustible and eternal, and therefore nothing can separate us from his love as it is revealed in Christ Jesus our Lord.[23]

Meanwhile, with the long perspective and inner stability of faith, and with the dynamic impulsion of love for God and man, we work together, with all men of good will, for peace and justice and abundant life on earth. The Spirit of the Lord is upon us, he has anointed us: that the blind may see, the lame may walk, and the poor may hear good news; that men may have beauty for ashes, the garment of praise for the spirit of heaviness; that the bands of wickedness may be loosed, the heavy burdens undone, the yokes broken, and that the oppressed may all go free.[24]

[23] Ps. 102:25–28 (cp. Heb. 1:10–12); Is. 40:6–8; 51:6; Rom. 8:38 f.
[24] Is. 35:5 f.; 58:6 f.; 61:1–3; Mt. 11:5; Lk. 4:18 f.

ABBREVIATIONS

Am.	Amos	Jer.	Jeremiah
A.S.V.	American Standard Version	Jn.	John
		1 Jn.	First John, etc.
A.V.	Authorized (King James) Version	Josh.	Joshua
		Ju.	Judges
1 Chr.	First Chronicles	1 K.	First Kings
2 Chr.	Second Chronicles	2 K.	Second Kings
Col.	Colossians		
1 Cor.	First Corinthians	Lam.	Lamentations
2 Cor.	Second Corinthians	Lev.	Leviticus
		Lk.	Luke
D	The Deuteronomic source	LXX	Septuagint
Dan.	Daniel		
Dt.	Deuteronomy	1 Macc.	First Maccabees
		2 Macc.	Second Maccabees
E	The Elohistic source	Mal.	Malachi
Eccl.	Ecclesiastes	mg.	marginal note
Ecclus.	Ecclesiasticus (Sirach, ben Sira)	Mi.	Micah
		Mk.	Mark
Eph.	Ephesians	Mt.	Matthew
2 Esdr.	Second Esdras (Fourth Ezra)		
		Na.	Nahum
Est.	Esther	Neh.	Nehemiah
E.VV.	English versions	NT	New Testament
Ex.	Exodus	Num.	Numbers
Ezek.	Ezekiel		
		Ob.	Obadiah
Gal.	Galatians	OT	Old Testament
Gen.	Genesis		
		P	The priestly source
H	The Holiness Code	1 P.	First Peter
Hab.	Habakkuk	2 P.	Second Peter
Heb.	Hebrews	Phil.	Philippians
Hg.	Haggai	Phmn.	Philemon
Ho.	Hosea	Prov.	Proverbs
		Ps.	Psalm, Psalms
Is.	Isaiah		
2 Is.	Second Isaiah	Rev.	Revelation
		Rom.	Romans
J	The Yahwistic source	R.S.V.	Revised Standard Version
Jas.	James	Ru.	Ruth

s.	section	V., v.	verse
ss.	sections	*v.i.*	see below
1 S.	First Samuel	*v.s.*	see above
2 S.	Second Samuel	Vv., vv.	verses
Sir.	Sirach (Ecclesiasticus)		
S.S.	Song of Solomon	W.S.	Wisdom of Solomon
1 Th.	First Thessalonians	Zc.	Zechariah
2 Th.	Second Thessalonians	Zp.	Zephaniah
1 Tim.	First Timothy		
2 Tim.	Second Timothy		

BIBLIOGRAPHY

The few books here listed are those which seem to the present author the best now available for the general student of biblical theology. Books on the history and literature of the Old and New Testaments are omitted, though some of them include an account of religious ideas and developments, because some work in these fields is assumed as a prerequisite for the study of biblical theology. Only a few books on the history of Hebrew religion and early Christianity are named, some acquaintance with these subjects also being presupposed. Books in other languages than English are mentioned only when there is nothing in English to take their place. Fuller bibliographies will be found in some of the works in this list.

GENERAL

For the theology of the Bible as a whole by all odds the best book we now have is

Fosdick, H. E., *A Guide to the Understanding of the Bible* (Harper, 1938).

While not always quite abreast of the most recent research, being written by a great preacher and pastor rather than a specialist in biblical studies, this is a work of genuine scholarship. It fills admirably a long-felt need.

OLD TESTAMENT THEOLOGY

On the theology of the Old Testament there is no satisfactory book in English. The historical development of the religion of Israel is well presented, though with some lack of proportion and with a few unfortunate excursions, by

Robinson, T. H., and Oesterley, W. O. E., *Hebrew Religion* (Macmillan, 2d edition, 1937).

The best treatment in English of many of the basic ideas of Old Testament theology is that given in

Pedersen, J. T. E., *Israel I–II* (Copenhagen and London, 1926) and *III–IV* (1941).

For thorough, comprehensive, and up-to-date presentations of Old Testament theology we are dependent upon German works. The best of these, in spite of an annoying tendency to harp on a few pet ideas, is

Eichrodt, W., *Die Theologie des Alten Testaments* (Leipzig, 3 vols., 1933–1938).

Useful also and valuable in different ways are two briefer works:

Köhler, L., *Die Theologie des Alten Testaments* (Tübingen, 1936),

and

Sellin, E., *Alttestamentliche Theologie auf Religionsgeschichtlicher Grundlage* (Leipzig, 2 vols., 1933).

Inter-Testamental Developments and New Testament Background

The standard treatise in English on rabbinic Judaism is

Moore, G. F., *Judaism* (Harvard University Press, 3 vols., 1927–1930).

For Hellenistic Judaism one may refer especially to

Goodenough, E. R., *By Light, Light* (Yale University Press, 1935),

or the same author's briefer and more popular

Introduction to Philo Judaeus (Yale University Press, 1940).

For the apocryphal writings, including those commonly called the pseudepigrapha, we now have

Torrey, C. C., *The Apocryphal Literature* (Yale University Press, 1945),

a very important and useful little book, which unfortunately appeared too late to be used in the preparation of the present volume.

A very helpful elementary presentation of the Jewish and Hellenistic backgrounds of the New Testament, unfortunately out of print but accessible in libraries, is

Macgregor, G. H. C., and Purdy, A. C., *Jew and Greek: Tutors Unto Christ* (Scribner, 1936).

New Testament Theology

The situation in New Testament theology is even less satisfying than it is in the theology of the Old Testament. There is no good book on the whole subject which takes into account the very significant recent developments in New Testament criticism, especially in the study of the gospels. Brief summaries of the religious ideas in the main divisions of New Testament history and literature may be found in

Parsons, E. W., *The Religion of the New Testament* (Harper, 1939),

and

Scott, E. F., *Varieties of New Testament Religion* (Scribner, 1943).

For thoroughness nothing has ever quite taken the place of

Holtzmann, H. J., *Lehrbuch der Neutestamentlichen Theologie* (Freiburg and Leipzig, 1897),

though a great deal of water has gone under the bridge since it was written. Much less exhaustive but more recent (and somewhat more conservative) are

Feine, P., *Die Theologie des Neuen Testaments* (Leipzig, 6th edition, 1934),

and

Büchsel, Fr., *Die Theologie des Neuen Testaments* (Gütersloh, 1935).

For the rest, we are largely dependent on separate works concerning the major divisions or particular books of the Bible. To enumerate even the most important books on the law, the prophets, and the other parts of the Old Testament, and on the teachings of Jesus, Paul, the Johannine literature, and the rest of the New Testament, would necessitate a much more extended bibliography than this is intended to be.

It should be emphasized that first-hand study of the Bible itself, using standard introductions, commentaries, and above all a good concordance, is more important than the reading of many books. Reference may be made also to

Joy, Charles R., *Harper's Topical Concordance* (Harper, 1940),

a convenient compilation of texts, quoted according to the A.V., under more than two thousand topics, arranged alphabetically.

For those who cannot use the original languages, attention may be drawn also to the importance of consulting the marginal notes in the A.S.V. and the R.S.V.

INDEX OF SCRIPTURAL REFERENCES

OLD TESTAMENT

Ecclesiastes
23, 114, 277

Song of Solomon

Isaiah

I *Corinthians*

INDEX OF NAMES AND SUBJECTS

(NOTE: For references to authors of books in the Bible see Index of Scriptural References.)